HUMAN TERRITORIAL FUNCTIONING

Environment and Behavior Series

Editors

DANIEL STOKOLS
University of Calfornia, Irvine

IRWIN ALTMAN
University of Utah

HUMAN TERRITORIAL FUNCTIONING

An empirical, evolutionary perspective
on individual and small group territorial
cognitions, behaviors, and consequences

RALPH B. TAYLOR

Department of Criminal Justice
Temple University

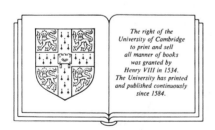

The right of the
University of Cambridge
to print and sell
all manner of books
was granted by
Henry VIII in 1534.
The University has printed
and published continuously
since 1584.

CAMBRIDGE UNIVERSITY PRESS

CAMBRIDGE

NEW YORK   NEW ROCHELLE   MELBOURNE   SYDNEY

Published by the Press Syndicate of the University of Cambridge
The Pitt Building, Trumpington Street, Cambridge CB2 1RP
32 East 57th Street, New York, NY 10022, USA
10 Stamford Road, Oakleigh, Melbourne 3166, Australia

First published 1988

Printed in the United States of America

Library of Congress Cataloging-in-Publication Data
Taylor, Ralph B.
Human territorial functioning : an empirical, evolutionary
perspective on individual and small group territorial cognitions,
behaviors, and consequences / Ralph Taylor.
p.   . – (Environment and behavior series)
ISBN 0–521–30776–7.   ISBN 0–521–31307–4 (pbk.)
1. Human territoriality.   2. Environmental psychology.   3. Spatial
behavior.   4. Interior decoration – Human factors.   I. Title.
II. Series.
GN491.7.T38   1988   87–16825
304.2 – dc19   CIP

British Library Cataloguing in Publication applied for.

To the three lovely
leading ladies in my life:
MICHELE, MARA, and NYSSA

CONTENTS

FIGURES, TABLES, AND BOXES

Figures

xvii

SERIES FOREWORD

In recent decades the relationship between human behavior and the physical environment has attracted researchers from the social sciences – psychology, sociology, geography, and anthropology – and from the environmental-design disciplines – architecture, urban and regional planning, and interior design. What is in many respects a new and exciting field of study has developed rapidly. Its multidisciplinary character has led to stimulation and cross-fertilization, on the one hand, and to confusion and difficulty in communication, on the other. Those involved have diverse intellectual styles and goals. Some are concerned with basic and theoretical issues; some, with applied real-world problems of environmental design.

This series offers a common meeting ground. It consists of short books on different topics of interest to all those who analyze environment-behavior links. We hope that the series will provide a useful introduction to the field for students, researchers, and practitioners alike, and will facilitate its evolutionary growth as well.

Our goals are as follows: (1) to represent problems the study of which is relatively well established, with a reasonably substantial body of research and knowledge generated; (2) to recruit authors from a variety of disciplines with a variety of perspectives; (3) to ensure that they not only summarize work on their topic but also set forth a "point of view," if not a theoretical orientation – we want the books not only to serve as texts but also to advance the field intellectually – and (4) to produce books useful to a broad range of students and other readers from dif-

ferent disciplines and with different levels of formal professional train-
ing. Course instructors will be able to select different combinations of
books to meet their particular curricular needs.

Irwin Altman
Daniel Stokols

PREFACE

The major themes of this volume are captured in the subtitle: the evolutionary origins of protohuman and later human territorial functioning. For such a system to have survived, albeit significantly altered, it must have "benefits" for humans. I suggest that it does; territorial functioning has psychological, social psychological, and ecological outcomes that contribute to orderly person–place relationships and to the well-being of individuals and small groups. My treatment of human territorial functioning is grounded in empirical social science research. Consequently, I circumscribe the concept to microscale, usually delimited locations ranging in size from furnishings (e.g., a chair) up to the scale of a streetblock. I maintain, based on theory and lack of evidence, that the concept does *not* work well when applied to macroscale settings, such as neighborhoods or nations.

The reader may think this treatment of the concept too confining or specialized. Nonetheless, the confusion surrounding the concept of human territoriality will be reduced only if we look carefully at how empirical findings illuminate the concept. And, the findings simply do not extend to larger-scale settings than the ones discussed here. I admit that my view is at variance with the perspective of other writers on this topic.

In addition, whereas others, from Klineberg, who discussed an instinct or drive for possessiveness, to Malmberg, who more recently placed the territorial instinct in the limbic system, have viewed territorial functioning as instinct-based or "hard-wired," I attempt to show that it is, rather, a set of learned, goal-oriented processes. Across times and cultures there is considerable variability, but also notable similarities.

I also differ sharply with the many earlier writers who have suggested that territorial functioning is a source of interpersonal or intergroup aggression and violence. I attest, instead, that research supports the view that human territorial functioning plays crucial rules in smoothing interpersonal and person–place transactions.

My divergent views on human territorial functioning do not, I hope, simply reflect a specialized use of the concept, or my "liberal" biases. I think the usage accords well with everyday meanings. And, in developing the view presented here, I have tried to look at the corpus of relevant research. Much of that has become available only in the last few years. This is the reason, I believe, for the contrast with interpreters who have preceded me.

Although this volume presents a particular model of human territorial functioning, and indicates how research supports this model, the reader should not be misled. The model developed represents an effort to achieve some personal closure on an area of research that has claimed my attention for some time. As a former mentor and colleague recently said, it is much easier to start an area of research than it is to finish one. The perspective developed here represents my attempt to tie up a conceptual bundle, to finish and round out my own contribution to the area. But there is much more work to be done, enough to keep dozens of researchers busy for dozens of years.

In fact, future research on territorial functioning may be much more exciting than the previous work. Once the outlines of relevant processes are understood, investigators can begin to apply the concept to extant problems. Indeed, researchers have already done so as indicated by the work in the areas of disorder and resource conservation. It is to be hoped that this process of application will flourish in the future. Application or more specifically, action research is particularly worthwhile for at least two reasons. It reduces social and environmental problems. Social scientists *do* have tools with which to dissect such problems and guide the implementation of solutions. And, application spurs theoretical clarification and model development.

As of this writing, the globe is dotted with armed clashes of varying intensity, from the Persian Gulf to Afghanistan, Sri Lanka, South Africa, El Salvador, and Nicaragua, to mention just a few. It was less than six years ago that Mrs. Thatcher settled a difference of opinion with Argentina using "the military option." Perhaps it is not too much to hope that as a result of this volume, one less person will be willing to say such violence is due to "territoriality" or the "territorial instinct."

ACKNOWLEDGMENTS

Acknowledgments customarily conclude with remarks regarding all the helpful sources mentioned earlier, and assignment of sole responsibility for egregious errors to the author. I prefer instead to dispense immediately with such a disclaimer. Therefore, the numerous valuable people mentioned here should not be held responsible for errors, untoward omissions, or sloppy thinking found in this volume. Blame for such blunders rests only with the author.

It is also standard practice to acknowledge the encouragement and support of immediate family members after recognizing other sources of assistance, with whom one usually spends much less time. Again, I prefer to concede such invaluable contributions up front. Michele has been supportive, forebearing, and encouraging in divers ways for quite some time. As initial plans for the book took shape, she helped convince me it was a task worth doing and within reach. In later stages, as a radically revised version emerged, she assisted me in focusing on the task at hand, even as a bewildering array of other events were descending upon us. I also thank Nyssa and Mara for the inspiration they have provided in little and big ways. They thought the book sounded like a good idea on the whole, and perhaps of interest to some.

Irv Altman and Dan Stokols were instrumental in getting the project airborne, and in guiding the pilot back on course as the ponderous contraption strayed repeatedly. Irv provided thorough, provocative, and challenging comments on the first draft; Dan made several crucial suggestions that resulted in a more coherently organized revision. Their encouragement and patience during the preproduction phase were most welcome.

Several scholars provided feedback on portions of the first draft. Doug Candland reviewed chapters on nonhuman territorial behavior and sociobiology; his comments, particularly on the latter, have led, I hope, to a more lucid exposition. Richard Boyd offered incisive criticisms on the discussion of evolutionary processes, and human–nonhuman parallels. He also brought to my attention his considerable body of work with Richerson. Their theoretical model of cultural evolution plays a key role in driving some of the major arguments concerning the emergence and evolution of human territorial functioning. The work of Glenn King is also important to that exposition. Paul Stern cogently dissected the chapter on resource conservation. As a result, I was able to reorganize the chapter and to focus more clearly on the central issues. Mark La Gory commented on two chapters covering attachment to place, a concept linked to, but distinct from, territorial functioning. He indicated that a fair treatment of the former topic would require an expanded analysis. This was simply not possible, and that material was dropped. He thereby steered me clear of covering even more material in too little space.

The actual physical production of various drafts was deftly handled by Percival Clarendon Wright, my personal scribe. Tirelessly and without complaint he modified, filed, and printed reams of text. A quiet and unassuming, but very speedy, assistant, he deserves the highest praise for never losing text, a flaw for which his predecessor was summarily dismissed. My office manager, Callie Erin Sparrow, always seemed to know what was where; her memory, albeit not limitless, was more than adequate. WBJC in Baltimore helped keep the atmosphere in the home office sane during a long summer of rewriting and editing by playing copious amounts of Boccherini, Vivaldi, and Bach.

At Cambridge University Press Susan Milmoe, Russell Hahn, and their colleagues have been patient, committed, and professional throughout. Mary Byers provided careful, consistent, and graceful copyediting.

In addition to the entities directly involved in the current volume, a gallery of persons have had, over the past dozen years or so, a major impact on my thinking about human territorial functioning. Sidney Brower deservedly heads the list. He took me on as a research assistant in the summer of 1974, and since then we have had the pleasure of collaborating on sundry research enterprises. Sidney had been thinking about human territorial functioning for a long time before we began working together. I have benefited immensely from the ideas he developed before our partnership, and the ideas on territorial functioning

in the urban residential environment I have developed since that time
are at least as much his as mine. In addition, I am indebted to Sidney
for his relentless obsession with issues of application. It is a fetish that,
luckily, has rubbed off a bit.

Other colleagues over the years have played instrumental roles in
nudging me along. Roger Stough threw me into field research before I
knew what it was about. Clint DeSoto and Bob Hogan presented (respectively) social psychological and personological problems in ways that
were fruitful and incisive, and thereby contributed to how I conceptualize issues. Lois Verbrugge took me and some of my wayward research ideas under her wing and, in an astonishingly brief time, oriented
me to the basics of research grants and survey research. During my short
stay at Virginia Tech, E. Scott Geller, Haller Gilmer, Lynda Schneek-
loth, and Jack Hamilton moved me closer to understanding what it
meant to be an "applied" investigator.

Over the years I have been fortunate enough to have a raft of energetic
co-workers and assistants on various research projects. Although space
does not permit the acknowledgment of all of their individual benefits,
I am indebted to all of them.

More recently, during the last few years I have been fortunate enough
to work with two careful and challenging collaborators: Steve Gottfredson and Sally Shumaker. Their contributions to various analyses and
conceptual developments are numerous, and go far beyond the articles
where their names appear with mine.

Some of the pictures used in this volume come from a gallery of more
than eight hundred slides that were collected as part of a research project
on urban territoriality conducted by Steve Gottfredson, Sidney Brower,
and myself, from 1978 through 1981. Photographers to whom we owe
the pictures include Kathy Young, Whit Drain, Sidney Brower, and
several others.

Much of the research carried out by myself and colleagues described
in chapters on disorder (Chapter 11) and the urban residential environment (Chapter 8) would never have been possible without generous
research support. I am indebted to the National Institute of Justice, in
particular personnel in the defunct Community Crime Prevention Division – Alan Wallis, Fred Heinzelmann, and Richard Titus – for some
early pivotal support (grants 78-NI-AX-0134, 80-IJ-CX-0077).

At Temple University, Alan Harland facilitated arrangements that,
at a crucial time, allowed the timely completion of the first draft. Also
at Temple, George Rengert, through brief chats and longer discussions,
continues to stimulate my own thinking on physical environment, territorial functioning, and disorder.

Finally, this volume owes much to Julian J. Edney, who began researching human territorial functioning before I had an inkling as to its nature. His empirical and theoretical contributions to this area have been numerous and important. His work plays a key role in guiding this field.

Jamestown, Rhode Island, December 1986
Havertown, Pennsylvania, July 1987

1
INTRODUCTION

The present volume examines human territorial functioning, a closely linked constellation of place-specific, socially determined and influential cognitions, behaviors, and sentiments. Territorial functioning encompasses a class of environment–behavior transactions concerned with issues of personal and group identity, cohesiveness, control, access, and ecological management. This functioning applies largely to small groups, and the individuals in those groups, and is limited largely to small-scale, delimited spaces. The present chapter outlines the purposes of this book, sketches its major recurrent themes, and presents in capsule form a low-level theory, or model, of human territorial functioning. The materials to be covered in the various sections are also introduced.

Focus

The concept of human territorial functioning addresses the question: How do people "manage" the locations they own, occupy, or use for varying periods of time? Approaching this question is difficult, for two reasons.

Some problems

First, everyone knows something about territoriality, based on personal experience. Children at camp vie for the top bunks, siblings get upset and scream when a sister or brother enters their room unannounced,

1

and in some households no one is allowed in the kitchen when dad is baking a cake. Frequently, territorial issues are resolved in the legal arena (see accompanying box). Further, territoriality is ensconced in our everyday lexicon with references to "turf battles" or phrases such as "a man's home is his castle." (But see Figure 1.1.) Movies may trade on everyday notions of how people are territorial, Sam Peckinpah's *Straw Dogs* of the early 1970's or the more recent *The Warriors* being cases in point. In our experience, language, and media, territorial issues are ever-present. Consequently, whatever social scientists may have to say on the topic is constantly juxtaposed with this common or everyday knowledge.

"Free George Yant"

In 1984 or 1985, if you stopped at a truck stop along a major route in the United States, you may have seen some "FREE GEORGE YANT" flyers, soliciting donations. You probably wondered, Who is George Yant? George Yant is a landowner in Blackduck, Minnesota, who has been sentenced to five years in prison for chasing trespassers off his property.[1]

On November 6, 1983, George Yant encountered two hunters on his land, two miles inside the boundaries of his property. In his area during hunting season it is not unusual for hunters to break fences, chop wood, and sometimes even shoot cattle and horses. This has been a source of considerable frustration to George Yant and other landowners. Yant, a trucker, raised horses and may, in the past, have had one killed by hunters. When he crossed paths with two hunters on November 6, he became upset. He marched them off his property, his rifle pointing at their backs. He also reportedly cursed and kicked them, and marched them half a mile down the road beyond his property before releasing them. Although Yant had never been arrested before, the judge, who was known for his stiff sentences, gave him five years in prison. The judge felt that although Yant may have been a peaceful, law-abiding citizen prior to the incident, on the day of the encounter " 'George Yant, like so many perpetrators of violent-person crimes, went berserk. He went headhunting.' "[2]

Second, territoriality is deemed relevant to a vast range of situations. Large-scale historical events, such as Napoleon's extremely costly victory at Borodino and the victory of North Vietnam in the Vietnam War,

---

[1] Jailing of Minn. landowner outrages others tired of forgiving trespassers (November 22, 1984). *Baltimore Sun*, pp. 1A, 27A.

[2] Ibid., p. 1A.

Figure 1.1. Although a man's home is his castle, such possession may have unanticipated consequences. *Source: Sally Forth.* Copyright © 1985 by News America Syndicate. Reprinted with permission of the publisher.

have been linked to human territoriality, as have less grandiose matters such as the seating arrangement in the boss's office, or the behavior of patrons in a gay bar. Such a broad-gauged application of the concept of human territoriality, spanning widely different levels of analysis, makes it difficult to determine exactly what territoriality *is*.

Empirical grounding

To surmount these difficulties the current volume takes an *empirical* approach. Findings from experiments, analyses, and observations in psychology, sociology, anthropology, and other social science fields are used as touchstones for formulating a perspective, definition, and understanding of human territorial functioning. Such empirical grounding is necessary to derive a clear-cut view of human territorial functioning, and helps us eschew the fuzzy or overgeneral conceptualizations that have predominated in the past.

A consequence of the grounded approach used in this volume is a treatment of human territorial functioning that is more restricted in scope than those offered by previous analysts. To be more specific, the evidence on territorial functioning is clear-cut only when considering individuals or small groups, rather than larger agglomerations such as neighborhoods, regions, or nation-states; and when the spatial focus is on specific, delimited, small-scale locations. These limitations may be a cause of consternation to some, but they are needed at this time. The evidence goes no further.

Perhaps more important, the restricted treatment of territorial functioning is warranted for an altogether different reason – for an evolutionary reason.

Grounding in evolutionary approach

In the past 25 years debate has flourished concerning linkages between animal and human social behavior. Territorial functioning has been included as one relevant cluster of behaviors in the larger category of social behaviors. Further, there have been advances in thinking about the biological and cultural evolution of social behaviors, with concomitant insights into the social and spatial organization of protohominids and early humans. These inquiries underscore the small group basis of nonhuman and human territorial functioning. Consequently, from an evolutionary perspective, human territorial functioning can only be soundly discussed in relation to small groups, and the individuals that compose them. From this viewpoint, application to larger-scale units (regions, nation-states, etc.) is not warranted.

Thus, the purpose of the current volume is to develop and apply the concept of human territorial functioning which illuminates how and why people manage different kinds of spaces, and the consequences of that management or lack thereof. The use of the territorial concept is grounded in an evolutionary perspective, and in current, empirical social science findings.

Introduction of major themes

Throughout the volume several different themes will occur regularly. It is useful to apprise the reader of these early on. These themes do not represent specific hypotheses but rather general conclusions consistently suggested by the evidence.

1. *Territorial functioning is highly place specific.*

Territorial cognitions, sentiments, and behaviors are often specific to particular, small-scale, and delimited sites. Small shifts in spatial location may result in major changes in territorial cognitions or behaviors, or both. For example, as will be discussed in the material on the urban residential environment (Chapters 8 and 11), cognitions regarding the front yard, or even steps, are quite different from those regarding the public sidewalk in front. Consequently, two corollaries follow:

a. *Territorial functioning varies markedly across sites*; and
b. *Territorial functioning may play key roles in maintaining ongoing behavior patterns in particular settings or sites.*

Turning from the physical or geographical, to the social, two points are consistently supported:

2a. *Territorial functioning is socially structured or conditioned,* and,
2b. *Territorial functioning is socially influential or relevant.*

In other words, territorial functioning is bound up in a pattern of systemlike influence with ongoing small group social parameters. Behaviors such as decorating or beautification may flow from, and at the same time reinforce, social cohesiveness among residents who live near one another, for example. Or, focusing on the "vertical" or power- and stratification-relevant dimensions of social transactions, territorial functioning of particular individuals in a group may emerge from existing stratification, and at the same time serve to reinforce these existing hierarchies.

3. *Consequently, the bases and consequences of territorial functioning are largely linked with small, face-to-face groups.*

Previous treatments of human territorial functioning have concentrated largely on its relevance to the "vertical" or power- and stratification-relevant dimensions of group interactions. Nonetheless, as the evidence will show, territorial functioning is *not* largely a competitive, individuocentric set of processes. Rather, it is a *group-based process*. It is as relevant to the "horizontal" or cohesiveness and solidarity dimensions of human interaction and sentiment as it is to the "vertical" ones. Further, it is relevant both to within-group relations and to between-group relations, for example, how members of a block club feel about each other and about members of another block club.

A corollary suggested by the preceding point is that

4. *there is an upper limit to the group sizes for which territorial functioning is relevant.*

Territorial functioning, being dependent upon and at the same time feeding into the social climate, cannot operate unless there are some minimal bonds of acquaintanceship or interaction among the members of the group in question. An issue to surface later will be whether or not territorial functioning applies to neighborhoods. I will argue that it does not, although it may easily apply to the smaller groups – corner gangs, block clubs, and so on – that are an important part of a neighborhood's fabric.

At the other end of the scale we can ask, Does territorial functioning apply to individuals? Most certainly, particularly when those individuals are considered *in the context of* particular groups to which they belong, or individuals with whom they interact. The personological relevance of territorial functioning, for example, enhancement of personal identity, is mainly important from the perspective of that individual person as a member of a group, or in interaction with one or more others.

5. *The place-specific and socially linked characteristics of human territorial functioning are a product of our evolutionary heritage.*

The grounding of territorial functioning in specific, delimited locations, and its intimate intertwining with small group processes, are features of the system that were shaped in our environment of evolutionary adaptedness, when protohominids wandered the high savannas of East Africa, and also much later in the early years of cultural evolution. That is, the contours of the territorial processes we observe today are, in general terms, evolutionary carryovers, shaped by biological and, more important, cultural evolution.

This does *not* mean, however, that the *consequences* of territorial functioning are the same now as they were tens of thousands, or hundreds of thousands of years ago. It is a well-accepted axiom in evolutionary biology that behavioral systems can persist even after they no longer serve the "purposes" for which they initially evolved. As long as the system is not detrimental, causing it to be selected against, it can persist.

Further, to say that territorial functioning has an evolutionary basis does *not* mean that it is "wired" into our genes, nor does it mean that it is inextricably linked with aggression.

These then are some of the themes that will be developed, and will periodically resurface throughout the volume.

Capsule statement of approach and model

Chapter 5 presents a detailed model of human territorial functioning. The theoretical perspective is put forth as a causal model, suggesting how particular factors shape territorial functioning, and how this functioning, in turn, has certain consequences. Thus the model presents hypotheses linking three classes of concepts: antecedents, territorial functioning, and consequences. This section contains a brief overview of the approach to human territorial functioning, and an outline of the model used.

Working definition

Territorial functioning refers to an interlocked system of sentiments, cognitions, and behaviors that are highly place specific, socially and culturally determined and maintaining, and that represent a class of person–place transactions concerned with issues of setting management, maintenance, legibility, and expressiveness.

Territorial functioning spans both (1) purposive behaviors, explicitly concerned about setting management, maintenance, and so on, like putting up a "No Trespassing" sign, as well as (2) sentiments and cognitions that are nonpurposive but largely responsive to current conditions, such as feelings of annoyance toward people who loiter in the alley behind your house and throw beer cans into your yard. Midway between these purposive and passive components are elements of the system that, (3) although not directed at setting management, legibility, and so on, end up contributing to the local ecology. For example, a person who works hard at keeping his front yard neatly planted with geraniums, impatiens, and pansies may do this simply because he finds it fun and relaxing. Nonetheless, by contributing to the overall impression "given off " by the block, to other residents as well as passersby, the gardener is playing a key role in the local territorial dynamics. His behaviors have consequences for the local setting that were unintended. The person is contributing inadvertently. Likewise, persons who, merely out of convenience, throw mattresses and broken TVs into their backyards are unwittingly weakening the local territorial dynamic.

The consequences of territorial functioning are diverse; they vary depending upon which level of analysis we wish to focus on, and the specific site in question. Almost all of the consequences, however, are relevant to the immediate local sociophysical ecology. Intentional territorial behaviors seek to preserve or change the position of the individual or group within the immediate ecology; behaviors with unintended territorial consequences have this effect ex post facto, and territorial cognitions and sentiments reflect such positions. Stated differently, territorial behaviors can clarify and support the immediate local social order. It is worth reiterating that the spaces in question are extremely delimited, and thus the term "local" refers to small-scale spaces, ranging from chairs and portions of a room, on up to streetblocks or comparably sized areas.

Outline of model

The conceptual model developed more fully in Chapter 5 is outlined here. An abbreviated schematic of the model appears in Figure 1.2. It delineates several classes of factors that shape how a particular, delimited site is perceived and defined by the individuals in a group. The subjective definition of the site, or perception, is a shared one, analogous to social perceptions of a particular individual (e.g., a leader) that persons (e.g., members of a group) may share. This shared view of the site in turn shapes the particular behaviors, both intentionally and unintentionally territorial, that occur there.

When considering these behaviors we can choose one of two "lenses" through which to view them. We can either consider events from a group-based perspective, focusing on how the group acts vis-à-vis outsiders, or other groups. Or, we can focus internally on how the behaviors influence the dynamics of the group itself, and the individuals composing it.

On the outcome side, territorial behaviors indicate, for individuals

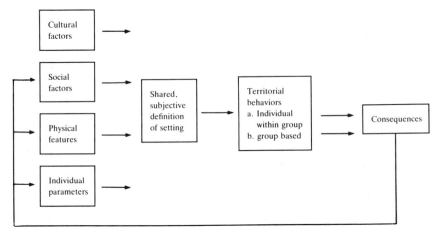

Figure 1.2. Capsule statement of conceptual model.

within groups, and for groups, relative positioning, involvement, and influence in the setting. These clarifications have *psychological, social psychological,* and *ecological* consequences. For example, they may help reduce stress, foster better ties among members of a group, and/or help the setting itself function more effectively.

Organization of the volume

Following the introduction, the remainder of the volume is organized into five parts.

Part I investigates the origins of human territorial functioning. Chapter 2 describes territorial systems operating in various nonhuman species, ranging from those evolutionarily furthest removed from humans, such as ants, to those most similar – primates. The purpose of these descriptions is to demonstrate, across a wide variety of species, that territorial systems (a) are not linked in any deterministic fashion with physical violence, (b) depend upon relations between individuals and the groups they constitute, (c) are highly context specific, operating in relationship to available resources, and (d) are "functional" in several different ways. Chapter 3 provides a specific model of the emergence of territoriality among humans. Chapter 4 explores the various explanations of human territorial systems that have been offered. Instinct-based, group selection-based, sociobiologic, and cultural evolutionary perspectives are reviewed. The latter is a particular extension of sociobiology. It considers how both genes and culture can work together to facilitate the evolution of functional social behaviors such as territoriality, and seems a particularly promising explanation for the initial emergence of human territorial functioning.

The reader may well wonder about the relevance of such material in a book primarily about humans in "modern" contexts. The discussion in Part I is needed, however, for two reasons. First, it provides a larger context or baseline against which human behaviors, sentiments, and cognitions can be assessed. It provides a larger framework for "making sense" out of the human patterns, explaining where such patterns are "coming from." Second, the material is needed to counteract fallacious arguments that, even today, are accepted by many in part, perhaps, because these ideas fit well with some "everyday" notions about territorial functioning. Of course, those not interested in evolution or human–nonhuman linkages may skip Part I with no ill effects.

Part II includes two chapters detailing my conceptual approach to human territorial functioning. Chapter 5 defines territorial functioning and indicates how it overlaps with, but also differs from, related environment–behavior concepts such as attachment to place, personal space, and others. Links between territorial functioning and social, psychological, personal, and cultural factors are indicated. Connections between territorial functioning and the larger social order are noted.

Chapter 6 introduces two theoretical perspectives in psychology that nicely complement the territorial perspective being developed, and provide added insight into the consequences of territorial functioning. Dan Stokols' place-specific analysis of how settings exacerbate or ameliorate stress is introduced. His analysis clarifies the means by which territorial functioning reduces stress.

The second theoretical perspective introduced is ecological psychology's behavior setting theory. Ecological psychology, developed by Roger Barker and later refined by Allan Wicker and others, is concerned with identifying the extant "natural" units in the environment. These researchers succeeded in identifying such units and called them *behavior settings*. In the outdoor, residential environment I will argue that territorial functioning plays several roles in shaping and maintaining the functioning of these behavior settings.

The utility of these two perspectives can be stated differently. Throughout, as exemplified in the conceptual model presented in Chapter 5, my approach to human territoriality is functionalist, in the Parsonian sense. That is, I focus on how territoriality helps groups, and individuals in groups, get along. I do not wish to imply that conflict never comes into play. But without the territorial system there would be even *more* conflict. Relations within groups, and across groups, in particular settings, would be even more strife-torn without territorial functioning.

The functionalist perspective is complemented by the stress perspective. The latter is, in a way, the reverse of the former.

The focus on behavior settings moves us away from groups and individuals in groups to focus solely on the settings themselves, to consider what is happening "out there" in the environment, regardless of whom it is happening to, or why.

Part III is the empirical "heart" of the volume. The chapters progress from discussions of the most intimate, central, and prototypical territories, such as are found in the home, to the most public, least central, and least prototypical territories, such as are found in public spaces, like a seat on a train or in a library. The material is ordered using the concept of *centrality*. We start with settings where the person–setting links are of *high* centrality and progress to settings where it is *low*.

The concept of centrality refers to how critical a particular space is to the overall "lifespace" of the individual or group.[3] *Centrality* focuses on the importance of the setting as a supportive context for daily functioning. Spaces whose loss is more upsetting to the individual or group, or where disruption has a more deleterious impact on healthy functioning, causing more stress, are more central locations. Centrality is not a characteristic of a place; it is an attribute of the *transactions* between an individual (or group) and a place: It is an aspect of person–place bonds. Thus, two people may feel differently about the centrality of a particular place. Nonetheless, across a broad range of spaces, many people may concur about the *relative* differences in centrality. This agreement is indicated in Figure 1.3.

Degree of centrality is chosen as the organizing framework for the empirical material because as we move from more central to less central settings there are shifts in the specific consequences of territorial functioning. More specifically, as we move from places where person–place transactions are of high centrality to places where they are lower, psychological consequences of territorial functioning lessen, and ecological consequences become more important. Further, such an organizing scheme highlights one of the major themes of the volume, namely, the place specificity of territorial functioning.

Chapter 7 examines territorial functioning in settings that are often highest on the centrality continuum (see Figure 1.3), that is, settings within the household. The empirical literature, albeit scant, reveals that territorial functioning within the household is shaped by the ongoing

[3] Lewin, K. (1936). *Principles of topological psychology*. New York: McGraw-Hill.

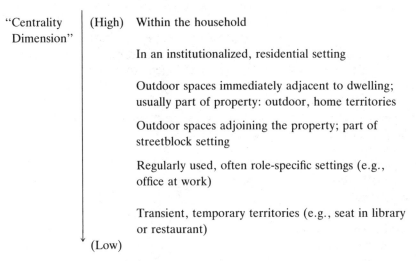

"Centrality Dimension"

(High) Within the household

In an institutionalized, residential setting

Outdoor spaces immediately adjacent to dwelling; usually part of property: outdoor, home territories

Outdoor spaces adjoining the property; part of streetblock setting

Regularly used, often role-specific settings (e.g., office at work)

Transient, temporary territories (e.g., seat in library or restaurant)

(Low)

Figure 1.3. Spaces arrayed along centrality continuum.

social and cultural dynamics of the setting, and limited by the lexicon of available isolable locations within the household. In experiments and observations carried out in institutional or experimental residential settings, social dynamics, in the form of group composition and social position of particular individuals, emerge as key forces shaping territorial processes. Place specificity is relevant as territorial behaviors are contingent upon the subjective importance of location. Finally, persons' territorial behaviors when "at home" and visited by others are examined. Highlighting the influence of social context, group climate (cooperative vs. competitive) emerges as one determinant of these interactions.

Chapter 8 considers spaces immediately outside the home. These outside locations buffer the individual or household from the immediate local society on the streetblock, but at the same time allow the person or household to contribute in pivotal ways to the continued maintenance of the streetblock setting. The chapter explores how the streetblock functions as a behavior setting, and how the behaviors of individuals and households in their exterior home and near-home territories help maintain the setting.

Chapter 9 moves into regularly used territories, where one often encounters familiar others. Territorial functioning in workplaces, such as offices, is examined. Uses of territorial processes to convey "messages" regarding social position, and the links between social position, territorial functioning, and physical attributes, merit attention. Outcomes of sports contests are also considered, and the social dynamics resulting in a home court *disadvantage* noted.

Chapter 10 concludes Part III by considering territories that are the least prototypical – what have been called temporary or public territories. These are places where very "stripped down" or minimal territorial functioning is evident. Territorial functioning is so minimal in these settings because a supportive group context is lacking. In these types of places territorial functioning is often maintained by an individual in a context that is socially unfamiliar. Some of the studies highlight again the theme of place specificity, observing that the claiming of a territory is more vigorous the more valued the spot.

Part IV includes two chapters that explore applications of territorial functioning to "real-world" problems. These two chapters highlight the continuing evolution and unfolding of theory and research on human territorial functioning. Chapter 11 examines the relationship between territorial functioning in the urban residential environment, and crime, fear of crime, and vandalism. The general model introduced in Chapter 5, and used as an organizing framework in Chapters 7 through 10, is *extended* to address problems of disorder more clearly.

Chapter 12 explores the theoretical linkages between territorial processes and resource conservation. Laboratory studies using *territorializing strategies* in a "tragedy of the commons" situation find that these approaches result in more resource conservation. Territorializing strategies used in lab settings bear important similarities to territorial functioning in the "real world." Suggestions are made concerning how territorial strategies could be developed, on a small group basis, for the latter settings. Although much more work is needed, territorializing strategies might be useful in various "real-world" situations where conservation is an issue. Issues relevant to possible implementation are discussed.

Part V closes out the volume. In Chapter 13 the general line of argument advanced in the book is reviewed. Chapter 14 considers the future of research and application. Three particular areas of fruitful application are outlined: stress reduction in households, privatizing streets to reduce disorder, and energy conservation.

Before leaving the outline of topics, a few words are in order regarding some material *not* found in the volume. Closely related to the concept of territorial functioning, but nonetheless distinct from it, is the concept of *attachment to place*. Such material, although intriguing (at least to the author), did not fit cleanly with the rest of the material. As a result, the current volume overlaps less with mainstream urban sociology than I would like.

Summary

This chapter touched on several key features of the approach to human territorial functioning that will be adopted in this volume. The approach will be grounded in two ways. An evolutionary perspective will be used to guide the delineation of human territorial functioning. As a result, the present treatment of human territorial functioning is somewhat circumscribed, compared to previous conceptualizations. The evolutionary perspective indicates that territorial functioning is *small group based* and highly *place specific*. The approach is also grounded in current social science research on the topic, focusing primarily on the areas of sociology and psychology, with other contributions coming from anthropology, geography, and criminology. Major themes in the current treatment of territorial functioning were introduced, and the conceptual model to be later developed was presented in capsule form. The contents of the volume were outlined. Following consideration of the evolutionary origins of human territorial functioning, a conceptual model of human territorial functioning is presented. Several chapters present the major results from social science investigations on the topic, and are organized by type of setting.

PART I
ORIGINS OF HUMAN
TERRITORIAL FUNCTIONING

Previous treatments of human territorial functioning have either ignored the issue of its origins, or handled it badly or in too abbreviated a fashion. At the risk of repeating the second error, the three chapters in this section seek to investigate the matter. Achieving a perspective on the origins of human territorial functioning will serve to clear away misconceptions that surround the concept and to clarify its evolutionary origins.

Chapter 2 provides some details on the range of territorial behaviors displayed by various species. Territorial functioning in ants, birds, and primates reveals several commonalities, most particularly links between the local ecology and territorial functioning, and between territorial functioning and group processes. The material addresses questions such as: What forms does territorial functioning take? What ends does it accomplish? Is it universally present in all species? Does it guarantee high levels of conflict?

Chapter 3 addresses the following question: Since our evolutionarily closest "relatives" do *not* engage in widespread territorial behavior, might territorial functioning have provided an advantage to early hominids as they emerged and diverged from other primates? Using conceptual pieces from C. O. Lovejoy and Glenn King, a case is made for a home-based, male provisioning, social carnivore model of early territorial functioning.

Chapter 4 addresses the question: What theoretical framework is most appropriate for explaining territorial functioning and its evolution? Ardrey's instinct-based arguments, still influential, are considered. The essence of a sociobiological interpretation of territorial functioning is outlined. Particularly useful are recent models of cultural evolution and group selection that help explain (respectively) how territorial functioning was elaborated and disseminated among humans. Some speculations are offered regarding the evolution of territorial functioning in humans subsequent to the emergence of a capacity for culture.

Note to the reader. The reader should feel free to skip the next three chapters. Some may find the material somewhat more difficult than that presented in the other chapters. If the reader is willing to accept the conclusions emerging from Part I (see the introduction to Part II), and my assertions that territorial functioning is evolutionarily driven, small group based, and contextually sensitive, he or she can bypass the next three chapters.

2

TERRITORIAL FUNCTIONING AND RELATED PROCESSES IN DIFFERENT SPECIES

But animals do not move at random throughout the world, and most cling to some piece of earth, which they know intimately. Throughout the study, I plotted the routes of travel of the various gorilla groups on a map, and soon it became apparent that there were some boundaries beyond which a group did not roam.
– George Schaller, The Year of the Gorilla *(p. 191)*

In this chapter territorial functioning and related sociospatial processes, such as uses of a home range, are described for different species, ranging from ants to primates. Some of *Homo sapiens's* nearest primate relatives, however, do not show evidence of territorial functioning, although they do use home range areas and are probably attached to them. This brief consideration of different varieties of territorial functioning underscores several points, including the variable, conflict-inhibiting, place-dependent, and group-linked nature of territorial functioning.

Before moving into this descriptive area, some basic concepts in evolutionary theory are presented along with key terms relevant to different evolutionary mechanisms.

Some key points in evolutionary theory

Darwinian theory seeks to explain the evolution of characteristics of species. Some of the key concepts of evolutionary theory are defined in the following box. Darwin suggested that *natural selection* played a primary role in determining which organisms survived and had offspring, and which did not.

All members of a particular species, at a particular time and in a particular location, are not equal. Due to their individual makeups, members have different capacities (some otters may be stronger swimmers than others, for example), and due to varying experiences, may

17

behave differently (some lions may be better hunters because they learned from parents who were more adept).

Key terms in selection theory[1]

Forces driving evolution:
1. *Mutation pressure:* pressure resulting from genetic mutations within a population. These changes are unrelated to their adaptive value in the environment.
2. *Gene flow:* a migration pressure, resulting from the introduction of genetically different individuals into the population.
3. *Genetic drift:* "the alteration of gene frequencies through sampling error."[2] This is more likely to occur in smaller populations.
4. *Natural selection.* "Occurs whenever some types of genes [or traits] are replicated and transmitted to the next generation consistently more often than others."[3]

Three ingredients needed for natural selection to occur:
1. Heritable variation.
2. Variants (specific behaviors, traits, or physical features) must have an impact on the phenotype (individual organism).
3. "Phenotypic differences [differences among various individual organisms] must affect individuals' chances of transmitting the variants they carry."[4]

Levels at which natural selection can occur: (1) genes, (2) individuals, (3) kin, or (4) populations or groups.

   Individual selection processes occur over generations and "operate on" direct progeny (e.g., through daughters or sons). (Cf. *group selection.*) The processes result in *direct fitness.*

   Kin selection processes working through related as well as direct progeny (e.g., sons or daughters of brother or sister) result in *indirect fitness.*

   Inclusive fitness (direct + indirect fitness) refers to "the sum of an individual's own individual fitness plus all effects the individual's activities have on the individual fitness of relatives other than direct descendants."[5]

---

[1] Pertinent sources for this material came from: Richerson, P. J., & Boyd, R. (1984). Natural selection and culture. *BioScience, 34*, 430–434.
   Wilson, E. O., & Bossert, W. H. (1972). *A primer of population biology.* Stamford, CT: Sinauer.
   Wittenberger, J. F. (1981). *Animal social behavior.* Belmont, CA: Wadsworth.
[2] Wilson & Bossert (1972), p. 83.
[3] Wittenberger (1981), p. 26.
[4] Richerson & Boyd (1984) p. 431.
[5] Wittenberger (1981), p. 62.

Genotype: the genetic material, or makeup, of particular or subsequent generations. Selection at the genotypic level is rarely observed. Most often we observe selection of:

Phenotypes: the outward behavior and makeup of individual organisms. Selection always acts on phenotypes, even though, in genetic form, the selection theory focuses on genotypes.

Fitness: "the tendency for a trait . . . to increase or decrease in a population."[6] Alternative terms are *selective value* or *adaptive value*, meaning that these traits help the organism adapt or propagate more successfully than others in the population.

Group selection: processes operating at the group level such that the progeny of one group are more fit than the progeny of another group.

Role of selection pressures

These differences, or variations, are important because most species in most environments experience *selection pressure.* That is, the environment in which they are living puts pressure on them to adapt capably to the setting. The simple fact that a particular species plays a role in the food chain, gobbling up smaller creatures and being gobbled up by larger ones, can become a selection pressure if the density of predators is high, and/or the density of prey is low. Consequently, in a particular niche, some members of a species survive and have progeny, and others do not. The fitter organisms, through their progeny, have passed on their genetic heritage.

Over succeeding generations, those organisms with the genes or traits that are associated with a higher level of *fitness* will become, relative to other organisms in the population, more prevalent. Consequently, those genes or traits will "spread" through the population, and the population as a whole will become more adapted to the context in which it finds itself. (Matters get more complicated when the organisms' niche changes, but let's ignore this problem for the moment.) So, if at one particular time there were lions in a particular setting, some of whom had parents who were adept hunters and some of whom had parents not adept at hunting, and if over successive generations the prey on which those lions fed was sparse, many generations later the adept hunters would predominate in the population.

Darwin originally suggested that selection could occur at the individual level, *or* at the group level. In the case of group-level selection, (a) subgroups of a species are separated from one another, (b) some subgroups have more of a particular trait than another group, and (c)

---

[6] Ibid., p. 46.

the trait is such that it would not be selected for at the individual level – it would not help the individual organism survive, but it might help the *group* survive (e.g., the "trait" of cooperation). (There are also many additional special conditions that must be present for group selection to operate adequately using genetic mechanisms, but we need not be concerned with those just yet.) Thus, over successive generations, assuming selection pressure in the niches in question, the group in which more members have the trait of cooperation will have more progeny, thus demonstrating their enhanced fitness.

Varying uses of evolutionary theory

When Darwin originally formulated evolutionary theory, genes were not yet known. Thus, the mechanisms that would actually carry out the selection were unspecified. With the discovery of genes, and the development of genetic theory, processes of selection became linked to genetic mechanisms. The bulk of attention, in the midpart of this century, was given to selection for various *physical traits*, through genetic mechanisms. Individual organisms with genetic material resulting in traits with high survival value would have more progeny, and thus their genes, relative to the genes of other individual organisms, would "spread," via processes of *individual selection*, throughout the population over successive generations.

Extending the framework even further, for about twenty years researchers have been applying genetic, evolution-based ideas to social behaviors. This field is referred to as *sociobiology*. They have sought to explain social behavior using a consistent, evolutionary perspective. Many researchers have relied on a genetic framework to explain the transmission of social behaviors across generations. A variety of social behaviors have been investigated.

A good case in point is altruism. An individual organism helping others in a group is not benefiting him- or herself directly. Actually, he or she may be putting him- or herself at risk by helping another (e.g., a male gorilla, running from a hunting party, and pausing to pick up an infant gorilla he has not sired). Such behavior can be explained, however, with the concepts of *kin selection* and *inclusive fitness*. The individual passes on some traits through progeny of brothers and sisters, as well as his own progeny. Processes of individual selection, making it more likely to have more progeny, and processes of kin selection, making it more likely for related others to have more progeny, result, together, in greater inclusive fitness.

Even more recently, sociobiologists have "broken out" of the genetic framework and have begun to consider how *cultural transmission* might also be explained by evolutionary processes. In the next chapter we will explore this *coevolutionary perspective*, which says that traits may be passed on through *both* genes and culture.

Clearly, the evolutionary perspective is enormously powerful and is capable of explaining both the development of physical traits and social behavior patterns, at the individual or group level, using genetic or cultural-based mechanisms. Consequently, it is important to be able to understand territorial functioning, in nonhuman species, from this powerful perspective, and to see how human territorial functioning may have been adaptive, three to six million years ago, when hominids were emerging in East Africa.

Territorial functioning and related processes in other species

A rough working definition of a territory, for nonhuman species, is as follows: "a fixed area from which intruders are excluded by some combination of advertisement, threat, and attack."[7]

The behaviors involved in maintaining these territories are what we mean by territorial functioning when referring to nonhuman species. The result of a territorial arrangement is "site-dependent dominance."[8] That is, the individual or group possessing the territory has certain advantages over other individuals or groups of the same species, and sometimes even over members of different species. These advantages pertain mainly to access to a variety of resources located within the territory, and greater familiarity with the site. Consequently, the "holders" can better evade predators. In the case of insects such as ants the main type of resource of interest is food supplies. When we turn to other types of organisms such as birds we shall see that other types of resources, such as nesting sites, are also important.

Territories, core areas, and home ranges

For nonhuman species holding territories there is a continuum of types of sites, from home ranges to core areas to territories.[9] Territories are related to areas called *home ranges*. These are the bounded or circumscribed areas within which the individual or group spends most of its time.[10]

---

[7] Brown, J. L. (1975). *The evolution of behavior*. New York: Norton. Cited in Barash, D. P. (1982) *Sociobiology and behavior*, 2nd ed. New York: Elsevier, p. 370.

[8] Barash (1982), p. 370.

[9] Ibid.

[10] Wittenberger (1981), p. 247.

Within the home range are certain heavily used *core areas*. These are usually centered on sleeping areas and sites where desirable food resources are available on a routine basis (e.g., watering holes).[11] As we go from home ranges to core areas to territories there is decreasing overlap between the different "user groups," and an increasing emphasis on exclusive use. That is, the resident individual or group becomes less willing to tolerate "outsiders" in that area.

As we go from home ranges to territories the quality of the space increases; there are more benefits gained from using and defending the location. An animal or group of animals is acting territorial if they "(1) restrict some or all of their activities to a defended area, (2) advertise their presence within that area, and (3) maintain essentially exclusive possession of all parts of that area."[12]

Territories represent something valuable; they must contain something that helps the occupying individual or group to survive. The more valuable the site in question the more likely it is that the occupying individual or group will demand exclusive use. The value of the locale is not only a function of what is in it; what is outside is important as well. The survival-enhancing quality of resources within the territory is determined by their value relative to resources available elsewhere.

Even this preliminary attempt to "pin down" the nature of nonhuman territories makes it clear that the type of space in question is not easily defined and isolated. There are no absolute dividing lines between home ranges and core areas, or between core areas of the home range and territories. Nonetheless, using a criterion of excludability of competitors allows us to classify sites with a fair amount of certainty.

Ways of defending territories

There are many different ways of defending a territory. Sometimes occupant and intruder may actually come to blows. But, as some of the following examples will illustrate, more often than not less violent measures suffice. There may be a "mock" combat where the individual (or group) occupying the territory makes threatening motions and acts as if it (or they) will actually engage the trespasser. And in many, many instances simple "advertisements" are all that is necessary. These may include various secretions (e.g., urination in the case of wolves), bird songs, and other mechanisms. In short, these examples will indicate that there is no necessary, unconditional link between nonhuman territoriality and physical aggression.

[11] Ibid., p. 249.
[12] Ibid.

These examples also provide evidence on some other general points. Maintenance of territories is not universal across species. Some of our closest "ancestors" do not exhibit territorial functioning. Second, territorial functioning is highly specific to particular locations, and the environmental contingencies operating there. As the contingencies shift (e.g., resources become more plentiful during a wet season), territorial functioning may alter, or disappear altogether. The functioning is dependent on the setting, and the circumstances in the setting at a particular time.

Some different forms of territorial functioning

Ants

Ants are most unlike us in size and social organization.[13] Much is known about ants; the kinds of territorial functioning they exhibit are diverse. Further, their forms of territoriality are intimately connected with the nature of their food resources.

Two features of ant colonies help explain their territorial functioning (see Table 2.1). First, ant colonies are socially complex and exhibit an elaborate division of labor, which makes complex communication strategies necessary. Second, the colonies are largely stationary; for each individual, most if not all of its life is spent in and around a particular location. Therefore, they get to know their locale and what it has to offer.

The three types of ants discussed in Table 2.1 have different types of food supplies – uniformly distributed in time and space, spatially patchy but temporally stable, and spatially and temporally unstable. Consequently, the type of territorial defense that has evolved for each type is different, and is "tailored" to the particular food supply. That is, each territorial strategy maximizes benefits, such as access to the food source, and minimizes costs, such as energy spent in territorial defense. Thus, each strategy is adaptive to the particular situation of the colony.

A second feature illustrated by all three examples is the social nature of the territorial strategies. The complex strategies are dependent upon communication structures, such as a forager returning to the nest site and "recruiting" others, or members of the nest following chemical signposts laid down by others. Without such communication structures the strategies could not be pursued.

---

[13] The discussion of ant territories and territorial behavior relies on Holldobler, B., & Lumsden, C. J. (1980), Territorial strategies in ants. *Science, 210,* 732–739.

Table 2.1. *Territorial strategies in ants*

African weaver ants

Type of territory	Live in trees in the forest canopy. Average colony covers 17 trees, 1,600 square meters. Capture insects that wander into their trees, also hunt on the ground. Build leaf nests where queen lives under guard.
Boundary defense	"Absolute." Respond to any invasions within the perimeter of the territory. "Border guards," in reaction to intruder, will return to leaf nest site and "recruit" defenders.
Resource/prey distribution	Prey are evenly distributed over time and space, in the trees, and along the ground.
Links to resources/ prey	Territorial strategy maintains integrity of the boundary, thus ensuring that all resources distributed within the territorial sphere are available to the host colony. Border maintenance strategy maximizes ratio of returns (resources available) to costs (energy expended in maintaining territorial integrity).

Harvester ants

Type of territory	Spatially complex trail system. Colonies lay out "recruitment" trails leading from nest site to newly discovered seed fall. Foraging ants from the nest move along these trunk trails. Trails have chemical "signposts" that are largely resistant to fading. Each colony follows its own highway system. Discovered food site is used as point of origin for new foraging expeditions.
Boundary defense	Ants from two different colonies only fight when their two trails cross, as happens when the trails are being laid out. Fighting ceases when trails diverge.
Resource/prey distribution	Spatially "patchy" and unpredictable, but temporally stable. Location of seed falls is unpredictable. But, once landed, they represent a stable resource that can be exploited over time.
Links to resources/ prey	Trails lead other members of the colony to a discovered resource (seed fall). Thus, each member of the colony need not rediscover, on its own, the food supply. Foraging energy is conserved. Energy is also conserved because unproductive or barren space is not defended.

Honey ants

Type of territory	"Temporary." Defend an area only if food sources have recently been discovered nearby. "Scout" finding supply returns to nest, recruits others. They

Table 2.1. *(cont.)*

	will then defend against other colony if it is located near the discovered food source. Engage in "display tournament," with other colony – a stylized mock combat – while nestmates carry off the food. Once food is removed, contest is broken off. Usually no casualties from the contacts.
Boundary defense	There is no defense of fixed boundaries. Area near located food source is defended while source is being removed.
Resource/prey distribution	One of their main food supplies is termites. These have an unpredictable spatiotemporal distribution.
Links to resources/ prey	Particular area is defended only if and while it is near food source. Minimal temporal duration of defense procedure results in energy "saved" for the ants.

Birds

Birds are "preadapted" to being territorial.[14] They have good vision and fly, which enables them to survey a large land area. Although many types of birds hold and defend territories, not all do. Whether or not territorial functioning is evident depends upon the way the resource (e.g., food or nesting sites) is distributed. Is it plentiful or scarce? Is its location fixed and predictable or random? And, it depends upon how much competition there is. Seagulls swirling around a garbage dump, where the resources are plentiful, provide an example of birds that do not hold territories.

The word "territory" was first applied to birds about 200 years ago by Oliver Goldsmith. The most significant modern study is Eliot How-ard's *Territory in Bird Life*.[15] An English businessman and amateur birdwatcher, Howard spent years trooping over the moors and through woodlands and fields observing a whole range of birds. His specialty was the warbler. He concluded from his observations that birds spend much time and energy defending and holding territories. Songs, he suggested, were part of the territorial system, serving both to warn off

---

[14] Barash (1982), p. 374.

[15] Nice, M. M. (1941). The role of territory in bird life. *American Midland Naturalist, 26,* 441–487.

Howard, H. E. *Territory in bird life.* London: John Murray.

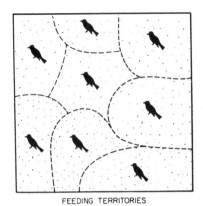
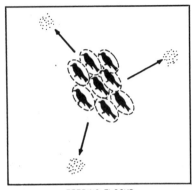

FEEDING TERRITORIES   FEEDING FLOCKS

Figure 2.1. Link between territorial functioning and resource distribution. "Horn's principle of group foraging. If food is more or less evenly distributed through the environment and can be defended economically, it is energetically most efficient to occupy exclusive territories [*left*]. But if food occurs in unpredictable patches [*right*], the individuals should collapse their territories to roosting spots or nest sites, and forage as a group." *Source*: E. O. Wilson (1980), *Sociobiology: The abridged edition*. Cambridge, MA: Harvard University Press, p. 27. Reprinted by permission.

challengers and to invite female companions to share a nesting site. Although his publication attracted little notice when it appeared, and the first printing eventually had to be remaindered (i.e., sold at a discount by the publisher), his work was important. It established, based upon extensive observation, that much of bird life was organized around the defense and advertisement of territories.

As with ants, the link between territorial functioning and resource distribution is quite clear-cut. This is evident from Horn's principle, which "applies to many kinds of colonial birds, from blackbirds and swallows, to herons, ibises, spoonbills, and other seabirds."[16] Horn's principle of group foraging, based on geometric analysis, suggests that whether birds hold individual territories or forage in groups depends upon the distribution of food in the environment (See Figure 2.1) When resources are unevenly distributed, group foraging makes more sense.

[16] Wilson, E. O. (1980). *Sociobiology: the abridged edition*. Cambridge, MA: Harvard University Press, p. 27.

The less experienced birds in the group save energy by following the more experienced birds, who have a better chance of locating food.

The link between territorial functioning and resource distribution is further demonstrated in the relationship between *territory size*, competition, and ampleness of resources. A number of bird studies have shown an inverse relation between the availability of food supply and size of territory.[17] For example, as the abundance of insects increases, the territory size of winter wrens decreases. As the quality and quantity of the heather plant increase, the territory size of the red grouse decreases.[18] Territorial extent thus appears, to some degree, to be a function of resource density.[19]

In fact, across species, the issue of territory size is quite amenable to an evolutionary perspective. As territory size increases, so do several costs. They increase directly and linearly with size. First, with a larger territory there will be more intrusions per unit time, simply because the border is more extensive. More time will be spent chasing trespassers off the property. Second, the costs of detecting each intruder will increase. A longer distance must be travelled from the sleeping site to the border, and more time will be taken up patrolling. Third, in the case of group territories (discussed later in this section), it will become progressively harder to expel intruders. Repelling intruders often involves summoning fellow group members for assistance (as discussed in Table 2.1). As the territory becomes larger group members are spread out more thinly, and thus recruiting them and getting them to the invasion site is more difficult and time-consuming. All of these costs will increase linearly with the size of the territory.

Putting these different costs and benefits together results in the scheme shown in Figure 2.2. There is a certain range of territorial sizes that will be optimal for a species in a given ecological situation. The size will be

---

[17] Wittenberger (1981), pp. 275–276.

[18] Ibid.

[19] Unfortunately, territory size also varies with some other factors in addition to food supply, such as the density of the species competing for the same food supply. Where territories are smaller there is a higher density of competing species. Wittenberger suggested that since abundant resources would attract more species relying on the same food supply, decreased territory size is a response to the increased competition pressure, not to more abundant supplies per se. It is also the case that the larger individual members of a particular species hold larger territories. This had led to a discussion regarding the "adaptive significance" of territories. Since animals can hold territories that serve many different functions (e.g., providing a nesting site, a mating site, a safe place to raise young, and an adequate food supply), it is very difficult exactly to determine the main reasons (functions) for holding territories.

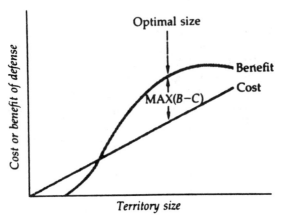

Figure 2.2. Predicting optimal size for territories. "An individual's fitness is maximal when territory size is adjusted to maximize the difference between benefits (*B*) and costs (*C*) of defense. Hence, optimal territory size occurs at *MAX (B − C)*." Consequently, the size of territory held is predictable. *Source:* J. Wittenberger (1981), *Animal social behavior.* Belmont, CA: Wadsworth, p. 286. Reprinted with permission of the author.

optimal in that the extent to which the benefits of the territory exceed the costs of defending the territory will be maximized.

Not only will individual birds hold and defend territories; so too will groups or flocks of birds. Certain species establish *group territories.* An example is the *acorn woodpecker,* found in California.[20] These woodpeckers live in extended family groups. They make holes in trees, fence-posts, and telephone poles into which they jam acorns. Since the acorns are tightly wedged in they can't be pilfered by squirrels, which also like acorns.[21] A storage granary can be a tree with up to 11,000 holes dug in it. Since it takes about half an hour to dig (or peck) each hole, such granaries represent a sizable energy investment on the part of the woodpeckers. It is not surprising then that the granaries are strongly defended against intruders, even when they are empty. The woodpeckers will also defend other areas of their home range, but not as strongly as they defend the granaries. In areas where acorn woodpeckers do not peck holes for their stores, but simply put acorns any old place (e.g., under

[20] Wittenberger (1981), p. 265.
[21] This is an example of a territorial strategy adapted to inter- as well as intraspecific competition. Since the woodpeckers and the squirrels compete for the same food, the woodpeckers defend against the squirrels, even though they are a different species.

a piece of loose bark), empty stores are not defended. Thus, where woodpeckers spend lots of energy building a store, which is reusable, they will "mind the store" when it is stocked *and* when it is empty. This is an economical strategy in that it saves them the energy they would have had to expend next year to build (or peck) another storehouse.

Birds will hold territories to ensure access to a variety of resources such as food or nesting and mating sites. A group of birds, or individual birds, may defend a territory. Defense can be accomplished in a variety of ways such as advertisement through plumage or song.

Primates

It is only in the last twenty years that extensive field observations of primates have been completed. The work in the late 1950's and early 1960's of Jane Goodall with chimps, and George Schaller with mountain gorillas, has been followed by many other excellent studies of primates in their natural habitats. Prior to this work, most observations had been based on captive primates in zoo settings, or had been done by hunters, from behind a gunsight.[22] These earlier studies had suggested that primates, particularly gorillas, were fierce and highly aggressive. The naturalistic studies of the last quarter century have painted a different picture.

Although violence and even murder do occur in primate life, the incidence is low. Many primate species are territorial. Thus, in the primate realm as with other vertebrates, and with invertebrates, there is no inexorable or even strong connection between territorial functioning and violent behavior. Primate species, like other species, have many different and more efficient means, other than physical violence and contact, for preserving territorial integrity.

As primates are, in evolutionary terms, our closest "relatives," whether or not they exhibit territorial functioning, and if so in what way, is of particular interest. Examination of these species indicates, as with ants and birds, that territorial organization is highly resource dependent. Further, it is abundantly clear that territorial functioning in primates is linked with patterns of social organization.[23]

---

[22] Washburn, S. L. (1978). Human behavior and the behavior of other animals. *American Psychologist, 33*, 405–418. An excellently organized review of primate territorial behavior can be found in Jolly, A. (1972), *The evolution of primate behavior*. New York: Macmillan, Chapter 7.

[23] This is vividly illustrated in Jane Goodall's most recent work. See:
Goodall, J. (1986). *The chimps of Gombe: Patterns of behavior*. Cambridge, MA: Belknap Press of Harvard University Press, Chapter 17.

The territorial functioning–resource linkage is best demonstrated by contrasting *arboreal leaf eaters* such as *gibbons* and *howler monkeys* with some other species.

Perhaps the most general type of spatial arrangement adhered to by primates is that of the home range: the area occupied by an individual or group throughout its or their adult life, excluding long migration routes (e.g., between summer and winter feeding areas). As mentioned earlier, the entire area within the home range is not necessarily defended against other individuals or groups. A large part of it, however, may be. A portion within the home range can be described as the core areas – those portions of the home range frequently used for eating, sleeping, and drinking. The area within the home range that is defended against outsiders is the "defended territory." Other groups or individuals may occasionally wander into and attempt to feed in another's defended territory, but they are likely to be chased off. The "exclusive territory" is that area within the defended territory where there is no tolerance whatsoever for outsiders, and outsiders are unlikely to enter there, except briefly. Many more primates exhibit patterns of behavior indicative of home range use of space than territorial use of space.

Diurnal, arboreal leaf eaters such as gibbons or howler monkeys live in small groups or families. Distance between troops is maintained by long-distance signals between troops, such as a dawn chorus. This form of "Reveille" allows groups to locate other groups, and then move off in a direction that minimizes the chances of contact. Some primates in this group such as gibbons will usually move from the center of their territory to the boundary area where another troop was heard, and then engage in mock combat with that other group at the edge of the territory. Actual physical contact between males during these territorial displays is rare. The "tournament" may go on for one or two hours. Long-distance calls are also used at other times of the day, such as when two troops approach one another. Through these mechanisms exclusive "rights" over most of a territory are maintained.

For such species, territorial strategies are fitness enhancing, i.e., they "make sense" from an evolutionary perspective. The food supplies of such species, as compared, for example, to omnivores, or terrestrial leaf eaters, are less varied and more spatially predictable. Given the more restricted nature of their diet there is probably more competition between groups for food resources. Whenever competition over a resource is higher, a territorial strategy is more likely to be energy efficient. And, in addition, the resource in question is more spatially "predictable." Trees and bushes do not migrate. The resources are more easily defended, once an area is learned. Their foliage may vary over time, but is likely to follow predictable seasonal cycles. Therefore primates who

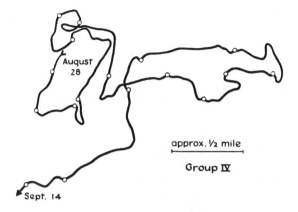

Figure 2.3. Gorilla group travel patterns. The figure illustrates the home range travel pattern of a group of mountain gorillas followed by Schaller from August 28 to September 14, 1959. The *circles* represent a nest site used for one night. The *lines* between the circles indicate the route travelled during a day by the group. *Source*: G. Shaller (1964), *The year of the gorilla*. Chicago: University of Chicago Press, p. 115. Copyright © 1964 by the University of Chicago. Reprinted by permission of the University of Chicago Press.

are mainly leafeaters, in contrast to omnivores, can be more assured of exactly what they are defending, and where it is.

The territorial strategy of howler monkeys contrasts nicely with the home-range strategy of mountain gorillas, which are semiterrestrial leaf eaters. George Schaller spent a year in East Africa observing mountain gorillas in 1959 and 1960.[24]

The mountain gorillas lived in small groups, ranging in size from 5 to 27, with a small number of adult males in each group. Each group covered a particular home range, an area with which it was familiar, foraging much of the day, and travelling in midafternoon. New nest sites were occupied each evening. The spatial behavior of one group of gorillas, for a two-week period of time, is shown in Figure 2.3.

Overlapping home ranges between two troops were common. There were no long-distance spacing mechanisms but rather short-distance ones. When two troops met the males would "glower and chest-beat" at one another.[25] Sometimes, however, the groups would socialize (e.g., groom one another), and individuals might even switch troops, although

[24] Schaller, G. B. (1964). *The year of the gorilla*. Chicago: University of Chicago Press.
[25] Jolly (1972), p. 123.

Schaller's observations suggest this is probably rare. These varied responses to outgroups suggest that "neighbors" are recognized and responded to differentially.

Schaller noted that one group had a highly variable response to meeting neighboring groups. "With group III it peacefully shared a common nest site; it approached group V to within fifty yards but made no attempt to mingle; and it behaved antagonistically toward group XI."[26]

The fact that several gorilla groups occupy the same section of the forest, and that, when groups meet, their interactions tend to be peaceful, was of considerable interest to me. Once it was generally thought that each monkey and ape group lived in a territory, the boundaries of which were defended vigorously against intrusion by other members of the same species. But the gorilla certainly shares its range and its abundant food resources with others of its kind, disdaining all claims to a plot of land of its own.[27]

Chimpanzees are considered, in terms of biological structure, to be our closest relative; that is, this is the primate group we "branched off from" some three to five million years ago. They exhibit home range spatial behavior. Semiterrestrial omnivores, also living in small groups, chimps do appear to form regional troops ranging in size from around 30 to 80 members. All within a troop are acquainted with one another. One troop may stay in a particular home range for a long period of time, or may migrate between home ranges as food availability shifts.

Until recently it was generally accepted that chimps were *not* a territorial species. But Jane Goodall's latest observations suggest that this is still an open issue. Based on the chimp troops she and her co-workers have observed over a number of years, Goodall concludes that, in several respects, chimps demonstrate "classic territoriality." Intruders "are expelled ... boundaries are monitored ... auditory displays may be exchanged ... boundaries may be respected over a number of years." At the same time, in contrast with the classic definition, outcomes of encounters between parties from neighboring groups are determined more by relative size than by location. Chimps have "a large home range with

---

[26] Schaller (1964), p. 200. It is interesting to note that there is a perfect rank order correlation between the degree of hostility with which group VII greeted the neighboring group in question, and the size of that neighboring group. Group II was 5 members, group V was 11 members, and group XI was 16 members. Group VII itself comprised 18 members. The group size figures are taken from Table 1, p. 111. Goodall's most recent observations confirm this point with chimps (1986, pp. 526–527). In fact, she suggests that the relative size of two neighboring parties may be a more important determinant of degree of violence during the encounter than the location.

[27] Ibid., p. 201.

considerable overlap between neighboring communities," and demon-strate more *violent* hostility towards neighbors than would be expected. Clearly, the extent and nature of chimp territorial functioning, and its use relative to home range strategies, are still open questions.[28]

In short, since the diets of mountain gorillas and chimpanzees are less spatially predictable, and more diverse, the former, and perhaps the latter, rely primarily on home range strategies. By contrast, arboreal leaf eaters, such as howler monkeys, whose resources are less diverse and more spatially predictable, rely mainly on territorial functioning. Thus, for primates, as with other species, territorial functioning is evi-dent and relied on most heavily if resource distribution is such that the functioning enhances fitness.

Conclusions

Territorial strategies are evident in species ranging from ants to primates. In all of these species, whether or not territorial strategies are pursued, as well as the exact type of strategies adopted, depends upon resource distributions and competition levels. The evolutionary perspective il-luminates the rationale behind these patterns of spatial behavior, sug-gesting how territorial strategies may maximize the ratio of benefits (resource availability and security) to costs (energy spent defending boundaries, finding new food sources, and so on). Individuals or groups may establish territories. Communication between groups or individuals is critical to efficient territorial maintenance.

In some of the primates evolutionarily close to human beings, home range rather than territorial strategies are primarily pursued. This raises an interesting issue. If these primates did not engage in territorial strat-egies, why did early humans do so? Is territorial functioning in any way implicated in the emergence of early human beings? And, if it is, in what ways did it promote successful adaptation? It is to these issues we turn in Chapter 3.

[28] Goodall (1986), pp. 525–528.

3
THE ORIGINS OF HUMAN TERRITORIAL FUNCTIONING

If some of our nearest evolutionary relatives, such as mountain gorillas, exhibit a home-range-based system of sociospatial behavior, then why did humans evolve a system of territorial functioning instead? Stated differently, what was the value of a system based on territorial functioning in our environment of evolutionary adaptedness, several million years ago on the savannas and in the forests of East Africa? This chapter sketches an answer to this question, drawing on recent anthropological theorizing. A territory-based spatial organization, coupled with a particular group/family structure, probably had significant adaptive value for primitive hominids.

The importance of territorial functioning in protohominid emergence

Anthropologists have long wondered what physical, cultural, and behavioral changes allowed the protohominids, emerging before *Homo erectus* and *Homo sapiens*, to flourish and compete successfully with pongids (gorillas, chimps, orangutans).[1] Current evidence suggests that

---

[1] The line of argument presented here is C. O. Lovejoy's (1981). The origin of man. *Science, 211*, 341–350. Reprinted in R. L. Ciochon & J. G. Fleagle (Eds.) (1985), *Primate evolution and human origins*. New York: Benjamin Cummings. The earliest hominids emerged four to six million years ago; they were preceded by protohominids, such as the Dryopithecines. Both hominids and man-apes or pongids emerged from this earlier

bipedality, the emergence of material culture involving toolmaking, and the expansion of the neocortex and the concomitant larger braincase, although applicable to later species, did not spur the emergence of *early* protohominids.

When protohominids emerged during the Miocene epoch (which began about 25 million years ago and ended roughly 7 million years ago), they lived not only in high savannas or grasslands but also in canopy forest and woodlands, and all these settings were characterized by marked seasonality. A selective advantage would have accrued to protohominids if they engaged in a pattern of behavior that allowed decreased infant mortality from environmental hazards in these varied settings.

Given the extended helplessness of infants, adaptations that allowed more intensive parenting behavior, permitting the infant to learn more, and more quickly, and permitted decreased parental travel, would have increased infant survival. Travelling and parenting are obviously exclusive activities for the parent. Further, travelling requires that the mother expend calories that then cannot be allocated to lactation. Further, when travelling the infant is constantly in danger of being injured. The best way to ensure infant survival is to sequester offspring "at locations of maximum safety."[2] But such sequestration is not possible if the mother and infant must forage for food. Schaller's mountain gorillas foraged from the time they woke up, till late morning, and then again sometimes before nesting down for the night. Foraging is a time- as well as energy-consuming activity. How could sequestration be possible?

Sequestration allowed more parenting, less travelling

Sequestration would be possible, allow more parenting time and less travel time for the infant, and would be safe and energy efficient if the mother–infant pairs occupied a particular base, *and* if related males foraged farther away from the base. There would be many advantages to such an arrangement. The separation of male and female feeding areas reduces competition between the two parents. Females forage close by and the male can bring food back to the female thereby increasing her protein intake and calories available for lactation, while at the same time reducing *her* foraging time. Furthermore, "lowered mobility of females would reduce accident rates during travel, maximize

line. J. A. Moore (1972). The evolution of life. In J. A. Garraty & P. Gay (Eds.), *The Columbia history of the world.* New York: Harper & Row.

  E. P. Lanning, Human evolution, in Garraty & Gay (1972), p. 36.
[2] Lovejoy (1985), p. 292.

familiarity with the core area, reduce exposure to predators, and allow intensification of parenting behaviors."[3] Thus, staying put and foraging close to home was safer, allowed more "quality time" between infant and mother, and ensured ample food supplies.

Male would forage afar if paternity assured

But, for the male of the "family" to go along with such an arrangement, in which he had to travel farther each day to a foraging area than the female so as to benefit his offspring, there must be some advantages. Such a strategy would "make sense" for him if, and only if, he is assured of the paternity of the infant who is benefiting from increased parenting and relative protection. This assurance is available in monogamous pair bonding, which would be associated, over time, with a roughly equal sex ratio. Under a monogamous arrangement the male would not be missing opportunities with available females to sire additional offspring when he travelled to and from his foraging area. Paternity for an individual male would not be assured under a polygamous bonding arrangement, where females would outnumber males, and other males could sire offspring while he is out foraging.

The male can also intensify his bonds with the "family" by spending time with his offspring, allowing for even more directed parenting, when he is not foraging. This time investment also serves to highlight the male's paternity, and the social structure based on the monogamous pair bond. The offspring also benefits from closer links with the parents.[4]

Male provisioning, home-based model

What has been outlined is a *male provisioning, home-based* model, where the male brings back food to the home site for the infant and nursing mother, thereby increasing the male's direct fitness. According to this model, mother–infant sequestration, with the male foraging farther afield and bringing home provisions, allows the mother to devote more time and calories to the offspring and reduces exposure to danger.

---

[3] Ibid., p. 293.

[4] An interesting example of the kinds of things the offspring can learn from watching the parents is correct food habits. Schaller [1964, p. 181] observed among mountain gorillas that "infants stay with their mothers and probably learn what to eat and what not to eat by watching them. In this way, food habits are handed down from generation to generation, a primitive form of culture. . . . When another infant began to gnaw on the petiole of a Hagiena leaf, which adults do not consume, its mother reached over and took the leaf away from it."

The model provides an evolutionary advantage to the male if and only if the groups are organized around a monogamous pair bond. The salience of this bond is heightened by male parenting with offspring. In other words, a sex-role-dependent, home-based system resulted in an optimal relationship between the protohominids and the available resources.

But a home-based system does not necessarily imply territorial functioning. One of the hallmarks of territorial functioning among primates and other species is the excludability of others. Attempts to exclude others and utilize a territorial system provide advantages if there is competition for available resources. Among early hominids this was probably the case. Starting out as omnivores they probably competed with members of the same species, and with other species, for the same food sources. Thus, if members of one group were able to exclude others, using some type of territorial strategy, they were preserving more resources for themselves and thus enhancing their fitness. In light of such concerns the optimal territory may have been an area for one family. So, in order to guarantee resources for exclusive consumption, a territorial system based on "single families" would have been a sensible strategy for protohominids.

Nonetheless, two additional factors need to be taken into account before we can come to closure on a model of protohominid territorial functioning: predation and diet.

Avoiding predation: group needed to maintain territory

Undoubtedly, the early hominids were preyed on by carnivores. Many carnivores as discussed later in this section operate in groups. A single male hominid, or a male and a female, would not have been much of a match for a pack of eight Miocene tigerlike beasts. Lacking sophisticated weaponry, they would have been sitting ducks for a foraging pride. Consequently, in order to detect and drive off predators, it made evolutionary sense for the early hominids to maintain a territory as a group. If the members in the group were kin, such territory defense and predator repulsion provided for kin selection and enhanced the inclusive fitness of all individuals involved. You were helping your own offspring, and your brother's offspring, and your sister's offspring, and so on. So, to repulse predators some territorial group-based arrangement was probably advantageous.

Group needed to support dietary habits

The second reason for a group-based territorial arrangement, instead of a single-family arrangement, derives from protohominid eating habits.[5] They, and hominids who came later, probably ate a lot of meat. Investigations of hominid remains from ancient campsites at the Olduvai Gorge in Africa, and elsewhere, have revealed piles of deliberately broken animal bones along with human fossils and tools used to cut up animals. The animals in question range from those that were considerably smaller than humans at the time to those that were considerably larger (elephants and saber-toothed tigers). Estimates from modern hunter–gatherer populations have suggested that about a third of their diet comes from meat. This stands in stark contrast to meat intake by primates, which is about 1 percent of their diet. But this dietary profile of protohominids and hominids is quite similar to that of *social carnivores*. Another difference between protohominids and pongids is that the former group routinely hunted and killed animals much larger than themselves; pongids have not been observed doing this. Thus, as protohominids evolved they may have adapted a hunting-gathering modus vivendi, eating more meat than their ancestors and going after bigger game.[6]

But protohominids and early hominids did not go after big game alone. Lacking weaponry such as fire or projectiles, they relied heavily on cooperation. The game hunted could outweigh individual hunters by 10 to 1 or 100 to 1. For example, early hominids going after bison went in a sizable group, isolated one animal from the rest of the herd, and drove it, with noise, shouts, and rocks, towards and over a cliff to its death. Once the animal was killed, assistance was needed to transport it back to the campsite where it could be shared with other members of the group, the most important being the women and children. Thus, cooperative hunting, with small groups fanning out from or fragmenting from a larger group, was probably how protohominids and, later, early hominids brought home the bacon.

---

[5] The key arguments presented here are those of Glenn King. King, G. E. (1975). Socio-territorial units among carnivores and early hominids. *Journal of Anthropological Research, 31*, 69–87.

King, G. E. (1976a). Socioterritorial units and interspecific competition: Modern carnivores and early hominids. *Journal of Anthropological Research, 32*, 276–284.

King, G. E. (1976b). Society and territory in human evolution. *Journal of Human Evolution, 5*, 323–332.

[6] King argues that an alternative to hunting live game, such as eating animals that others had killed, was probably not viable for the following reasons: (1) Carrion is scarce; (2) there is likely to be little meat left on the bones by the time the original killer is through with it; and (3) scavenging is dangerous because other animals are also attracted to the carrion site and could decide that the human scavenger is acceptable fare.

Social carnivores use territorial arrangements

Given this likely arrangement, it would be important to know the spatial systems used by current-day social carnivores. Such carnivores, in terms of their large meat intake, are similar to early hominids. If these social carnivores all exhibit the same type of spatial organization, it is likely that protohominids and early hominids may have used a similar system, given the comparable requirements of their heavy reliance on cooperative hunting to support dietary habits.

Social carnivores include lions, timber wolves, spotted hyenas, and the Cape hunting dog. All except the last do exhibit strong territoriality, by which is meant "the system in which a stable group occupies a stable home range and controls access to the prey animals that it contains."[7] The territorial arrangements used by different social carnivores are described in the accompanying box.

Territorial arrangements in social carnivores

Hyena clans, which can number up to 80 members, maintain nonoverlapping territories. Intruders, even if they are not hunting, are attacked or scared off; sometimes large between-clan fights can develop. Large fights between clans can also ensue if there is a dispute about the group to which killed prey belongs. Larger territorial groups, therefore, mean that the territory can be more successfully defended against other clans. This can happen if a hyena starts chasing an animal in its own territory but runs over into another clan's territory. The animals hunt alone or in small groups. But the larger the animal they are chasing the more likely they are to hunt in a larger group. Some instances of migratory hyena clans have been observed, but the predominant and most stable organization appears to be the territorial one.

Lions hunt in small groups – rarely more than 8 – but also belong to larger groups called prides of up to 40. Each pride has a stable, definite area, although the entire area is not defended against all lions from other prides. Main activity areas, and primary sources of food are, however, well defended.

Wolf packs are much smaller than hyena clans and lion prides, usually containing seven or fewer wolves. Larger packs have also been observed. Again, as with the preceding social carnivores, the pack breaks into smaller groups of one, two, or three animals for most hunting, unless very large

---

[7] King (1975), p. 73.

prey, such as moose, is being chased. It does appear from some limited evidence that larger packs are able to control a wider foraging area. Although timber wolves do migrate, their main form of organization is stable territorial groupings.

Hyenas, lions, and wolves share several similarities in territorial functioning.

1. *Two levels of social organization are apparent*: the larger grouping, which controls access to resources over an extensive area, and smaller subgroups devoted to hunting. The size of the latter group depends in part on the size of the prey sought. Since animals switch quite freely between hunting subgroups, it is safe to interpret the larger grouping as the main social unit.

2. *The smaller hunting groups represent optimal sizes for search and capture of prey*. They are small enough to be relatively unobtrusive, yet large enough so that when they cooperate they can bring down the desired animal.

3. *The spatial organization of the animals is stable*. That is, over time a clan or pride or pack will retain dominion over the same area. In some of these species, cubs may "inherit the estate." Some prides stay in the same location for two or three generations. Remaining in an area allows the occupants to become expert at predicting where and when they might find prey within their domain.

The organization is territorial in that the larger occupying group by and large controls who has access to the available resources – prey – within the area. Thus the important point about the territorial organization is not exclusivity – which may or may not be strictly maintained, depending on the species – but rather, that (4) *the territorial system allows each group to control who has access to the vital resources*.

The larger, community-level organization, from which the hunting groups branch off, confers an important advantage. Namely, if there is an all-out attack by the neighboring group on the territory, a large social entity is needed to defend against the intruders and prevent eviction. In such melees the larger group clearly has an advantage. Although these assaults may be rare, the availability of a larger potential group, which can be assembled if needed, allows the individuals to stay in a familiar area in the face of concerted challenges. This is an important advantage.

To sum up: Social carnivores eat a lot of meat, which means they must hunt a lot. Seeking prey that may be their own size or larger, they must cooperate with others in their group. Therefore they form small hunting groups. These smaller groups can coalesce into larger socioterritorial units. The larger units are useful in the event that large-scale defense of the territory is needed. The availability of such large potential groupings confers an advantage on the resident group in that they can resist being overrun and evicted, and therefore need not continually be searching out new hunting grounds and "learning the lay of the land" all over again.

Socioterritorial arrangements would have been adaptive for protohominids and early hominids

It seems likely that protohominids and, later on, early hominids displayed the same pattern of socioterritorial organization. Groupings would probably get to know an area and its wildlife and stay on that range for a period of time. They could, of course, have separate summer and winter ranges and spend some time migrating in between. In each area smaller hunting parties would move out and, having made a kill, transport the remains back to a central place or campsite. Should a hunting party make contact with an invading troop, they could return to the central location and summon other hunting groups who are also part of the larger group. Assembled, they could challenge the invaders. Barring vastly superior numbers, or untoward circumstances, they would probably be successful in defending their territory and its resources. Thus, the socioterritorial organization, based on moderate-sized groups off which smaller hunting parties branched as needed, provided direct and indirect fitness advantages, thus increasing inclusive fitness.

Summary

To sum up then: Inasmuch as some of our phylogenetically closest relatives do not exhibit territorial functioning, arguments must be offered, in an evolutionary framework, explaining why protohominids and early hominids demonstrated territorial functioning, outlining the advantages this provided them, as compared to their pongid relatives, and thus allowed them to further evolve. A rationale for a home-based, sex-differentiated, male provisioning model, based on monogamous pair bonding, can be developed. The advantages of such a system include reduced exposure of offspring to predators, more time for parenting, and decreased hazards from travelling. Consequently, the individual fitness of the male and female adults was enhanced, as their offspring received caloric, safety-related, and social benefits. To explain why occupants should demand exclusive use of an area centered on a home base requires only that we posit a spatially and temporally stable distribution of resources.

But, in order to provide for cooperative hunting of meat, and adequate defense against predators or resource competitors, the territorial system needs to be based on small groups (of 10–40), rather than individual male-female-offspring families. Such group-based territorial arrangements have been observed among social carnivores, whose diet is more similar to that of early humans than was the diet of early humans to that of primates. The large group provides for adequate defense of the territory against intraspecific or interspecific competition. The group can break into smaller hunting parties for the particular prey sought. Provided the group members are related, the group-based arrangement would enhance the indirect fitness of the individuals involved, and thus the overall inclusive fitness.

Thus, assuming competition and particular resource configurations, a territorial system demanding some degree of excludability, and based upon small groups, may have increased the inclusive fitness of proto-hominids and early hominids and allowed them to evolve. Stated more simply, the evolution of territorial functioning represented an elaboration of the home range system of closely related pongids and played a key role in the emergence of hominids several million years ago.

4

THEORETICAL PERSPECTIVES ON INTERPRETING TERRITORIAL FUNCTIONING: Exactly how did it evolve?

Social learning or cultural transmission can be modeled as a system of inheritance.[1]

"Don't you understand? If they get in we're dead."
– Dustin Hoffman, Straw Dogs

Chapter 2 described territorial strategies in several different species. As the examples suggested, the specific forms of territorial functioning adopted were contingent upon resource distribution and social organization. Turning to primates, we saw that although some do engage in territorial functioning, other species, including some of our nearest phylogenetic neighbors, do not rely primarily on a territorial arrangement. Consequently, the question emerged: In what ways might territorial functioning have enhanced the fitness of early hominids as they evolved from pongids? In Chapter 3 Lovejoy's male provisioning model provided the rationale for a home-based spatial organization, and considerations of diet, hunting, and defense from predation suggested that a small group, territorial–based system may have enhanced the inclusive fitness of protohominids and, later, early hominids.

Organization of the chapter

In this chapter we attempt to go further, more clearly specifying the exact forms of evolutionarily driven mechanisms responsible for the transmittal, development, and elaboration of territorial functioning. Within an evolutionary framework, there are three perspectives directly pertinent to territorial functioning. Very loosely, these are the *instinct, group-*

---

[1] Richerson, P. J., & Boyd, R. (1984). Natural selection and culture. *BioScience, 34,* 430–434.

based conservation, and *sociobiology* perspectives. The first, albeit dismissible, deserves mention given the popularity it has had. The second is noteworthy because it focuses attention on the relationship between the organisms in question, and their impacts on the ecology. The third perspective, sociobiology, is one on which we shall spend some time. Among sociobiologists, three "schools" can be distinguished: those focusing on genetic transmission, those focusing on gene–culture interactions, and those focusing on cultural transmission. The latter variant of the perspective, I will argue, is an extremely useful model for pinpointing the processes by which territorial functioning was shaped and transmitted.

The instinct perspective

Ardrey's view: the territorial imperative

In the early 1970's, the late Sam Peckinpah directed *Straw Dogs*, a deeply disturbing, violent movie. Dustin Hoffman, playing a distant, distracted astrophysicist who hopes to find quiet to complete his theoretical research, returns with his young wife (Susan George) to her father's farmhouse in western England. Animosities mount between "the Yank" and a group of young local men, fueled in part by his wife's seductive behavior and past popularity. She is subsequently raped by two of the men while her husband is decoyed away. Later, while driving on a foggy night he hits a local mentally retarded man and takes him to the farmhouse. The injured man has just inadvertently killed a young village girl. In pursuit, several local toughs, drunk, come to take him away and "ask him a few questions." The professor, over his wife's protestations, refuses to give the man up and orders them out.

The siege begins with window breaking. The local magistrate arrives but is killed while trying to disarm one of the attackers. The transformation begins; the bespectacled professor turns into a calculating, shrewd, and appallingly brutal defender of his house. One by one, with wire, burning acid, and an enormous, antiquated animal trap, the attackers are killed. The professor's wife shoots the last one. As the professor drives the retarded man home, the latter says, "I don't know my way home." "Neither do I," replies the astrophysicist.

The film is deeply troubling. Putting aside the gratuitous physical and sexual violence, there is an undeniable air of plausibility as the professor's transformation unfolds. The ease with which the veneer of civilization falls away from one of its most "advanced" members conjures up a most unwelcome image of ourselves. It seems to deny that civilization has had any positive effect on "human nature," to suggest that when we get right down to it we are not much better than our protohominid and primate forebears who, some argue, survived millions of years ago because they able to kill before they got killed. Robert Ardrey, author of *The Territorial Imperative* and proponent of "open instinct" theory, holds just such a view.

Before launching into a detailed consideration of Ardrey's views, some justification is needed. Some have suggested that no one takes his ideas, quite popular in the late 1960's and early 1970's, at all seriously any more. Nonetheless, even as recently as two years ago I had students who strongly espoused Ardrey-like beliefs, which suggests that his ideas were not simply a fad, or, if a fad, have not yet run their course.

Adherents to Ardrey's main line of thought – that territoriality applies to behaviors on vastly different scales, ranging from interactions between two people to clashes between nations, and that territoriality is instinct based – have even recently shown up among credentialled writers. Torsten Malmberg's 1980 volume *Human territoriality* is a good case in point.[2]

According to Malmberg, there are fundamental similarities between the structures that motivate mammalian behavior and those that regulate human behavior;[3] territorial functioning applies to everything from personal spaces to nation-states; and territorial functioning is innate and instinctually driven. "So it seems reasonable to assume that territoriality is innate and should be placed in the limbic system."[4] So, the treatment of territorial functioning is sweeping, applying to spaces of vastly differing scales. The parallels between Malmberg's and Ardrey's views suggest that Ardrey's view of territorial functioning is somewhat more enduring and attractive than many would wish.

Ardrey felt that current human behaviors are as much driven by the "territorial imperative" as were the behaviors of our prehistoric ancestors. "If we defend our title to our land or the sovereignty of our country, we do it for reasons no different, no less innate, no less ineradicable, than do lower animals."[5]

According to this view, territoriality is instinctual, "hardwired," just like our physical characteristics, with inescapable consequences. Reference to it explains a broad range of phenomena from how property owners act to how nations behave. As an example of the latter, Ardrey suggested that because of territorial factors America would lose,

---

[2] Malmberg, T. (1980). *Human territoriality: Survey of behavioral territories in man with preliminary analysis and discussion of meaning.* New York: Mouton.

[3] Ibid., p. 308.

[4] Ibid., pp. 317–318.

[5] Ardrey, R. (1966). *The territorial imperative.* New York: Dell, p. 5.

and the North Vietnamese would win, the Vietnam War.[6] In short, the territorial "principle" was expanded by Ardrey until it was all-encompassing, and forceful beyond restraining. He granted that these instincts were "open"; the final form they took was influenced by learning.[7] But the forces of the "innate design," although more labile in the case of "open" as compared to "closed" instincts, were no less avoidable.

What is the territorial instinct? According to Ardrey it is, very simply, "the command to defend one's property."[8] "When we discuss behavior patterns, such as the territorial, we discuss these open programs of instinct. The disposition to defend a territory is innate. The command to defend it is likewise innate."[9] Thus, in Ardrey's view, to appropriate and protect space is the territorial principle, or "imperative."

Ardrey identified three psychological factors that "motivate" territorial behavior: security, stimulation, and identity. Security is provided by the safe locus of the territory. Stimulation is provided by the defense and interchanges that occur at the boundary. Identification is provided by the overall meaning of the territory. Besides territory, war also satisfies all three of these "needs."

Ardrey's view of human territorial functioning is essentially this: People are aggressive, even murderous, like our killer ape ancestors. We need to be secure, to be stimulated, and to identify with something larger. In higher animals such as primates these "psychological" needs are met by territory and conflict. The territorial imperative is an open instinct, part design, part learning, which drives us to claim and defend territories. Territories range in size from the very small – a seat – to the very large – a nation. As long as distinctions can be made between an in-group and an out-group, the space defended by the in-group can be called a territory. Hatfield–McCoy disputes, Napoleon at the gates of Moscow, people putting up fences, and gang warfare in Brooklyn are all interrelated in one seamless conceptual web.

The trilogy of needs discussed by Ardrey are like fluid in a hydraulic cylinder; they build and need to be bled off by certain behaviors. If they are released by small-scale competitions they will not build up pressure to the point where they can only be let off by large eruptions such as wars. The territorial imperative is pervasive, demanding, and unavoidable, according to this view.[10]

---

[6] Ibid., pp. 293–294.
[7] Ibid., pp. 24–26.
[8] Ibid., p. 232.
[9] Ibid., p. 23.
[10] Although Ardrey's ideas may seem simplistic to many in hindsight, they were quite

Extending this argument, Ardrey implies three points:[11] (1) Conflict and competition are inevitable because we are just "built that way"; (2) we really don't have much choice about how we act in various situations, although we may concoct elaborate rationalizations for our behavior in an effort to mask its causes; and (3) differences in society, such as between the rich and the poor, merely mirror internal, genetically based differences in heritage.[12] The "have-nots" in our society somehow "deserve" their position. Consequently, efforts at social reform, such as a "war on poverty," are fundamentally futile.

Problems with the structure of the argument

Ardrey relies on incidental parallels between nonhuman and human social behavior. But a few parallels do not establish comparability.[13]

popular at the time. Why? A couple of reasons have been suggested. First, the ideas came at a time when social unrest was widespread in this country. The ideas proposed by Ardrey, and, in different form, by Desmond Morris in *The naked ape*, and by Konrad Lorenz in *On aggression*, seemed to "explain" why things tended to be running amok (Bay of Pigs, the Kennedy assassination, riots, Vietnam, and so on).

Another reason for the popularity of these reductionist views may have been the fact that they countered the "oversocialized" and largely rational perspective on human nature and society that had been popular in academic circles in the 1950s. (Suttles, G. [1972]. *The social construction of communities*. Chicago: University of Chicago Press, pp. 114–115.) In sociology, "functionalist" views were popular at the time. According to these views, promulgated by Talcott Parsons and his students, every institution in society existed because it served a purpose in that society, and helped keep things going. In social psychology several popular, rational, cost–benefit models of small group behavior were circulating (e.g., Homans, G. C. [1950]. *The human group*. New York: Harcourt Brace & World; Thibaut, J. W., & Kelley, H. H. [1959]. *The social psychology of groups*. New York: Wiley). These suggested that people rationally calculated whom they should interact with, what they should do for others, and what groups they should belong to; and also that they enacted the course of action that gave them the largest ratio of benefits to costs. The message of Ardrey and colleagues directly rebutted this view of social life and societal structures. Their message suggested that matters were not so open and flexible, but rather quite constrained by our biological heritage. Theirs "is a message which reemphasizes the harshness of competition and aggression, the sacrifices of group life, and the enduring biogenetic bases of social differentiation" (Suttles [1972], pp. 115–116).

[11] Suttles, G. (1972), Chapter 5.

[12] This last point is very close to what has been labeled "social Darwinism." For a discussion of this school of thought see Hofstadter, R. (1959), *Social Darwinism in American thought*. New York: Brazilier. Social Darwinism, in essence, has very little to do with Darwin's evolutionary framework, however.

[13] "There is always a danger in such abrupt projections: substantiation for one's theories

Where there appear to be parallels between animal and human social behavior – barking dogs and fence-building property owners – this is taken as evidence of homology, or underlying structural similarity. This assumption of homology, however, is exactly what the authors are trying to prove. Analogy (surface similarity of the same process in two different species) does not necessarily imply homology (underlying structural similarity, which determines the process in the two species).

In short, Ardrey assumes the fundamental similarities between humans and nonhuman species. But it is exactly this point he is trying to prove.

An additional problem with the argument is an inherent contradiction.[14] Although humans are "just like" animals there is something wrong with humans. Instincts that work fine in animal societies cause problems and strife in the human context. It is not clear why this should be so. It is also not clear how this view of a fundamental difference between animals and humans can be reconciled with the view of fundamental similarity, which is held at the same time.

And, finally, it is assumed that the animal kingdom contains the key for understanding humans.[15] If we understand biology we can understand human social behavior. This is a reductionist, oversimplified view of human social behavior.

Problems with the treatment of territorial functioning

Focusing specifically on the treatment of territorial functioning, the views of Ardrey and Malmberg are problematic in several respects. First, both Ardrey and Malmberg expand the concept to so many different levels that it becomes, in practical terms, useless. When territoriality explains everything from how we respond to invasions of personal space, to why nations go to war and who wins, it becomes conceptually diffuse and amorphous.

Second, Ardrey ignores that many species, including some of the

---

and hunches is drawn from one source [nonhumans], and the theories and hunches are applied elsewhere [to humans]. This amounts to a kind of gross extrapolation in which nonhuman organisms are substituted for humans with very little conceptual justification . . . each author has tried to demonstrate his argument only by showing how generalizations drawn from studies of nonhuman organisms can be selectively applied to some incidents among humans. Such incidental parallels between man and animal do not prove their general comparability but assume such comparability" (Suttles [1972], p. 119).

[14] Ibid., p. 121.

[15] Ibid., p. 125.

primates "closest" to us, do not exhibit territoriality. If territoriality were as driving as the impulse to reproduce, it would surely be evident among all species. It is not. This suggests, as discussed earlier, that territoriality refers to a set of strategies that are adopted under certain conditions, and not to an instinct or an imperative.

Third, the strong linkages between aggression, predation, and territoriality that, Andrey suggests, are an iron triangle, are in reality more weakly coupled than he proposes. Territoriality does not necessarily imply physical contact between "owner" and invader, with consequent violence and/or injury to the latter. The territorial system provides for a broad range of displays and communications that obviate the need for physical contact or violence. And, the link between aggression and seeking prey (predation) is also much weaker than he suggests.[16] Carnivores are no more violent towards other members of their own species than are herbivores or omnivores. An animal holding a territory so that it can hunt prey in that space will not necessarily be more violent towards its neighbors than an animal holding a territory because it contains a noncarnivorous resource. Hunters kill their prey, not each other.

Finally, both Ardrey and Malmberg ignore the small group, evolutionarily determined basis of territorial functioning. Failure to recognize this connection in part explains their broad-gauged, multilevel, and inappropriate use of territorial concepts.

In sum, both because of flaws in argumentation, and misconceptualizations regarding the evolutionary foundations of territorial functioning, Ardrey's instinct-based view of human territoriality, and Malmberg's similar view, can be rejected.

Group selection and ecology-conserving behavior

A perspective that develops a group-selection, ecologically preserving evolutionary perspective on nonhuman social behavior patterns was put forth by Wynne-Edwards in the mid–1960's. Although not explicitly applied to human territorial functioning, the viewpoint offered suggests a specific, Darwinian-based set of processes to explain territorial behavior in nonhuman species. It is worthwhile to consider how the proposed processes apply to territorial behavior among nonhuman species,

---

[16] "Ardrey . . . traces the aggressive behavior of man back to the predatory ways of his australopithecine ancestors. He overlooks the fact that there is no necessary connection between aggression and predation. After all, plant eaters are no more peaceful against their own kind [than meat eaters]." Eibl-Eibesfeldt, I. (1974). *Ethology: The biology of behavior*, 2nd ed. New York: Holt, Rhinehart and Winston, p. 349.

and then to consider how well they might apply to human territorial functioning.

The mechanisms

Sea lions, which actually are large seals, are phylogenetically related to terrestrial bears; they roost in colonies, often on islands or ice packs where their relatively defenseless offspring will be safe from predators. The favored social arrangement is a harem, with a single dominant male having charge of several females. Dominant male sea lions will defend territories near where females are congregating, thus increasing their direct fitness by securing access to the breeding females. Periodically, subdominant males will emerge from the water and attempt to overthrow the dominant male. Inflating the air sacs around their nostrils, and propping themselves up, the two will butt heads and roar at each other, sometimes for several hours. The contest is energy intensive. Eventually one of the contestants tires and slithers into the sea.

Clearly such a strategy increases the direct fitness of the winning male. He is assured of continued easy access to breeding females, in a relatively safe location. This kind of territorial strategy, benefiting a particular individual, fits with our common conception of the phenomenon.

But Wynne-Edwards would suggest that these strategies also help to preserve the breeding ecology. By holding down the number of males, the offspring do not become so excessive that pups are constantly trampled by adults.

In fact, Wynne-Edwards argues, there are some types of territorial strategies that clearly and mainly benefit the participating group. Sika deer, which force weak members of the group out of a territory and into a no-deer land prowled by wolves, would be one example. Wynne-Edwards also provides a detailed analysis of territorial strategies of red grouse, which nest on the moors. As the summer wanes, and feed becomes scarcer, surplus males are systematically segregated, deprived of a territory, and harassed for the purpose of expelling them.[17] "More and more are driven out altogether; and since they can rarely find a safe nook to occupy elsewhere in the neighbor-

---

[17] Wynne-Edwards, V. C. (1962). *Animal dispersion in relation to social behavior.* New York: Hafner.

Wynne-Edwards, V. C. (1963). Intergroup selection in the evolution of social systems. *Nature, 200,* 623–626.

Wynne-Edwards, V. C. (1965). Self-regulating systems in populations of animals. *Science, 147,* 1543–1548. For those who may be intimidated by Wynne-Edwards' weighty tome, the *Science* article provides an informative and much briefer introduction to some of the main ideas.

hood, they become outcasts, and are easily picked up by hawks and foxes, or succumb to malnutrition."[18]

Wynne-Edwards suggests that territorial strategies constitute one cluster of processes that keep a subpopulation from overfeeding in a particular niche. Other strategies serving the same purpose include epideictic displays (such as lightning bugs flashing to each other) and pecking orders or social hierarchies. But most important, he proposed, were territorial systems.

The functionality of these group-based territorial strategies hinges on the concept of *carrying capacity*. This refers to the density or overall population that an area's resources can support and continue to renew themselves.

Since, in the past, disaster has followed when the carrying capacity of the ecological niche was overreached, there has been strong selection pressure for the evolution of mechanisms that keep organisms from exceeding the carrying capacity of their niche.

Territorial functioning limits the population of the group so that members will not overconsume their food supply, thereby exhausting the resource, reducing future yield to zero, and leaving themselves prey to starvation. By each animal or group having a territory, and the consequent spreading out of the animals at a lower density, and control of overall group size, the survival possibilities of the group are enhanced.

The actual selection mechanisms by means of which these limiting strategies evolved center on intergroup selection. This is a type of natural selection discussed originally by Darwin, and later attended to by geneticists such as Sewall Wright. The basic idea is that some groups of individuals, in a species, are more likely to survive than other groupings, and thus are more likely to pass on their genes (or culture) to subsequent generations of the species. By their overall behavior, groups, rather than individuals, are "selected for." The origins of this mechanism may have been as follows.[19]

Group selection

Evolutionary pressures drive individual organisms to reproduce as much as possible. Animals, however, live in groupings that are often spatially separated from one another. And groupings of animals often stay in one location for a considerable period of time. Thus, at some time in the prehistoric past of each species, there were probably many groupings, the members of which were reproducing as much as possible. In the ecological niches occupied by the most fecund groupings, however,

---

[18] Wynne-Edwards (1963), p. 625.
[19] For more details on the proposed dynamics see Wynne-Edwards, ibid.

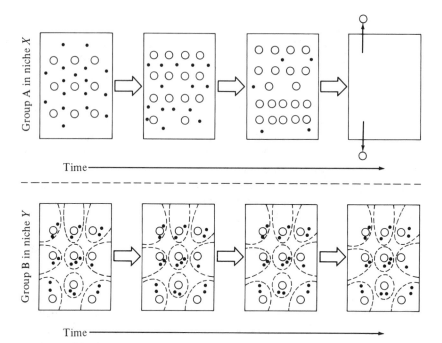

Figure 4.1. How group selection operates. Two sets of one type of an organism start out at time 0 (T_0). Each *O* represents ten organisms. Group A is isolated in niche *X*, and group B is isolated in niche *Y*. The two niches are comparable, with similar resources, at T_0. Initially, in each niche, there are 90 *O*'s and 180 *dots*. *O*'s feed on dots. Each dot in the figure is equal to 10 dots. Over time, group A does not implement a territorial arrangement sorting out subsets of organisms within the niche. Thus, over time the group exceeds the carrying capacity of the niche, and eats up all the dots. Most *O*'s die; a few survive and migrate elsewhere. By contrast, group B in niche *Y does* adopt a territorial arrangement within the niche, as indicated by the *dashed lines*. As a result of this arrangement, the ratio of *O*'s to dots is stabilized, and the population of *O*'s does not exceed the carrying capacity of the niche.

local resources were depleted. Consequently, many of these groupings became extinct due to starvation.

In contrast, there may have been other groupings in which genetic combinations emerged that encouraged self-restraint on reproduction, via social and spatial behavioral systems such as territoriality. Over time, members of such groupings were more likely than members of the maximally reproducing groupings to survive because they were not overusing their food resources. Consequently, intergroup selection was occurring, with the restraining groups being favored (i.e., they were more likely to leave more offspring) over the unrestrained groupings. Those who controlled themselves were more likely to be in groups that survived. Thus, genes favoring maintaining group size or density below the carrying capacity of the ecological niche were passed on to subsequent generations and groups. Groups in which individuals cooperated for the good of the whole group were more likely to survive. Groups with these behaviors were *selected for* over generations (see Figure 4.1).

We can extend the preceding model to primates and, in particular, early hominids by allowing for selection pressures to operate on cultural transmission as well as genetic inheritance. (How cultural transmission can operate in an evolutionary perspective will be explained later in the chapter.)

A note on the controversy surrounding group selection

Group selection is controversial. Dethroned by Wilson and genetically oriented sociobiologists, it has recently gained considerable theoretical and empirical support.

The model of intergroup selection poses a paradox: Does it make sense for an individual organism to constrain itself for the good of the group? Forces of group selection appear to be directly at odds with those of individual selection. For the good of the group an individual is required to compromise his or her own individual fitness. E. O. Wilson has argued that such a situation is unlikely to develop.[20] He maintains that in such an ecologically conscious group an individual with "selfish" genes would seek to have as many offspring as possible, or consume as much of the resources as possible. Consequently the genes propagated down through the generations by the "selfish" individual would overwhelm the genes propagated by the individuals that "restrained for the good of the group," resulting, eventually, in the extinction of the "restrained" genes and the total dominance of the "selfish" genes.

---

[20] Wilson, W. O. (1975). *Sociobiology: The new synthesis*. Cambridge, MA: Harvard University Press.

In short, according to Wilson, group selection is a superfluous mechanism; mechanisms of individual selection are sufficient, by themselves, to explain the social behavior of organisms. On these grounds, notions of intergroup selection, according to genetically focused sociobiologists, can be rejected.

Other, more technical arguments have been proposed against the idea of group selection as well. Mathematical modelling using computer simulations has suggested that group selection can work, but only under a very restricted set of conditions, conditions that are not likely to exist on a wide scale in real-world settings.[21]

But, contravening the arguments of the genetic-minded sociobiologists are three important points.

First, Wilson, in his arguments against group selection, ignores *inclusive* fitness. When we consider inclusive fitness, as in the sketch of early hominid territorial organization, it is clear how an individual can benefit from furthering the maintenance of the group to which he or she belongs.

Second, mathematical analyses of cultural transmission driven by evolutionary forces point toward group selection as a "strong force."[22] These analyses imply that group selection of culturally transmitted traits, such as cooperation, can occur in a broader range of situations than heretofore expected.

Third, recent experimental evidence points towards the robustness of group selection processes. Controlled experiments with flour beetles have suggested that group selection mechanisms can be efficient and can work in a broader set of situations than those prescribed by simulation studies.[23] The implications of this recent work are that group selection is a potentially more robust mechanism, applicable to a wider set of conditions than heretofore suspected. And, in some cases it may even be more efficient than mechanisms of individual selection.[24]

---

[21] These conditions are as follows: The groups must be small; there must be a high extinction rate among the various groups in order to keep up the selection pressure; and there must be a low rate of migration among groups, otherwise the "selfish gene taking over" scenario may come about. Levin, B. R., & Kilmer, W. L. (1974). Interdemic selection and the evolution of altruism: a computer simulation study. *Evolution, 28*, 527–545.

[22] Boyd, R., & Richerson, P. J. (1982). Cultural transmission and the evolution of cooperative behavior. *Human Ecology, 10*, 325–351 (abstract).

[23] Craig, D. M. (1982). Group selection versus individual selection: an experimental analysis. *Evolution, 36*, 271–282.

[24] Ibid., pp. 279, 281. The increased efficiency is due to the fact that since group selection depends on the group mean, rather than individual attributes, it is a better estimator of the underlying genetic distribution.

Summing-up on group selection

A reasonable case can be made for the viability of group selection processes and their involvement in genetically based evolution in response to selection pressures (see the preceding box). Intergroup selection can enhance inclusive selection, assuming some degree of kinship in the various groups, and may be more efficient than individual selection.[25] Further, once we take into account cultural transmission via evolutionary processes, an extremely strong case can be made for group selection. We will get to these cultural transmission processes in a moment. But first, let's return to the early hominid model of the evolution of territorial functioning, and elaborate it so as to include group selection processes.

Incorporating group selection into the early hominid territorial model

In the last chapter we outlined a group-based, territorial, male provisioning model of sociospatial organization for protohominids and early hominids. To explore how group selection might explain the emergence of territorial functioning, consider the following thought experiment.

There are three groups of early hominids, each existing in a different "niche." The distance between the groups is such that there is little migration between groups. Further, these niches exist in an overall ecology, where due to, say, a severe drought, there is very strong competition for food. All three groups are of equal size, about 40 each, at Time 1. The major difference between the three groups is the extent to which they exhibit territorial functioning.

Group I exhibits a *full territorial strategy*. Border guards are constantly on patrol, and warn of dangerous predators or of other groups attempting an incursion. When trouble is evident they summon others from nearby hunting parties and repel the threat. (Imagine the advantage accruing to a group whose members can communicate symbolically concerning present or anticipated dangers.)

Group II exhibits a *partial territorial strategy*. Conspecifics are excluded from the main campsite, but are allowed to roam about the feeding area used by the group, hunting prey and consuming other resources. After a member is eaten by a predator, they employ a system of border guards for a period of time, to warn of incursions of these animals.

Group II exhibits a *home range strategy*. Conspecifics are not excluded

---

[25] It may be more "accurate," since it is based on the group's "mean" response to environmental conditions.

Table 4.1. *Plight of different hypothetical hominid groups: group
selection for territorial functioning*

	Time 2 (T1 + 6 mos.)	(T1 + 9 mos.)
Group I (full)	Group size still at 40. Resources are maintained. Predation largely avoided. ($N = 40$)	Group continues successfully in original niche; group size remains constant.
Group II (partial)	Some of foraging area has been given up to group invading from another drought-stricken area. Some members killed by predators, a couple in fights with in-migrating group. ($N = 30$)	After protracted struggle with invading group, original group members are ultimately overwhelmed by superior numbers; almost all are killed.
Group III (none)	In-migrating group has taken over control of half of the foraging area. Many group members lost to predators. ($N = 18$)	Original group reduced to 5. They out-migrate from original niche; new group has replaced them. Almost all original group members ultimately starve; a couple are taken in by another group, in another niche.

Note: Group I employed a full territorial strategy, II a partial territorial strategy,
and III a home range strategy but no territorial strategy.

from the foraging area or main campsites. There is no systematic arrangement to warn of predator incursions, so the latter may approach until spotted by an adult present at the main campsite. There is little in the way of large-scale cooperative behavior to exclude others (see Table 4.1)

Table 4.1 indicates what might happen to these three different groups over a period of time, assuming competition for resources. The group using a full-fledged territorial strategy fares much better than the other groups, staying at full strength and utilizing and preserving the resources in its niche. Over generations, more progeny of members of group I, as compared to groups II and III, will be likely to grow to adulthood, and perhaps move out and occupy other niches, possibly moving into them at a time when competition for resources is slack, and maintaining their "right" to them in tougher times through a territorial strategy. Through such group selection mechanisms then, territorial strategies among early hominids may have spread, over time, across a progressively larger number of niches.

How was territorial functioning shaped and transmitted?

At this juncture it is necessary to focus more closely on the mechanisms that, among early hominids, transmitted behavior patterns such as territorial functioning from one generation to the next, and that allowed such patterns to adapt to the particular situations they confronted. Such mechanisms are the focus of sociobiology, which is an attempt to interpret the social behaviors of numerous species, including humans, within a consistent, evolutionary perspective. Emerging in the late 1960's and early 1970's, sociobiology provided a unitary framework for understanding a broad range of social behaviors – altruism and courtship, for example. Since that time it has evolved further, in an effort to dovetail with anthropology.

The ideas of sociobiology pertinent to our inquiry here can most easily be presented by discussing three different foci of sociobiologists. Some have concentrated largely or solely on mechanisms of genetic inheritance, and how selection pressures modified subsequent genetically based phenotypes. Some, to understand better the application of sociobiology to humans, have concentrated on the interactions between genetic material and culture; still others have focused on how culture evolved. This tripartite division is by no means clear-cut. What researchers working on cultural evolution conclude has implications for gene–culture transactions, for example. And in some cases, particular researchers have focused on different issues at various points in their career. Nonetheless, this division is helpful because it helps us at least organize the considerable volume of material in this area.

The major features of these different portions of sociobiology are outlined. After reviewing these perspectives we will consider the implications of each for understanding the evolution of human territorial functioning.

Genetic transmission

Espoused by E. O. Wilson (in the early to mid-1970's), and David Barash and others, one "school" of sociobiologists concentrates on the genetic mechanisms by which social behavior evolved. That is, its central focus is on natural selection for particular genotypes, which are associated with adaptive phenotypes, passed from one generation to the next.

According to the sociobiological perspective, we can understand how animal species (including humans) behave towards other animals by focusing on the advantages to individual genotypes resulting from these behaviors. To the extent these complex social behaviors make it more likely for genes to be reproduced in subsequent generations, they increase fitness and are thus understandable.

Some have suggested that the genetically focused variant of sociobiology has limited applicability to higher primates because it does not consider the roles of social learning and culture. But there are difficulties even in applying it to "lower" species. The relevant points are discussed in the following box.

Limitations of genetically focused sociobiology

First, environmental conditions directly influence phenotypes (behaviors and structures of individuals), not genotypes. Individual selection works directly on individuals, not on genes. As mentioned earlier, Darwinian fitness refers to the relative frequencies of specific genes and how they change; individual fitness refers to an individual's ability to leave more offspring than other members of the species. These two types of fitness and these two types of selection are distinct. A problem arises in that the theory focuses mainly on the genes and Darwinian fitness whereas the available data report only what happens to the individuals, i.e., on the effects of individual fitness.[26] In short, there is a dramatic slippage between the units on which data are available and the focus of the perspective. Consequently, in most instances only indirect evidence of key constructs is available.

The linkage between individual fitness and Darwinian fitness is complicated for several reasons. For example, there is not a one-to-one correspondence or mapping between many of the traits underlying social behavior, and the genetic makeup. A particular gene that influences the trait of dominance, for example, may also influence other traits such as level of stimulus seeking or ability to remember particular routes through a landscape. Although there are many instances where traits have been cleanly tied to one or two genes (e.g., the ability to roll your tongue up at the sides when you stick it out), in many cases, particularly when we

---

[26] Wittenberger (1981), pp. 41–47.

are discussing traits relevant to complex social behaviors, the connections between genes and traits are indirect at best and hopelessly turbid at worst. Consequently caution must be used when making inferences about changes in gene pools on the basis of individual selection data.

In addition, sociobiological analyses to date have been forced to rely on very crude and imprecise estimates of the costs and benefits of particular strategies.[27] Unable to pinpoint the adaptive value – which is what they would really like to know – of particular behaviors, researchers of necessity have fallen back on the notion that some behaviors or strategies incur higher or lower costs to the organism or confer higher or lower benefits on the organism than do others."While it is reasonable to assume that there is a cost to aggression and a benefit to grooming, attaching precise values to discrete acts in order to generate cost–benefit ratios is difficult if not impossible."[28]

A third problem, related to the preceding and emerging from field studies of primates, is that the sociobiological perspective does not, as yet, have much predictive power.[29] The perspective has been useful in putting a post hoc framework around findings and patterns already in hand, but has been less successful in predicting what will happen in particular instances. This is due to a variety of problems in operationalizing some of the important concepts in the perspective, such as exact measures of costs and benefits, or tracing exact lineages of particular individuals. But it is also due to some oversimplifications inherent in the perspective that need to be, but have not yet been, elaborated.[30]

The point of these comments is not to discredit a sociobiology focused on genetic transmission. It is a powerful perspective. At the same time its problems seem to be no fewer than those that plague other approaches.

Gene–culture evolution

More recently, Wilson and Lumsden, and others, have suggested that genes and culture may interact to produce adaptive behaviors.

[27] Richard, A. F., & Schulman, S. R. (1982). Sociobiology: primate field studies. *Annual Review of Anthropology, 11*, 231–255; see pp. 245–246.

[28] Ibid., p. 245.

[29] Ibid. See, for example, the description of the macaque study on pp. 235–236, and the description of the baboon study on p. 237.

[30] "We do not know enough, in most cases, to estimate with confidence the actual values of many of the parameters fundamental to almost all sociobiological models. A corollary of this . . . is that as more data accumulate it is likely that many of the simplifying assumptions of current models will be shown to be inapplicable to long-lived social species such as primates." Ibid., p. 244.

In essence the coevolutionary perspective is a further clarification of a certain problem in the area of sociobiology as applied to humans, namely, what are the links between culture and genetic selection?[31] There simply is not room here to consider in detail the various perspectives on this issue, which differ sharply in several crucial respects. In this section we will simply outline the most pertinent features of gene–culture coevolution. We will then consider how culture itself evolves, a topic so far neglected. The analysis of cultural evolution has implications for the gene–culture interface, and these will be mentioned in the next section.

The coevolutionary variant of sociobiology starts with some simple premises. First, people have a capacity for culture.[32] Given this capacity

[31] For a standard view of the gene–culture interface see Barkow, J. H. (1978). Culture and sociobiology. *American Anthropologist, 30*, 5–20, or Durham, W. H. (1979). Toward a coevolutionary theory of human biology and culture. In N. A. Chagnon & W. Irons (Eds.), *Evolutionary biology and human social behavior: An anthropological perspective*. North Scituate, MA: Duxbury Press, pp. 39–58.

Other versions of the perspective, however, allow for genes to continue to play a dominant role vis-à-vis culture. Lumsden and Wilson are the main proponents of the view. The mathematical basis of their perspective is contained in Lumsden, C. J., & Wilson, E. O. (1981), *Genes, mind and culture: The coevolutionary process.* Cambridge, MA: Harvard University Press. A review that points out problems and limits of the mathematical models used by Lumsden and Wilson is found in Smith, J. M., & Warren, N. (1982), Models of cultural and genetic change. *Evolution, 36*, 620–627. A popular version of their perspective is contained in Lumsden, C. J., & Wilson, E. O. (1983), *Promethean fire: Reflections on the origin of mind.* Cambridge, MA: Harvard University Press. For a discussion of problems with this work see Gould, S. J. (June 30, 1983). Genes on the brain. *New York Review of Books*, pp. 5–10. For an interesting comparison of the Lumsden and Wilson view of the gene–culture interface, with other views, see Boyd, R., & Richerson, P. J. (1983), Why is culture adaptive? *Quarterly Review of Biology, 58*, 209–214.

The Lumsden–Wilson view radically proposes that culture can amplify the consequences of genetic selection, that culture allows genetic selection to occur at a faster rate. Thus they develop a "thousand year rule": Traits can be selected for and become predominant in a population within this period of time.

The most satisfying and integrative perspective on gene–culture coevolution is offered by Boyd and Richerson. Boyd, R., & Richerson, P. J. (1985). *Culture and the evolutionary process.* Chicago: University of Chicago Press. Perhaps of greatest interest is their conclusion, based on their analysis of cultural evolution, that cultural evolutionary processes can favor outcomes that are counter to conventional sociobiological predictions.

[32] "The term 'capacity for culture' is a shorthand way of referring to a host of behavioral characteristics, including, but not limited to, symbolic ability and accurate mapping of the physical and social environments; the capacity to inhibit aggression and to bond

people are constantly innovating and trying new things. They put up houses or igloos or tents in different ways, treat each other in new ways, explore new routes, and so on. Second, there is a bias built into the processes of socialization and development. As a result of this bias people are more likely to learn behaviors that are in their own self-interest.[33] Learning and doing those things that are more clearly in our self-interest result in feelings of satisfaction.

In prehistoric time, populations that developed and used a capacity for culture were more likely to survive. Natural selection favored and furthered the development of culture because such development resulted in populations increasing their inclusive fitness – passing on more of their genes to subsequent generations. Think of fire. Groups that learned to make and control fire were safer from night predators, and could cook their meat, making it last longer. This knowledge was then passed down, by imitative learning and communicated symbols, to subsequent generations.[34]

This does not mean, however, that people consciously engaged in the behavior so that and only so that they could survive. Nor does it mean that the significance of the behavior must reflect its survival value. People may have made fires in large part because it made them feel safer at night; it may have provided a sense of security. The meaning of the event may have centered on notions of a fire god. Because a behavior has adaptive significance it is not necessary that people perceive or revere that significance.[35]

Thus, in the environment of evolutionary adaptedness natural selection processes favored the development of a capacity for culture, and many cultural innovations. The people (or perhaps groups) that engaged in these innovations – who were more flexible, and thus adapted more to local conditions – were more likely to survive, and thus pass on their genotypes to subsequent generations.[36] In this way, through genetically

peacefully to conspecifics; the ability to use and ultimately to make tools; the tendency to acquire information from the older generation and to transmit it to the young; the ability to communicate, culminating in verbal language; and specific learning preferences and the tendency to find certain categories of experience 'rewarding.' These abilities, in sum, constitute the emotional-cognitive potential of our species." Barkow (1978), p. 80.

[33] Irons, W. (1979). Natural selection, adaptation, and human social behavior. In N. A. Chagnon & W. Irons. (Eds.), *Evolutionary biology and human social behavior: An anthropological perspective*. North Scituate, MA: Duxbury Press, pp. 4–39.

[34] Durham (1979), p. 43.

[35] Ibid.

[36] This selection for flexibility, allowing quicker adaptation to local conditions, is a key element in the Lumsden and Wilson view of gene–culture coevolution.

based mechanisms influenced by natural selection, the capacity for culture spread.

Over a long period of time, there may be several factors operating that keep culture adaptive. As mentioned earlier, people are biased towards doing things that are in their own interest and that are satisfying. And, people continue to be selectively receptive to cultural innovations; all new cultural patterns are not embraced by everyone. Thus, cultural maintenance and innovations may still have significant adaptive value, even though we live in civilized times, selection pressure in many countries is not intense, and the value of these sentiments and behaviors is not put to the test every generation.[37]

The overall implications of this perspective are startling. Durham, and others such as Boyd and Richerson, suggest that culture is as capable – and in some cases more capable because it can respond more rapidly to changes in the external environment, and because of the particular way it evolves – as genetic processes of selection in producing behavior patterns and sentiments that have biological adaptive value, i.e., that maximize the inclusive fitness of individuals or groups. Therefore, simply because a behavior pattern has adaptive value does not mean it is strongly genetically determined; *it could just as well be culturally determined*. This is a crucial point. Thus, it is extremely difficult to ascertain, even if a behavior or constellation of sentiments (e.g., xenophobia) has survival value, whether the origin is predominantly genetic (through natural selection), predominantly cultural (through cultural evolution), or both.

A model of cultural evolution

Perhaps even more important than the rudiments of the coevolutionary "school" of sociobiology are the recent refinements by Robert Boyd and Peter Richerson of work on how culture evolves.[38] The model they

---

[37] This is particularly possible, if, as Wynne-Edwards suggested for animals and Durham suggested for humans, these cultural traits were in the past selected for partly on the basis of intergroup selection processes.

But, as we will see with Boyd and Richerson's model of cultural evolution, culture can evolve toward variants that result in *less* fitness.

[38] Boyd, R., & Richerson, P. J. (1983). Why is culture adaptive? *Quarterly Review of Biology, 58*, 209–214. Boyd, R., & Richerson, P. J. (1982). Cultural transmission and the evolution of cooperative behavior. *Human Ecology, 10*, 325–351. Boyd, R., & Richerson, P. J. (1985). *Culture and the evolutionary process*. Chicago: University of Chicago Press. Richerson, P. J., & Boyd, R. (1984). Natural selection and culture. *BioScience, 34*, 430–434.

develop can be considered within a coevolutionary perspective, but it comes to some very different conclusions.

The purpose of the Boyd and Richerson model can be stated simply. They seek to explain cultural evolution in a Darwinian framework. That is, to what extent, and in what ways, do natural selection processes influence the evolution of culture? Stated differently, Boyd and Richerson propose that "cultural transmission can be modeled as a system of inheritance."[39]

It is important to bear in mind, when discussing cultural evolution, that in some respects we have shifted gears. First, no longer is the focus simply on the survival of individuals or groups. Rather, the focus is on particular *cultural variants*, or manifestations (e.g., reading). Second, generation time is variable. A "cultural parent" may teach another person something he has recently learned (e.g., one sibling teaching another how to roller-skate), or something that was learned years ago (e.g., a parent or teacher showing a child how to bake bread).

The definition of culture adopted by Boyd and Richerson is broad. "By 'culture' we mean the transmission from one generation to the next, via teaching and imitation, of knowledge, values, and other factors that influence behavior."[40] Thus playing the piano, reading signs, or showing solicitousness for sick people are all reflections of culture.

What are the ways that aspects of culture are transmitted or modified? Several processes may be at work. In order to illustrate these forces, several of which are analogous to genetically based processes, we will use the following example.

A hypothetical working example

Imagine a small group (approximately 50) of primitive hunter-gatherer humans during the Upper Paleolithic period (some 25,000–35,000 years ago) in a mountainous, partially wooded area in Europe. It includes about 15 adult males, each bonded to one of 15 adult women, and 10 infants. There are a half dozen very old males, and a half dozen "teenagers" also in the group. Let's call this troop group A. Imagine that the group maintained a moderate-sized home range of several square kilometers. The range is valuable to them for several reasons. It contains, periodically, prey that they hunt, such as wildebeest. It also serves as home to a range of alternative food sources: small game, many different kinds of roots and berries, and several varieties of birds. These smaller food resources are distributed evenly throughout the locale.

[39] Boyd & Richerson (1984), p. 430.
[40] Boyd & Richerson (1985), p. 2.

Adjoining group A is a comparably sized group, which we will call group B. Lately A has been troubled by B. Members of the latter group have taken to coming over to A's area, in small groups of four to six, and running off with some wildebeest or small game. Adult male members of group A spend much of their time, when they would otherwise be hunting or foraging, chasing off the intruders. Once an intruding group is spotted by a patrolling member of group A (often the older males get this job), he returns to the main site and dispatches the teens to go fetch a couple of the closest hunting parties. The recalled hunting parties then pursue the intruders, sometimes catching them before they reach the border and forcing them to drop their take so they can run away faster. But often the intruders can slip away before their pursuers arrive. Group A wants to come up with a better way to protect their territory.

After putting their heads together they come up with a system whereby they put up "signposts" – a cross between totem poles and street signs – at the boundaries of their home range, along well-used paths through the forest. Crowned with fierce-looking painted designs, the signposts are intended, by their imposing height and intense colors, to convey the message: "Keep out if you know what's good for you!!" Placed slightly inward from each signpost is a trap: a pit, camouflaged with grass and sticks, with crude spears at the bottom. After a few days of work the posts and traps are in place.

The next week, an intruding band of five from group B comes upon one of the signposts. After some concerned consultation they decide to ignore it and proceed. They continue stealing down the path when suddenly the leader of the group screams and disappears. The others turn and run. Back at B's main site, after the other hunting parties come in, they recount their tale to their concerned comrades. Some refuse to believe the story. The next day a group of four unbelievers sets out; only three return, with the same tale as the day before. In a very short time the neighboring group will learn to "respect" the signposts of the resident group and will cease their incursions.

Over a period of time, let us now imagine several subsequent developments in this scenario.

1. A teenager, teen B–1, in group B, coming of age a couple of years later, asks his father about the markers at the boundary. His father, who has not gone on any of the incursions, says the signs do not mean anything. But the teen asks a prominent hunter in the group about the signs and receives dire warnings. Given the status and prestige of the hunter, the teen decides to believe him and concludes that the signs are dangerous and should be avoided. The hunter has acted as a "cultural parent." (These conversations take place in a very primitive "language.")

2. Teen B–1's brother, teen B–2, who hates authority figures of any kind, parental or nonparental, has a hunch. He approaches the boundary area with a peer; they get off the trail when they see the sign, stay off it for about 50 meters, then get back on. Nothing happens to them. They harvest some truffles and then return to their territory, using the same procedures. But when teen B–2 comes back and "tells" what has happened, few believe him. His social position in the group militates against his acting as a "cultural parent."

3. A few years later, at a time when competition for local resources is relatively low, a few young adults from group A strike out on their own, and set up a new territory. Let's call this group A–1. When competition with neighboring groups increases during a dry spell, they put up the signposts along the trail as they have seen their parents do. But they do not make the posts very tall, and do not do a good job at covering up the traps on the trail. Consequently, the warning posts are not highly effective in keeping out adjoining groups.

4. Imagine another group of males, A–2, that strikes out from group A about the same time as group A–1 to set up their own area. When competition increases they put up signposts with pits. Two of the adult males construct and paint the signposts. They happened to have better learned the strategy, and be better painters, than the others in the group. Consequently, the posts they construct have extremely frightening designs and are most impressive. They turn out to be effective at warding off intruders. Children in this subgroup who, as adults later forming group AA–2 learn the pits-and-posts strategy, or out-migrants from the group subsequently joining other groups, are more effective users of this strategy than those descending or migrating out from group A–1.

5. Over a couple of generations, group A, relative to group B, prospers. Young adults emerging from group A learn the value of the posts-and-pits strategy and are instructed in the elements of the strategy. The strategy, over time, is honed. For example, the value of placing the pit sometimes on the trail, sometimes on the side, and of sometimes using multiple pits, emerges. In group B, whose area is also raided sometimes by an even worse-off group (group C), no widespread posts-and-pits strategy emerges. Some group members are in favor of it, but general dislike and distrust of group A hinders the widespread acceptance of it. Groups of males and females striking off from group B do not, in general, do as well as those striking off from group A.

The elements shaping cultural development

Using Boyd and Richerson's framework, we can "unpack" this example. We start with the idea that there are *operating forces that make particular cultural variants more or less popular.* The posts-and-pits strategy, contrasted with a no-posts-and-pits strategy, represented a particular cultural variant. Its popularity can be determined by the frequency with which it is adopted by subsequent groups, including A, B, C, "splinter groups," and other groups, in the larger population. These forces derive from enculturation patterns, and patterns of social interaction. Several of these forces are *analogous* to particular *genetic forces* (see the following box).

**Forces shaping cultural evolution, and genetic analogs
(from Boyd and Richerson)**

A. There are two forces of *random variation.*

1. *Errors in transmission* refer to mistakes in enculturation that people make while learning particular cultural variants. Someone whose mother never corrected his sloppy floor-washing techniques will pass on the same sloppy habits to his children, should they "choose" to learn from him. The genetic analog to this is *genetic mutation*, where genetic material, due to, for example, ionizing radiation or chemical mutagens, mutates over generations. Errors in transmission are illustrated in the case of group A–1. They do not implement the pits-and-posts strategy effectively.

2. *Sampling errors* refer to the fact that, in a subpopulation, some are enculturated less well than others, and in a small group, those less well enculturated may predominate over those better enculturated in a particular cultural variant, or vice versa. Splinter group A–2, compared to splinter group A–1, contains a higher proportion of males who learned the pits-and-posts strategy *well*. These differences are due to sampling error. The genetic analog to this process is *genetic drift*. Gene frequencies are altered through sampling errors, particularly when the populations in question are small.

B. In addition, there are also forces of *guided variation.*

1. *Decision-making forces* refer to

(a) *biased transmission*, as a result of which a person is more likely to imitate one model than another. Teen B–1 was biased in favor of learning from the hunter, instead of his father. He made a *biased choice* of who would be his "cultural parent."

(b) *Individual learning*, contrasted with social learning, occurs when a person modifies existing behavior patterns learned from others. Cultural characteristics acquired by a particular individual can be passed on to another. (This can*not* happen genetically; the Lamarckian idea of transmission of physical characteristics is incorrect.) Teen B–2 learned how to *avoid* the pits and posts. But, his individual learning, since it was in conflict with the more widely held *social* learning, was not accepted in Group B.

Through decision-making forces, *natural selection can have an indirect influence* on the inheritance of cultural variants because natural selection shapes the neurological equipment used to make decisions, and may shape the very rules by which we make decisions (e.g., causal attribution processes).

Natural selection can have a *direct* influence on cultural variation.

We choose to imitate those behaviors, all else equal, that are most frequent in the environment. These most frequent behaviors are, under certain conditions, probably most adaptive. Stated differently, what we learn socially is frequency dependent; we imitate what is popular. The groups splintering off from A routinely adopted the pits-and-posts strategy, while those striking off from group B did not. This natural selection is a particularly strong force influencing cultural evolution and determining which cultural variants are passed on to others, as long as the cultural variation is heritable, and decision-making rules are weak, i.e., over-matched by the complexity of the environment. Given the latter condition, it is more cost effective to imitate. Consequently, social learning keeps adaptive traits in a high frequency. But under certain circumstances (homogeneous environments), these adapted traits may *reduce* genetic fitness (e.g., the tradition of small families, or a celibate priesthood).

Major points

The major points of the Boyd and Richerson model, which has extensive mathematical underpinnings, can be summarized as follows.

1. Natural selection influences which cultural variants are passed on. It can operate indirectly or directly (as indicated in the preceding box). The direct impact of natural selection on which aspects of culture will be transmitted will be strong under particular conditions. By imitation and social learning, from biological parents and other "cultural parents," the elements of the culture are passed on.

2. Aspects of culture learned from nonbiological parents may or may not increase our genetic or Darwinian fitness. It depends upon whether the environment is relatively uniform, or more variable. The culture can, in some situations, get "off track."

3. Our current sociocultural makeup is a result of a "dual inheritance"

model: what has been passed down to us by genetic transmission, and what has been passed down to us via cultural transmission. Cultural inheritance has introduced "novel evolutionary forces" that "can lead to behavior that would not be predicted on the basis of conventional neo-Darwinian theory" (e.g., the perpetuation of a celibate priesthood).[41]

4. All else equal, what is imitated is frequency dependent. We imitate what is most popular. Under particular conditions then, particular traits, such as cooperation, will "spread" throughout a particular subgroup, even if the group is composed of unrelated individuals. And, further, under certain other conditions, the spread of the trait will result in increased genetic fitness of the adopting group. Consequently, some groups may be fitter than others, resulting in intergroup selection along Darwinian lines.[42]

Back to the working example

Each of these four points can be illustrated by expanding our posts-and-pits example. Consider the following respective extensions of the four points.

1. Other groups, such as group X, which have some contact with group A, at a time when resources are plentiful and there is no need for poaching, may learn about the posts-and-pits strategy and, at some future time of need, attempt to implement it themselves.

2. Group A–1, due to a shift in the location of their main large food supplies, moves out of the forest ecology and into a grassland ecology. The group, over a period of years, gains some members from nearby groups. New members in the group go along with the pits-and-posts strategy, and do their part in setting up such a system. But there is little utility to the strategy since there are no well-used trails on the grasslands, as there were in the forest and woodlands. Thus, the demarcation of selected points on their boundary is not effective in keeping out intruders. And, it may actually decrease their fitness because time spent digging pits and carving posts is time taken away from hunting and foraging. The social learning of the newcomers to the group was not effective because of the varied environmental context.

3. New persons joining group A–2, still residing in the forest, such as a male–female pair unrelated to any group members, would not be expected to contribute the time and energy to constructing the pits and posts, if we consider only issues of genetic (direct and indirect) fitness.

---

[41] Ibid., p. 2.
[42] Boyd & Richerson (1982).

Their time would be better spent if he hunted and she prepared a homesite. But when the time of the month comes around for the group members to freshly paint the signposts, and redig and camouflage the pits, he may go along and help because he's conforming to the activity pattern of the others in the group. New persons joining group A–1, recently moved to the grasslands, would still participate in the strategy, even though it was useless.

4. Imagine, a few biological generations hence, several splinter groups derived from our original trio (AAAA, BBBB, and CCCC), and some amount of migration between them. Imagine that in group AAAA slightly more than half in the group are in favor of putting up scary signposts each season along well-used trails in the woods near their boundary, and slightly less than half in group BBBB are in favor of this practice. The strategy will spread throughout group AAAA, and the splinter groups to which it gives rise. And persons coming into the group will, for the most part, contribute to the strategy. By contrast, in group BBBB, the practice will fade out, and new persons joining the group will not take it up. Assuming some amount of selection pressure, and that all the groups continue to reside in forested areas, group AAAA and groups deriving from it will be selected for genetically, at the group level, over group BBBB and the groups splintering or descending from it. Darwinian intergroup selection will operate.

The advantages of the Boyd and Richerson model

The coevolutionary perspective has suggested that culture, as well as genes, can produce adaptive behavioral patterns. Thus, not all adaptive behavior patterns are necessarily genetic in origin. Culture can produce behaviors that enhance survival and thus genotypic transmission. As put forward by Durham and Irons, most of the time cultural adaptations are "on track," facilitating the emergence of behavior patterns that enhance genetic fitness.

The Boyd and Richerson model provides a significant elaboration of the coevolutionary or dual inheritance perspective.

1. It clearly specifies the evolutionary-based cultural transmission mechanisms.
2. It clarifies how cultural evolution may or may not produce behaviors that are adaptive in the sense of enhancing genetic (inclusive) fitness.
3. It indicates how, through frequency-dependent imitation, behaviors such as cooperation can spread within a group, enhancing its fitness and resulting in intergroup selection.
4. And, the model indicates how the particulars of transmission and

adaptability of certain cultural variants *depend upon the local ecology* and the trait in question.

The evolution of human territorial functioning

Macrolevel

Earlier we sketched out how hominid territorial functioning may have emerged, and the advantages it may have provided to hominids emerging several millions of years ago. Now, with the aid of the Boyd and Richerson model, we can also sketch the outlines of how human territorial functioning may have evolved in the last few thousands of years, as humans acquired and elaborated their capacity for culture, resulting in outcomes such as language, tools, signs, farming, cities, and so on. (These suggestions are listed in Table 4.2.)

In prehistoric times, territorial functioning probably was only practiced in times and places where ecological conditions made it advantageous. When resources were only moderately plentiful, and one could predict where to find them, a territorial system seems likely to have emerged.[43] In short, when it was economically defensible, the territorial system of sociospatial organization was probably exhibited and "selected for." Since it was an arrangement of groups vis-à-vis one another, much selection probably occurred at the intergroup level. This line of argument is fully in keeping with the Boyd and Richerson model.

The territories defended were probably at two levels. Most proximate was the *homesite*, and the immediately adjoining area, where female adults engaged in extensive parenting, small children played, and all members of the group slept. It may have been a cave, as in Europe after the last Ice Age. To ensure the safety of the offspring it was necessary to exclude members of strange groups and to repel predators.

Overlying this was a larger area: the *feeding territory*. It was here, as described in the early hominid example, that the group hunted prey and perhaps gathered different types of roots, berries, and so on. Its size was probably variable, depending upon resource density and degree of competition from neighboring groups. And the degree of excludability demanded probably was also variable, being contingent upon local conditions. So, the territorial strategy at this level was *specific to the ecology*.

If, for example, the group hunted some variety of fox, and one year foxes were particularly plentiful, the group members may not have responded consistently to incursions from other groups. In some situations,

---

[43] Dyson-Hudson, R., & Smith, E. A. (1978). Human territoriality: An ecological reassessment. *American Anthropologist, 80*, 21–41.

Table 4.2. *Suggested milestones in cultural evolution of territorial functioning*

Macrolevel changes

1. From the emergence of early hominids, several million years ago, to the emergence of *Homo sapiens sapiens* a couple of hundred thousand years ago, territorial functioning centered on the excludability of other groups from the food source area (*feeding territory*). Excludability might *not* have been called for when resources where plentiful, or when the type of prey (e.g., very large wandering game) made defense uneconomical. *Homesites* where the group ate and rested were defended from predators and from other groups. Family units within the main group might have defended portions of the homesite against other group members.

2. With the domestication of animals and the beginnings of agriculture around 9,000–7,000 years ago, feeding territories and homesites became more clearly defined.

3. As homesites of a small band of hunter-gatherers evolved into villages, the importance of spaces allocated to particular families might have increased, along with the size of the primary group. Agricultural developments permitted both these changes.

4. As more complex agglomerations such as cities developed around 7,000 B.C., accompanied by elaborate divisions of labor, (a) the importance of defending the primary group's feeding territory waned completely. Functional groups replaced primary groups; (b) salience of family-based territory increased; (c) territories specific to small, face-to-face functional groupings emerged.

5. Shift occurred in the relative predominance of benefits offered by territorial functioning; importance of resource conservation and safety from predators waned. Conflict-reduction benefits, within and between groups, increased, as necessitated by a more complex social organization.

Microlevel changes

1. Reliance on signs, symbols, and other forms of communication to indicate occupancy or ownership increased.

2. This permitted more efficient territorial functioning, with fewer conflicts and more energy allocated to other tasks.

3. The symbology developed was specific to particular locales.

---

the defense of the group territory may have vanished altogether and been replaced by a home range situation. As glaciation from the last Ice Age retreated, when human groups spread out to hunt very large game that wandered quite widely, it would not be economical to defend a particular area that did not contain a significant food source.

As the final glaciation of the *Pleistocene epoch* ended, people turned from big game hunting to small foodstuffs, fish, and game. The importance of defending a food territory probably increased. Then, it probably increased further around 9,000 B.C. when groups shifted from foraging and hunting, expending energy on the collection of vegetables and seeds.[44] In light of the higher spatial and temporal predictability of the latter food sources, boundary defense was an "economical" strategy.

Groups probably still engaged in seasonal migrations, but within another few thousand years (7,500–3,000 B.C.) plants and animals had been domesticated, agriculture was developing, and villagelike arrangements evolved into larger agglomerations, eventually cities. With this agglomeration came, inevitably, a division of labor. Given this increase in complexity the notion of a feeding territory lost meaning. What probably emerged at this time, in conjunction with the waning importance of the hunting-gathering group, were (a) a more family-specific notion of *homesite*, and (b) the replacement of the feeding territory with role-specific, small-group territories (e.g., the soldiers' barracks, the king's palace, the priests' temple, and so on), organized round functional groups rather than primary groups; and (c) the relegation of defense matters to political units (e.g., kings) rather than territorial units.

It is unwise to label whole cities or empires as territories. To do so pulls us away from the evolutionary origins of the behavioral system, which clearly lie in small, face-to-face groups. It was these groups that maintained excludability, and thus they are at the core of this level of territorial functioning.

In sum, as dietary patterns, ecologies, and modes of social organization shifted, so too did the areas over which excludability was demanded.

A final point on macrolevel functioning: Through culturally transmitted processes of adaptation to particular local ecologies, territorial functioning was shaped, in many instances, to fit particular situations and locales. That is, the Boyd and Richerson model helps us understand why there can be so many diverse arrangements, in different cultures, of territorial functioning.

Microlevel

Also occurring was a series of microlevel changes, through cultural evolution, language, communication, symbology, and other features. All of these changes, overall, probably resulted in more efficient (i.e., less energy-intensive) territorial functioning.

With painting and totems, boundaries could be symbolized, and these

---

[44] Hoebel, E. A. (1966). *Anthropology*. New York: McGraw-Hill, p. 183.

symbols would be recognized by conspecifics (but of course would be of no help against predators). Boundaries of both feeding areas and homesites could thereby be delineated. The use of such symbols could have spread through cultural transmission in direct response to natural selection pressures, as the Boyd and Richerson model indicates.

Such symbols carried two messages. They signalled ownership or occupancy of a site. Furs on the floor of a cave indicated where a particular male–female couple slept, for example. The pits-and-posts strategy signalled the boundaries of the feeding area in the working example developed earlier. In addition, signs or symbols carried the threat of consequences should the signals not be respected; when and if the signaller returned and discovered the intrusion, there could be unpleasant consequences. In these two ways, then, such symbols served as a proxy for the presence of the occupant.

Table 4.2 summarizes these possible steps in the evolution of territorial functioning.

The culture-dependent elaboration of territorial functioning, in more general terms, is notable in several respects.

1. In the era preceding the rise of cities, when primary groups were still the significant core of social life, the elaboration, through signs and symbols, made for more efficient within- and between-group functioning.

2. Between-group conflicts were reduced as members of other groups respected the boundary markers. When competition for food sources became very intense such markers were probably more likely to be ignored (a situation that has an analog in modern territorial functioning), but on the whole they probably reduced border scraps, allowing members of each group to devote energy to more fitness-enhancing activities, such as intensive parenting, or more careful mapping of food sources.

3. Following processes of intergroup selection, groups using the more elaborate, complex form of territorial functioning were more likely to have higher rates of genotypic transmission, explaining the eventual adoption of a more elaborate territorial system across different niches.

4. Similarly, within groups, particular individuals or nuclear families could go about their daily routines without worrying about running back every half hour to defend their sleeping site. So, again, except in times of very intense competition for, say, sleeping sites, conflicts overall were lessened by the symbols, and energy could be devoted to more fitness-enhancing activities. Further, analogous to the adoption of cooperation, within each group such sign-observing behaviors would spread, following conformist transmission.[45]

[45] Boyd & Richerson (1982).

A final question

Territorial functioning, in different ecologies and times, represents the adaptation of individuals and groups to particular situations. Is territorial functioning always adaptive? That is, is it a system that enhances our genetic fitness?

Unfortunately, there are two different answers to this question. Durham argues that cultural adaptations are usually "on track" and keep cultural variants in tune with the ecological situation. Boyd and Richerson argue otherwise. In certain situations, they suggest, it is possible for cultural variants to evolve that decrease genetic fitness. In other words, it is possible for culture to get "off track."

Given the formidable mathematical and conceptual underpinnings of their line of reasoning, and a recognition of cultural inertia, I find it difficult to fault Boyd and Richerson's conclusion. Thus, territorial functioning, treated as a cluster of cultural variants based on cultural transmission mechanisms, may or may not be adaptive, that is, may or may not increase the genetic fitness of the individuals or groups engaged in it. On the whole, however, it must in the past have been highly adaptive for many groups and in many situations. Otherwise, territorial functioning would not be as widespread, across many different cultures, as it is today.

Summary

This chapter has examined the evolution of human territorial functioning. Ardrey's argument that a territorial instinct derived from our prehistoric ancestors causes us to run amok was examined and found wanting in several respects. Wynne-Edwards' idea that, based on group selection processes, we have evolved social mechanisms such as territorial functioning that avoid overuse of resources in a particular ecological niche was considered. His argument appears sound and dovetails well with certain points of the cultural evolution model. Among sociobiologists, selection mechanisms focusing only on genetic transmission are limited in key ways, although intergroup selection based on genetic fitness may have played a role in the spread of territorial functioning among early hominids, before their capacity for culture was fully developed. Boyd and Richerson's model of cultural evolution highlights the role of natural selection in the spread of particular behaviors. Their emphasis on social learning underscores how territorial functioning must be tied to small, face-to-face groups. Their focus on selection pressure points up how, in many circumstances, territorial functioning spread because it was a behavior pattern adapted to the particular environmental and social contingencies confronting a particular group. Further, it is a very useful model for considering how, with the rise of civilization, the nature of territorial functioning was elaborated and changed.

PART II
A CONCEPTUAL MODEL OF
HUMAN TERRITORIAL
FUNCTIONING

Part I outlined the emergence and evolution of human territorial functioning, indicating how, before the development of a capacity for culture, it was fitness enhancing and consequently was "spread" throughout the gene pool, its dissemination probably relying in part on mechanisms of intergroup selection. Territorial functioning was a key element in the sociospatial behavior system of early hominids that allowed them to compete successfully with pongids. Subsequent to the development of a capacity for culture, territorial functioning evolved and was elaborated in response to direct and indirect influences of natural selection. The Boyd and Richerson model explains how such evolution occurred. The fundamental spatial units on which territorial functioning centered probably were the feeding area and the homesite. Later, as civilization emerged and larger groups of people started living together, first in villages and later in larger groupings, and a more elaborate division of labor materialized, the importance of the feeding territory declined, and the homesite was transformed from a primary group site to a nuclear family site. Territories based on functional groupings emerged.

There are two hallmarks of the evolutionary origins of territorial functioning. First, it is highly place specific. This means (a) that the territorial functioning will be tailored to the locale, and (b) that the "decision" of whether to engage in territorial functioning depends upon local conditions, such as the amount of competition and scarcity of resources. Second, it is fundamentally a group-based mechanism, relying for most of our past on face-to-face primary groupings. Consequently, since face-to-face groupings are limited in size, the space defined as a territory must of necessity be delimited.

This section serves as a bridge between an evolutionary perspective and "modern-day" empirical investigations of human territorial functioning. The evolutionary framework sets the parameters on a model of human territorial functioning. Chapter 5 proposes this model. It indicates the causal antecedents of territorial functioning, and the proximal and distal functional impacts. An extended example, based on a fictional fraternity house, illustrates the causal processes described and appears in the Appendix that follows Chapter 5.

The functional impacts of territorial functioning are varied and include consequences for both individuals and settings, as well as groups and individuals within groups. *Territorial functioning has psychological, ecological, and social psychological impacts.* To deepen understanding of the impacts of territorial functioning on individuals *qua* individuals, and on settings, Chapter 6 introduces two theoretical perspectives. These are meshed with territorial functioning to better clarify those impacts. Stokols' model of place-specific stressors clarifies the processes linking psychological impacts with territorial functioning. Barker's ideas on behavior settings, later elaborated by Wicker, provide key concepts specifying territorial functioning's ecological role.

The antecedents and consequences of territorial functioning discussed in this part will be further illustrated in Part III, which contains the empirical bulk of the volume.

5
A PERSPECTIVE ON HUMAN TERRITORIAL FUNCTIONING

A six-year-old girl is sitting on the beach, near the waterline, digging a hole with a clamshell. She has been working diligently for about fifteen minutes. Her younger sister, four, saunters over and watches silently. Her foot, slowly and deliberately nearing the edge of the hole, pushes some sand back in. The older sister looks up, starts yelling and tries to hit the younger one with the clamshell in her hand.

In an off-campus apartment shared by four men, three of them are sitting in the living room drinking beer, talking about their absent roommate. They complain that he never cleans up the kitchen or helps in the picking up and cleaning of common areas like the living room and bathroom. As they are talking the fourth roommate, returning from studying at the library (on a Friday night), comes in. He nods to the three others and, without taking off his coat, retreats to his bedroom and closes the door. The other three look at each other, shake their heads and laugh quietly, then turn to a discussion of plans for the upcoming weekend.

In a lower-income neighborhood, residents on a block have organized for a massive cleanup and beautification campaign, sponsored by a local newspaper. They have gone down to the paper and gotten paint, of two colors, to represent their official block colors. Over the next several days they have removed six truckloads of trash from two vacant lots, put out planters all along the block, and painted the curbs. Two mothers are sitting out front on the steps, watching their children play on the sidewalk. Across the street a young male crumples up a soft drink cup and drops it as he is walking along. The two mothers, who didn't seem to be paying attention, get up immediately and start shouting at the male. He pretends he doesn't hear. Two men come out and join the women. They start walking toward the litterer, who darts hurriedly down an alley.

Introduction

Instances of human territorial functioning abound in everyday life. Yet it is important to *delineate* the bounds of human territorial functioning. In what particular situations is it likely or unlikely to be operating? What determines whether or not someone or some group acts territorial? What "shape" does territorial functioning take, and what determines this? And what are the consequences of territorial functioning? This chapter addresses these questions.

In formulating a perspective on human territorial functioning the "lessons" gleaned from our examination of the evolutionary origins of this environment–behavior system will be useful. Working in an evolutionary framework delimits territorial functioning to face-to-face groups. It is in such groups that territorial functioning has its origins. Second, such a framework recognizes it as highly place specific, treating territorial functioning as a system of adaptations to particular social and physical contingencies operating in particular locales. Related to this is a third point: Given forces of cultural evolution and adaptation to specific ecologies, the shape of territorial functioning will vary across cultures, across settings within cultures, and even across time within a particular setting. These broad parameters of territorial functioning can serve as useful guidelines in formulating a specific framework.

Organization of the chapter

A specific definition of human territorial functioning opens the chapter. This definition is then placed in a context with other approaches to human territoriality. This juxtaposition is accomplished in the following manner. Themes inherent in some of the major definitions of human territorial functioning are considered and are organized into four continua. The placement of my definition of human territorial functioning along each of these continua is indicated.

This definitional groundwork sets the stage for a "low-level" causal model of human territorial functioning. The antecedents of territorial functioning are indicated, as are the component parts of the functioning. The nested nature of territorial operations is noted, applying to both individuals within groups, and relations between groups.

Extensive attention is given to the social psychological, psychological, and ecological consequences of territorial functioning. These consequences are broken down into two groups: those that are *proximal,* evident soon after or during the territorial functioning, and those that are *distal,* emerging over a longer period of time, and of which individuals and groups may be less aware. (An extended example, illustrating the hypothesized causal processes described in the model, can be found in the Appendix for those who wish elaboration.) The model outlined here can be used as a schema for pinpointing and organizing causal processes discussed in the future chapters that review empirical findings in various settings.

Defining territorial functioning

A brief definition of territorial functioning was offered in Chapter 1. Specifically, territorial functioning refers to:

- an interlocked system of attitudes, sentiments, and behaviors that are
- specific to a particular, usually delimited, site or location, which,
- in the context of individuals in a group, or a small group as a whole,
- reflect and reinforce, for those individuals or groups, some degree of excludability of use, responsibility for, and control over activities in these specific sites.

Consequently:

1. *Human territorial functioning involves a tightly coupled system of person–place transactions.* How people feel about a location is often reflected in how they act there. Those who feel strongly about a setting (e.g., an "old-timer" who has lived on a block for a long time) are likely to show this behaviorally (e.g., sweep the alley daily).

2. *These transactions have implications for the setting and for the individuals and groups involved.*

3. *The scale of sites in which territorial functioning is usually evident is limited.* This point deserves some amplification.

As is evident from the consideration of the outlines of territorial functioning in earlier times, it was linked to small face-to-face groups, and subgroups within those primary groups. Members of a primary group defended a feeding territory because it provided them with needed resources. Within the primary group, subgroups, probably centered on the male–female adult pairs, "claimed" certain portions of the homesite, allowing them to use such spots for rest, storage, or whatever, with minimal conflict within the primary group. Initially then, two clear-cut levels of territorial functioning were probably evident. Both of these levels of functioning relied upon the bonds between the small group members. All members of such face-to-face groups were acquainted, and there was probably a fair degree of mutual liking, resulting in high group cohesiveness. People in the group got along. If they did not, or were unhappy, individuals or subgroups may have left the group to join another.

At the level of the feeding territory, it is only because such social bonds existed that people actually contributed to the public good by defending the locale. Mancur Olson's analysis of collective behavior unreservedly concludes that people will not contribute to the production of a public good, even when it is in their own best interests to do so.[1] There must be "something extra" operating. That something extra came in two parts for primitive persons. First, there was a knowledge of the other members and a confidence that they would contribute to the group effort. Predictability hinged upon knowing others in the group. Such

[1] Olson, M. [1965]. *The logic of collective action.* Cambridge, MA: Harvard University Press.

acquaintanceship was not easily acquired in larger groups. Second, the willingness to contribute to the public good was cemented by some degree of liking for the others in the group. As group size increases, overall liking for all other group members declines, simply because opportunities to get to know comembers must be divided up among more comembers. So, the defense of areas larger than a feeding territory was probably not possible until the emergence of early civilization and the establishment of basic political units, e.g., a ruler over a city.

Some might propose that the modern analog of the feeding territory is the neighborhood. Although in urban situations it is much smaller than the feeding territories of primitive groups, due to higher-density living conditions, neighborhood populations, ranging from the hundreds to the tens of thousands, are much larger.

In addition, primitive primary groups were defending what was, for them, a selective benefit. That is, to the extent outside groups partook of the benefit (food sources) in the area, the goods left for the occupying group were diminished. Of course, in times of plenty when competition between groups was low, outside and occupying groups could both "harvest" or hunt in the feeding territory. And, under such conditions, groups probably reverted to a home range strategy, no longer demanding excludability. But most of the time early hominids were probably in a highly competitive situation. Exactly the reverse is the case with the neighborhood. Most of the time neighborhood quality is a public good that all in the neighborhood, and the immediately surrounding areas, can freely enjoy without "using it up." Most of the time, there is no selective benefit to defend by excluding.

There are situations where neighborhood quality does become a selective benefit, and this is in times of neighborhood change, such as, for example, racial turnover, or when there are major changes in land use. In such cases residents may become hostile towards those who, in their eyes, threaten to "use up" their neighborhood quality. In such instances *in*formal actions of residents may appear, parallel to primitive primary group defense of a feeding territory.[2] Human ecologists, Suttles and Bursik in particular, have made much of such instances of the "defended neighborhood."[3] And there are times when neighborhoods

---

[2] *Formal* aspects of neighborhood responses to threat are well explained by political theory, and territorial concepts need not be invoked.

Henig, J. (1982). *Neighborhood mobilization.* New Brunswick, NJ: Rutgers University Press.

Crenson, M. (1983). *Neighborhood politics.* Cambridge: Harvard University Press.

[3] Suttles, G. D. (1972). *The social construction of communities.* Chicago: University of Chicago Press.

Figure 5.1. An urban neighborhood. *Source*: Baltimore City Department of Planning. Given the evolutionary perspective underlying our approach to human territorial functioning, in most situations territorial functioning does *not* operate at the neighborhood level. But it may be operative at the streetblock level. (For illustrations of streetblocks see page 174.)

do change. But, most of the time, neighborhood quality is a public good, and it is not economical for residents to exclude others from it.

Given the much larger group sizes of neighborhood populations compared to primitive groups, and the fact that, most of the time, neighborhood quality is not a selective benefit but rather a public good, in most situations territorial functioning does *not* apply to neighborhood sentiments and actions.

For several reasons, a much closer analog to primitive primary groups' feeding territories is the *streetblock* or a portion of a streetblock (see Figure 5.1). First, among people on the streetblock, or a portion thereof, there are social bonds. People are likely to see one another regularly. Barring bizarre or discourteous behavior, this may lead to minimal levels of acquaintanceship. People are at least familiar with one another. Thus,

Heitgard, J. L., & Bursik, R. J., Jr. (1984). The defended community and patterns of spatial autocorrelation. Paper presented at the annual meeting of the American Society of Criminology. Cincinnati, OH, November.

there is something of a face-to-face group quality. In addition, problems on a block are more immediate to all residents than are neighborhood problems. Thus, we may be able to model territorial functioning at the streetblock level.

In sum, there is an upper limit to the spatial scale for the application of territorial concepts. This delimitation is not arbitrary but rather is grounded in an understanding of the face-to-face group basis of territorial functioning. This essential ingredient of territorial functioning is a hallmark of its evolutionary heritage.

4. *Since territorial functioning is highly place specific, the benefits emerging from it vary across settings.* Although there is a family resemblance between the different benefits of territorial functioning, the specific advantages accruing depend upon the nature of the site.

Themes in definitions others have offered

Major themes

There are at least as many definitions of human territorial functioning as there are researchers in territoriality. (In some cases, researchers have even promulgated different definitions on different occasions.) In part, the definitional clutter is due to the complexity of the territorial idea. Needless to say, this has resulted in considerable confusion.[4]

Nonetheless, some common themes can be discerned. Not all definitions encompass all themes, and certain definitions emphasize some themes at the expense of others. We delineate the range of issues that people have treated as relevant to human territorial functioning by touching on some of the definitions offered.

1. The theme of *active defense* and, if necessary, aggressive behavior has been emphasized by many writers, particularly those who see close links (i.e., homology) between animal and human territorial functioning.

2. Some definitions allow that territories may be defended but not necessarily through direct aggression; other processes involving *laying claim* may be more pertinent. Laying claim may involve activities and statements of a wide variety. Creating, maintaining, or highlighting boundaries; signalling use or ownership through signs, markers, and

---

[4] For a listing of some of these definitions, see Altman, I. (1970), Territorial behavior in humans: An analysis of the concept. In L. Pastalan & D. H. Carson (Eds.), *Spatial behavior of older people*. Ann Arbor: University of Michigan Press, pp. 1–24. Or: Edney, J. J. (1974), Human territoriality. *Psychological Bulletin, 81*, 959–973, or Brown, B. (1987), Human territoriality. In I. D. Stokols & I. Altman (Eds.), *Handbook of environmental psychology*. New York: Wiley.

labels; or communicating warnings of varying levels of indirectness and subtlety to potential intruders may be involved. These devices not only signal tenancy, they also communicate, perhaps indirectly, expectations about who should or should not enter, and how one should behave when inside the territory. This process succeeds to the extent that the appropriate people are successfully kept out or, if allowed to enter, the extent to which the entrants conform to behavioral expectations about how to act in the setting. Accompanying success, therefore, are likely to be psychological feelings and attitudes reflective of control. Sundstrom's definition of territoriality as concerned with who has control over a particular space, and the activities that go on there, emphasizes this theme.[5]

3. Some definitions expand territoriality to include *defense of or control over concepts or nonspatial, nonphysical entities*. Bakker and Bakker-Rabdau, who define a territory as "that area of an individual's life which he experiences as his own, in which he exerts control, takes initiative, has expertise, or accepts responsibility," emphasize this theme.[6] This is a cognitive or abstract approach, as opposed to an explicitly geographical or spatial treatment of territorial functioning.

4. *Association with a place due to repeated usage or the passage of time* is another theme in some definitions of territorial functioning. This theme is dominant in Edney's definition of territories: those places with which persons or individuals are linked by a more or less continuous association.[7] Looking at territories in this light implies that territorial functioning is an accretive process emerging from temporally stable linkages between people and particular locations.[8] Such a view treats territorial functioning as similar to attachment to place.

The varying views of territorial functioning testify to its complexity. Some order can be brought to this complexity by pinpointing four continua. These are analytic dimensions, each of which is anchored by different and usually (but not always) exclusive attributes of territorial

---

[5] Sundstrom, E. (1977). Interpersonal behavior and the physical environment. In L. Wrightsman, *Social psychology*. Monterey, CA: Brooks/Cole.

[6] Bakker, C. B., & Bakker-Rabdau, M. K. (1976). *No trespassing! Explorations in human territoriality*. San Francisco: Chandler and Sharp, p. 4.

[7] Edney, J. J. (1976a). Human territories: Comment on functional properties. *Environment and Behavior, 8*, 31–47.

[8] This perspective on territories is interesting on two counts. First, by pinpointing the time variable as crucial, territorial functioning becomes very similar to attachment to place, which also emerges from long-term association. Second, it raises the question of whether people will treat "assigned" locations, such as a seat at the opera, as territories. Whether people do treat these spaces as such is overlooked by the focus on continuous association.

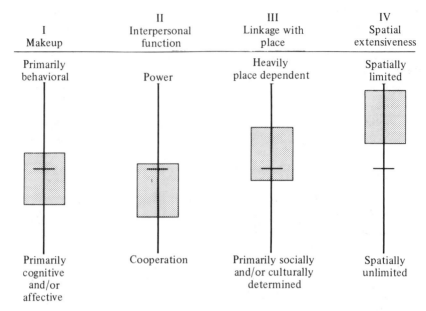

I Makeup	II Interpersonal function	III Linkage with place	IV Spatial extensiveness
Primarily behavioral	Power	Heavily place dependent	Spatially limited
Primarily cognitive and/or affective	Cooperation	Primarily socially and/or culturally determined	Spatially unlimited

Figure 5.2. Differences in conceptualizing territorial functioning. Four continua along which definitions used by writers of territorial functioning have varied. The author's perspective on territorial functioning is indicated by the *shaded portions* along each continuum.

functioning. Various definitions of territorial functioning can be spotted at particular points along one or more of these continua.

These four dimensions are presented in the next section. Following the presentation of each dimension, the placement on each of my definition of human territorial functioning is indicated and explained (see Figure 5.2).

Four organizing dimensions

Continuum I. *Territoriality is a primarily cognitive and affective process versus a primarily behavioral process.* Those emphasizing the nonbehavioral components of territoriality would suggest that how people view a particular territory – the meaning, associated affect, and perception of that location – would be a critical determinant of how they behave there, and that these views can develop and become significant over time. Those emphasizing the behavioral end of this dimension would argue that certain behaviors simply occur in certain situations, given the physical, social, and cultural characteristics of the situation.

My perspective on territorial functioning is located near the midpoint, slightly more on the cognitive end. That is, territorial functioning includes both behavioral and nonbehavioral components. The nonbehavioral components are slightly more important because they represent necessary (albeit not sufficient) precursors of territorial behavior. Stated differently: How a person perceives and feels about a particular location is a prime determinant of how he or she acts there.

Continuum II. *Territorial behaviors and sentiments accrue power to one individual or group at the expense of another individual or group versus territoriality promotes orderly social interaction between individuals or groups.* Those individuals who place themselves at the "power" end of this attitude dimension emphasize aspects of territoriality such as the "home court advantage" (see Chapter 9). They feel that territories in the main make it easier for groups and individuals to dominate others, and may also see close links between animal and human territoriality. Territoriality has individuocentric, egocentric qualities. Sacks' recent book on human territoriality is an excellent reflection of this viewpoint.[9] He argues that territorial functioning serves as a perpetrator of and cover for power relationships.

Countering such a view are those who suggest territoriality allows people to get along better, avoid conflict, and get on with other business, as expressed in "good fences make good neighbors." Territoriality facilitates social organization and social life at many levels of functioning. Gold and Edney's viewpoints both lie at this end of the continuum; they both emphasize how territoriality reduces disorder and complexity.[10]

On this dimension the present interpretation of territorial functioning is clearly closer to the "cooperation" end and emphasizes territoriality as an organizer and facilitator of social life. This is not to deny that there are numerous situations where territorial functioning allows some individuals or groups to "have something" over others. But there are even more situations and instances where territorial functioning allows individuals and groups to get along better with one another. The socially constructive consequences of territorial functioning are illuminated later in this chapter.

Continuum III. *Territorial behaviors, attitudes and sentiments are highly place dependent versus predominantly socially and culturally determined.* (This is the one dimension where the two endpoints are not

[9] Sacks, D. (1987). *Human territoriality*. Cambridge: Cambridge University Press.
[10] Gold, J. R. (1982). Territoriality and human spatial behavior. *Progress in Human Geography, 6,* 44–67.
Edney, J. J. (1976b). The psychological role of property rights. *Environment and Planning A, 8,* 811–822.

exclusive.) Those researchers at the "place" end of this dimension are primarily concerned with how the physical features of a space – size, degree of boundedness, proximity to other valued spaces, etc. – influence the territorial behaviors that go on there. They emphasize how certain kinds of locations allow or promote certain kinds of territorial functioning. Researchers such as Brower[11] and others who emerge from a predominantly architectural or planning background would be placed towards the physical end of this dimension. Researchers at the other end of this dimension tend to focus on how territorial functioning is a product of social and cultural dynamics. In their analyses of territorial functioning they would tend to emphasize how social factors such as role expectations or the nature of the relationship between two people, such as whether they agree or disagree on the topic being discussed in a certain territory, would influence territorial dynamics. Kubzhansky and Sundstrom are appropriately placed towards the social/cultural end of this dimension.[12]

The view of territoriality promulgated here, although explicitly admitting the roles of social and cultural factors in shaping territorial functioning, gives more emphasis to the role of place. This is because territoriality is telling us about a relationship between a person or group, and a particular place. The very high degree of place specificity is one of the paramount features of the concept.

Continuum IV. *Territories are limited in scope, and actually quite small, versus territories can be any size, ranging from personal space to nation-states.* This dimension is basically concerned with the extensiveness of territories. At the small end of this dimension are investigators who focus on interactional territories that are created by and surround small groups such as a couple talking, or a family group sitting in the living room. Scheflen, who has suggested that a territory is "a unit of space defined for a time by some kind of human behavior,"[13] would fall at the circumscribed, behaviorally dependent end of this dimension. According to his view, two people looking at each other are creating a territory. At the other end of the dimension we have investigators who

---

[11] Brower, S. The signs we learn to read. *Landscape, 15*, 9–12.

[12] Kubzhansky, P. E., & Bar Tal, Y. (1984). Social role factors in resident advantage. Paper presented at the annual meeting of the Eastern Psychological Association, Baltimore, April.

Conroy, J., & Sundstrom, E. (1977). Territorial dominance in a dyadic conversation as a function of similarity of opinion. *Journal of Personality and Social Psychology, 35*, 570–576.

[13] Scheflen, A. E. (1976). *Human territories: How we behave in space-time.* Englewood Cliffs, NJ: Prentice-Hall, p. 6.

emphasize large-scale, extensive territories, extending perhaps even all the way up to countries. Malmberg is such an investigator. He regards territorial attitudes towards home and country as one of the causes of war.[14]

The view of territorial functioning put forward in this volume is spatially limited. The focus is on small, usually circumscribed or delimited spaces that can be taken care of or looked after by a face-to-face group, or by an individual within a group. Territories range in size from chairs, seats, or sides of a table, to streetblocks. Territorial functioning emerges from and is supported by social dynamics in small groups. These dynamics do not exist, or they change radically, as soon as groups larger than face-to-face ones are considered.

A conceptual model of territorial functioning

In this section an orienting model for approaching human territoriality is proposed. A model is a "low-level" theory that proposes how various concepts are tied together. The particular form of the model presented is a *causal model*. The logic of causal models is explained, with the help of an example, in the following box.

The proposed model suggests classes of variables that influence territorial functioning. It also suggests what kinds of impacts come about as a result of territorial functioning. It is by no means 100 percent empirically validated; some of the connections suggested have received considerable empirical attention, some only modest attention, and others none at all. And there has been no overall "test," if that were possible, of the entire model. Consequently, the model contains some hypotheses that are speculative. Given these limitations, it is probably best to treat the model as a rough map of a partially known locale. Nonetheless, despite these limitations, the orientation provided by the framework may prove useful, and can at least be used as an organizing scheme.

Logic behind causal models

The essential logic behind causal models is straightforward. In fact, we think about many things using causal models. Causal models depict how events unfold over time.

The simplest causal model is of the form:

---

[14] Malmberg, T. (1980). *Human territoriality: Survey of behavioral territories in man with preliminary analysis and discussion of meaning.* New York: Mouton, p. 109.

$$A \quad \rightarrow \quad B,$$

where one cause is linked with one effect. But multiple causes can also be included, as in the case:

$$\begin{matrix} A_1 & \rightarrow \\ A_2 & \rightarrow \end{matrix} \quad B$$

Intermediate consequences can be considered as well:

$$A \quad \rightarrow \quad B \quad \rightarrow \quad C$$

In this instance we would say that factor A has a *direct* impact on B and B, in turn, has a *direct* impact on C. The impact of factor A on C is *indirect*, since it is "channelled" via factor B.

Let's consider the case of "good grades" in college. You might have a simple model about the factors that lead to such an outcome. Your model might be something like this: Those who spend a lot of time studying, and have a high level of intelligence, will be the ones who get good grades in college. Graphically, your model could be depicted as follows:

$$\begin{matrix} \text{Intelligence } (X_1) & \rightarrow \\ \text{Time spent studying } (X_2) & \rightarrow \end{matrix} \quad \text{Good grades } (Y_1)$$

Your causal model contains several hypotheses: More intelligent people get better grades; people who work harder get better grades; and persons who are smarter *and* who work harder get even better grades than people who are either just smart or hard workers.

But, upon reflection, you decide that your model about college grades is more complex. You decide that there are certain factors that "lead to" a person's being more intelligent. And you also consider that "good grades" have some important impacts you would like to include. For example, on the antecedent side you might propose that parents' intelligence (X_0) influences the college student's intelligence level (X_1). On the outcome side, you might propose (and perhaps this is a bit of wishful thinking) that grades in college (e.g., GPA) translate into salary level ten years after graduation; that smarter people are more likely to seek and find higher-paying jobs. Taking into account both the added antecedent and consequent factors your model now looks like this:

Parents' intelligence (X_0)	$\rightarrow$ Student's intelligence (X_1)	$\rightarrow$ Good grades (Y_1)	$\rightarrow$ High pay (Y_2)
	Hard work (X_2)	$\underline{\qquad\qquad\uparrow}$	

Now X_1 and X_2 represent intermediate predictors, and Y_1 represents an intermediate outcome, all of which link X_0 and Y_2. Again, as with the simpler model, this more complex model contains several hypotheses. (Since this is just an example, they need not all be listed here.) But, again, this model represents the kernel of a theory; it suggests processes that link various concepts in particular ways; more of X_0 leads to more of X_1, which leads to more of Y_1 and in turn Y_2, and so on.

Overview

The theoretical framework proposed is depicted in Figure 5.3. On the left are four classes of exogenous or predictor variables: cultural, social, individual or intrapersonal, and physical. These factors influence the type of territory available, how it is viewed, and how individuals and groups feel about that location. That is, these factors shape the "meaning" or "image" of a particular location – the extent to which it is viewed as a territory, and if so, of what type.

The particular image of a location may be subjective only, as when one person has a claim, as yet unrecognized by others, to a space. Or, the definition may be more widely shared, as when several people in a group agree (e.g., a group of small girls thinking about *their* clubhouse). These territorial cognitions suggest, support, or justify particular territorial behaviors. The behaviors may be of an "everyday" or routine nature (e.g., sweeping out the clubhouse on Saturdays), or in response to a particular situation (e.g., the girls chasing boys away from their clubhouse).

The link between cognitions and behaviors, although strong, is not ironclad. There may be times when territorial cognitions do not "translate" into behavior. Nonetheless, in most circumstances, and at most times, there is a noticeable correspondence between the two.

These territorial behaviors then have a range of consequences. Which consequences are salient depends upon the level at which we wish to focus. At a very general level we can say that the various consequences enhance the functioning of individuals within groups, and the relations between groups. These consequences are detailed next.

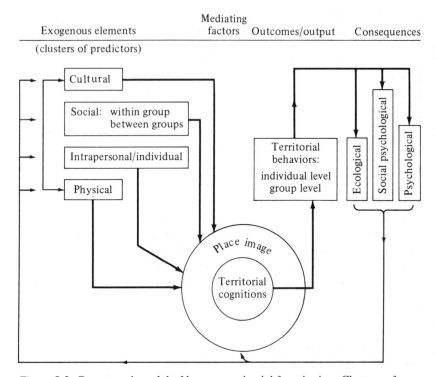

Figure 5.3. Conceptual model of human territorial functioning. Clusters of predictors appear on the *left*, and proximal and distal outcomes appear on the *right* and *far right*, respectively. Linking the two are territorial cognitions pertinent to a location. The territorial cognitions are part of the broader place image of the location held by the individual or group.

Individual elements

Predictors

Cultural. Territorial functioning operates differently in different cultures.[15] In some cultures (e.g., certain groups in Nigeria), visitors to the home are not allowed to look into the kitchen; the viewing of food before it is served is considered unhealthful, and perhaps bad luck. A field experiment by Worchel and Lollis[16] found that Greeks, as compared

---

[15] Altman, I., & Chemers, M. (1980). *Culture and environment.* Monterey, CA: Brooks/Cole.

[16] Worchel, S., & Lollis, M. (1982). Reactions to territorial contamination as a function of culture. *Personality and Social Psychology Bulletin, 8,* 370–375.

to Americans, defined the sidewalk adjoining their property as more public, and thus were more reluctant to pick up garbage "planted" there. The same location, in different cultures, may be categorized quite differently. These different categorizations are then reflected in territorial behaviors.

Cultural and *physical* features are clearly interconnected. For example, different traditional housing designs were favored among different American Indian tribes. There can be an interplay among the different factors influencing territorial functioning.

Physical. The physical parameters of a location influence its salience as an identifiable and separate space, its defensibility, and the extent to which particular behaviors in the space can be carried out. Persons occupying particular sites are aware of physical characteristics, and how they shape the functional potential of the space. To take a very simple example, in a field experiment conducted in a library, carrels, seating one and providing more privacy for more efficient studying, were perceived by students as more valuable study sites than tables, and were more likely to be defended when usurped by another.[17]

Social. Roughly, social factors can be divided into two groups: between-group and within-group factors. A good example of the latter is the social position of an individual within a group. Studies dating as far back as the late 1950's, usually conducted in institutional settings, have investigated whether individuals "higher up" in a group translate that position into a spatial advantage of one sort or another (e.g., occupying a top bunk in a cabin). The reverse has also been investigated: whether spatial advantage can translate into temporary social advantage. Other within-group factors, such as homogeneity, cohesiveness, and size, also influence territorial functioning. In considering this class of social factors it is important not to dwell exclusively on power-related aspects of group structure.

Between-group factors such as increasing social distance can lead members of each group to define a territory more sharply, or defend a boundary more vigorously. Or, as in a case of wayward teens taking over a small vest-pocket park after dark, a group such as residents may "cede" a territory altogether – giving up using it after dark.

Individual. People differ in their needs for privacy, security, control, and contact with others. Consequently, within a particular group

---

[17] Taylor, R. B., & Brooks, D. K. (1980). Temporary territories: Responses to intrusions in a public setting. *Population & Environment, 3,* 135–145.

or setting the territorial functioning of two different people may be remarkably different. In a small business two partners may each have separate and identical offices. But one partner may keep her door open most of the time, while the other usually keeps his shut. In an identical setting two people may evince different territorial functioning.

Territorial cognitions

The four classes of predictors influence territorial cognitions. Territorial cognitions are a subset of the total attitudes and sentiments that a person or group holds about a location; they are a portion of the place image. With regard to a specific location (e.g., my front porch) I may hold several attitudes and sentiments. A portion of these are properly labelled territorial cognitions: how responsible I feel for what happens there; how concerned I am about its appearance and upkeep; how much privacy I expect to have there; what kinds of persons I expect to encounter, and how I may respond to them, and so on.[18]

Territorial behaviors

Territorial cognitions shape territorial behaviors. Territorial behaviors are broad and include a host of paraverbal, nonverbal, verbal, and setting-changing or -maintaining behaviors.

Most prototypical are those intentional behaviors aimed towards notifying others of occupancy, excluding others, asserting control, or asking others to conform to setting standards. Such behaviors aim to directly influence the behavior of others in the setting.

In addition are those behaviors that have an indirect influence on others in the setting. A pedestrian walking past a well-kept front yard may hesitate to discard a gum wrapper, for example. In the residential context, behaviors such as maintenance and beautification can have indirect effects on the behaviors of others.

Consequences

Consequences or functions served by territoriality can be grouped into two classes: the *proximal,* or immediate consequences experi-

---

[18] Often, at least in residential contexts, issues such as control and privacy are difficult to investigate because people, particularly with regard to outdoor locations, often do not use those terms. Consequently, it is sometimes necessary to investigate these issues in a roundabout way, asking about expected and experienced problems.

enced by a particular individual or group, and the *distal* consequences, which follow later and are less likely to be immediately
evident to the individual or group in question, and influence groups
in a more general way.

Proximal functions served. (1) Territorial behaviors allow certain
groups, or individuals within those groups, to enjoy or "consume" certain selective benefits of the place they are or will be occupying. The
site can be used more effectively for particular purposes. This ability to
freely carry out the activities associated with the site is a fruit of having
some degree of control over who can enter the site, and/or control over
what they can do there. (2) Territorial behaviors make social interactions
more organized and predictable. You know what people are associated
with what places, whom you are likely to meet where: in various rooms
in your dorm, on the street where you live, in the building where you
work. Encountering unknown persons there can result in awkward interactions. As one moves from location to location, the linkage of people
to sites means that a predictable social matrix is coupled with the various
locations. This predictability occurs at the molar level (who am I likely
to find on the playground at this hour?) and the microlevel (who will
be sitting in this seat at the table?). Further, in one particular group,
in one particular location the predictability may be coupled with and
amplify the influence structure within the group (the boss who sits at
the head of the table).[19]

Distal functions served. The preceding immediate consequences have
more long-term or more general impacts. These consequences are social
psychological, psychological, and ecological in nature. The *social psychological* functions served relate to a reduction in conflict within a
particular group, or between two different groups. (See the following
box for an example of the latter.) Within and between groups, and for
particular individuals, linking particular persons or classes of persons
with sites results in predictability of others' behavior within that space,
and/or predictability of interaction patterns.

Peanut Park

In his investigation of a multiracial, multiethnic area in Chicago in the
early 1960's, sociologist Gerry Suttles observed that a park, located "be-

---

[19] Lyman, S. M., & Scott, M. B. (1967). Territoriality: A neglected sociological dimension.
Social Problems, 15, 236–249.

tween" several different ethnic groups, was "carefully" used.[20] Particular
ethnic groups restricted themselves to only a portion of the park, or used
it only at certain times. Consequently, conflicts between the different
groups were reduced.

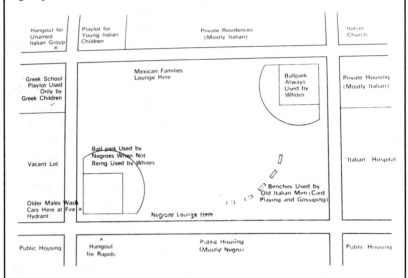

Usage patterns in Peanut Park. *Source*: G. D. Suttles (1968), *The social
order of the slum*. Chicago: University of Chicago Press. Copyright © 1968
by the University of Chicago. Reprinted by permission of the University
of Chicago Press.

The *psychological* consequences center on a reduction in place-specific
stressors. Stokols' contextual-stress model will be used in Chapter 6 to
clarify the linkage between territorial functioning and stress reduction.

The *ecological* consequences emerging are a more efficient carrying
out of the behavior-setting program (see Chapter 6) when the site in
question is a behavior setting. What needs to get done in the setting
can be accomplished more easily. The "business" of the setting is less
interrupted.

Comment. Individuals engaged in territorial functioning are probably
not aware of the distal consequences to which we are referring in this
section. A recognition of the impacts is probably somewhat "out of
awareness" of most of those involved in the behaviors. This lack of

[20] Suttles, G. D. (1968). *The social order of the slum*. Chicago: University of Chicago
Press.

awareness and intentionality, however, in no way diminishes the impacts themselves.

(An extended example, further illustrating the connections between the concepts used in the conceptual model, can be found in the Appendix that follows this chapter. It focuses on a hypothetical college fraternity, relations among members in the fraternity, and between that house and other fraternities.)

Territorial functioning and related concepts

In this section territorial functioning is compared and contrasted with some related environment–behavior concepts. The concepts considered are personal space, jurisdiction, privacy, home range, and attachment to place. The major points of overlap and contrast are summarized in the final box in this chapter.

Personal space

Surrounding individuals and in some cases even very small groups, such as a couple conversing, is a personal space.[21] This surrounding zone or series of zones is an area others are not usually allowed to enter; unwanted entrances are usually interpreted as intrusive and may cause the person whose space was invaded to feel uncomfortable and/or annoyed. This surrounding zone is not totally rigid. Rather, it is flexible. We "use" particular zones to distance ourselves from particular other individuals in certain situations. Individuals with whom we have intimate relations can approach more closely before we feel "invaded." Acquaintances are felt to be invading at somewhat greater distance than close friends, and strangers are felt to be intruding at an even greater distance. Or, a particular individual may be approached less closely in a formal than in an informal context (e.g., at a large company board meeting instead of in a living room at a party).

How is the concept of personal space similar to the concept of human territoriality? There are several points of overlap. First, both concepts

---

[21] Sommer, R. (1969). *Personal space.* Englewood Cliffs, NJ: Prentice-Hall.

   Hayduk, L. (1978). Personal space: An evaluative and directive review. *Psychological Bulletin, 85,* 117–134.

   Sundstrom, E., & Altman, I. (1976). Personal space and interpersonal relationships: Research review and theoretical model. *Human Ecology, 4,* 47–67.

   Altman, I., & Vinsel, A. M. (1977). An analysis of E. T. Hall's proxemic framework. In I. Altman & J. Wohlwill (Eds.), *Human behavior and environment,* vol. 2. New York: Plenum, pp. 181–259.

refer to *exclusive* space. The person whose space is in question feels that he or she has some sort of superior claim to that space; it is mine more than it is another's. This excludability is not total and absolute across all situations, but rather is relative and context dependent; nonetheless, in both concepts some space is "claimed."

Further, in the cases of both personal space and human territoriality, people coming into the "claimed" space can be upsetting, causing arousal and stress in the person who has been intruded upon. Having one's personal space invaded, or invading another's, can cause physiological signs of arousal such as increased heart rate, sweating, or increased blood pressure.[22] Although the point has not been carefully documented in the case of territorial intrusions (perhaps because it is too obvious), considerable anecdotal evidence is available. Recall your feelings last time you saw someone you did not know, perhaps a friend of your roommate's, sitting on your bed when you returned to your dorm room or apartment.

A third point of similarity: Our reactions to an approaching other depends on that person's identity and the nature of our relationship with that person.[23] When you see a perfect stranger walk into your front yard, approach your front door, or come up and stand close behind you at the supermarket checkout, your reaction is different than when the approaching person is a neighbor or a friend. In the case of the stranger there are immediate questions of motive. These questions do not come up in the case of a known person – unless the intrusion is at a very odd hour. The approaches of persons who are more liked, or of persons with whom we are acquainted, are interpreted and reacted to differently.

A fourth and final point of overlap is that in both processes, aspects of the physical environment can be used as props to help delineate or clarify boundaries. Generally speaking, this is a fairly central part of territorial functioning. People erect fences or put up hedges; in an open office they may pile books or other items on their desk to obscure the line of sight between the occupant and passersby. In some instances viable territories are crucially dependent upon the existence of physical boundaries. And people may do similar things to preserve their personal space. In a library, for example, people may pile books between themselves and those sitting close by, or turn their body away. Thus, the configuration of the physical environment, and modifiable elements of the physical environment, can play a part in personal space functioning as well as territorial functioning.

[22] Hayduk (1978).
[23] Sundstrom & Altman (1976).

At the same time, there are important differences between the concepts of personal space and human territoriality. First, and perhaps most important, a person always occupies the center of his or her personal space, whereas territories can be left behind. Your personal space, like your shadow, can*not* be left behind. But a person is rarely at the exact center of his or her territory, and need not always be occupying a territory for his or her claim to be legitimate. When a student comes back to the dorm room after pizza, it is not necessary to "reestablish" territory. When an executive returns to his or her office at the beginning of the workday, it is not necessary to reclaim the location in question. Although territorial claims are in some senses "weaker" when the occupant is not present, there is no question about who does or does not have a "right" to access that space. The claim persists overtime and when one is elsewhere.

A second point of difference, which flows out of the more portable nature of personal space as compared to territoriality, is that territorial spaces are usually more bounded and delimited than are personal spaces. Walls, hedges, fences, doors, and other physical elements are often used to mark where one territory ends and another begins. As such they represent more or less distinct indications of where different claims to space are seamed together, and clues that we are entering or leaving a domain. No such clues are available for personal space; there are no distinct bounds. Whether one has violated another's personal space can be determined solely from the response of the person in question. There are no external referents other than distance to the person.

A third point of disparity has to do with size. In most cases, although there are exceptions, personal space encompasses a smaller region than does a territory. This difference is not necessary. There can be cases where a personal space is larger than a territory (e.g., the personal space surrounding a monarch at a formal function vs. a temporary territory in a library), but in most instances, the latter is more extensive.

Jurisdiction

A concept less popular than personal space, but still deserving of attention, is that of a *jurisdiction*.[24] Jurisdictions are larger than personal spaces, but smaller and more fleeting than territories. Jurisdictions are areas to which individuals can lay claim because of their job role requirements.

Perhaps the best way to approach this concept is to think of instances

[24] Roos, P. D. (1968). Jurisdiction: An ecological concept. *Human Relations, 21,* 75–84.

where servicepeople have come to your home – the TV repairwoman, the plumber, or the electrician. Upon arriving these individuals are granted access to particular areas within the house where they are required to be, given their job and what they have to accomplish. The TV repairwoman has access to the living room and the area surrounding the ailing device, for example. She can be there as long as it takes her to effect the desired cure. For that period of time her presence is accepted. While there, the repairwoman's access is limited to locations required to complete the job. Once the job is done, the right of access to the location is withdrawn.

The points of similarity with territorial functioning are several. First, in the case of both jurisdictions and territories, an individual has right of access to a particular location. Others can be excluded. Second, both territories and jurisdictions are bounded. The distinctness of the boundary depends upon the actual setting. A radio room on a ship is a more clearly bounded jurisdiction than the area in the living room around the TV repairwoman. Nonetheless, in both cases the jurisdiction is spatially circumscribed.

Finally, at a general level, jurisdictions and territories assist in working towards the same goal: increasing the legibility or clarity of social settings. Certain people have a "right" to be in certain places at certain times. This greatly enhances the predictability of social settings, and allows the person holding the jurisdiction or territory to accomplish more things in the setting with fewer distractions.

But, these similarities notwithstanding, there are several differences between jurisdictional and territorial processes. Perhaps the most significant difference is that jurisdictions, compared to territories, are much more dependent on the role of the holder, and that role is assigned. A person is entitled to hold a jurisdiction by virtue of the functional role he or she fulfills. The claim is job dependent. Who the person is – in terms of age, sex, race, or class – is unimportant; what is important is what the person is supposed to be carrying out given his or her job or role in the situation: the assigned role.

Related to this first difference is a second one. Inasmuch as jurisdictions are more dependent upon job or assigned role functions than are territories, they tend to be shorter lived and more delimited. When the repairwoman is finished resuscitating the TV set – or perhaps has admitted failure – she is not expected to stay in the living room chatting with the occupant, drinking coffee and waiting for lunch to appear. The job is completed and with it the right to a jurisdiction. The person is expected to leave. On average, then, jurisdictions are more temporary than territories.[25]

---

[25] With repeated access, however, it seems possible that a jurisdiction can evolve into a

Implicit in the preceding two considerations is a third point of difference between jurisdictions and territories. The link between the holder and the location in question is based on different forces. In territories, time, heritage, familiarity, and sentiments of attachment may help establish and maintain a link between an individual or group and a location. In jurisdictions it is simply job requirements that forge the link between the holder and the location. The "meaning" of the location, per se, to the individual, is not important. What is important is how that location fits into the individual's assigned work functions.

Home range

Whereas the concepts of personal space and jurisdiction reflect processes that usually are more spatially restricted and limited than territoriality, the concept of *home range,* as applied to humans, is more spatially inclusive than territoriality. An individual's home range includes the set of places in the environment that he or she uses and is familiar with.[26] The application of this term to humans is quite similar to its application to animals. Spaces included in the home range of a primate might include sleeping site, feeding ground, and watering hole. The home range of a person might include home and adjoining spaces, office or other work-site, and bar (watering hole) where the person stops off after work. Planners and geographers often refer to this domain as an activity space. It encompasses the locations that are visited on a more or less regular basis. Of course, some sites within the home range may be used more intensively than others. The more heavily used areas may be referred to as "core" areas within the home range.

Determining whether a location is best classified as a territory or a home range is difficult for two reasons. First, the home range clearly adjoins and surrounds viable territories. Territories are nested within the home range.

Second, some definitions of territory further blur what distinction there may be between the two concepts. For example, defining territory as that place with which we are more or less regularly associated over a period of time, obscures the distinction between a territory and a home range. Probably the most honest way of attacking this problem is to admit that the differences between home range and territory are to some extent relative. Given the partially relative nature of these differences, there may be situations where it is difficult to tell where a home range

---

territory. The proverbial janitor's closet that gets decorated with pictures or stickers may be an example of such blurring.

[26] Stea, D. (1970). Home range and use of space. In L. A. Pastalan & D. H. Carson (Eds.), *Spatial behavior of older people.* Ann Arbor, MI: University of Michigan Press.

ends and a territory begins. This may be particularly true in certain sections of a residential context, such as a college campus or a neighborhood. Nonetheless, moving away from these murky situations, there are numerous instances where territoriality applies more clearly than home range (e.g., the front yard or front steps), and vice versa (e.g., the route I walk to school).

And, perhaps the clearest-cut difference between a territory and a home range is the difference in excludability demanded and achieved. It is more difficult to keep others out, or to control what they are doing, in a home range. This is so for several reasons, which also represent differences between the two concepts. First, a home range is more extensive than a territory, making surveillance more difficult. Second, no excludability can be exercised when the occupant is not present in a home range because, third, one's "rights" in a home range are more minimal than in a territory.

Stated more conceptually, the resources in home ranges are *public* in nature, whereas those in territories are *selective*. In the former, they can be equally enjoyed by all and thus need not be defended; in the latter, one person's or group's enjoyment of the benefit interferes with another's enjoyment of it. Thus, some degree of excludability is attempted.

Attachment to place

Attachment to place refers to a positive "affective bond or association between individuals and their residential environment."[27] People become attached to neighborhoods and cities, or areas of the country, or sections of a state. When they leave, Coloradoans may miss their mountains, New Yorkers their streets, and watermen the Chesapeake Bay. These sentiments bespeak deep-seated feelings of individuals towards locale.

The similarities between the sentiments of attachment and territorial functioning are several. First, both feelings of attachment and territorial cognitions are heavily influenced by the qualities of the locale in question. There are some places to which individuals can become more easily attached than others.[28] Physical and social qualities of some locales

---

[27] Shumaker, S. A., & Taylor, R. B. (1982). Toward a clarification of people–place relationships: A model of attachment to place. In N. Feimer & E. S. Geller (Eds.), *Environmental psychology: Directions and perspectives.* New York: Praeger, pp. 219–256, p. 233.

[28] See, for example, Taylor, R. B., Gottfredson, S. D., & Brower, S. (1985). Attachment to place: Discriminant validity and impacts of disorder and diversity. *American Journal of Community Psychology, 13,* 525–542.

generate greater affection or satisfaction; similarly, physical and social qualities, albeit perhaps different ones, make it easier to establish territories, and feel a sense of territorial control or responsibility.

A second point of similarity: In both territorial functioning and attachment to place, disruption of the extant person–place bonds can have serious negative consequences for the individual or group affected. Disruption of territorial control processes may engender higher fear levels, for example.[29] In the case of attachment, persons who are more attached to current residence may suffer more (e.g., have a lowered sense of well-being) if forced to move.[30] Thus, in both instances, interference with the processes in question can be deleterious.

A third, less well-established point of similarity: For both processes, the dynamics in question may occur at the group as well as individual level. Groups can establish and hold territories, as in the familiar case of the street corner gang. Groups of people may also become attached to a location, and respond collectively when that location is threatened. Both person–place processes may operate simultaneously at the group as well as individual level.

Balanced against these points of similarity are, of course, the inevitable areas of contrast; two are particularly important. First, attachment can apply to locations that are larger than territories; people can be attached to neighborhoods, cities, states, and even countries. It does not make sense, however, to speak of the same spatial units as territories. Foci of attachment can be and often are larger, and less clearly spatially defined and delimited, than territories.

This distinction in spatial extent is not arbitrary but rather emerges from the different evolutionary origins of the two processes. Although the development of territorial functioning was largely dependent on small group processes, this was not the case for attachment. Group-based processes may have fostered some feelings of attachment for some areas, but they were not crucial. It was through psychological and behavioral processes that people became comfortable with a locale over time, learned to appreciate its "good points," and thus became attached to a location. An individual saw a location repeatedly, and moved through it regularly, these repeated viewings giving rise to familiarity and liking. Not being linked to small group processes, the sentiments of attachment can be devoted to areas much larger than a small group

[29] Taylor, R. B., Gottfredson, S. D., & Brower, S. (1981). Territorial cognitions and social climate in urban neighborhoods. *Basic and Applied Social Psychology, 2,* 289–303.

[30] Stokols, D., Shumaker, S. A., & Martinez, J. (1983). Residential mobility and personal well being. *Journal of Environmental Psychology, 3,* 5–19.

could protect. But sometimes people become attached to locales that can later be defended as territories (e.g., a house, or a portion thereof). Thus, with spatial extensiveness, there is some overlap between attachment and territorial functioning. But in the prototypical situation, people are attached to areas more extensive than territories.

A second difference, related to the first, is that most of the time sentiments of attachment are not linked to desires for excludability. These sentiments reflect enjoyment of a public good not a selective benefit.

A final, less significant difference between territoriality and attachment to place: The latter is viewed as a more accretive process than the former. The passage of time appears to be more crucial to the development of sentiments of attachment than it is to territorial cognitions.[31] Although linkage overtime between an individual or group and a territory strengthens territorial functioning, the exercise of territorial control and the development of attitudes reflecting proprietorship appear to be less time dependent than the sentiments of attachment. It may take me five years to feel that my new neighborhood is a real home, whereas I may be willing to exercise territorial control and chase unwanted intruders off my lawn after being there only a few days.

Although overlapping with territoriality, attachment to place is by no means a redundant concept. Rather, it complements notions of territorial functioning by clarifying the larger shell of sentiments, usually referring to larger-scale spaces, within which, in spatial terms, territorial functioning goes on. Although place dependent like territorial functioning, attachment is not inextricably linked to group processes.

Privacy

Like territorial functioning, privacy is concerned with issues of excludability and access. Delineating the relationship between privacy and territoriality is tricky because different perspectives on the problem exist.

Privacy as an interrelated set of boundary-regulation processes

Irwin Altman and his colleagues have suggested that privacy is a more comprehensive set of person–person and person–place processes than

---

[31] For an example of the impacts of time on the sentiments of attachment, see Kasarda, J. P., & Janowitz, M. (1974), Community attachment in mass society. *American Sociological Review, 39,* 328–339.

territoriality.[32] Through a variety of privacy mechanisms, they have suggested, one can receive more or less "information" from others, or one can impart to others more or less "information" about oneself. Privacy mechanisms encompass a range of behaviors: spatial behavior, manipulations of the environment, verbal and nonverbal communication, and so on. According to this view territorial functioning is simply one set of processes, among others, by means of which people match their desired and achieved levels of privacy. For example, a recluse, by putting up warning signs at the boundaries of his property, can scare off visitors and salespersons and thus have the desired amount of privacy. Or, alternatively, a person desirous of contact can leave her office door open and perhaps thereby achieve the desired amount of (low) privacy. According to this view, privacy is a two-way, multichannel cluster of boundary–regulation processes.

A variety of evidence supports the Altman perspective. For example, a study by Vinsel et al. found that the use of various privacy behaviors among college students was associated with whether or not they subsequently dropped out.[33]

Privacy and territorial experiences as distinct

Contrasting with Altman's view is one held by Edney, which states simply that privacy and territorial experiences are distinct. Having privacy and being in a territory result in different experiences and different outcomes. If one is in a territory, one's mood, and how one interprets behavior, are different depending upon whether one has privacy. Experiments by Julian Edney and Michael Buda have supported this perspective and successfully disentangled territorial and privacy experiences in a laboratory setting.[34]

Their findings imply that having a territory "felt" different to the participants than having privacy, and produced some different results. Therefore, although territoriality and privacy may overlap substantially in our everyday environment – we are most likely to also have privacy in a territory of our own – territorial experiences cannot be treated merely as a subset of privacy experiences, because the two phenomena have distinct effects.

---

[32] Altman, I. (1975). *The environment and social behavior.* Monterey, CA: Brooks/Cole.

[33] Vinsel, A., Brown, B. B., Altman, I., & Foss, C. (1980). Privacy regulation, territorial displays, and effectiveness of individual functioning. *Journal of Personality and Social Psychology, 39,* 1104–1115.

[34] Edney, J. J., & Buda, M. A. (1976). Distinguishing territoriality and privacy: Two studies. *Human Ecology, 4,* 283–296.

Proposing a linkage

A third position on the question of the linkage between privacy and territoriality represents something of a compromise between the view that privacy and territoriality are indissolubly linked, and the view that they offer distinct experiences. This perspective makes one crucial assumption: For most people, privacy experiences are more central than privacy behaviors. That is, when most people think of privacy, they consider the experience of having privacy, not the behaviors that lead up to or ensure that privacy. This assumption is supported by the definitions of private as "a state of being private" or "a place of seclusion from company."[35] Reference to privacy behaviors, although conceptually appealing and supported by empirical evidence, is not common in everyday usage.

In understanding the nature of the linkage between territorial functioning and privacy experiences, the following points should be taken into account.

First, there are many different types of privacy experiences.[36] Most prototypical are probably the experiences of *solitude* and *intimacy*.[37]

Solitude refers to a privacy experience where one is alone, and away from others; there is a physical distance or separation between the ego and the rest of the social world. The most paradigmatic uses of the privacy concept center very explicitly on individuals.[38] Intimacy, however, refers to the situation where a small group of individuals withdraws from the social world for the purpose of confidential communication. The intimate privacy experience is exemplified in two friends walking far down a beach, away from the crowd, for a chat; or a boss summoning a troublesome employee to his or her office and closing the door. The "boundary" between the two persons in the group is permeable, but the group itself presents a relatively impermeable boundary to those outside the group.

---

[35] (1983). *Webster's New Universal Unabridged Dictionary*. New York: Dorset & Baber, p. 1432.

[36] Westin has proposed four. Westin, A. F. (1967). *Privacy and freedom*. New York: Atheneum. Marshall has proposed six. See Marshall, N. J. (1972), Privacy and environment. *Human Ecology, 2*, 93–110, or Marshall, N. J. (1974), Dimensions of privacy preferences. *Multivariate Behavioral Research, 9*, 255–271.

[37] These labels are Westin's (1967).

[38] Altman, I., Vinsel, A., & Brown, B. B. (1981). Dialectic conceptions in social psychology: An application to social penetration and privacy regulation. In L. Berkowitz (Ed.), *Advances in experimental social psychology*, vol. 14. New York: Academic Press, pp. 107–160. See esp. p. 151.

The second point to consider is that territorial functioning is evident in a range of settings. In some locations the occupant of a territory can exercise greater control over who does and does not enter. Consequently, one is more likely to experience the desired level of privacy in some types of territories than in others. The varying "strength" of different types of territories may explain the strong natural covariation or co-occurrence of territorial functioning and privacy experiences.

Some results from a field study by Taylor and Ferguson support this proposed linkage between privacy experiences and territorial functioning.[39] In that study students reported that they were likely to go a more secure location, or a "stronger" territory when they wanted to be alone with another (the "intimacy" privacy experience) than when they sought to be alone and away from all others (the "solitude" privacy experience). For example, if a student wanted to be alone to think over plans for the future, or to introspect, he or she would be most likely to go to a place where he or she had little territorial control, but was outside and away from others. A relatively secluded, parklike setting on the Virginia Tech campus was a favorite spot for solitude seekers. But if the student wanted to be alone with another to talk over personal, confidential matters, inside spots where one could establish "stronger" territorial claims, such as one's dorm room or apartment, were chosen. In other words, if the type of privacy desired demanded confidential communication, "stronger" territories were viewed as better places to go. Participants also reported that the kind of territory gained influenced the quality of the privacy experience. In "stronger" territories (e.g., in one's room or apartment as compared to being outside), occupants felt a greater sense of control.

These patterns suggest a "two-stage" linkage between privacy and territorial processes. When a person desires a particular type of privacy, the experience sought is considered in conjunction with the resources available. Imagine an undergraduate premed major who, already having questions about his choice of major, just finds out that he has failed miserably on a midterm in organic chemistry. The student may not only be depressed but may also wish to be alone to have some time to think about the possibility of switching majors, reevaluating career goals, and how significant others might react to such moves. Given these desires the student will probably do a rough inventory of places where he could go. Dorm room or apartment may or may not be a possibility depending upon whether the student has his own bedroom, the number of roommates, how well he gets along with them, whether the roommates have

---

[39] Taylor, R. B., & Ferguson, G. (1980). Solitude and intimacy: Linking territoriality and privacy experiences. *Journal of Nonverbal Behavior, 4*, 227–239.

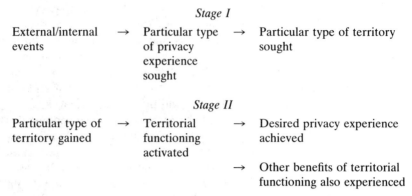

Stage I

External/internal → Particular type → Particular type of territory
events of privacy sought
experience
sought

Stage II

Particular type of → Territorial → Desired privacy experience
territory gained functioning achieved
activated
→ Other benefits of territorial
functioning also experienced

Figure 5.4. Two-stage model linking territorial functioning and privacy experiences.

other friends visiting at the time, and so on. Other, perhaps more distant or soothing places – downtown, a nearby beach or woods, the mountains – may be considered, depending upon how much effort it would take to get there.

Say the student decides to go to his off-campus apartment because his roommates will probably be gone. Once the person is there, the benefits of territorial control serve to buttress the solitude that can be achieved. Barring roommates, unwanted intruders are unlikely or, should they show up, can at least be sent away. The phone can be turned off. A favorite record can be put on. Thus, being in a more central territory better supports or reinforces the privacy experience desired.

At the same time, being in a central territory affords more than just privacy; other benefits are conferred as well. Familiar objects may reinforce one's sense of identity. Should others be present, one may be more persuasive with them than would be the case if one were elsewhere. One may simply feel relaxed and at ease there. In short, "strong" territories are multipurpose; although they may make possible or perhaps even safeguard or enhance privacy experiences, they facilitate many other outcomes as well (Figure 5.4).

In sum, a cleaner link between privacy and territorial functioning can be established if we focus on privacy *experiences*. The type of privacy sought shapes territorial functioning, leading the person or group to occupy a particular type of territory, i.e., a place where the person or group can have control over excludability, deciding whether to bar or invite others. Once in a location where the desired amount of territorial functioning can be exercised, other benefits, besides just the privacy experience, accrue.[40]

It is premature to attempt a clearer conceptualization of the link between territorial functioning and privacy *behaviors,* the centerpiece of Altman's privacy model. There simply is not enough evidence at the current time to clarify the possible connections. For the most part, privacy researchers have shown little interest in territorial functioning, and vice versa, making it difficult to bridge the gap between the two concepts.

Nonetheless, some general distinctions can be made between territorial functioning and privacy behaviors. First, as conceptualized by Altman, privacy behaviors constitute a more general class of activities than the behaviors involved in territorial functioning. The relevant processes cover a wider variety of mechanisms. Second, territorial functioning more clearly constitutes an environment–behavior *system* than do privacy behaviors. Although privacy-seeking and privacy-avoiding scales have been constructed by researchers in this area, it has not yet been established that the full range of behavioral privacy mechanisms envisioned by Altman work together in a systemlike fashion. This point has, however, been demonstrated in the case of territorial functioning (see Chapter 8 for example).

And, finally, the concept of privacy behaviors, albeit context sensitive, is inherently less place dependent than the concept of territorial functioning. In other words, privacy mechanisms, those behavioral sequences used to increase or decrease contact with others, are more generalizable and less place specific than territorial behaviors. Territorial functioning is more "driven" by particular setting characteristics than are privacy behaviors. The latter, albeit setting linked, are "driven" to a greater extent by personal characteristics than the former. Privacy researchers have developed privacy scales that indicate how some individuals use more or fewer privacy mechanisms than others. But such scales have not been developed for territorial functioning.[41]

Although the link between territorial functioning and privacy behaviors is not clear, what is clear is that the two concepts are not redundant. Privacy, with its more person-specific focus and, as conceptualized by

---

[40] For empirical support of this last point, see:

Taylor, R. B. (1977). Territorial cognitions and the structure of centrality. Paper presented at the annual meeting of the Eastern Psychological Association, Boston, April.

[41] Privacy scales have been generated by Marshall, McKechnie, and others. For a good example see Ferguson, G. (1979), The development of a privacy scale. Master's thesis. Department of Psychology, Virginia Polytechnic Institute and State University.

Altman, more general nature, provides an interpretation of boundary-regulation processes that is quite different from a concern with territorial functioning.

Territorial functioning and related concepts: most important differences

Personal space. Person is at the center of one's personal space. It cannot be left behind.

Jurisdiction. Completely dependent on functional role assigned to holder. Also, usually held for a more delimited time.

Home range. Much less excludability demanded and achieved. Others usually allowed free use of the area and "resources" in question. Location and goods within it treated as a "public" good, rather than selective benefit.

Attachment to place. Applicable to larger-scale domains. Usually, no excludability demanded. May provide larger shell of sentiments within which territorial functioning operates.

Privacy experiences. May be linked to territorial functioning in a "two-stage" fashion. Type of experience sought may determine territorial functioning. But, once in a territory, occupant enjoys other benefits in addition to desired privacy experience.

Privacy behaviors. Linkage with territorial functioning not clear. Altman has suggested that privacy mechanisms may include many aspects of territorial functioning.

Summary

The chapter opened with an elaborated definition of territorial functioning, and a clarification of the dominant themes in definitions offered by various researchers. The definition used here highlights the spatially delimited, small group-based, place-specific attributes of territorial functioning. These attributes emerge from the evolutionary origins of the system in question. A model of territorial functioning was introduced, highlighting the determinants and consequences of territorial functioning. The model places territorial cognitions in a central role, as key shapers of territorial behaviors. Immediate and longer-term consequences of territorial functioning were highlighted, including psychological, social psychological, and ecological outcomes. Finally, territorial functioning was compared and contrasted with related environment–behavior concepts. Although there are obvious points of overlap between territorial functioning and these other notions, territorial functioning does provide a unique focus and thus is not a redundant concept.

Appendix: An extended example illustrating the conceptual model

Consider the following hypothetical example. At a major midwestern university (Big State University, or BSU) there are about fifteen fraternities. Most are located on a long street, known as "Fraternity Row," at the edge of campus. Each is a three-story home, with single and double rooms on the second and third floors, and two large rooms, for parties and meetings, on the first floor. In each basement there are Ping-Pong tables, a bar, and a separate TV room. Membership in each fraternity ranges from 30 to 50 students, although each house accommodates only 15–25 on a live-in basis.

Each fraternity attracts a fairly distinct membership. Football and lacrosse "jocks" favor one house, math and engineering types another, prelaw students appear to gravitate to two or three in particular, one house appears to be drawing mainly gays, and one fraternity has a reputation as being mainly for "heads": those who are heavily into different kinds of drugs. It is not surprising, given the rough "sorting" of different types of students into different houses, that there is strong rivalry between some of the fraternities. This is manifested in several ways. There are interfraternity sports leagues in touch football, softball, rugby, and basketball. During Ice Carnival Weekend there is an interfraternity ice sculpture contest, judged by a committee composed of faculty in the art department and college officials. The winning statue gets a front-page write-up (with photo) in the college newspaper. During Red Cross blood drives the Interfraternity Council keeps track of how much is contributed by the various organizations, who compete to be the highest donor.

But the competition can also take less constructive forms. During the sculpture competition houses have been known to incite their youngest members to carry out late-night raids on the artwork of rival houses. These raiders, armed with buckets of hot water, tire irons, and crowbars, have left many ice statues dismembered (or worse). At other times of the year raids may be carried out in which paint is thrown on a rival house, or its windows are soaped or covered with shaving cream. Needless to say, the college administration disapproves of such antics, and from time to time will levy modest fines on the miscreants. But these actions appear to have little deterrent impact.

Located at the far end of "The Row," the fraternity called "Bones' Fence" typifies what life is like in many of the other houses. This house severed or lost (the details are unclear) its national affiliation several years back, and has been a successful nonaffiliated fraternity since that time. Many of its members appear to be potential yuppies or yumpies. They are largely middle to upper middle class. Many are prebusiness and prelaw majors. The house prides itself on being fairly selective; although it is rushed by many underclassmen every year, only a fraction are selected. Total membership in the house is 35, and about 17 of those actually live in the house. Although the membership is not as rowdy as Sig Ep, the football/lacrosse frat, "the Fencers" have occasional outbursts. Their chief rival is "Lambda House," located at the opposite end of The Row. Whether geographical juxtaposition or competition for some of the same rushees accounts more for their traditional rivalry is not clear. But, being a "class" frat, the Fencers try very hard to be imaginative. For example, in one raid the Fencers, with the help of someone "inside" Lambda House, succeeded in turning off the basement heat in Lambda, and filling one entire room with snow. (Lambda later retaliated by gracing the Fencers' basement floor with three inches of Jello when the house members were away for a basketball game.)

Within "B.F." there is an interesting residential arrangement. The rooms on the third floor are singles. Their greater privacy makes them more desirable than the doubles and triples on the second floor; they are also warmer in the winter. Therefore house officers, who are required by bylaws to live in the house, and members of the frat who are seniors, and/or very good buddies with an officer, compete for the third-floor rooms. Lowly juniors and some seniors are relegated to the second floor. Sophomore brothers are not allowed to live in the house.

Given these introductory facts, how does this illustrate the dynamics proposed in the preliminary framework indicated in Figure 5.3? The linkages proposed by the framework can be examined one by one.

Cultural factors influence subjective definition of territory. Sociocultural factors influence how a particular territory is defined. A certain type of territory may simply not exist in certain types of cultures. For example, in British universities, there are social clubs and societies, and each "college" is a unit that undergraduates identify with to some extent, but there is no clear counterpart to the fraternity, with its live-in status and peculiar blend of social activities. This type of institution within the university, and the territorial arrangement that accompanies it, is distinctly American.

Social factors influence subjective definition of territory; social factors influence individual and group territorial functioning. Two clusters of social features are relevant to these linkages: differences between the various groups in question (i.e., between the various fraternity houses), and differences within the various groups (i.e., intrahouse differences). With regard to *between-group* differences in the current example, part of what makes each fraternity distinct, and allows each member to think that his fraternity is somehow special and different from the others, is the "sorting" of different student "types" into different fraternities. Certain types of rushees (e.g., computer jocks, lax jocks, gays, etc.) were attracted to certain fraternities; at the same time, each fraternity was looking for potential brothers who would "fit in." As a result, the social composition of each group is to some extent unique, in terms of the background of its members. This allows the members of each group to identify, and sometimes exaggerate, how their fraternity is different from another. At the same time these differences strengthen the extent to which the individual members identify with and value their particular fraternity. These differences in sentiments and cognitions are then reflected in behaviors, such as spending more or less time at the fraternity, or showing up at more or fewer fraternity functions. Stated differently: The fraternity houses (territories) that are used most heavily by the membership, and that are most valued, are those providing the clearest and most distinct group identity for their members. Thus, for example, members of the one black fraternity on campus, and the one Jewish fraternity on campus, may value their fraternity more, and spend more time in the territories available within and created by the fraternity, than the members of the Bones' Fence fraternity.

Another way to focus on the impact of between-group social factors is to consider the differential access to spaces within the Bones' Fence house afforded to members versus nonmembers. As a rule, nonmembers are not allowed in the house, except during rush week, or unless invited by a member. When a social function such as a dance or social hour is held all brothers are admitted free, but nonbrothers must confront the bouncer at the door and either cough up the requisite three dollars to get in, or go away.

With regard to *within-group social differences:* the internal group dynamics of each house are different, and those factors influence subjective definition of territory, and actual territorial functioning. For example, in fraternities where the membership is more homogeneous, and where there is more agreement about the goals of the fraternity, the territories provided by the fraternity will be more valued by and used by its members. Further, the extent to which individual members are actively involved in the social dynamics of the fraternity (attend meetings reliably, volunteer to participate in or head up special functions such as the Red Cross blood drive, show up consistently at social functions) will reflect the degree to which they value the territories created by the fraternity. The position of each individual in the social network created by the fraternity membership influences how that individual views and uses various locations within the fraternity. Thus, the overall structure of each fraternity group influences how the members of the group perceive and use the fraternity territories, and the relationship of individual members to that group structure also influences individual perceptions and actions.

Individual factors influence subjective definition of territory, and territorial functioning. Interindividual differences among members of a particular fraternity influence how territories within the fraternity are perceived, and how people behave in various territories. For example, in the case of Bones' Fence the officers of the fraternity perceive that they have a right to occupy the most desirable residential rooms in the house, the third-floor singles, and they do so. Or, to take another example, those who have lived in the house longer may have a more proprietary attitude towards the house, and be more involved in its care and upkeep. Seniors who have been living in the house since their junior year, as compared to seniors who do not and have not lived in the house, may think it is more important to turn out for a "paint-up and fix-up weekend," and may be more likely actually to do so.

Physical environment influences subjective definition of territory. Various features of the physical environment may enhance or detract from the extent to which people can think of it as a territory or a set of territories. A fraternity, as a social group, centers on its house. Without a house there is no central meeting place. The size and quality of the house and its location influence how members feel about it. Some fraternities at BSU are not located on Fraternity Row, and are of wooden-frame construction instead of stately brick. Members of the former may feel that their house is not a "quality place," and that their fraternity does not somehow measure up to the ones on the Row. Being of lesser quality, these fraternities may not be able to attract the top-notch rushees. Bones' Fence, being both brick and on the Row, is perceived by its members as a bona fide, "class" house. The Fence is also somewhat smaller than other houses on the Row, reducing the size of its live-in population. Whereas other houses are able to accommodate all or almost all of their members who want to live there, the Fence cannot. Consequently, since there is some selection in determining residency in the house, those who do live there value it more. And, being a smaller group than residential populations in other houses, they are more cohesive and work together better as a group when it comes to doing things about house maintenance, cleanup, or yardwork. This is but a minor example of how the physical environment can influence perception of territory, and individual and group territorial functioning.

Individual and group territorial functioning operate simultaneously and are mutually influenced. The proposed framework suggests that territorial functioning at two levels can be discerned and are linked: the individual within the group, and the relations between groups. Examples of individual territorial functioning within a group include how much time an individual member spends in various territories within the house. Does he use his room as a place to study or socialize, or only to sleep in? How many evenings a week does he spend in the TV room or in the basement bar? Group territorial functioning focuses on the activities of interacting members that are focused towards a common goal, that is, relevant to relationships between groups. For example, how many members of the house turn out to work on the annual snow sculpture, and how much time do they put into the effort? In essence, the sculpture serves as an elaborate, stylized symbol or marker of the group territory. Overall, how well kept is the house? Do members let the house degenerate to the point where there are broken windows throughout, the toilets don't flush, and the leaves are knee-deep in the front yard? Or do they routinely get together and do serious spring cleaning and painting, agree as a group to get structural repairs done when needed, despite the cost, and set aside two Saturday afternoons a fall for raking up the yard? All of these activities represent aspects of group territorial functioning.

Obviously, individual and group territorial functioning is linked because individuals must contribute to the functions of the group. In the case of activities where interacting individuals are involved, one can focus either on individuals or groups as the unit of analysis. One might look at how many hours various individual members of Bones' Fence contributed to working on the ice statue, and try to predict this using individual scores on scales tapping attitudes towards the Fence, and measures of social involvement with other house members. If one were seeking to understand group functioning, total personhours (including hours girlfriends contributed) put in by each house on its ice statue, or hours per capita, could be predicted using house-level information such as number of members per house, percentage of art majors in each house, and so on. Thus, individual versus group is in this instance simply a matter of focus.

But there may be other aspects of territorial functioning that are amenable to analysis only at the individual level, that is, analysis of the individual within the group. Time spent by various members in various settings and territories within the house (own room, kitchen, etc.) would be one such example.

Group and individual territorial functioning contribute to social order. Effective territorial functioning clarifies the social order within Bones' Fence. Consider the following examples. Bouncers' ejection of non-members trying to gain entrance to Saturday night dances keeps the dance floor (and bar) from becoming hopelessly overcrowded. It may also reduce the chances of fights breaking out. By seeking to recruit "like-minded" rushees, and successfully doing so, high levels of group cohesiveness are maintained, which translates into stronger identification of brothers with the house, and more group involvement in maintenance projects. Thus, the house overall is better kept up.

The purpose of this example has been to provide a hypothetical illustration of how the processes depicted in the proposed model on human territoriality might operate in a particular situation. As an exercise, the reader might want to think of a familiar situation and consider how, or to what extent, territorial functioning in that setting exemplifies the linkages proposed.

6
CLARIFYING PSYCHOLOGICAL AND ECOLOGICAL CONSEQUENCES

Streets, boundaries, forecourts, and entrances are key areas for self-expression. All those who enter a house must pass through some forecourt. Creating a good impression, a powerful impression, or a friendly, welcoming one depends very much on this "front." This area is also very susceptible to pressure from neighbors. A resident who fails to mow the lawn regularly or to paint the house, or who leaves old cars outside will soon incur the ire of neighbors in most communities. It may be property values that people worry about or it may be simply the sense of street identity.
– Don Appleyard, "Home" (1979)

The conceptual framework introduced in the preceding chapter associated human territorial functioning with four classes of consequences: social psychological within group, social psychological between group, psychological, and ecological. That framework is more fully specified in the current chapter.

Organization of the chapter

Two additional perspectives are introduced that clarify how the psychological and ecological consequences of territorial functioning, depicted in the preceding chapter, emerge. A *context-specific stress model* developed by Dan Stokols is outlined. This perspective delineates the process leading to stress-related consequences. It is particularly helpful in considering spaces where the person–place bonds are of high centrality. In relatively private locations, where the person–place bond is of high centrality, territorial functioning accomplishes a spatiotemporal sorting, *reducing* conflicting functional demands and thereby *de*creasing experienced stress.

The second perspective introduced is ecological psychology's *behavior setting theory*. It identifies the relevant components of public settings, and explains the persistence and focus of particular activities in locations. In outdoor residential locations, such as the streetblock, territorial functioning plays several key roles in maintaining behavior settings.

Purpose of additional perspectives

The introduction of these additional perspectives serves two purposes. A stress perspective clarifies the processes linking territorial functioning and intraindividual or psychological consequences, illuminating precisely the facilitation or thwarting experienced by individuals in various locations. An ecological psychological perspective indicates how territorial functioning contributes to ongoing ecological units – behavior settings (defined later). These are the building blocks of the public environment. In short, with the inclusion and integration of these additional conceptual domains we can better specify the underlying processes linking territorial functioning with particular outcomes.[1]

Second, this conceptual integration helps to build more powerful, truly interdisciplinary theoretical perspectives. Many of the issues that environment–behavior researchers wish to tackle are exceedingly complex. Later in this volume, for example, we will turn to issues of disorder (Chapter 11) and resource conservation (Chapter 12). The far-reaching nature of these issues demands a sound but broad-gauged theoretical perspective. Such holistic coverage cannot be achieved by any one narrowly defined theory but rather demands a carefully integrated approach. Territorial functioning can be fused with additional theoretical perspectives, such as the two discussed in this chapter, to produce a useful, articulated viewpoint.

Perspective relevance and centrality

The relevance of the two perspectives introduced here varies as a function of centrality. (Recall that centrality is an attribute of person–place transactions, not settings per se. For locations where centrality is higher, the loss of that setting results in a greater disturbance of the overall lifespace of the individual or group.) One aspect of centrality is its private versus public nature.[2] Sites affording more privacy usually have greater functional importance for an individual, or satisfy "higher-order" needs, than more public locations. They are also more multifunctional. And, this public versus private nature is linked to the consequences of territorial functioning.

More specifically, the intraindividual, stress-related consequences

---

[1] A third perspective already built into my treatment of territorial functioning is a group dynamics focus. Since this concern is so basic to my treatment of territorial functioning it is not viewed as "added on."

[2] Taylor, R. B. (1977). Territorial cognitions and the structure of centrality. Paper presented at the annual meetings of the Eastern Psychological Association, Boston, April.

of territorial functioning are most salient in relatively private settings. It is in these settings that territorial functioning allows the execution of behavioral sequences important for the individual *qua* individual or as a member of a group. The psychological consequences of territorial functioning predominate in these more private contexts such as spaces within the home, private offices or work spaces, and so on.

By contrast, the ecological consequences of territorial functioning are most salient in more public settings. Territorial functioning may reduce stress for individuals, but the more sizable impact is on the settings themselves. In settings that qualify as behavior settings territorial functioning plays pivotal roles in maintaining the setting program (see the section entitled "Behavior setting theory"). At church suppers, fraternity parties (see the Appendix), in drugstores and in shops, territorial functioning channels behaviors appropriately and reduces the incidence of behaviors that might threaten the setting.

Across all varieties of settings, social psychological consequences occur and are salient. This is in contrast to the prominence of the ecological and psychological consequences, which are more place specific.

The linkage between salience of functional consequences associated with territorial functioning, and centrality, is indicated in Figure 6.1.

A contextual-stress perspective

Some terminology: what are stress and coping?

Before examining the specifics of Stokols' congruence model of setting-specific stress, some more general terminology on stress and coping is needed.

Stressors are any demands or threats in the external environment that challenge our ability to adapt.[3] Psychologists have investigated impacts of a range of stressors: noise, air pollution, and crowding, to name a few.

The *stress response* is complex and includes physiological responses, such as arousal or elevated blood pressure, affective responses such as fatigue or depression, and cognitive responses, such as decreased attention.

Responses to the stressor are *mediated* by a range of *psychological factors*. There has been considerable work on how people respond physiologically to stressors and on the psychological dynamics that

---

[3] Lazarus, R. (1966). *Psychological stress and the coping process*. New York: McGraw-Hill.

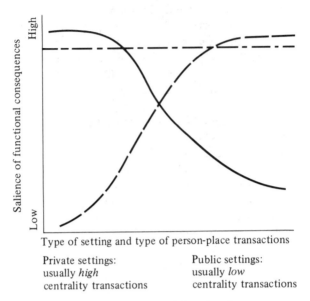

Type of setting and type of person-place transactions

Private settings: Public settings:
usually *high*   usually *low*
centrality transactions   centrality transactions

Figure 6.1. Type of setting and functional consequences. The figure suggests how the relative salience of the psychological (———), ecological (– – – – –), and social psychological consequences (— - — -) varies as a function of the centrality of the person–place bonds relevant to the location in question.

make a particular stressor appear more or less threatening.[4] Our stress response is determined not only by the nature of the stressor itself (how loud the noise is, how packed the room is) but also by our psychological interpretation or appraisal of the stressor: How controllable does it appear to be? Is it going to last for a short or a long time? Is it escapable?

In response to a stressor people may show *coping responses.* These are the cognitive and behavioral strategies used to lessen the demands of the stressor. These responses are quite varied and may include cognitive efforts to adapt to the stressor, as when people try to tune out the noise that is bothering them, as well as behavior adaptations (e.g., wearing ear plugs). Coping responses may be *palliative,* such as tuning out the stressor, or *instrumental,* as when people seek to eliminate the stressor (e.g., by turning the noise off). Coping efforts may also include the garnering of *social support* – when others proffer aid, of one sort or another, to the person experiencing the stressor. Often, coping re-

---

[4] Baum, A., Singer, J., & Baum, C. (1982). Stress and the environment. In G. W. Evans (Ed.), *Environmental stress.* Cambridge: Cambridge University Press, pp. 15–44.

sponses lessen the impact of the stressor, resulting in diminished stress responses.

Stressors, however, can have consequences even after they have ended. These *poststress responses* include *decrements* in performance and cognition.[5] Even after the noise to which we have been subjected has been turned off, for example, we may find ourselves feeling very tired, or having trouble concentrating on a task like reading or problem solving.

A congruence model of stress

Although stress research has furnished insight into what kinds of stressors are more or less bothersome for what kinds of people, Stokols has criticized it for its placelessness. That is, most of the research has viewed stressors as isolated events or chains of events and has failed to consider the importance of the *context* in which they occur. And yet, stressors always occur someplace. Stokols has suggested that it is important to investigate systematically the functional impact of stressors by examining where they occur.

Any particular setting can either facilitate or hinder the accomplishment of certain goals; it supports or constrains activities.[6] A situation of *congruence* exists between the person and the setting when the setting allows the individual to accomplish the goals or functions that he or she thinks are appropriate to accomplish there. Settings differ in that different behaviors are appropriate or expected in different locations.[7] We expect to be able to sleep in our bedroom at home; we do not expect to be able to (or to be allowed to) sleep in a classroom. Consequently, what is bothersome varies from setting to setting. The fact that someone is talking may not be bothersome in a classroom (unless it interferes with hearing a lecture), but the same talking might be very bothersome, and thus stressful, in a bedroom late at night when one is trying to get to sleep. Stokols' analysis considers how stressors are experienced within particular settings, and thus how the impacts of particular stressors are setting specific.[8]

---

[5] Glass, D., & Singer, J. (1972). *Urban stressors.* New York: Academic.

[6] Chein, I. The environment as a determinant of behavior (1954). *Journal of Social Psychology, 39*, 115–127.

[7] Wicker, A. (1979). *An introduction to ecological psychology.* Monterey, CA: Brooks/ Cole.

[8] Stokols, D. (1979). A congruence analysis of human stress. In I. G. Sarason & C. D. Spielberger (Eds.), *Stress and anxiety*, Vol. 6. Washington, DC: Hemisphere, pp. 27– 53.

Stokols has suggested that this person–environment congruence actually has several components (see the following). First, there is *environmental controllability;* a setting is controllable to the extent that it facilitates, and does not thwart, personal needs relevant to the setting. The ratio of actual facilitation of personal needs to ideal facilitation (i.e., preferred level of need attainment) less the amount of thwarting that goes on, summed across all the relevant needs in the setting, represents an environment's controllability.

Components of person–environment, stress-related congruence: key terms in Stokols' model

Relevant needs. In a particular setting, a person or group seeks to satisfy particular needs or functions. The needs are relevant to the setting in that the setting is the location in which they can be satisfied.

Ideal facilitation (IF) refers to the preferred level of need attainment a person seeks to achieve in that particular setting. It reflects "the individual's appraisal of the optimal or desired level of facilitation associated with that need" for that setting. Thus, there are specific levels of ideal facilitation for particular need-setting combinations. The level of ideal facilitation for a privacy–office combination – how much privacy is desired in the office setting – is different from the level for privacy–bedroom, for example.

Actual facilitation (AF) reflects the extent to which an individual in a setting perceives that a particular need is actually facilitated within a particular setting. In other words, to what extent can the setting actually permit the achievement of certain conditions or behaviors that allow the satisfaction of a particular need? Since actual facilitation will always be less than ideal facilitation, the ratio of actual/ideal, for each pertinent need, cannot be greater than 1.0, and will most often be far less than 1.0.

Thwarting. The satisfaction of various needs, in various settings, is thwarted or hindered to various degrees. There are social and physical features in settings that prevent the attainment of a particular desired need-setting combination. For example, the attainment of privacy in an office is thwarted by the role demand of being accessible to co-workers. *Actual thwarting (AT)* reflects the extent to which the person perceives that satisfaction of a particular need in the setting is hindered.

Environmental controllability (C) is a setting-specific attribute, reflecting the extent to which a particular setting is controllable by an individual or group. "The controllability of a setting concerns the degree to which it can be modified or maintained in accord with personal preference and well-being, and the extent to which one's exposure to the environment can be personally regulated." It is a product of several factors:[9]

$$C = \frac{d_f(AF_{nf}) - d_t(AT_{nt})}{df_f(IF_{nf}) + d_t(IF_{nt})},$$

where n_f refers to the needs that are perceived to be facilitated, and n_t refers to the needs that are perceived to be thwarted in the setting. Thus, it is a "composite" of several different needs, some of which may be satisfied, others of which may be hindered.

Different needs have different levels of *motivational significance* for various individuals. In a work setting, for example, privacy may be much more important for one supervisor than for another. Environmental controllability can be adjusted to take this into account.

In addition to facilitating needs, settings also place *demands* on individuals: "the degree to which a setting constrains personal goals or activities." It is, in essence, the reverse of adjusted controllability. That is, it is the ratio of thwarting to facilitation, across needs, rather than the ratio of facilitation to thwarting. In other words, as controllability decreases, demand increases.

The *demand* associated with a particular *stressor* in a setting can be computed by determining environmental *controllability* when the stressor is *present* versus when it is *absent*.

The second part of Stokols' congruence model of environmental controllability is *environmental salience*. This refers to the extent to which the needs suggested as appropriate by the setting, or the needs usually associated with that type of setting, are *motivationally significant,* or subjectively important. Simply put: It is more important to be able to do some things rather than other things in a setting. For example, suppose that in Olly's case (see the next box), the need to create novel environments, as represented by his tunnel, was much greater – more important to him – than his need for self-expression through his building ability. In this case the environmental controllability of his messy room would be reduced much more by his parents' request to take apart the tunnel and put the chairs back where they belonged, than it would by their request to put the blocks away. What he can or cannot do, in terms of activities relevant to each need, is important to him only insofar as that need itself is important. Being thwarted on less "motivationally significant" needs is less stressful.

[9] This is equation (1) from Stokols (1979).

Not only is the degree of thwarting or facilitating situation- or setting-specific, so too are the relevant needs. Satisfaction of different needs is more or less appropriate depending upon the setting. Olly would probably not expect that he could create novel environments like tunnels in his sister's or brother's bedroom.

An application of Stokols' model: Olly's room

The Awful Mess depicts the plight of a young boy named Olly.[10] In Olly's room there was "a tunnel, and two tall towers, and a bad traffic jam. Wild animals lived in a deep, dark cave," formerly the closet. Olly is ostracized by his older brother and sister who think the clutter is too much. His mother and father entreat Olly to clean up, but he refuses and instead builds another tower. The parents say: "Well, after all, it's *his* room." The baby-sitter takes matters in hand, but her thorough cleaning is undone as soon as she leaves. One day a boy, David, comes to visit. Olly and David go up to his room and have a grand time stalking through the jungle, past the traffic jam, and crawling through the tunnel. David proclaims: "I like your room; it's *neat!*"

Let's consider the personal needs relevant to the setting. Olly's room was important as a place where he could express himself. Artworks such as his towers were achievements symbolizing his engineering and planning abilities, as well as physical coordination. The room was also important as a place to imagine. The placement of the beasts in the cave – the closet – facilitated his pretending that the room was a dark and dangerous place. It was also important as a place where he could create and experience novel physical settings. The creation of the tunnel made a small, enclosed, dark space. With the flashlight, the new and different situation could be explored. Thus, three needs were satisfied by the messy room – and not by the neat one: self-expression, pretending, and novelty.[11]

For each of these three needs one can consider the extent to which the setting either facilitated or thwarted its satisfaction. In the messy room the satisfaction of all three needs was quite close to the desired or preferred amount. And the needs were not thwarted much by the situation. Thus, focusing just on these three needs, the messy room would get a very high score on environmental controllability.

---

[10] Rockwell, A. F. (1973). *The awful mess*. New York: Four Winds Press.

[11] Of course, the room also met other needs, such as a place to entertain friends, or to be alone, away from the rest of the family. But, these needs were satisfied equally well by a messy or a neat room. The preceding three needs, by contrast, were satisfied by the messy room but not the neat room.

In the neat room, by contrast, thwarting levels were much higher, and actual need-satisfaction levels were much lower. The environment was not at all novel, there being no tunnel; there were no towers to testify to Olly's abilities since the blocks were all put away; and it was hard to think about dangerous beasts in the jungle since his animals were all neatly tucked in. Focusing on these three needs then, the environmental controllability score would be much lower in the neat room.

Controllability concerns the extent to which need facilitation exceeds the thwarting of needs in particular situations. The focus can also be reversed. Focusing on the degree to which the need thwarting outweighs or overcomes the need facilitation considers the extent to which the environment places *demands* on the individual. Stokols suggests that the extent to which the setting is demanding reflects its incongruence with behavior, and thus the degree to which it is stressful.

Stokols' model introduces us to the concept of stressors, and associated demands, by focusing on "need-in-setting" elements. To the extent the need in question is important for that individual and that setting, and it is thwarted, the person experiences stress; to the extent the need is important and is facilitated in the setting, the person experiences satisfaction in the setting.

Links with territorial functioning

Territorial functioning includes a range of setting-specific behavioral strategies geared towards increasing need facilitation, and reducing thwarting, in a particular setting. When these strategies are inadequate, ignored, or fall into disuse, need facilitation may decrease and thwarting may increase, resulting in increased demand on the individual by the setting, and hence stress. In other words, territorial functioning reduces stress-related outcomes by helping "manage" the demand placed on the individual by the setting in question, thereby increasing environmental controllability.

Territorial functioning influences environmental controllability by reducing actual thwarting of various needs, by increasing actual facilitation, or both. Lacking such functioning, demands in the setting increase, and higher levels of stress are experienced.

Moving away from the technical terms presented in Stokols' model, his perspective leads us towards a general point: *Territorial functioning allows people to achieve what they want to achieve in particular settings, with minimal interference.* It reduces factors impeding these accomplishments, and/or may simply make it easier to do things in the setting. Consequently, the friction between the setting itself and the individual in the setting is lessened. Being in the setting is a more satisfying experience, and more is achieved there. Less demand and consequent stress are experienced.

Stokols' model also explains, in part, why territorial strategies employed in a setting may differ across individuals and groups. Different needs may be motivationally significant, in the same setting, for various individuals. Thus, the type of thwarting concerned will differ and, consequently, the approach to reducing demand. Two supervisors in identical offices may act quite differently because for one the most motivationally significant factor may be getting her work done, whereas for another the greatest need may be to tune in to employees' concerns.

Moving from interindividual to intersetting variation, Stokols' model helps us understand why territorial functioning varies across settings. Not only are different settings physically and socially variable, but one also seeks to facilitate different needs, and protect against different types of thwarting, in those different contexts. If we assume that territorial functioning, working in a systemlike fashion, not only reflects environmental controllability but also shapes it, then territorial functioning may adapt itself to the particular needs and threats pertinent to specific settings. Territorial behaviors can be modified so as to maximize environmental controllability. *It is this systemlike linkage between environmental controllability and territorial functioning that generates the highly place specific nature of territorial functioning.*

Finally, Stokols' model illuminates why the psychological consequences of territorial functioning will be more salient in private and semiprivate settings than in more public settings. In more public (as compared to private) spaces, the motivational significance (subjective importance) of the needs "brought" to the setting is less. The needs satisfied in more public spaces (e.g., excitement, novelty, needs specific to the setting such as carrying out tasks like banking or shopping) are less central to the well-being of the individual than are needs such as privacy, intimacy, or freedom from distractions met in more private spaces. As the motivational significance of the needs in question for the setting diminishes, the thwarting experienced is less stressful, and territorial functioning becomes progressively uncoupled from environmental controllability.[12]

---

[12] It is also the case that the "effort" required to coordinate and implement effective territorial strategies excluding others or controlling activities increases in public as compared to private settings, and the probable efficacy of the strategies themselves

The stress perspective delineated by Stokols will be useful in subsequent chapters examining territorial functioning in the home, and in regularly used spaces like work sites, offices, and so on, and will illuminate the benefits of territorial functioning accruing to individuals.

In the next section we examine a theory that moves us from the *psychological* to the *ecological consequences* of territorial functioning, focusing on settings rather than individuals.

Behavior setting theory

Background

For over 30 years, Roger Barker and his associates worked out of a small field office, recording data about events occurring in public settings in a small Kansas town. Information about schools, churches, drugstores, town meetings, and many other places and events was examined. Their data set was so extensive they had to rely on NASA computers to analyze it.

Their initial focus had been on individuals. Barker had sought to understand the factors that made different individuals behave differently in the environment. For example, in his book coauthored with Herbert Wright, *One Boy's Day*, he reported the stream of behavior of one individual over a day.

But in the process of observing individuals Barker noted something rather unexpected. Two observations of the same person in the same place, even if separated by a considerable period of time, were more similar than two observations of the same individual separated by a short period of time, recorded in two different locations. This discovery led him to shift his focus from individuals to settings. The bulk of his research career was devoted to discovering and describing fundamental units in the external social environment. He called them *behavior settings*. Over several decades Barker recorded information about all the behavior settings in the small Kansas town in which he was working. Behavior settings are the building blocks of public life.

A behavior setting is a small-scale social system composed of people interacting with one another and with inanimate objects to carry out a regularly occurring, prescribed behavioral sequence, or program, within specifiable time and place boundaries. Collectively, settings constitute the immediate contexts of everyday life. They include offices, workshops, club

decreases. These factors further the uncoupling of psychological consequences from territorial functioning in progressively more public spaces.

meetings, retail stores, worship services, instructional classes, and many other places and events.[13]

It is in behavior settings that businesses, organizations, and institutions function. And, from the perspective of individuals, it is by participating in sequences of behavior settings that daily public life is carried out: at the office, on the assembly line, at church, or at the Lions Club monthly meeting. (See the following box for key terms in behavior setting theory.)

Key terms in behavior setting theory

Behavior settings are regularly occurring, temporally and spatially bounded person–environment units. The three major components are:
1. The participants in the setting;
2. The *standing pattern of behavior* or behavior setting program. This includes the behavioral sequences that are integral to the functioning of the setting. For example, for a person working in a gift shop key behavioral sequences might include greeting customers, providing information on items in the store, making change, and wrapping purchases;
3. The *surrounding (or circumjacent) physical milieu* bounds the behavior setting and supports activities within the setting itself. For effective functioning the physical milieu must be *congruent* with the behavior setting program. Primary elements of the physical milieu in a gift shop, for example, would include a cash register, display shelving, and supplies of wrappings and bags.

If there is congruence between what people do in the setting, and the arrangements of physical objects in the setting, then a state of behavior–environment *synomorphy* or congruence is said to exist.

Different behavior settings are relatively independent of one another. What happens in one usually has little impact on what happens in another. For example, if a gift shop is located next to a restaurant, and the restaurant is forced to close early because of a small fire in the kitchen, this will not influence the closing time of the gift shop.

But, within a behavior setting are smaller, interdependent parts called

---

[13] Wicker, A. W. (1987). Behavior settings reconsidered. In D. Stokols & I. Altman (Eds.), *Handbook of environmental psychology*. New York: Wiley (abstract).

The most basic text on behavior settings and the field of ecological psychology is Barker, R. G. (1968), *Ecological psychology*. Stanford, CA: Stanford University Press.

Somewhat less technical and more up-to-date is Wicker, A. W. (1979), *Introduction to ecological psychology*. Monterey, CA: Brooks/Cole.

synomorphs. For example, a restaurant might include synomorphs such as the kitchen, main dining area, reception area, and bar. If there is a fire in the kitchen *all* of the other synomorphs in the setting will be affected. Sometimes the internal dynamics of behavior settings are threatened, or go awry. For example, a setting may be *understaffed* in particular roles; in a restaurant, two waitresses may call in sick. Remaining participants may compensate by working harder. A setting may also be *overstaffed* in particular roles, for example, there may be too many waitresses in the restaurant. Consequently, hiring standards may be raised, and already-hired waitresses may work more slowly.

Further, participants may not conform to the setting program. Others may respond in one of two ways. They will first engage in *deviation countering*. In such instances they encourage the person to conform to the setting requirements. A dilatory waitress will be reprimanded, for example. Should such actions fail, *vetoing mechanisms* may be enacted, and the person in question will be asked to leave the setting. The dilatory waitress may be fired. These deviation-countering and vetoing mechanisms keep the setting running smoothly.

Participants in a behavior setting can be distinguished according to *levels of penetration* in the setting. Some are leaders, some are co-workers, some are audience members, and so on.

Streetblocks as behavior settings

I have suggested elsewhere that streetblocks in the urban residential environment function as behavior settings.[14] The reasons for this are several. (1) The streetblock is bounded, by housefronts and cross streets, like a behavior setting. (2) The physical milieu surrounds and encloses the behavior setting, and supports activities therein. (3) A standing pattern of behavior, or program, exists; certain behaviors occur on a routine, predictable basis: lawn mowing, the delivery of mail, kids going to school, adults driving off to work, and so on. Although not advertised, these activities are predictable and routinized. (4) People participate to varying degrees in the setting. There may be a block leader or block captains, or well-known figures on the block. And, there are deviation-countering and vetoing mechanisms on the streetblock.

The notion of a setting program implies agreement on what behaviors

[14] For full details on this line of argument see Taylor (1987), Toward an environmental psychology of disorder. In D. Stokols & I. Altman (Eds.), *Handbook of environmental psychology*. New York: Wiley.

are acceptable and when and where they are acceptable. It implies setting-specific norms. Working on cars may be acceptable in the alley but not out front. Undoubtedly, the norms themselves, as well as their clarity, varies from block to block. Furthermore, norms are likely to be less clear, or less widely shared in more heterogeneous and/or changing blocks. Nonetheless, despite variation in norm clarity, and in the norms themselves, they still do operate from block to block and reflect the underlying setting program.

Ecological consequences of territorial functioning

In the case of the residential streetblock, dovetailing the behavior setting concept with territorial functioning illuminates how the latter contributes to the setting program, and thereby setting maintenance. This linkage is described in this section. The reader may find it useful to conceptualize how such linkages might work in other types of behavior settings. The processes pinpointed here indicate how the ecological consequences of territorial functioning emerge.

The main function served by territorial functioning, from the perspective of the behavior setting itself, is *setting maintenance*. Various components of territorial functioning serve to maintain the environment–behavior congruence or synomorphy extant in the setting. Stated differently, as territorial functioning weakens, or is more widely ignored, the behavior setting program devolves.

The territorial functioning–behavior setting connection is carried via two channels. First, territorial markers, elements of the physical environment, provide cues to insiders and outsiders regarding the setting program. Territorial markers are indicators of ownership, occupancy, investment, or caring, and include, in this context, explicit elements such as "Keep Out" signs and locked gates, as well as less explicit elements of upkeep and beautification. These serve as nonverbal messages or cues to people in the setting about how to behave there.[15] Through social learning processes individuals learn the association between these physical cues and appropriate behavior.[16] In the same way that people learn to be quiet in church, they learn not to throw litter into a well-kept flower garden on a well-kept block. (Of course, there are some who never learn either lesson.) Simply put, physical features produced by or reflective of territorial functioning cue people into the setting, suggesting the kind of behavior that is appropriate and in keeping with the setting program.

[15] Rapoport, A. (1982). *The meaning of the built environment.* Beverly Hills: Sage.
[16] Wicker, A. (1979), Chapter 4.

The second linkage between the behavior setting and territorial functioning is a behavioral one. Territorial behaviors function as deviation-countering and vetoing mechanisms. Behaviors that, from the viewpoint of the individual or group, regulate access or control the behaviors of those therein, serve the setting by maintaining the program. Excluding others from the setting (e.g., asking a pushy kid interrupting the play of some smaller children to leave) is *vetoing*. Correcting others while they are in the setting is *deviation countering* (e.g., "You can play ball out front but if the ball goes in the flowers again you have to stop"). The requester asks others in the setting to bring their behavior into line with the behavior setting program.

Thus, by physical and behavioral processes territorial functioning supports the behavior setting program. Such "assistance" to the program can be important because behavior settings do not exist in a vacuum. They can be under pressure from outside forces.[17] There is often a load or demand, of exogenous origins, impinging on the behavior setting, and its program. Such forces play important roles in the evolution or shift of setting programs over time. For example, the population of households on a block may change dramatically, or the block may experience an influx of children. In the face of these changes, over the long run the setting program will probably be modified. But, in the short run the program will be "backed up" and reinforced by territorial functioning.

As we move from more private to more public settings the ecological consequences of territorial functioning become more salient, in part because the functioning affects a larger number of people. More persons are involved in the setting, broadening the relevance of program maintenance. More persons are influenced if the setting program degenerates or changes. Consequently, in more public settings involving more than a small primary group, such as family or close friends, the salience of the ecological consequences of territorial functioning and malfunctioning increases.

Summary

This chapter has introduced two additional perspectives – a stress perspective and an ecological perspective. These perspectives clarify processes linking territorial functioning with psychological and ecological consequences. These additional perspectives can be fruitfully integrated with the focus on territorial functioning, and portions of that integration were outlined.

---

[17] Wicker (1987).

PART III
TERRITORIAL FUNCTIONING
IN SETTINGS OF VARYING
CENTRALITY

The following four chapters comprise the empirical heart of the volume. Territorial functioning is examined in settings of varying *centrality*. (Recall that centrality refers to an aspect of person–place transactions, namely, how important a setting is. The higher the centrality of the setting in question, the more the person or group would suffer or be stressed were they to lose that setting, or unwillingly to lose control of it.) Starting with settings that are at the core of the lifespace and usually of highest centrality – locations inside the home – we move progressively outward. The organization of spaces by centrality does not reflect ad hoc groupings of spaces according to various objective attributes. Rather, it represents relative differences in *perceived importance* of the settings to the overall lifespace of the individual or group.

Roughly, we will group settings into four levels of centrality, from highest to lowest:

1. Spaces within residential settings (Chapter 7);
2. Spaces immediately outside residences (Chapter 8);
3. Regularly used settings, such as work spaces (Chapter 9); and
4. Public locations used for short periods of time, where temporary territories are created (Chapter 10).[1]

---

[1] The reader might wish to reverse the position of numbers 2 and 3, feeling that regular settings are more important for the individual than spaces immediately adjoining the residence itself. And for some individuals this may well be true. Nonetheless, since the

This range of spaces reveals both continuity and variation in territorial functioning. The *variation* will be evident in several ways. (1) The types of territorial strategies used will vary, (2) as will the consequences of territorial functioning. Nonetheless, in the case of both strategies and consequences, there are strong family resemblances as we move along the centrality continuum. And, as mentioned earlier, (3) the relative salience of different types of consequences – psychological versus social psychological versus ecological – also shifts as we move across the centrality continuum. The rationale for the variations probably lies in specific attributes of the locations themselves. As we go from spaces where person–place transactions are of highest centrality to locations where they are lower, the following differences are evident.

1. *The spaces become less multifunctional.* The locations examined become increasingly geared towards specific purposes, and less capable of supporting a wide range of activities relevant to daily functioning. Stated differently, the nature of the "resource" available in each setting becomes increasingly specific. Space in the public library can be used for reading, writing, or studying. A similarly sized space in the home can be used for a much broader range of activities.

2. *Group boundaries and the properties of the occupying groups themselves vary as a function of centrality.* Group boundaries between occupants and nonoccupants become less clear as centrality decreases, and the strength, duration, and multiplexity of the bonds between individuals in the setting decrease.[2,3] This shift in social dynamics has implications for the kinds of territorial strategies (e.g., marking) one can employ, and for the success one can expect strategies to have.

But, perhaps more important, there is also *continuity* in territorial functioning in locations where centrality varies. We will demonstrate this continuity using the theoretical framework outlined in Chapter 5. In each chapter links between territorial functioning and each cluster of predictors will be illustrated by empirical studies. Links between territorial functioning and important outcomes also are outlined. Such

outside residential environment is so physically proximate to the interior residential spaces, disturbances in the former can seriously disrupt individual and household functioning in the latter. And such disturbances are often inescapable.

[2] The point being made here is related to the earlier suggestion by Altman (1975) that, as one proceeds from primary to secondary to public territories one encounters, respectively, members of one's primary reference group, one's secondary reference group, and strangers.

[3] Multiplexity refers to the role complexity of the ties in a social network. The more "roles" in which you know someone (friend, neighbor, co-worker, relative, and so on), the more multiplex the tie.

points of continuity *indicate that similar causal processes are at work in settings of varying centrality.* In other words, empirical results support the application of territorial concepts to an array of spaces.

Some general themes surfacing repeatedly in the following chapters, and to which the reader may wish to be attuned, are (1) the highly place specific operations of territorial functioning, and (2) the inexorable dependence of territorial functioning on the immediate social climate, i.e., the social bonds existing among the persons in and adjacent to the setting in question.

Finally, there is some material that does *not* appear in the following four chapters. Given the breadth of the volume, it is not possible to include considerable detail on cross-cultural differences in territorial functioning. Although such differences will be touched on, detailed analysis and descriptions are not included. Such exclusion does not represent a bias per se, but is rather in keeping with the empirical focus, and heavy reliance on psychological and sociological findings, which are integral to the volume.[4]

---

[4] The anthropological literature on territorial functioning, particularly within households, is extremely rich. See, for example:

Altman, I., & Chemers, M. (1980). *Culture and environment.* Monterey, CA: Brooks/Cole.

Altman, I., & Gauvain, M. (1981). A cross-cultural and dialectic analysis of homes. In L. Liben, A. Patterson, & N. Newcombe (Eds.), *Spatial behavior and representation across the life span.* New York: Academic, pp. 283–320.

Gauvain, M., Altman, I., & Fahim, H. (1983). Homes and social change: A cross-cultural analysis. In N. Feimer & E. S. Geller (Eds.), *Environmental psychology: Directions and perspectives.* New York: Praeger, pp. 180–218.

Rapoport, A. (1969). *House form and culture.* Englewood Cliffs, NJ: Prentice-Hall.

7
INTERIOR RESIDENTIAL SETTINGS

But, you may say, we asked you to speak about women and fiction. . . .
All I could do was to offer you an opinion upon one minor point – a
woman must have money and a room of her own if she is to write
fiction.
– Virginia Woolf, A Room of One's Own *(1929)*

How does territorial functioning operate in settings where people live?
This is the main question addressed in this chapter. A range of interior
residential settings will be examined, spanning intact households, dorm
settings, institutional residential settings, and experimental groups in
isolation.

These various sites share three characteristics. (1) For a period of
time, small groups, ranging in size from two to more than a dozen, live
in these settings; they take up residence there and share space. It is
there that the "strongest" territories exist.[1] These spaces represent the
core of the group's spatial activity system. (2) Interior residential settings
are strongly multifunctional. (3) And, in these settings, co-occupants
have frequent contact over a period of time. The objective diversities
of the settings examined here are outweighed by the similarities in subjective significance and individual and group functioning.

Investigating territorial functioning in interior residential settings is
frustrating for two reasons. First, the settings in question are highly
private, causing operational as well as ethical problems for researchers (see the following box). Consequently, there is a paucity of solid
data for some of the settings considered. Second, territorial functioning is often latent; one is not aware of it unless changes impinge
(see Figure 7.1). This submerged nature of territorial functioning
makes its examination all the more difficult. Given these constraints,

---

[1] Appleyard, D. (1979). Home. *Architectural Association Quarterly, 11* (no. 3), 4–20.

Figure 7.1. A kitchen takeover. In well-used spaces, territorial dynamics often operate out of awareness. *Source*: *Sally Forth*. Copyright © 1985 by News America Syndicate. Reprinted with permission of the publisher.

we know a lot less about territorial functioning in interior residential settings than we do about territorial functioning elsewhere, such as exterior residential settings. Nonetheless, these limitations aside, this chapter demonstrates that enough is known to reliably link territorial functioning with particular classes of predictors, and to outline significance consequences.

Organization of the chapter

The first portion examines the four clusters of predictors of territorial functioning: cultural (including subcultural), physical, social, and intrapersonal. The second part examines specific consequences of territorial functioning. The third section considers what happens when residents meet "outsiders" in an interior residential setting, and discusses why and under what conditions the former party is at an advantage.

Determinants of territorial functioning

Cultural and subcultural factors

Particular cultures associate specific functions and meanings with locations within the interior residential setting. Going along with this culture-specific "meaning" are norms about who is allowed where, when. This point is illustrated in a modern-day example from a working-class Greek neighborhood[2] where cultural requirements specified symbolic arrangements in interior spaces.

For example, when a daughter was married, the father of the bride was required to provide a separate dwelling as part of the dowry, and since the kitchen was the physical marker of autonomy, the bride's dwelling unit would have to have a kitchen. Thus, many times the father would excavate a basement for the additional living unit and would ensure that a second kitchen was added to the house.

Another example had to do with the type of furniture required in various rooms. Even though the houses in this neighborhood were very small, a large, formal dining room table was "required" equipment. The table would be used to entertain guests, and for special family celebrations such as baptisms, weddings, or name days. At a microlevel, then, the table symbolized the tradition of the family.[3] It was used infrequently, took up lots of room, and added significantly to the cramped nature of the living space, but could not be removed.

The findings of this Greek study can be considered using the contextual-stress perspective outlined in Chapter 6. Tradition specifies that certain rooms in the household or sections in the household will facilitate particular motivationally significant needs, whose significance rests upon tradition. These needs are significant at the level of the household. The actual facilitation of these tradition-specified needs, however, results in increased thwarting of other, more mundane "everyday" needs, of individuals, and perhaps of the household as a whole, in those same settings.

A study by Al Scheflen and colleagues (see the following box) investigated territorial functioning in black, Hispanic, and Italian lower-income households.[4] Differences in territorial functioning in interior residential settings across the three ethnic groups illustrate how, at the subcultural as well as cultural level, uses of particular spaces within the household are culturally defined.

The groups defined various interior spaces differently. For example, among black households the female head of household would usually define the living room as a "parlor," a formal area to be

---

[2] Hirschon, R. B., & Gold, J. H. (1982). Territoriality and the home environment in a Greek community. *Anthropological Quarterly*, 55, 63–73.

[3] Jacobi, M., & Stokols, D. (1983). The role of tradition in group–environment relations. In N. Feimer & E. S. Geller (Eds.), *Environmental psychology: Directions and perspectives*. New York: Praeger, pp. 157–179.

[4] Scheflen, A. E. (1971). Living space in an urban ghetto. *Family Process, 10*, 429–450.

McMillan, R. (1974). Analysis of multiple events in a ghetto household. Unpublished doctoral dissertation. New York: Columbia University Teachers' College.

used only for the greeting and entertaining of important guests from outside the household. Plastic covers might be on the furniture most of the time; there might also be narrow plastic runways on the carpet, and the children and other adults would be expected, unless "company" was present, to stay out. The living room was used as a "front" region for formal interaction, where the household could put its best foot forward when interacting with important others from outside the household. Maintaining such a region meant that levels of physical density were higher elsewhere within the household. Thus, as in the Greek households in the preceding example, satisfaction of individual needs is thwarted so as to accommodate household-level, symbolic "needs."

Issues of methods and ethics

In the late 1960's Al Scheflen and colleagues carried out a federally funded study of "ghetto" households. The question they were interested in was simple. How do lower-income households manage to carry out their daily activities given that they live in such cramped quarters? Cameras were placed in the apartments of black, Puerto Rican, and Italian households. Thousands of hours of interaction were taped and subsequently coded. Assistants would come in every few days and change the tapes. Methodologically, the study presented a sizable challenge. (As an aside, it is interesting to note that Roger Barker's concept of the *stream of behavior* was a pivotal tool in analyzing the findings.)[5]

The following findings emerged from the Scheflen study.

1. Children's behavior patterns were quite dispersed. Since their bedroom was likely to be shared with at least a couple of siblings, it was impossible, for example, for them to do their homework there. Thus, they might gravitate to the kitchen, and the eldest might grab the best spot. Or they might lie on the floor of the entranceway. Children, being weakest in the household's "power structure," had their activity patterns the most dislocated as a result of minimal available space.

2. Who actually got to occupy a particular space was a complex function of time of day, time of week, the nature of the activity in progress, and the others present. For example, if relatives were over for a Sunday afternoon visit, the women might be sitting in the living room on the sofa, a couple of older men sitting on the remaining chairs, younger men stand-

---

[5] An example of the use of the stream of behavior concept can be found in McMillan (1974). For background on the concept see Barker, R. G. (Ed.) (1963), *The stream of behavior*. New York: Appleton-Century-Crofts.

ing and talking; the children, banished from the room, might take the opportunity to watch TV in their parents' bedroom.

3. Given the limited available space, rules or behavioral adaptations were developed that prescribed certain patterns of exclusion under certain circumstances. Among certain ethnic groups violations of these rules were severely punished. If a father routinely had a friend over from work on Friday night, for example, these two would have access to the living room, and all children were excluded. Or, to take another example, if a mother was about to begin a complex activity like baking a cake, the kitchen would be cleared of all children. They simply could not go in there until that activity was completed.

4. Given the larger household size in a lower-income context, and the smaller size of the living unit, enduring territorial arrangements become less likely or, at the least, much more delimited. Simple present occupancy might outweigh any standing claim, as was demonstrated in the case of the father who came home, found three children sitting in his living room chair watching TV, wandered around the room for a bit, and then left the apartment because there was, he said, "no place" for him.

Scheflen's study raises some major ethical issues.

Doing research in the household constitutes a major invasion of privacy. Is such an invasion justified? In the language of human subjects' concerns, such an invasion constitutes a major "cost" for the participants. Such a cost can only be justified if, resulting from the study, or the researchers' interactions with the participants, benefits will accrue to the participants that outweigh the costs imposed on them. For example, they might get to find out about the research process, or, on a more practical level, the researcher might be willing to use the study findings to advocate better housing conditions.

The participants in the Scheflen study did *not* feel that the benefits of participation outweighed the costs, and thus they forced an early termination of the study. Participants complained that their privacy was being invaded, and that what was being found out was not advantageous to them in any way. Further, they suggested that what was found might even hurt them because, lacking comparable studies of middle-class families, the results would be used to compare lower-income households to middle-class stereotypes, resulting in further denigration of the former group. That study was carried out in the late 1960's; as of this date I know of no comparable study of middle-class households.

The home is a very private place. Respect for this privacy constitutes a strong barrier to research, and deservedly so. Yet, for theoretical and practical reasons, it is important to understand spatial behavior patterns within the home. An understanding of these patterns might lead to insights that can be used to improve household functioning. Given this situation, research in this context needs to be carried out with a special sensitivity to ethical concerns, and participants' welfare.

Although space does not permit an in-depth examination of cultural and subcultural influences on territorial functioning in interior residential settings, the preceding examples suggest that cultural and subcultural factors define the "role" of certain locations within the household, and these microscale environmental cognitions subsequently shape territorial functioning.

Physical factors

The capability of sites within the household to function as territories, i.e., as locations where the occupant or occupants can exercise some degree of excludability and control over activities, is dependent upon physical features of the sites in question. Several findings from a study of 45 middle-class Israeli families point up the importance of physical features, in particular the relevance of *physical boundaries, and boundary permeability.*[6]

Household members were asked: "To whom does each place in the apartment belong?" Household members agreed with one another on the "assignment" of various locations within the household. Certain areas were perceived as belonging to individuals, such as a child's bedroom, or group of persons, such as the parents' bedroom. Other areas were perceived as open to all, like the dining room, even though within that space a particular individual might habitually sit in one chair. Most likely to be labelled as territories, belonging to an individual or subgroup, were locations within the household with clear boundaries. Thus, rooms and pieces of furniture were the main types of territories identified in the household.

The importance of boundary permeability was revealed in two findings. (1) An outside terrace separated from the living room was used as a bedroom in many households, but the extent to which people felt they could express themselves in such a location, or carry out various activities, was less than in the interior bedrooms. (2) As the number of

[6] Sebba, R., & Churchman, A. (1983). Territories and territoriality in the home. *Environment and Behavior, 15,* 191–210. In this study all members of each household were interviewed.

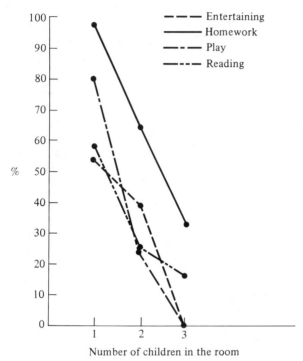

Figure 7.2. Percentage of children reporting that they use their own room for particular activities is influenced by the number of children sharing the room. *Source*: R. Sebba and A. Churchman (1983), Territories and territoriality in the home. *Environment and Behavior, 15,* 191–210. Copyright © 1983 by Sage Publications, Inc. Reprinted by permission of Sage Publications, Inc.

siblings sharing a bedroom increased, thus lowering the extent to which one youth could "control" access to the bedroom, the functionality of the bedroom as a territory decreased (Figure 7.2). Children who were sharing a bedroom with a sibling, compared to those children who had a room of their own, were less likely to expect that they would assert their dominance there if a conflict came up. They were also less likely to feel that a part of the home was theirs.

The Israeli study indicates that physical boundaries are used to define territories, and that lower permeability due to lack of physical surrounds, or due to a larger user group, interfered with use of territories within the household for a variety of functions.[7]

[7] This last point may not apply equally in different cultural contexts. In many cultural groups households appear to function satisfactorily in a context dominated by semishared spaces. The lack of nonshared spaces within the household does not adversely affect

Thinking about the results of the Israeli study from a psychological, context-sensitive stress perspective suggests that in shared space such as a bedroom, the lack of guaranteed sole access implies a higher potential for conflict over how the room will be used. Thus, siblings anticipate that *less* need satisfaction and *more* thwarting are likely there.

Increased thwarting can come about not only as a result of incomplete or permeable physical boundaries; it can also result from increased *load* on a particular space, as occurs if a space a person would like to control (e.g., a study) is also used for another purpose (e.g., family TV room). Where bounded spaces are subjected to conflicting use requirements, or put under a heavier "load," and territorial functioning at the scale of bounded rooms is not possible, household members may attempt to cope by engaging in more microlevel territorial strategies.[8]

In sum, physical factors in interior residential settings are clearly tied to territorial functioning. Territorial strategies controlling entry and activities are most feasible in physically bounded, enclosed spaces that are not shared and that "belong" to just one user. Multiple users, or conflicting uses of such bounded spaces, increase boundary permeability and interfere with territorial functioning. Household members may revert to more microscale territorial strategies in such cases. In the context of Stokols' stress model, such physical characteristics are associated with higher actual thwarting levels, and lower actual facilitation levels.

Personality factors

The links between personality and territorial functioning in interior residential settings have not been firmly established, although there are some tantalizing findings from two different studies with undergraduates. One such study suggested that the territorial functioning–person-

them. This is the case because alternative behavioral systems have had time to develop in these cultures, permitting efficient privacy regulation even though physical boundaries are minimal. See:

Altman, I. (1977). Privacy regulation: Culturally universal or culturally specific? *Journal of Social Issues, 33,* 66–84.

But, in Western, middle-income, and lower-middle-income households, where expectations that nonshared spaces will be available in the household operate, the lack of such spaces, reducing the behavioral options, may be associated with negative consequences. These outcomes will be delineated later in the chapter.

[8] Schiavo, R. S. (1977). Family use of the environment, related psychological experiences, and evaluation of environmental features. Paper presented at the annual meeting of the American Psychological Association, San Francisco, August.

ality linkage may be sex dependent.[9] Among women sharing a room with a roommate, those who were more self-assured reported a smaller portion of the room being their own territory. Among men, the reverse held: More self-assured men reported a larger portion of the room being their own territory. A second study, with only male participants, examined connections between personality and sociability of future living arrangements, and found that those who were more sociable were more likely to choose living arrangements involving more shared living space with others.[10] Such a result suggests that those with more sociable personalities had less of a need for nonshared living space.

More strongly indicated are links between the *congruence* of the personalities of those sharing living space, and territorial functioning. One study of college roommates found that the pairings reported conflict or were less likely to remain together if their personality profiles were incompatible.[11] Since the shared living space was the main arena in which the roommates interacted, it is plausible that spatial conflicts, associated with an inability to agree on appropriate territorial strategies, were part and parcel of incompatible roommates' decisions to switch.

A study of Navy men isolated in groups of two found more direct linkages between territorial functioning and personality congruence. In dyads whose members were incompatible on personality variables such as dominance or affiliation, individuals used locations within the living space in an increasingly exclusive way as the mission – living in isolation – wore on.[12] This pattern suggests participants attempted to limit or dampen interpersonal friction by adopting very clear-cut allocations of spaces within the living unit.

Related to the notion of individual personality is the concept of group style. Particular groups may just do things certain ways, out of habit, preference, tradition, or whatever. In middle-class, intact households two "styles" of territorial functioning in interior residential settings were identified in one study.[13] Although some "universals" were observed,

[9] Mercer, W., & Benjamin, M. L. (1980). Spatial behavior of university undergraduates in double-occupancy residence rooms: An inventory of effects. *Journal of Applied Social Psychology, 10*, 32–44.

[10] Switzer, R., & Taylor, R. B. (1983). Predicting privacy vs. sociability of residential choice: Impacts of personality and local social ties. *Basic and Applied Social Psychology, 4*, 123–136.

[11] Williams, J. E. (1976). Conflict between freshman male roommates. Research report no. 10–67. College Park, MD: University of Maryland Counseling Center. Cited in Holland, J. L. (1973), *Making vocational choices*. Englewood Cliffs, NJ: Prentice-Hall, p. 67.

[12] Altman, I., & Haythorn, W. W. (1967). The ecology of isolated groups. *Behavioral Science, 12*, 169–182.

[13] Altman, I., Nelson, P. A., & Lett, E. E. (1972). The ecology of home environments.

such as knocking before entering bedrooms if the door was closed and the room occupied, there appeared to be two different approaches to privacy regulation and space use. One approach was exemplified by "open" households where bedroom doors were open all day, special function rooms such as workshops were open to all, family members visited one another in bedrooms frequently, and particular activities were not confined to particular rooms. Guests could be entertained in the kitchen as well as the living room; dining could occur in the TV room as well as the dining room. In opposition to these open, informal households were closed, more formal households. Bedroom doors were closed during the day, special rooms were closed off to others, there was less visiting in bedrooms, and particular activities were always restricted to particular rooms; entertaining always occurred in the living room, eating always in the dining room or kitchen.

These two different patterns are indicative of the different ways households can develop environmental practices that reflect the ongoing social dynamics of the unit.[14] To speculate somewhat further along these lines, it sounds to me like the families using the "closed" arrangement have a rigid, cold "personality"; each member is concerned about maintaining what is his or hers, and there is a rigid linkage of functions to rooms, reducing behavioral flexibility in the households. By contrast, it sounds like the families using the "open" strategies have a more flexible, warmer personality; more sharing and social support go on.

In sum, the link between personality and territorial functioning is largely unsubstantiated at this point, although results suggest links between personality and flexible territorial functioning in interior residential settings. More substantial are connections between personality *congruence* and territorial functioning. It also seems possible that household groups, controlling for social class, size, and space factors, develop particular "styles" of territorial functioning in interior household settings. Whether those styles are linked to objective measures of household "personality" remains to be determined.

Social factors

The research linking territorial functioning to social factors in interior residential settings is substantial, allowing us not only to be sure of the linkage itself but also to go further and pinpoint particular relevant

JSAS Catalog of Selected Documents in Psychology. Washington, DC: American Psychological Association.

[14] Altman, I. (1977). Research on environment and behavior: A personal statement of strategy. In D. Stokols (Ed.), *Perspectives on environment and behavior.* New York: Plenum, pp. 303–324.

aspects of group structure and interpersonal relationships. Two classes of small group characteristics will be examined: horizontal and vertical. *Horizontal* social features refer to issues of cohesiveness, degree of liking or disliking, communication, and so on. *Vertical* relationships refer to differences in social power, influence, or dominance.

Social power refers to the potential social influence of one person in a group over another, the ability of an individual in a group to bring about behavioral or attitudinal changes in another person or set of persons in the group.[15] There are many approaches that an individual can use to influence another, or to exercise social power.

And, of course, in a group all individuals do not seek to exercise the same amount of power over others. In groups of animals dominance hierarchies develop; among barnyard chickens, animals that are higher in the hierarchy are more likely to peck those who are lower, and less likely to be pecked by the underlings.

Social dominance . . . is a priority system based on either overt or implied aggression. Dominant individuals gain prior access to resources or mates, while subordinate individuals must settle with the leavings. Physical fights are frequently unnecessary for establishing dominance relationships. Morphological traits indicative of size, strength, or fighting ability usually suffice.[16]

But, although dominator–subordinate relationships appear straightforward in the barnyard, observations of primate groups in natural environments have raised some serious questions about the validity, generality, and unity of the dominance concept.[17]

[15] French, J. R. P., & Raven, B. H. (1959). *The bases of social power.* In D. Cartwright (Ed.), *Studies in social power.* Ann Arbor: ISR, University of Michigan, pp. 150–167.
    Raven, B. H., & Rubin, J. Z. (1982). *Social psychology,* 2nd ed. New York: Wiley, pp. 402–443.
[16] Wittenberger (1981), p. 587.
[17] Ibid., pp. 591–594.
    (1) Animals in a group that are dominant in one situation (e.g., gaining access to desirable mates) may not be as dominant in another situation (e.g., gaining access to food resources or nesting sites). In other words, a group may have several dominance hierarchies, each of which is somewhat situation specific. (2) Dominance is not a single, rigid linear ordering (A > B > C > D . . .); it appears to be more complex. There can be intransitivities. Sometimes D may turn around and get away with pecking B. Further, establishment of a high-dominance position is not dependent solely on the outcome of aggressive or agonistic encounters; primates and other animals have lots of other ways of figuring out who's boss.
    From a sociobiological perspective, for an animal to engage in an aggressive encounter, the outcome of which it can estimate would probably not be in its favor, is a waste of energy and thus a behavior that would reduce its fitness.

Nonetheless, some of the research examined here has taken simplified ideas about dominance relations and applied them to human groups, in an attempt to observe a linkage between dominance position and territorial position or territorial strategies.

Horizontal social factors

Liking. A greater degree of liking between individuals sharing the same interior residential setting should result in more trouble-free territorial functioning. As liking increases there should be a more consensual spatial and temporal allocation of particular locations within the setting. Two studies, unfortunately limited to college-age populations, provide clear support for such expectations.

The *spatial allocation* of an interior residential setting was examined in a study of male and female undergraduates at a small Canadian college. Participants indicated on a room schematic what space was their territory, and what space was common or shared.[18] For both men and women, increased liking of the roommate was associated with indicating a larger common area or shared territory. Given the other predictors of size of shared territory, the authors suggested that it served as a social area for women, and as a neutral zone or "DMZ" for men. Liking of the roommate was also associated with a smaller "own" territory, but only for women.

The *temporal allocation* of shared residential space was examined in a study carried out by Glenn Ferguson and myself.[19] When asked where they would go to be alone with a friend for a confidential chat, participants were more likely to go to their dorm room or apartment if they got along better with their roommate(s), and/or had fewer of them. Further, once in the room or apartment, they were less likely to be intruded upon if they were better acquainted with the roommate(s). Thus social dynamics and usage norms in shared space were linked. In cases where roommates had a better understanding of one another, they appeared to develop consensual norms about who could use the room and when, and thus allowed each other to use the space for sensitive activities without fear of interruption.

Expected group longevity. The commitment of members to a group can

---

[18] Mercer, W., & Benjamin, M. L. (1980). Spatial behavior of university undergraduates in double-occupancy residence rooms: An inventory of effects. *Journal of Applied Social Psychology, 10*, 32–44.

[19] Taylor, R. B., & Ferguson, G. (1980). Solitude and intimacy: Linking territoriality and privacy behavior. *Journal of Nonverbal Behavior, 4*, 227–239.

be expressed in a temporal as well as a liking dimension. Groups where the members share a longer-term commitment to one another might use different territorial strategies. Anticipating a long-term shared living arrangement, in the early stages they might demand clear-cut partitions of the living space into zones of excludability. This imposes some minimum level of order on the living space. They may later "ease up" after a semblance of order is achieved. Results from two studies support this line of reasoning.

One study investigated use of *microlevel territorial strategies* among young cohabiting and married couples.[20] Strategies included exclusive use of a bed or side of bed, bureau or particular drawers, area of closet, chair at table, and shelf in bathroom. Married couples reported greater use of such strategies.

Young married couples perhaps experience higher stress levels than young cohabiting couples. For the former, a long expected time together stretches before them, and they feel a strong need to "make it." Expectations that they will survive the "long haul" contribute to the potential stressfulness of the living arrangements. Stated differently, these expectations and hopes for a long-term relationship, and the shame and disappointment that would accompany the failure of that relationship, influence the *primary appraisal* [21] of the potential stressfulness of living together, making it appear more threatening than in the case of unmarried couples. If the latter couples do not get along and go their respective ways, it is less of a letdown. Consequently, it is more important for married couples to cope with and manage sociospatial conflicts. So, early on they work out some territorial strategies that involve exclusive use of particular locations within the household.

A second study with very different participants – naval personnel – in a very different context (a multiday, isolation experiment) suggests the same dynamics.[22] In this study the spatial behavior of dyads was monitored under a broad range of isolation conditions. Territorial behavior was defined as the exclusive use of chairs, beds, or areas on a side of a table. Groups, of course, if it all got to be too much, could ask to get out before their time was up. When aborting and completing groups were compared, the latter showed high levels of territorial behavior in the first few days of the study, whereas the latter showed low levels of territoriality early on, with increasing levels as they moved

---

[20] Rosenblatt, P. C., & Budd, L. G. (1975). Territoriality and privacy in married and unmarried cohabiting couples. *Journal of Social Psychology*, *97*, 67–76.

[21] Lazarus (1966).

[22] Altman, I., Taylor, D., & Wheeler, L. (1971). Ecological aspects of group behavior in isolation. *Journal of Applied Social Psychology*, *1*, 76–100.

closer to aborting, particularly in the case of the groups expecting a long mission. When considered in conjunction with the data on social activity it appears that the territorial levels were a sign of tension or stress within the group. Those groups that realized early they were in a potentially stressful situation exhibited high levels of territoriality. They sought to establish spatial norms providing a clearer framework for social interaction, thus smoothing out the group dynamics. Once the group got into a routine, and the members got used to each other, territoriality eased off. The aborter groups assessed the situation differently. Underestimating the amount of stress they would be under, they did not seek to clarify the sociospatial ecology early on. As the mission wore on they tried to do this and became more territorial. But, having gotten off on the wrong foot, it was not possible to smooth things out, and under high levels of stress they terminated.

These two studies suggest that dyads, in everyday and experimental conditions, are more likely to resort to microlevel territorial strategies the stronger their desire is to "make it" in that context, and "survive" as an intact group. Part and parcel of this commitment appears to be a realistic expectation that stressful situations could develop, and the implementation of microscale territorial strategies to minimize possible conflicts.

Summary and remaining questions. Liking of coresidents, in very small groups, appears associated with clearer temporal allocation of shared residential space. Commitment to the group is linked with use of microlevel territorial strategies, apparently in an effort to reduce stress in the situation and develop a smoothly running living situation.

Many questions, however, remain. (1) How does sex composition of the group relate to the liking–territorial functioning link? One study of female and male undergraduates, in same-sex groupings, suggested that males and females viewed shared space differently. (2) Do territorial strategies vary as liking fluctuates? In Stan and Jan Berenstain's *The Berenstain Bears Get into a Fight,* Brother and Sister Bear draw a big red line down the middle of the tree house they are building on the day they have a big squabble. When they later make up, they rub out the line. (See Figure 14.1, p. 324.) It seems likely that as short-term conflicts wax and wane, territorial functioning would shift accordingly; but there is no evidence on this point. (3) The longer-term temporal development of territorial strategies is also in question. We know how territorial functioning develops in isolated groups overtime, but know little about spatial behavior patterns in naturally occurring groups, as they progress. (4) Finally, almost all of the studies have been done with couples. What goes on in larger groups? Studies of tripling-up in dorm rooms have suggested that complex social dynamics develop.[23] What is happening *spatially* in these settings?

Vertical factors: territorial dynamics and dominance

The hypotheses. Based on a loose interpretation of ethological findings, researchers of human territorial functioning have sought linkages between territorial behaviors of individuals and their relative standing or dominance position in a residential group. Most of this work has been carried out in institutionalized settings. Almost all of the work has used only male participants. Researchers have hypothesized that individuals holding a higher dominance position in a group will be more territorial. This leads to two specific hypotheses (see Figure 7.3):

First, it can mean that the individual with the "higher" position in the group has relatively greater access to valued locations within the group's living space, analogous to the greater access of dominant animals to better nesting sites. This is the *priority access hypothesis.* Behaviorally, more dominant individuals would show patterns of more frequent use of high-priority spaces, or more exclusive use of valued spaces.

Second, it can mean that the high-dominance individuals have greater access to *all* spaces within the group's domain; they travel more freely and in a less restricted manner. In this case spatial behavior patterns would be more dispersed; this is a *dispersion hypothesis.* High-dominance individuals would range more widely over the group's living space.

Some confused findings. A series of studies by Aristide Esser and colleagues, focusing largely on institutionalized male populations, has examined dominance and exclusive use of space.[24] The typical meth-

---

[23] Baron, R. M., Mandel, D. R., Adams, C. A., & Griffen, L. M. (1976). Effects of social density in university residential environments. *Journal of Personality and Social Psychology, 34,* 434–446.

Aiello, J. R., Baum, A., & Gormley, F. (1981). Social determinants of residential crowding stress. *Personality and Social Psychology Bulletin, 7,* 643–644.

[24] Deutsch, R. D., Esser, A. H., & Sossin, K. M. (1978). Dominance, aggression, and functional use of space in institutionalized female adolescents. *Aggressive Behavior, 4,* 313–329.

Esser, A. H. (1968). Dominance hierarchy and clinical course of psychiatrically hospitalized boys. *Child Development, 39,* 147–152.

Esser, A. H. (1970). Interactional hierarchy and power structure on a psychiatric ward: Ethological studies of dominance behavior in a total institution. In S. J. Hutt & C. Hutt (Eds.), *Behavior studies in psychiatry.* New York: Pergamon, pp. 25–59.

Esser, A. H. (1973). Cottage Fourteen: Dominance and territoriality in a group of

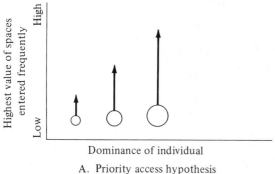

Dominance of individual

A. Priority access hypothesis

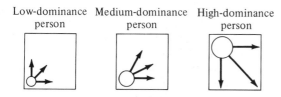

B. Dispersion hypothesis

Figure 7.3. Proposed dominance–territorial functioning links. A. The priority access hypothesis. Those individuals who hold a more dominant position in the group (as indicated by the relative size of the *circles*, the largest representing a high-dominance individual) have frequent and unimpeded access to more valuable locations within the group's living space. *Arrows* indicate scores of particular individuals on the "frequent access to high value locations" dimension. B. The dispersion hypothesis. Those individuals who hold a more dominant position in the group can range more widely across the sites within the group's living space. *Arrows* reflect real distance travelled, within home setting, from point of origin.

odology used in Esser's studies is to get caretaking staff to rate or rank individual patients in a group on dominance, to section the group's living space into arbitrarily defined squares, and then have observers, using a time interval sampling scheme, record who is where over a period of

institutionalized boys. *Small Group Behavior, 4,* 131–146.

Esser, A. H., Chamberlain, A. S., Chappel, F. D., & Kline, N. S. (1965). Territoriality of patients on a research ward. *Recent Advances in Behavioral Psychiatry, 7,* 36–44.

Paluck, R. J., & Esser, A. H. (1971). Controlled experimental modification of aggressive behavior in territories of severely retarded boys. *American Journal of Mental Deficiency, 76,* 23–29.

time. A person is defined as being "territorial" if he uses a particular space frequently.[25] Some of these studies have found that individuals in the top part of the dominance hierarchy were more territorial, while others have found that it was individuals in the bottom part of the hierarchy who were more territorial.[26]

Support for priority access. A few studies examining the dominance–territorial functioning linkage while attending to the value of the spaces in question have found support for the priority access thesis.

1. In a camp setting, Blood and Livant observed that members of cabin groups arranged themselves spatially so as to reflect and implement social relations. "Leaders" in a cabin group would claim top bunks, from which the rest of the cabin could be more easily surveyed and where their bunk would not be "accidentally" stepped on by others. From such a spot it was easier to traumatize others, particularly the person bunking right below, than it was to be traumatized.[27]

2. In a field study in a residential treatment facility for boys, Sundstrom and Altman observed that boys who were higher in the group structure, wielding power over a greater number of others, over a period of time were more likely to have access to the more valued locations

---

[25] Actually, one of the major problems in figuring out what Esser's studies add up to is that being territorial was defined differently in different studies. In the 1965 and 1973 studies, being territorial was defined as occupying an individual space for more than 25% of the observation time. In the 1968 study it was defined as occupying a space for 25% of the occupation time *and* successfully defending against intruders. In the 1970 study it was defined as occupying a space for 15% of the observation time and successfully defending against intruders who were higher up in the dominance hierarchy. In the 1971 study by Paluck and Esser, it was defined as demonstrating a mean occupancy time that was at least two standard deviations above the mean occupancy time for that territory. These different definitions make cross-study comparisons very difficult and would seem to increase the likelihood of contradictory findings across studies.

[26] As Edney (1974) has noted, the last finding could be spurious, low dominance and territoriality both stemming from self-isolation habits. Further, in these different studies perceived desirability of locations was not systematically assessed. Thus, if people were using a space a lot it was not clear if the location was valuable or not. Sundstrom (1977) has also pointed out that cross-study variation in the relative availability of desirable or high-quality spaces may have also contributed to inconsistent patterns of results. It also should be noted that the way the spaces were bounded in these observational studies was arbitrary in many cases. Defining sections of an open space as territories simply because they can be mapped out with grids on the floor seems artificial. The characteristics of a space in such a grid would be very different from a space such as in a single bedroom.

[27] Blood, R. O., & Livant, W. P. (1957). The use of space within the cabin group. *Journal of Social Issues, 13,* 47–53.

(e.g., the rec room) within the cottage setting.[28] This study also found that certain aspects of the dominance–territorial functioning link were dependent on overall group structure (see the following subsection).

3. A study of 45 inmates in a prison dorm developed behavioral indices of dominance rank based on social contact, nonverbal, and aggression data.[29] More dominant individuals had greater access to valued space as indicated by their proximate location to the TV set, and the fact that they were more likely to have a single instead of a double bunk. (Double bunks were less desirable because someone was likely to step on your bunk, "by accident," while getting to his.)

Support for the dispersion hypothesis. Two studies have provided support for the dispersion study. The study with prison inmates found that more dominant members of the group ranged more freely and extensively over the living space, while less dominant group members restricted themselves more, some of the low-dominance group members rarely leaving their bunks. The latter individuals, experiencing considerable stress, may have attempted to "cope" with the situation by drastically restricting their behavioral orbit. In this study, group membership was stable during the observation period. This may have been a key condition for the emergence of the two types of dominance–territoriality relationships observed.

Group structure was more fluid during the aforementioned field study by Sundstrom and Altman. During the ten-week study period the cottage group of about 20 boys passed through three different stages. In phase I, the first five weeks, the group was stable. In phase II, the group was in transition. Two highly dominant group members left and were replaced by two new, highly dominant boys. Two weeks later two more members (one high dominance, one medium dominance) left. In phase III, the last three weeks of observation, the group was in the process of reorganizing itself. Dominance rankings of group members, made by staff and boys, were obtained, as were participants' ratings of the desirability of various areas within the cottage. The results gave conditional support to the dispersion hypothesis. When the group composition was stable, higher-dominance boys were seen in a broader range of spaces. But when the group structure was shifting and then reorganizing, this relationship was not evident.

Thus, the link between relative social position and extensiveness of

[28] Sundstrom, E., & Altman, I. (1974). Field study of dominance and territorial behavior. *Journal of Personality and Social Psychology, 30*, 115–125.

[29] Austin, W. T., & Bates, F. L. (1974). Ethological indicators of dominance and territory in a human captive population. *Social Forces, 52*, 447–455.

spatial behavior patterns appears contingent upon stable group structure, and less likely to emerge lacking this setting condition. Support for priority access is not so contingent.

Are the two hypotheses contradictory? At first blush, support for both these hypotheses thus might seem contradictory; how can the high-dominance person range more freely over the living area, but at the same time have better access to desirable places? Doesn't it seem that others would take his valuable "spot" while he is ranging over the cottage?

A high-dominance person in the group can claim a valued spot (e.g., a good seat in a common TV room), then wander off, returning later to reclaim his spot and inflicting harm on any usurpers. Out of fear of retaliation others will not take the "good" but unoccupied spot. So, it does not seem contradictory to suggest that in an institutional setting an individual can have access to high-priority locations and, at the same time, maintain a dispersed activity pattern.

This line of reasoning also perhaps explains why the dispersion thesis is supported only when group structure is stable. It is only when there is such stability that people know whom to fear. Lacking such stability, and in the presence of a confused group ecology, the high-dominance person may not have a broad enough base of "respect," and thus is unable to reserve highly desirable locations.[30]

Summing-up on social factors and territorial functioning in interior residential settings

Both horizontal and vertical aspects of interpersonal relationships are linked to territorial functioning in interior residential settings. But the linkages are not straightforward. In the case of dominance relationships, the full mapping of social position onto spatial behavior patterns appears contingent upon the overarching group structure. Stated more generally, the overall group structure, as well as the position of the individual within the group, influences territorial behavior patterns; there are two levels – group and individual within group – of social factors influencing territorial functioning.

---

[30] This speculation leads to an interesting question. In noninstitutionalized settings, such as a fraternity or sorority, where members live in less fear of retaliation, would the same two hypotheses also be upheld? Would fear of more mild sanctions be sufficient to allow both priority access and dispersed behavior patterns of high-status persons? At this time there are no available data on this question.

In addition, the role of place specificity is underscored in the findings here. Territorial-dominance studies that ignore the perceived value of location yield inconsistent findings. It is only when the value for residents of the space itself is considered that consistent support for the priority access hypothesis emerges.

When we focus on the horizontal aspects of interpersonal relationships, clear patterns are somewhat more elusive. Certain aspects of territorial functioning appear socially linked, such as shared agreements on scheduling of space use. Links between social climate and microlevel territorial strategies, and size of exclusive versus shared areas in the setting have also been observed, but a precise interpretation of these connections is difficult because there is no specific orienting model. In interior residential settings, such as a dorm room, for example, one could argue that as liking increased, the size of the shared area would also increase. Unfortunately, one could also argue the opposite. Put territorial functioning first. One could reason that if each individual had an extensive area in the shared living space that was solely his or hers, and recognized as such, then such a spatial contract, and the concomitantly reduced level of spatial conflicts, all else equal, would result in the earlier emergence of liking among the coresidents, or the emergence of stronger liking. Attention to theoretical links between group cohesiveness measures and territorial functioning is needed.

Closing comments on predictors of territorial functioning

Studies have indicated that all four classes of predictors – cultural, personality, physical, and social – shape territorial functioning in the most multifunctional, subjectively important locations. And, as the model we have developed predicts, this influence operates via transformations of the image of the locus in question. Dimensions of cognition such as mine exclusively versus shared, important for symbolic reasons versus important for everyday functioning, and so on, shape territorial behaviors such as frequency and duration of use, shared versus exclusive use, ejection of others, and control over others while they are in the location.

Considering the predictors in toto, it is apparent that they are interdependent. Cultural practices, for example, prescribe particular physical arrangements in the setting. As the nature of the social relationships between residents shifts, so too may the physical arrangements. The clusters of predictors under examination mutually influence one another.

Table 7.1. *Outcomes of territorial functioning in interior residential settings*

	Related to daily functioning	Expressive/symbolic
Intrapersonal	Decreased thwarting Increased actual facilitation Decreased stress response	Identity display: reflect/deepen attachment individuate person-in-group
Interpersonal	Social organization "translated" into spatial organization Patterns of exclusive use reduce areas of potential conflict	Group identity display: communal rituals carried out heritage/status expressed

Consequences of territorial functioning

In order to organize this discussion of consequences of territorial functioning in interior residential settings, four broad types of consequences are proposed. First, and as discussed earlier, we can separate psychological, intraindividual consequences from social psychological consequences, affecting interpersonal ties or entire groups.

The individual/group dichotomy can be "crossed" with a functional versus symbolic dimension. Consequences that are functional have to do with daily behavior, task-oriented activities, or actions directly impinging on health and well-being. Symbolic or expressive concerns are less mundane and concern matters whose correspondence with behavioral patterns is sometimes less apparent. The consequences we will be reviewing are summarized in Table 7.1.

Psychological consequences: enhanced facilitation, reduced thwarting

By regulating access to particular locations, and/or exercising control over the activities therein, the individual in the residential unit is more assured that he or she can carry out the activities he or she wishes, in the space in question. Using Stokols' contextual-stress perspective, some of this benefit may be in the form of enhanced actual facilitation (e.g., homework concentration is easier when it is quiet), and some may be attributable to reduced thwarting, perhaps in the form of fewer interruptions, or at least increased predictability of interruptions. Consequently, the individual should experience more environmental controllability and less stress. Stated graphically:

Territorial	→	Enhanced	→	Less stress
behaviors		environmental		experienced
		controllability		

Support for such a proposed dynamic comes from two studies. A Baltimore study found that people were less bothered by the stressors of high levels of household density, or large household size, if they had a room where they could go and not be bothered by others.[31] The availability of a nonshared territory lessened the impact of the stressor, by reducing thwarting and/or increasing actual need facilitation.

Less directly supportive but nonetheless pertinent are results from the reanalysis of a national survey. Those with lower social positions, such as mothers and nonhousehold heads or spouses of heads, were more dissatisfied with living conditions within the household.[32] For example, mothers, when compared with fathers, in higher-density homes reported significantly lower levels of satisfaction with dwelling livability, and available space. Mothers' higher levels of experienced stress probably stemmed from expectations in traditional households that they be more accessible to others.[33] Claims to nonshared or shared spaces may be, therefore, less respected in the case of the mother as compared to the father. In other words, lower-status persons in the household, having less "guaranteed" access to nonshared locations within the residential unit, experience higher levels of thwarting and thus are less satisfied with the dwelling unit.

If we want to proceed with the causal logic and assume that the less stress experienced in a location, the less likely the person will be to leave it, additional studies are also relevant. The isolation study mentioned earlier found that if members of the group exhibited territorial functioning early in the mission, they were less likely to abort the mission later on.[34] Patterns of exclusive use adopted early resulted in less stress

---

[31] Verbrugge, L., & Taylor, R. B. (1980). Consequences of population density and size. *Urban Affairs Quarterly, 16,* 135–160.

[32] Baldassare, M. (1981). The effects of household density on subgroups. *American Sociological Review, 46,* 110–118.

[33] Smith, D. (1971). Household space and family organization. In D. Davies & K. Herman (Eds.), *Social space: Canadian perspectives.* Toronto: New Press, pp. 62–69.

[34] Altman, Taylor, & Wheeler (1971).

later. In a study examining the privacy-regulation mechanisms used by college students who later stayed in college, or dropped out, stay-ins were more likely to use contact avoidance mechanisms, several of which involved territorial functioning.[35] For example, stay-ins were more likely than dropouts to shut the door to their room or to go find a quiet place. By creating or seeking out nonshared or behaviorally constrained locations they were able to experience greater environmental controllability, and thus could continue functioning effectively in the college context.

Given the broad range of pertinent studies touching on the link between effective territorial functioning and less stress and stress-related consequences, it is clear that the psychological consequences of territorial functioning are substantial in interior residential settings.

Identity display and consequences

Another aspect of territorial functioning in interior residential settings concerns personal identity. Altman and his colleagues have maintained that people "use territories to display aspects of their personalities, interests, and values."[36] In other words, they suggest, territorial behaviors such as marker placement, and decorating, allow individuals to express their individuality. Such behaviors satisfy *expressive* or *symbolic* needs. Microlevel territorial strategies, such as claiming certain shelves in the closet, may also satisfy these same needs, as well as provide functional benefits. The consequences of these territorial behaviors are difficult to pin down.

Low levels of display may indicate a low level of commitment to the larger locale in question. A couple of studies involving college students indicated that displays in dorm rooms were linked with dropping out of college or staying in.[37]

It seems likely that there are also more immediate psychological and social consequences of personal displays in interior residential settings.

---

[35] Vinsel, A., Brown, B. B., Altman, I., & Foss, C. (1980). Privacy regulation, territorial displays, and effectiveness of individual functioning. *Journal of Personality and Social Psychology, 39*, 1104–1115.

[36] Ibid., p. 1113.

[37] Hansen, W. B., & Altman, I. (1976). Decorating personal places: A descriptive analysis. *Environment and Behavior, 8*, 491–504.

The first study by Hansen and Altman found that volume of personal display in dorm rooms was linked with staying in college. The later study did not replicate this finding. But the authors did observe that stay-ins as compared to dropouts had decorations reflecting a stronger commitment to the college environment.

(1) Most important, such displays or marking behaviors may symbolize, reflect, and perhaps even deepen the person's commitment or attachment to the *immediate* location. (2) The person may be more satisfied with his or her living arrangement if given the freedom to personalize his or her location. (3) The markers indicate to whom the space belongs, signalling possession. And (4), on an interpersonal level, the displays signal to others who the occupier is. Therefore, the role of the occupier, vis-à-vis others, is clarified. He or she is more clearly individuated. The clarity of the individual's position in the group is enhanced by these environmental manipulations.

Social psychological consequences

The social psychological consequences of territorial functioning in interior residential settings are several.

1. Through territorial functioning the group structure is "mapped onto" the space available. This connection is most obvious in the territoriality-dominance studies. Those "higher" in the group have more access to valued locations, and more access to spaces overall. Spatial resources are "distributed" according to social position. As a result, stress related to spatial issues is "distributed" differentially across the group members.

2. Patterns of exclusive use result in reduced conflict over spatial matters. Mutually recognized allotments of locations lessen competing claims for use, and thus reduce overall friction between group members. Spatiotemporal claims to sites within the living space become fixed. These matters are no longer ambiguous for group members.

3. Day-to-day functioning of the group itself is thus facilitated. If it is accepted that Father can kick the children out of the kitchen when it is time to prepare dinner, dinner ends up getting on the table sooner.

4. Through the allocation of spaces to special symbolic uses, group rituals are more easily carried out. Particular sites within the living space are put aside for special, symbolic occasions.

5. And the display of special symbols communicates the group's background to outsiders. In the same way that personal displays such as decorated dorm rooms communicate the background of the occupant, the "front regions" of households – parlors, living rooms – communicate to outsiders the background and values of the group. A picture on the mantle of Martin Luther King "says" something about the household very different from what a picture of Ronald Reagan would "say."

Insiders meet outsiders

Sometimes in interior residential settings we interact with those from outside who are not part of the residential grouping (as the story in the accompanying box illustrates).

Wendy tells off Peter Pan

When Peter Pan visited the Darlings' nursery for his first chat with Wendy, he explained to her all about the lost boys who fall out of their prams in Kensington Gardens and get sent to Neverland. "If they are not claimed in seven days they are sent away to the Neverland to defray expenses. I'm captain." While they were discussing differences between girls and boys (girls are never so stupid as to fall out of their prams) Wendy mentioned that John, her brother " 'just despises us.' For reply Peter rose and kicked John out of bed, blankets and all; one kick. This seemed to Wendy rather forward for a first meeting, *and she told him with spirit that he was not captain in her house.*"[38] This is actually one of the few times that Wendy does *not* defer to Peter in the course of their adventures.

It is built into the folk wisdom of our and other cultures that we have an advantage over others when we meet them on our ground. A variety of ethological evidence with different species supports this idea. But do we actually have such an advantage?

The empirical studies that have looked at this issue are field studies that usually run as follows. Groups of previously unacquainted persons meet in the dorm room belonging to one of the group members. They discuss some problem or issue and attempt to arrive at a group solution. The group size is usually two. The experimenter examines the group's decision to see if it favors the resident or the visitor more. Recording of verbal interaction may also be examined to see who talked more, who interrupted more, and so on. It is assumed that patterns of verbal interaction are reflective of the actual interpersonal influence dynamics.

A couple of studies have provided results that affirm the folk wisdom

---

[38] Barrie, J. M. (1911/1980). *Peter Pan.* New York: Scribners, p. 31.

surrounding the resident advantage.[39] One field study had dyad members playing roles of prosecuting and defending attorney in a hypothetical sentencing discussion. The resident advantage was evident in that group members who were residents talked more than visitors, and, when the resident was also the defense attorney, the group agreed on significantly lighter sentences.

A second study using groups of three found that the group solution to a university budget problem was most likely to match the solution of the resident, in whose room the group discussion was held, even if the resident was a low-dominance person. (Each group was composed of a high-, medium-, and low-dominance person.) Thus, even Caspar Milquetoast types, who are not used to being influential with others, can hold sway over others when on their own ground, and when outnumbered.

These two studies are similar in that the task assigned the group involves compromise. Some members of the group have to give something up in order to arrive at a group solution. Such a task structure seems likely to force the group into a competitive mind set. In a more cooperative context, however, the resident advantage may not appear.[40] In a field experiment Conroy and Sundstrom found that when residents and visitor had different opinions on the topic under discussion, for which they were preparing a class presentation, the expected resident advantage emerged. Residents talked more, and interrupted visitors more.[41] But, when opinions were similar, residents deferred to visitors, allowing them to talk and successfully interrupt more. The authors called this deferring of resident to visitor a *hospitality effect*.

This last finding is yet another instance of how territorial functioning is contingent upon the social dynamics of the group under consideration. It appears here that the exertion of the resident advantage, as reflected

[39] Martindale, D. A. (1971). Territorial dominance behavior in dyadic verbal interactions. *Proceedings of the 79th annual convention of the American Psychological Association.* Washington, DC: American Psychological Association, pp. 305–306.

  Taylor, R. B., & Lanni, J. C. (1981). Territorial dominance: The influence of the resident advantage in triadic decisionmaking. *Journal of Personality and Social Psychology, 41,* 909–915.

[40] Conroy, J., & Sundstrom, E. (1977). Territorial dominance in a dyadic conversation as a function of similarity of opinion. *Journal of Personality and Social Psychology, 35,* 570–576.

[41] The experimenters referred to interrupting as simultaneous control. B successfully overtalks A when B and A start speaking at the same time, A eventually desists, and B continues.

in talking and successfully interrupting more is a flexible strategy used only as needed.

So, in situations where there are differences of opinion, and potential conflict, can the resident advantage help the person who is "at home"? For several reasons I think such a conclusion is not yet warranted by available findings.

1. The underlying processes at work are not specified. Edney has suggested that the resident advantage works through cognitive channels, influencing attribution patterns – how people interpret the causes of behavior.[42] Others have suggested that it works primarily through social role expectations.[43] They argue that certain expectations about how to behave as a guest, or a host, are widely shared, and these preset dispositions shape behavior in the resident–visitor context.

2. The studies so far have only used previously unacquainted persons. Does the resident advantage come into play if people in the group are already acquainted?

3. The studies so far have used participants of equal ascriptive status; students have talked to other students. What would happen if individuals of different ascribed statuses were working on a problem, say a graduate student and an undergraduate student? Would the "underling" be more influential when "at home"? Would the higher-status person feel, when he was at home, that he did not need to "rely" on the resident advantage, and thus let the underling talk more? Or would he let the underling talk more but not be persuaded?

4. The studies so far have involved only males. What happens when women talk to other women? Do they "use" the resident advantage? What happens when men talk to women?

These are all uninvestigated questions. Consequently, the most appropriate conclusion at this time is probably that the resident can be more influential over visitors when the groups are previously unacquainted, equal-status males, and the task at hand involves resolving differences of opinion. This conclusion may be more limited than some would like. The reader may ask: "How can your conclusions be so circumscribed when the folk wisdom concerning this effect is so strong? Can the folk wisdom be wrong?" My feeling is that the folk wisdom may or may not be wrong; enough is not yet known. But, what is clear

---

[42] Edney, J. J. (1975). Territoriality and control: A field experiment. *Journal of Personality and Social Psychology, 31*, 1108–1115.

[43] Kubzhansky, P. E., & Bar Tal, Y. (1984). Social role factors in resident advantage. Paper presented at the annual meeting of the Eastern Psychological Association, Baltimore, April.

is that people very much want the folk wisdom to be right (see the following box).

A personal aside: people want to believe

People's strong desire to believe in the efficacy of the resident advantage came to my attention after Joe Lanni and I published an article on the topic in the usual obscure academic journal. Subsequent articles referring to it appeared in *Psychology Today* and *Reader's Digest*. Columns appeared in the *Philadelphia Inquirer* and the *Los Angeles Times*. I was asked to discuss it on radio talk shows in Washington, DC, and San Francisco.

Particularly revealing was the "slant" given to this issue in the coverage. The story line used was: here is an effective, less-than-transparent (i.e., crafty) way to manipulate people and get what you want. On one show the host wanted to concentrate on how the findings tied in to successfully getting a raise from your boss. (During the commercials the other station staff shouted at the host that no way would he be allowed to try this on their own boss at the station!) In other words, in people's minds the findings fit nicely into "Here's how to gain power and influence people and get things out of them you never dreamed of."

It would be comforting for the traditionally powerless, or those who find themselves more influenced than influencing, to think that there was some surefire strategy they could use to get what they wanted. Or to think, in a somewhat less grandiose fashion, that there were at least some places where they could be immune from the attempts of others to influence them. In other words, there are a lot of strong self-serving reasons why people want the resident advantage to "work for them." This underlying rationale helps to make the folk wisdom surrounding this phenomenon appear so strong. Unfortunately, we do not yet know if the phenomenon is as powerful, durable, and general as people wish it to be.

Closing comments

Territorial functioning in multifunctional, interior residential settings where person–place transactions are of high centrality has been examined. In these contexts territorial functioning plays a range of roles, the most important of which may be the reduction of the thwarting of motivationally significant needs, the enhancement of actual facilitation of needs, and the reduction of group conflict. This is accomplished by linking particular individuals with particular locations in the setting.

Space in interior residential settings is differentiated. There are some locations where, for an individual household member, the potential for access control, privacy, and management of the environment is high; there are other locations where this potential is nil. This differentiation can occur at the room level or at a more microscale, such as the side of a closet. At the most general level, territorial functioning, through such differentiation, is preserving the viability and multifunctionality of the spaces in question.

Such spatial differentiation is reflected in the physical markings, cognitions, and behaviors of group members. They recognize relative differences in proprietorship and occupancy. As the members of the group know or get to know one another, they come to rely on a set of behavioral norms to control and direct spatial behaviors. In spaces of lower centrality, where familiarity between co-occupants is weaker, reliance on physical supports for boundary regulation is more evident.

Within residential settings, some members appear to be more privileged, in terms of what locations they may claim, and the number of others they may exclude. In households the most disadvantaged appear to be children, particularly if they cannot have a bedroom to themselves, and mothers, who are expected to be highly accessible to other members of the family at all times. In nonhousehold, institutional settings, persons with higher rank in a group may have access to more places, and more access to higher-value locations, than others. Social position translates into spatial prerogatives.

Across households, there are differences in territorial functioning. Within class levels there appear to be differences in terms of how open and flexible, versus closed and rigid, the territorial arrangements are. There are differences also based on group structure. More cohesiveness seems to be associated with more clear-cut norms about use of shared space.

Nonetheless, several significant questions remain.

1. How do people react when there is a change in the layout or availability or quality of territories within the household? If the change implies increased thwarting, do people react with "learned helplessness," where they passively accept the situation and try to do nothing about it, or do they show "reactance" and try to reassert their behavioral freedom, and regain lost territory?[44] Or do they react some other way?

2. Over time, what are the links between facilitation, thwarting, stress, and microlevel territorial strategies? It seems reasonable to expect a

---

[44] Stokols (1979) points out that current theoretical integrations of reactance and learned helplessness theory suggest that a helplessness response will be more likely if initial levels of environmental controllability were low rather than high, and the ensuing thwarting is chronic rather than occasional.

temporal coupling between ongoing social dynamics, stress, and territorial functioning. But apart from studies with isolated groups, we have no evidence on this point.

3. How does territorial functioning shift across stages in the life cycle? As people move from single, to young married, to married-with-children, to empty nesters (or alternately, from married, to divorced, to new family), how do these changes create pressures and opportunities that are subsequently reflected in territorial functioning?

8
TERRITORIAL FUNCTIONING IN OUTDOOR RESIDENTIAL SPACES CLOSE TO THE HOME

If one is to tell what is going on in a residential area, it can be much more useful to look at the decoration of the windows, the cleanliness of the sidewalks, and the neatness of the lawns, than at the style and scale of the houses.
– Don Appleyard, "Environment as a Social Symbol"

"A lot of people say it's tacky... I don't know... One flamingo... maybe that's *tacky. I've got thirty-four."*
– Don Featherstone, of Union Products, Inc., inventor of the pink flamingo lawn ornament. Interview on National Public Radio's "All Things Considered," July 31, 1987.

In this chapter we move out of interior residential settings and into the spaces surrounding them: outdoor residential spaces close to the home. The locations to be considered include front steps, porches and front yards, driveways, backyards, alleys, sidewalks, and the street itself. These exterior locations not only encapsulate the interior residential spaces where person–place transactions are of highest centrality. They are also linked with interior settings in a number of important ways. Quality of life in the interior residential setting is shaped by events, people, and conditions in the adjoining outdoor spaces.

Transactions in outdoor residential spaces rank second highest on the centrality dimension for a simple reason: They are always there. In leaving the residence and returning home, occupants must traverse these spaces. Problems at the office or factory can be left behind when one heads home; problems around the home cannot be left behind unless one moves.

Furthermore, in a more subjective vein, these outdoor residential spaces are *part of home*. Home does not stop at the front door but rather extends beyond. The house is inextricably linked with its immediate setting, not only physically, but psychologically as well.

Finally, these near-home spaces constitute an essential bridge between the individual, or household, and the immediate local society. In spaces right outside the home the individual or household can put out "tentative social feelers," getting to know those who live close by.[1]

---

[1] Cooper, C. (1975). *Easter Hill Village.* New York: Free Press.

Organization of the chapter

Several preliminary issues are touched on in setting the context for the discussion: the historical background of urban and suburban neighborhoods, as well as evidence of psychological differentiation within the neighborhood arena, and of streetblock functioning. Social psychological reasons why social groups form at the streetblock or subblock level are marshalled.

The core of the chapter, relying on the framework presented in Chapter 5, considers the elements of territorial functioning, its predictors, and its consequences. Subsequently, the psychological, social psychological, and ecological consequences of territorial functioning on the streetblock are examined. One consequence – the impact of territorial functioning on disorder – is not examined here but is covered in Chapter 11.

Background

The recent nature of the residential environment as we know it

The urban and suburban residential environment as we know it is a relatively recent phenomenon, dating back less than 100 years. In the last 500 years, and more particularly in the last 50–100 years, street life in cities has changed. Lyn Lofland, a sociologist, has argued that one of the most significant differences between preindustrial and modern cities is that in the latter a "place order" – a segmentation of people and activities by location – predominates; this has superseded the much more chaotic situation found in preindustrial cities where, walking down the street, one would encounter all manner of persons – beggars, hawkers, waifs, hookers, and nobility.[2] In former times a "people order" predominated; all different classes of people were jammed together on the same city streets, and one identified others based on social factors (e.g., dress and retinue) rather than spatial factors. In the preindustrial cities people, by means of their attire, company, and language, clearly displayed their identities.

But with the advent of the modern city, and the emergence of mass-produced clothing, compulsory education, zoning laws, and subsequent settlement patterns, it became increasingly difficult visually to identify people as belonging to a particular class in society. Instead, people became identified based on where they lived. Where you were defined who you were. As innumerable singers have crooned, he couldn't be

[2] Lofland, L. H. (1973). *A world of strangers*. New York: Basic Books.

her boyfriend (or she his girlfriend) because he (or she) came from the "wrong side of town."

As part of this new order, we have witnessed in cities, and, more recently, in the suburban areas around major urban centers, the rise of predominantly residential locations. Urban and suburban neighborhoods are relatively recent, materializing only in the last 100 years or so. Their rise has been coupled not only with simple patterns of city growth but also with technological changes. With the advent of streetcars, as urban historians have documented, neighborhoods grew up along streetcar lines. It was no longer necessary to build worker housing near factories, or to arrange sites with residences on the upper floors and shops on the ground floor. Those who had a steady job at the other end of the streetcar line (i.e., middle-class households) readily occupied these neighborhoods at the fringes of cities, and in nearby towns.[3] Laborers, whose workplace shifted frequently, did not reside in such neighborhoods. And, of course, the car spawned much more extensive suburbanization. In urban areas, the car freed people from the streetcar line, allowing lower-income households to live in a wider variety of areas. So, even though the all-residential streetblocks discussed here may seem as permanent as they are familiar, it is important to recognize that they are, in historical perspective, relatively recent arrangements.

Some "old" evidence on the streetblock as a sociospatial arena

Much of urban sociology deals with neighborhood and community life. Yet there is strong evidence, dating back to the first quarter of this century, that the streetblock – the area bounded by the houses on the two sides of the street, and the cross streets – is an important sociospatial arena.[4]

In the years during and immediately after World War I, Roderick McKenzie, a member of "The Chicago School" of urban sociologists (Park, Burgess, Wirth, Shaw, McKay, etc.), carried out a study of "neighborhoods" in Columbus, Ohio. In one chapter he examined neighborhoods in detail.[5] *Of the five neighborhoods investigated, four*

---

[3] McKenzie, R. (1970; originally published 1923). *The neighborhood: A study of local life in the city of Columbus, Ohio.* New York: Arno Press.

    Warner, S.B. (1962) *Streetcar suburbs.* Cambridge, MA: Harvard University Press.

[4] For a historical and architectural view of streets, see:

    Anderson, S. (Ed.) (1978). *On streets.* Cambridge: MIT Press. For a commentary on these views see:

    Appleyard, D. (1979a). Review of *On streets. American Planning Association Journal,* 45, 342–344.

[5] McKenzie (1923/1970), pp. 344–363.

were based on just one street! Encompassing anywhere from two street-blocks to a distance of a quarter mile, the improvement organizations he discussed covered anywhere from a dozen to several dozen households, and promoted cleanup and beautification activities – putting distinctive boulders at the entrances to the street, fixing up a median street park, and so on. The organizations that covered a longer stretch would put out tabloids at irregular intervals, but the smaller groups, such as the Ninth Avenue neighborhood, covering only two short blocks, did not need a paper to disseminate information. The groups often held annual fetes such as beautification contests or fireworks displays. In several of the neighborhood groups described, the streets were uniform in terms of site features and housing quality, or distinct from adjoining land uses.

McKenzie observed that:

1. The larger the area covered, and the greater the number of people involved, the harder it was to generate interest in local projects;
2. Street groups for areas longer than two blocks tended to divide into subgroups, "especially when two different street car lines are used by the residents in communication with the down-town district"; and,
3. Most local activities were engineered by a very small number of energetic residents.[6]

At a more general level, McKenzie's findings indicated that the street-block, not what we think of today as the larger neighborhood or community, was the primary unit for formal and informal social ties and organizational activities.

This same point surfaces again in a study conducted right after World War II in a neighborhood housing married graduate students at MIT.[7] Half of the area studied was composed of one-story housing, where a number of apartments (two or three) would be side by side in a building, and six to ten buildings were arranged to form U-shaped courts (Figure 8.1). These courts, equivalent in terms of group size to a small street-block, functioned, in effect, as social groups. Friendship choices were much more likely within as compared to across courts, and when a rumor was planted it spread more quickly within than across courts. In other words, the courts served as "containers" of the local, face-to-face groupings, bounding the groups and separating them one from another.

The spatially limited nature of the predominant local social groupings observed in these two studies would suggest that residents felt differently

---

[6] Ibid., pp. 362–363.
[7] Festinger, L., Schachter, S., & Back, K. (1959). *Social pressures in informal groups.* Stanford, CA: Stanford University Press.

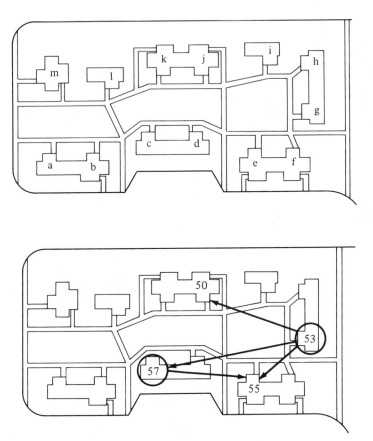

Figure 8.1. Arrangement of housing units and rumor transmission. *Upper panel*: Schematic diagram of the arrangement of the Westgate Court. Since households within each court were "turned in" on each other, this facilitated the development of face-to-face groupings within each court. *Lower panel*: The transmission of rumors planted by Festinger et al. was influenced by the arrangement of housing units into courts. Much of the information sharing occurred within courts. *Source*: Reprinted from *Social pressures in informal groups*, by Leon Festinger, Stanley Schachter, and Kurt Back with the permission of the publishers, Stanford University Press. Copyright © 1950 by Leon Festinger, Stanley Schachter, and Kurt Back (copyright renewed).

about their own block (or court) as compared to others. McKenzie found this to be the case; when he asked his students to define their neighborhood, many of them included just their streetblock, and perhaps adjoining ones. Similarly, more recently Suttles has suggested that people in lower-income, high-distrust areas may define their neighborhood as only their streetblock.[8]

A participant observation study carried out in the 1960's by Herbert Gans in a new suburban neighborhood found that residents first attempted to make friendships with other people on the block.[9] (In a participant observation study the investigator lives or works in the site he or she is studying.) Mothers would talk about child-care duties, and be invited to, or invite others to, "coffee klatches." Male adults would talk to other males while outside painting or mowing or cleaning up. In many cases these initial interactions would lead to later friendships. It was only when the person found the on-block climate uncongenial that he or she would "leapfrog" to the neighborhood level in search of acceptable locale-based friendships, and start attending community meetings. So, again, the block appears to be the more primary or basic container of local group formation and local ties.

In sum, these various studies, carried out in different places, and at different times in this century, suggest that in some respects the street-block is a more important arena than the neighborhood. It is more important in that:

1. The streetblock is more likely to be the locus of neighborly ties;
2. Communication among households is stronger within streetblocks than across blocks; and
3. Local improvement activities are as or more likely to be mounted on the streetblock than on the neighborhood level.[10]

The social psychological underpinnings of the emergence of small groups on the streetblock

There are interrelated social-spatial processes occurring on streetblocks that lay the groundwork for the emergence of small, face-to-face groups

---

[8] Suttles, G. D. ([1972]. *The social construction of communities.* Chicago: University of Chicago Press, p. 58) calls the streetblock the "face-block." He recognizes the streetblock as an areal unit but feels it is less important than the neighborhood for several reasons. (a) It is egocentric, defined differently by each resident. (b) It offers no residential identity, and (c) does not provide social solidarity (pp. 55–56). I disagree with (a) because streetblock physical boundaries can be much more clear-cut than neighborhood boundaries. I disagree with (b), and evidence of block clubs, such as were observed by McKenzie, and as can be found today in many cities, counters his proposition. On point (c), I feel that streetblocks provide much *more* social solidarity because there is at least minimal knowledge of coresidents, based on what can be gleaned in the daily round of comings and goings.

[9] Gans, H. J. (1967). *The Levittowners.* New York: Pantheon.

[10] This last point depends upon the social class level of the neighborhood, as will be elaborated later in this chapter.

in these settings. In other words, as a result of these processes, clusters of physically proximate coresidents develop into small social groupings.

We need to be clear about the nature of these groupings. Ties among group members need not encompass a strong degree of liking, or even be labeled as friendship. The ties in question are what sociologists call "weak ties."[11] In less technical terms, they are bonds of acquaintanceship.

Overlying the acquaintanceship tie is the neighbor role.[12] The neighbor role requires that one be civil and avoid nosiness. Should emergencies arise where help is needed for a brief time, one may proffer assistance; the recipient should do the same in a similar situation.

Proximity and passive contacts

There is much social psychology research on how friends are likely to be from among those who live close by rather than farther away.[13] The "friction" of distance is an impediment to acquaintanceship or friendship formation; proximity is a facilitator. Proximity may even allow acquaintanceship or friendship formation among dissimilar persons, overriding interpersonal differences.[14,15]

In a residential context the first stage of acquaintanceship formation involves *passive contacts*.[16] Passive contacts occur when coresidents have unplanned interactions with one another. They may see and greet each other when working on the yard, or walking to the bus stop. The frequency of passive contacts between two households is a function of proximity and siting arrangements – the layouts of entranceways, sidewalks and footpaths, driveways, and so on. Passive contacts, if accompanied by recognition and minimal familiarity with others, lay the cornerstone for the further development of acquaintanceships and neighborly ties.

[11] Granovetter, M. (1973). The strength of weak ties. *American Journal of Sociology, 78*, 1360–1380.

[12] Keller, S. (1968). *The urban neighborhood.*

  Mann, P. H. (1954). The concept of neighborliness. *American Journal of Sociology, 60*, 163–168.

[13] Secord, P., & Backman, K. (1974). *Social psychology.* New York: McGraw-Hill.

[14] Nahemow, L., & Lawton, M. P. (1975). Similarity and propinquity in friendship formation. *Journal of Personality and Social Psychology, 32*, 205–213.

[15] Not only are acquaintances more likely to be close by, so too are enemies.

  Ebbesen, E. E., Kjos, G. L., & Konecni, V. J. (1976). Spatial ecology: Its effects on the choice of friends and enemies. *Journal of Experimental Social Psychology, 12*, 505–518.

[16] Festinger et al. (1950).

On a typical streetblock, there are numerous opportunities for passive contacts among coresidents. Since they all live on the same block, they are close to one another. And, where front doors face the street, as is found on many blocks, people will be travelling frequently through the same zone.

Mere exposure

Further facilitating the strengthening of bonds with coresidents on the block are "mere exposure" effects. Social psychologists have established, in numerous experiments, that the more frequently one is exposed to another person, the more that other person is liked.[17] There are, of course, exceptions to this rule: Being exposed more frequently to someone who is unkind to us results in greater disliking. But, in general, the rule holds. On the streetblock then, barring persons who are disorderly, crazy, unbelievably nosy, or obnoxious, we can expect that as coresidents are exposed more frequently to one another in their daily comings and goings, bonds of acquaintanceship are progressively strengthened and perhaps infused with varying degrees of liking.

Norm emergence

As these weak ties develop the neighbor role becomes more firmly cemented to it. One feels more strongly about being civil, not intruding, and offering help should it be needed on a short-term basis. The grounds for offering help and being civil are not necessarily liking for the other person(s). Rather, as the ties develop one simply feels more strongly that this is how one acts. In fact, one is subscribing more strongly to the group-centered norms, and the norms themselves are strengthening.

Common fate

Coresidents on a block share a common fate. They are bothered by the same environmental conditions and immediate problems. To the extent the residents are aware of their common plight, their grouplike nature will be strengthened. Particular concerns such as a problem playground, a snow-blocked street, or an especially troublesome family may heighten residents' awareness of their commonality.

---

[17] Zajonc, R. (1968). Attitudinal effects of mere exposure. *Journal of Personality and Social Psychology*, monograph supplement, part 2, pp. 1–27.

Given these various spatial and social psychological processes at work, one might expect that physically similar, proximate blocks could develop very different personalities. This can happen, as the following story illustrates.

Two Worlds Apart

In an inner-city neighborhood in Baltimore are two blocks that, although right next to each other, are worlds apart. As the accompanying figures indicate, street length and housing characteristics are virtually identical on the two blocks. On "North Block," houses are always kept up, sidewalks swept, plantings put out, and parents always keep an eye on children who are out playing. One year the block won a citywide cleanup and beautification contest, overcoming stiff competition from other neighborhoods throughout the city. Neighborhood leaders speak highly of residents on the block, mentioning how they are always willing to help one another, willingly lending household goods or tools. On "South Block," however, life is rather different. Residents are constantly fighting and arguing, and every night from late spring to early fall the air is filled with the sounds of disagreements, taunts, and loud talk until all hours of the night. Neighbors distrust one another and constantly accuse other neighbors of "signifying" – spreading false, pernicious rumors. Neighborhood leaders point out how residents on the block never contribute to local neighborhood efforts. The block has one of the highest per capita crime rates in the city.

Two streetblocks, even though adjacent, can be as different as two neighborhoods.

Left: "North" block. *Right*: "South" block. *Source*: Urbter Associates. Copyright 1987.

Outdoor residential space is highly differentiated

So far we have suggested that the streetblock functions as a socio-spatial arena, distinct from the larger neighborhood. This distinctiveness should be manifested in how people view sites adjacent to their home. That is, in their spatial cognitions people should discriminate between spaces closer to home, and those farther away but still within the neighborhood.

Several studies provide evidence in support of such a differentiation. In a Toronto study high schoolers reported being much more willing to intervene in a street crime or a burglary if it happened close to home rather than somewhere else in the neighborhood.[18] In an Atlanta study participants reported feeling less afraid and worried when in the two-block area right around home rather than elsewhere in the neighborhood.[19] In a Minneapolis-St. Paul study residents were asked about territorial cognitions with respect to the sidewalk in front of their house, the sidewalk elsewhere on the block, and a nearby small commercial center.[20] There were significant and progressive drops in feelings of responsibility, recognition of users, and control over intruders as the space in question was farther from the home. Clearly, then, residents view spaces closer to versus farther from home differently, and expect they would act differently in the different locations.

Elements of territorial functioning in outdoor residential locations

Before delineating the specific determinants and consequences of territorial functioning in outdoor residential locations near the home, we can outline the elements of territorial functioning involved. Although the same basic elements are involved here as are evident in other settings where centrality of person–place transactions is different, the specific manifestation of territorial functioning is somewhat different. *The three basic elements are marking behaviors, cognitions or attitudes, and actual behaviors.* These three different elements are interwoven and support one another. (For an example, see the fol-

---

[18] Gillis, A. R., & Hagan, J. (1983). Bystander apathy and the territorial imperative. *Sociological Inquiry, 53*, 449–460.

[19] Greenberg, S., Rohe, W., & Williams, J. (1981). *Safe and secure neighborhoods.* Research Triangle Park, NC: RTI. Final Report.

[20] McPherson, M., Silloway, G., & Frey, D. L. (1983). *Crime, fear and control in neighborhood commercial centers.* Draft Final Report. Grant 80-IJ-CX–0073. National Institute of Justice. Minneapolis: Minnesota Crime Prevention Center, p. 285.

lowing box.) In a particular locus, attitudes or cognitions, behaviors, and markers will be congruent.

An example of the systemlike nature of territorial functioning in outdoor residential locations near home

From 1978 through 1981 my colleagues and I were involved in a study of streetblock functioning.[21] We investigated 63 streetblocks in 12 different neighborhoods in Baltimore. About eight heads of households were interviewed on each block. The interview protocol included extensive questions about outside home territories (steps or yard in front, backyard), near-home territories (sidewalk right in front of the house, alley right behind the house), and off-block territories (nearby corner store used by the resident, nearby playground familiar to the resident). In addition to the interviews, fronts and backs of the houses were photographed and the resulting slides subsequently rated on several dimensions by independent raters. One dimension rated was the extent of high-demand gardening visible. (All photographs were taken in the summer, when gardening efforts could be most easily detected.) In our analysis we used block means or proportions; the block was the unit of analysis. The interconnectedness of territorial attitudes and behaviors was clearly demonstrated by the results of our causal analysis predicting perceived problems.

Evidence of gardening, in this example, reflects both the behavioral as well as physical aspects of territorial functioning. Since we focused on high-demand gardening, not just lawn trimming, considerable efforts on the part of residents were necessary to produce the resulting physical markers. We hypothesized that if people gardened more extensively, they would become better acquainted with persons in the immediately adjacent, near-home spaces (alley behind, sidewalk in front). Our expectations were vindicated.

The relevant portion of our results is shown below. The figures shown are (standardized) path coefficients and are statistically significant. Controlling for racial composition, physical layout of the block, and average length of residence, blocks where high-demand gardening was more extensive were those where respondents could better recognize who did and did not belong in near-home spaces. For every unit (standard deviation) increase in gardening, recognition increased a quarter of a standard unit.

---

[21] Taylor, R. B., Gottfredson, S. D., & Brower, S. (1981a). Informal social control in the urban residential environment. Unpublished final report. Baltimore, MD: Center for Metropolitan Planning and Research, Johns Hopkins University.

And each of these elements of territorial functioning, gardening and recognition, served to decrease the perceived level of problems on the block. They each made a unique contribution to the outcome.

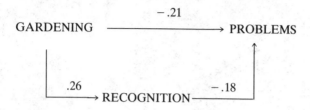

These results underscore the systemlike nature of territorial functioning, and the interconnection between behavioral, attitudinal, and physical components.

Markers

The concept of *markers* refers to a broad array of physical elements, which are in fact behavioral traces.[22] They are the observable consequences of behaviors such as maintenance, decoration, modification, and beautification. The markers may or may not be explicitly territorial in their "message." Explicitly territorial markers include "Keep Out" and "Beware of Dog" signs, locked gates, high fences, and so on. They signal a desire to regulate a boundary. Such markers carry *directive information*.[23]

Less explicitly territorial are signs of upkeep (e.g., swept sidewalks, scrubbed steps, trimmed lawns and bushes, well-painted houses) and beautification or embellishment (e.g., high-demand gardening such as flowers, ornaments such as witch balls, pink flamingos, pottery cats, donkey carts for flowers; see Figure 8.2). Seasonal decorations, at Christmas, Easter, or Halloween, are also relevant.[24]

Although less explicitly territorial markers do not convey a defensive "keep out" boundary-regulation message, they *do* convey information. How this information is decoded depends upon the specific perceiver,

[22] Zeisel, H. (1981). *Inquiry by design*. Monterey CA: Brooks/Cole.

[23] Appleyard, D. (1979b). The environment as a social symbol: Within a theory of environmental action and perception. *American Planning Association Journal, 45*, 143–153.

[24] Brown, B. B., & Werner, C. M. (1985). Social cohesiveness, territoriality, and holiday decorations: The influence of cul-de-sacs. *Environment and Behavior, 17*, 539–565.

Figure 8.2. A "marked" front yard. Can you find a swan? A frog? A pottery cat? Garden elves? A cart? Note that the yard is bounded with a symbolic barrier, as well. *Source*: Urbter Associates. Copyright 1987.

the context in which the message is sent, and other factors.[25] Nonetheless, nearby residents appear able to "interpret" reliably the messages "given off" by these markers.[26] What is symbolized by these messages depends in part upon the perspective. From the vantage point of the "sender," the markers may highlight themes of identity, power, or status. From the viewpoint of the "decoder," the themes of caring, vigilance, or how to behave appropriately may be picked up.[27]

Markers that are not explicitly territorial "carry a message" for both outsiders, persons who are strangers on a block, and other residents,

[25] Appleyard, D. (1973). Notes on urban perception and knowledge. In R. Downs & D. Stea (Eds.), *Image and environment*. Chicago: Aldine, pp. 109–114.

Appleyard, D. (1979c). Home. *Architectal Association Quarterly, 11* (No. 3), 4–20.

Rapoport (1982).

[26] Taylor, R. B., Brower, S., & Stough, R. (1976). User generated visual features as signs in the urban residential environment. In P. Suedfeld & J. A. Russel (Eds.), *The behavioral basis of design, Book 1*. Stroudsburg, PA: Dowden, Hutchinson & Ross.

Craik, K. H., & Appleyard, D. (1980). Streets of San Francisco: Brunswik's lens model applied to urban inference and assessment. *Journal of Social Issues, 36*, 72–85.

[27] Appleyard (1979b).

but the message may be different. The message decoded by coresidents, in the presence of extensive decoration and upkeep, may be: "He is a good neighbor who cares about where he lives, takes care of it, and can be called on if needed in a pinch."[28] Such signs contribute to the establishment of mutual trust and respect, and thereby facilitate the effective functioning of local social control. Outsiders may decode the message: "He is a vigilant resident who is always on the lookout to be sure that people don't mess up his property. You can't get away with anything around his place."

What are important, from the perspective of both coresidents and outsiders, are not only the signs evident at particular addresses. The overall distribution is also important. Is it extensive or shared across the streetblock as a whole? A street where 80% of the houses are well kept with trimmed lawns and shrubs gives a very different indication of resident attitudes to outsiders and coresidents, about the local involvement and caring of households, than does a street where only 5 percent of the addresses are similarly kept up. On the streetblock the relative prevalence of markers reveals qualities of the overall group and setting.

Behaviors

Relevant territorial behaviors include efforts to directly control access by, and activities of, others. Youth using the backyard as a shortcut may be chased off, or told just to be careful of the flowers while cutting through. Such efforts are clearly geared towards boundary control and/or internal regulation of the space in question. So too are efforts indicative of vigilance, such as surveillance behaviors.

Obviously as relevant are the behaviors required to produce markers explicitly geared towards boundary control. The building of fences, the planting of border shrubs with sharp thorns, and so on, fall into this category.

Also relevant but less clearly so are behaviors required to produce signs that qualify as markers, even though the markers may not be explicitly territorial. Painting, gardening, home improvement, planting, lawn trimming, and so on, qualify as territorial behaviors because they are required to produce markers. Such behaviors will increase the time the occupant actually spends in the exterior site in question. The actor need not be conscious that he or she is acting territorial while engaging in these activities.

---

[28] This assumes that the decoder does not have radically different tastes than the sender. If he did, the message decoded might be: "Boy, does he have bad taste!"

Cognitions

There are several dimensions to territorial cognitions relevant to outdoor residential locations near home. Territorial cognitions refer to people's perceptions of their relationship to a particular delimited location, or their perception of conditions in such a locus. Particular cognitions may be accompanied by affect; some may be accompanied by more affect than others. A perception of control may be accompanied by feelings of security or satisfaction, problems by frustration, social illegibility by concern, appropriation by attachment, and so on. Dimensions clearly relevant include the following:

1. *Issues of control versus problems.* People can perceive that they have more or less of a "say" about who enters a site, or what goes on there. They can perceive that there are more or fewer problems there such as littering, graffiti, drug dealing, loud noises at late hours, fighting, and so on. Perceived lack of control may be reflected not only in perception of problems but also in reported levels of concern.

2. *Issues of social legibility.* The extent to which a person can differentiate between who does and does not "belong" varies across different territories. This is, of course, contingent upon being able to recognize particular individuals in a location. Also related may be the extent to which, when the person is in the space in question, he or she is surrounded by familiar others.

3. *Issues of responsibility and caring.* A person may feel more or less responsible for events in a place, even if he is not legally or formally connected with the site in question. Usually we feel responsible for events in spaces we own or have been assigned, but our sense of obligation may extend further. Responsibility is often accompanied by caretaking behaviors. For example, I lived for several years on a block where a long-time resident, on a daily basis, would sweep the entire length of the alley, picking up glass, nails, bottles, and cans. His sense of proprietorship extended beyond his own property. Responsibility may also be accompanied by vigilance or surveillance behaviors.

4. *Issues of association.* An individual may spend more or less time in a site, or visit it more or less frequently, or view it as more or less familiar. Emerging from such association may be a sense of *appropriation*, a sense of caring and being psychically connected with the site.[29]

---

[29] Dovey, K. (1985). Home and homelessness. In I. Altman & C. Werner (Eds.), *Home environments*. New York: Plenum, pp. 33–64. See esp. pp. 47–48. The Latin root of appropriation is *appropriare*, "to make one's own."

Predictors of territorial functioning

In this section we consider empirical evidence linking our four clusters of predictors – cultural, physical, social, and "personality" – with territorial functioning in outdoor residential spaces near home. Again, as was the case with territorial functioning in interior residential settings, illustrative findings rather than extensive details on cultural linkages with territorial functioning are provided. For example, it is not possible to treat the topic of territorial markers, and how they vary and are decoded differently across cultures.

Cultural and subcultural factors

Cultural membership determines the spatial extent of the territorial region around the home site. Control and responsibility extend farther in some cultures than in others. This difference is well illustrated by a study on reactions to territorial contamination carried out in the United States and in Greece.[30] Experimenters placed bags of garbage in the front yards, on the sidewalk, and in the street, in middle-class neighborhoods in each country, then returned every three hours to see how soon the contamination was removed. When placed in the front yard, the garbage was removed equally promptly in both countries – about four to seven hours. But, when placed on the sidewalk right in front of the property, or in the street right next to the curb, it was removed more quickly in the United States (in about six hours, on average) than in Greece (average removal time there was about fifteen hours). These results suggest that territorial behaviors reflecting maintenance or up-keep, and probably perceptions of territorial control, extend farther from the home in the United States than in Greece.

Within cultures, there are also differences in extensiveness of territorial functioning in outdoor residential sites near home. Findings from a study of Slavic and non-Slavic households in a neighborhood in Kansas City underscore this point.[31] The authors found that in Slavic households sidewalk and house maintenance was higher, yard landscaping and attractiveness were higher, and plants were more extensive. The authors suggested that such signs of personalization communicated ethnic iden-

[30] Worchel, S., & Lollis, M. (1982). Reactions to territorial contamination as a function of culture. *Personality and Social Psychology Bulletin, 8*, 370–375.
[31] Greenbaum, P. E., & Greenbaum, S. D. (1981). Territorial personalization: Group identity and social interaction in a Slavic-American neighborhood. *Environment and Behavior, 13*, 574–589.

tity to coresidents, many of whom were members of the same ethnic group. Thus, the form and extensivenss of exterior displays and behaviors may vary across subcultural (ethnic) as well as cultural groupings.

Personality and related constructs

Vigilance

At the individual level, some households are more vigilant than others. In a field study by Julian Edney, residents responded to a visitor at the front door more quickly if they had "Keep Out" or "No Trespassing" signs posted.[32] Their heightened vigilance was expressed both through markers and behavior. Homeownership could not explain the level of vigilance observed.

Homeownership

An individual difference variable that can be loosely discussed under the concept of personality is homeowner versus renter status. One would expect that homeowners would have more extensively marked, better-kept properties, and report territorial cognitions reflective of more extensive or effective territorial functioning. And, indeed, this turns out to be the case. An analysis based on several hundred Baltimore households, and controlling for income and education levels, observed that homeowners:

Gardened more extensively, in front and in back;

Had housing units that were in better condition, and yards that were neater;

Reported experiencing fewer problems, greater social legibility, and more responsibility in near-home public spaces (e.g., sidewalk in front), immediately adjacent to the house site.[33]

Thus, on attitudes, markers, and behaviors, owners and renters exhibit different levels of territorial functioning.

Social class

In a pioneering study in the mid–1960's, Lee Rainwater examined attitudes towards home and neighborhood in lower- and lower-middle-

---

[32] Edney, J. J. (1972). Property, possession, and permanence. *Journal of Applied Social Psychology, 2*, 275–282.

[33] Taylor, Gottfredson, & Brower (1981a). Greenbaum & Greenbaum (1981) report comparable findings.

class households.[34] At lower social class levels residents experienced minimal levels of territorial control. They were concerned only with controlling what went on within their household. They felt they had no control over exterior events, and thus could not concern themselves with them. Residents who were closer to middle class in status reported a wider domain of concern, extending to the exterior property, the block, and the neighborhood. This finding was replicated in a Baltimore study.[35] Residents in middle-class as compared to lower-class neighborhoods reported stronger feelings of territorial responsibility in sites away from the home itself.

And, if we move to the upper region of the social class scale, territorial control may be very strong and may extend over an entire neighborhood of several hundred houses, as the accompanying box illustrates.

Social class and extent of territorial control: examples from the two ends of the scale

Residents at the very low end of the social class scale, because they live in neighborhoods where there is little stability and high levels of disorder, have a very restricted domain of territorial control. In a pilot interview for a study my colleagues and I were involved in, we spoke with a woman who lived in a part of town with a very high crime rate. She told us about several recent violent incidents that had occurred nearby, some of them taking place in the very hallway outside her apartment. But in a later part of the interview we asked her about problems experienced, and she insisted that there weren't any. But, the interviewer later discreetly inquired, how about all these goings-on you've told us about? She told us quite plainly that those problems were *out there*, and that she didn't bother with them. She just shut her door and minded her own business. Clearly her exercise of territorial control ended at the front door.

At the other end of the scale are high-income neighborhoods where residents have the means to exercise very strong territorial control over their entire neighborhood. Rolling Hills, on the Palos Verdes Peninsula not far from Los Angeles, is a good case in point.[36] It is a neighborhood

---

[34] Rainwater, L. (1966). Fear and house-as-haven in the lower class. *Journal of the American Institute of Planners, 32*, 23–31.

[35] Taylor, R. B., Gottfredson, S. D., & Brower, S. (1981b). Territorial cognitions and social climate in urban neighborhoods. *Basic and Applied Social Psychology, 2*, 289–303.

[36] Chapman, D. L. (October 28, 1984). Gated city: In Rolling Hills, prestige comes with the privacy and protection. *Torrance (CA) Daily Breeze*, p. A1.

of 662 homes and 2,049 residents and covers three square miles. It is walled, gated, and has round-the-clock security guards at each entrance. Residents have decals on their cars, and visitors have their car license numbers recorded. It is one of four "gated cities" in California, and is one of the highest-income communities in the state. Residents enjoy the neighborhood's relative privacy – low traffic levels, no door-to-door salespersons – and relative safety. Many residents leave their doors unlocked when at home. And, although they do not admit it, they probably enjoy the prestige, literally, the exclusiveness, that goes with such a location.

Clearly then, at higher social class levels, the domain of effective territorial control extends farther.

The linkage of social class and territorial extent is an analog to the dominance–dispersion linkage in interior residential settings. In the former, the relative position of the group in the larger metropolitan context, and in the latter the position of the individual in the small group, translate into a range of effective territorial functioning.

Appleyard has suggested that *degree of marking* or personalization varies with class.[37] At higher levels the extent, variety, and visibility of markers indicating personalization of the area around the home may decrease. Although I can think of a variety of impressionistic evidence in support of such a thesis, I am unaware of any solid supporting evidence.[38]

Urban versus suburban

In suburban neighborhoods, residents' sphere of effective territorial control is larger. In public spaces near the home, suburban residents report higher levels of control and social legibility.[39]

Although the differences between urban and suburban residents' territorial functioning may be clear-cut, pinpointing the key causal element in the residential context is not so simple. Length of residence is often

---

[37] Appleyard (1979b).

[38] Testing such a thesis would be problematic because the features of the house site proper vary also as a function of social class levels. At higher class levels yards are more extensive, houses are more differentiated, and so on. Such site features themselves may provide some degree of individuation, thus lessening the "need" for personalized markers.

[39] Taylor, R. B., & Stough, R. R. (1978). Territorial cognitions: Assessing Altman's typology. *Journal of Personality and Social Psychology, 36,* 418–423.

greater in suburban neighborhoods, residents are often more homogeneous on background factors such as income and education, and the actual physical design of the spaces in question is different. It is not known how much each (or any) of these factors contributes to the urban–suburban difference in territorial control.

In sum, several individual-level factors are associated with extent and strength of territorial functioning, most notably homeownership and social class. In the case of social class, however, the differences in territorial functioning are probably due more to the social composition and physical design of the residential context itself than to the individual householder. Likewise, it is also probably context that explains the more extensive territorial control and social legibility of suburban as compared to urban residents.

Physical design factors

Siting and land use

Land use arrangements can create "holes" in the fabric of resident-based territorial control in outdoor spaces near the home.

Institutional, commercial, or industrial land uses do not provide for continuous occupancy. Workers go home at night, and businesses close. Residents may perceive such vacated areas as "no-man's-lands."[40] In small commercial centers, for example, residents may feel unsafe at night and unsure of whom they might meet.[41] Thus they avoid such locations. Likewise for small, vest-pocket parks.[42]

Such fissures exist on an even smaller scale (see Figure 8.3). A vacant house where drug dealers gather, a vacant lot where abandoned cars might be pitched, and the sidewalk around a corner store after hours – all of these locations represent gaps in the residents' territorial control. Residents feel significantly less responsible for what goes on in such places, and also experience greater social illegibility, finding it harder to determine who does and does not belong in such sites.[43]

[40] Suttles, G. D. (1968). *The social order of the slum*. Chicago: University of Chicago Press.

[41] McPherson, M., Silloway, G., & Frey, D. L. (1983), p. 285.

[42] Brower, S. (1980). Territory in urban settings. In I. Altman, A. Rapoport, & J. Wohlwill (Eds.), *Human behavior and environment*. Vol. 4, *Environment and culture*. New York: Plenum.

[43] Taylor, Gottfredson, & Brower (1981b). In off-block territories such as the sidewalk in front of a nearby store, and a nearby playground, residents reported significantly lower levels ($p < .01$) of social recognition and responsibility than in near-home territories (sidewalk in front, alley behind).

Figure 8.3. Portion of a block where a row of houses has been razed. This area constitutes a "hole" in the fabric of residents' territorial control. Uncut grass, tall weeds, and litter indicate the site is not cared for. Note also the two vacant houses at right. On one, boards have been torn off a window, suggesting the house is frequented by "marginals." Person at *far left* with clipboard is collecting behavioral observation data. *Source*: Urbter Associates. Copyright 1987.

These slits in the fabric of territorial control constitute locations of convergence for those who are viewed by residents as "marginal" members of the local society – wayward youth, disreputable men, and others. Where these "marginal" persons gather is a reflection of the overarching texture of residents' influence. It "makes sense" for "marginal" individuals and groups to congregate where influence and surveillance are minimal: to drink on the playground, shoot craps in the alley behind some garages, and so on. In the territorial interstices they are less likely to be "hassled" by residents – as long as their behavior stays within some bounds. Since residents are less concerned about and able to regulate these locations, the "marginals" can gather in larger numbers and carry on more boisterously than they could elsewhere. They have greater freedom.

   In short, as a result partly of siting features, there are ongoing, micropolitical, low-level conflicts over use of space, with residents' territorial control being weaker in places that lack natural guardians,[44] and the "marginal" members of local society using such loci as points of convergence. (For further treatment of this issue, see Chapter 11.)

Volume of pedestrian and vehicular traffic

Higher levels of vehicular and pedestrian traffic reduce territorial functioning in outdoor spaces near the home. Having stores nearby that draw foot traffic results in residents' using their front yards less, and chatting less with each other in those spaces.[45] Higher levels of vehicular traffic likewise cause people to move indoors; thus they feel that their home includes a smaller fraction of the streetblock.[46] Traffic, vehicular or pedestrian, drives people into their houses, making them feel that less of the block is "theirs," and removing from their use an arena for informal socializing.

Appleyard's linking of street traffic and extent of territorial functioning may explain findings from a recent suburban Salt Lake City study investigating the impacts of *street form*.[47] Through streets and cul-de-sacs were compared. Territorial functioning was more evident on the latter. Halloween decorations were more extensive; residents felt more responsible for what happened on the block and spent more time there. Thus, on cul-de-sacs, markers and cognitions both reflected a more extensive territorial domain. Contacts with neighbors were also more frequent. These territorial and social differences probably emerged because on cul-de-sacs there was less vehicular and perhaps also pedestrian traffic.

[44] Cohen, L. E., & Felson, M. (1979). Social change and crime rate trends. *American Sociological Review, 44,* 588–688.

The solution, Robert Sommer has suggested, is to place occupants in these settings on a round-the-clock basis. Sommer, R. (1978). Developing proprietary attitudes towards the public environment. In *Crime prevention through environmental design.* Arlington, VA: Westinghouse National Issues Center/LEAA.

[45] Baum, A., Davis, G., & Aiello, J. R. (1978). Crowding and the neighborhood mediation of density. *Journal of Population, 1,* 266–279.

[46] Appleyard, D. (1979). *Livable streets: Protected neighborhoods.* Berkeley: University of California Press.

Appleyard, D., Gerson, M. S., & Lintell, M. (1976). *Livable urban streets: Managing traffic in residential neighborhoods.* Washington, DC: U.S. Department of Transportation.

Appleyard, D., & Lintell, M. (1972). The environmental quality of city streets: The residents' viewpoint. *Journal of the American Institute of Planners, 38,* 84–101.

[47] Brown, B. B., & Werner, C. M. (1985). Social cohesiveness, territoriality, and holiday decorations: The influence of cul-de-sacs. *Environment and Behavior, 17,* 539–565.

Boundaries

Physical boundaries separating the exterior home property from the adjacent public arena may support territorial functioning.[48] Conversely, if people feel more closely attached to a particular location, or engage in more activities there, or in activities that need protection from intruders, such as gardening, they may then construct barriers of one sort or another. The barriers may be substantive, such as fences, hedges, or gates, or they may be symbolic, as in a row of stones, a low railing, or a change in pavement height, texture, or materials.

This expectation appears realistic. For example, the analysis discussed in the second box in this chapter found such a linkage. On streetblocks where real and symbolic barriers were stronger and/or more extensive, high-demand gardening, carried on behind these boundaries, was more evident.[49]

The boundaries undoubtedly influence both those within and outside them. On the outside, they indicate an area where the resident is more vigilant and likely to respond to intrusions.[50] For those within, the boundaries may enhance behavioral freedom and perceived privacy, and perhaps attachment to the locus.

Summary

In sum, physical features have a multilevel influence on territorial functioning. As was the case in interior residential settings, these features serve to enhance or decrease the perceived utility of the space in question. In spatial terms, physical factors influence the contour of territorial functioning across spaces. Physical elements influence both cognitions concerning the space and behaviors there.

Social factors

Horizontal aspects of group structure were linked with territorial functioning, particularly microlevel strategies, in interior settings. Horizontal aspects of social structure also appear relevant outside. Their main im-

---

[48] Brower, S. (1965). The signs we learn to read. *Landscape, 15* (Autumn), 9–12.
   Brower, S. (1980).
   Newman, O. (1972). *Defensible space.* New York: Macmillan.

[49] The standardized regression coefficient was a significant .21, based on 63 streetblocks. Racial composition and average length of residence were used as control variables.

[50] Brower, S., Dockett, K., & Taylor, R. B. (1983). Residents' perceptions of site-level features. *Environment and Behavior, 15,* 419–437.

pact is a spatial expansion of the domain of territorial functioning, resulting in higher levels of concern and involvement farther from the home.

This social impact is evident in two studies examining public spaces immediately adjoining the housing site, such as sidewalks in front of the house, and alleys behind. The link with territorial cognitions was evident in a Baltimore study.[51] Respondents who felt that they were more similar to their neighbors on the streetblock reported feeling more in control (i.e., experiencing less trouble and fewer hassles) in these near-home spaces. Links have also been observed with behaviors such as maintenance and marking. In a Kansas City neighborhood, sidewalk maintenance was higher for households reporting more acquaintances in the neighborhood.[52] (All the sidewalks in the neighborhood were brick. Maintenance was evident if residents pulled the grass and weeds that quickly grew through the cracks.) In suburban areas outside Salt Lake City, houses where Halloween decorations were more evident reported knowing more of their neighbors.[53] Thus, all three aspects of territorial functioning are clearly linked, at the individual level, with the local social climate.[54]

Consequences of territorial functioning

In the same way that near-home spaces are physically interposed between the home and the larger neighborhood settings, territorial functioning there is sociodynamically interposed between the individual household and that local, on-block, society. And the linkage is bidirectional. Not only does territorial functioning "serve" or benefit the individual household, it also "serves" the immediate society; not only do social factors influence the territorial functioning of an individual household, but the characteristics of particular households influence the life of the street. This is indicated schematically in Figure 8.4.

This proposed linkage, however, suggests a paradox. At the same time that the territorial system distances or buffers the household from the local society, it also facilitates the joining and integration of that household with and into that society. Home and near-home territories

---

[51] Taylor, Gottfredson, & Brower (1981b).
[52] Greenbaum & Greenbaum (1981).
[53] Brown & Werner (1985).
[54] Group-level linkages have also been observed. For example, on streetblocks where respondents knew more people on the block by face or name, the group felt more responsible for what went on in near-home spaces.

Taylor, R. B., Gottfredson, S. D., & Brower, S. (1984). Block crime and fear. *Journal of Research in Crime and Delinquency, 21*, 303–331.

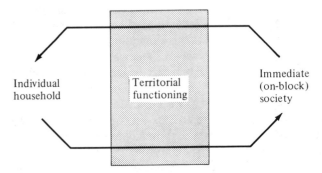

Figure 8.4. Territorial functioning in outdoor spaces near the home, like sidewalk in front of the house, simultaneously links the household to the immediately local, on-block society, and buffers the household from that society. *Source:* R. B. Taylor and S. Brower (1985), Home and near home territories. In I. Altman and C. Werner (Eds.), *Home environments*. New York: Plenum. Copyright 1985 by Plenum Publishing. Reprinted by permission.

help give each household "its own space" while at the same time providing an arena where "tentative social feelers"[55] can be put out or an individual can keep close watch on street life.[56]

But this paradox is resolved if one differentiates, in terms of functions, between those that serve the individual household, and those that serve the immediate local society. By discriminating between impacts on individuals or individual households, the immediate social group on the streetblock, and the behavior setting of the streetblock, we overcome the dichotomy between self-interest and public interest. The system can be both egocentric, buffering the individual household from local stressors, *and* public minded, assisting in the production of public goods such as local predictability.

In this section the consequences of territorial functioning are, as before, categorized as psychological, social psychological, and ecological. (Issues of disorder reduction are not examined here but are dealt with in Chapter 11.)

Psychological consequences

Stress reduction

Immediately adjacent public outdoor spaces constitute a zone over which the householder can have some degree of control in regulating

---

[55] Cooper, C. (1975).
[56] Jacobs, J. (1961). *The death and life of the great American city*. New York: Vintage.

the activities that occur there. Of course the extent to which such control can be exercised varies across different blocks and neighborhoods, and is dependent upon the specific predictors discussed earlier. By reducing noise, unwanted intrusions, and unregulated activity in these nearby outdoor spaces, the sense of security, orderliness, and the quality of life inside the house is enhanced. "Quiet" activities – reading, sleeping – are less likely to be disturbed. Attention need not be constantly diverted to what's going on outside. Worry is reduced. Very simply, life inside the home is better and less intruded upon. Thus, territoriality does for households what it does for individuals: enhance perceived and actual control[57] and privacy.[58] Using the contextual-stress model: As a result of territorial functioning, chances of future thwarting in the outdoor locations are reduced, and actual facilitation of interior and exterior behaviors such as gardening or maintenance is increased.[59]

Individuation

Territorial markers serve to differentiate (to *individuate*) the individual, or his or her household, from the surrounding context.[60] The exterior walls of the house, the front porch or yard, the backyard, and perhaps even the front fence or hedge allow for the expression of individual identity. Pink flamingos on the front lawn, or a large flag on July 4th, give coresidents and outsiders an indication of the characteristics of the individual household.

[57] Edney, J. J. (1976). Human territories: Comment on functional properties. *Environment and Behavior, 8,* 31–47.

[58] Altman (1975).

[59] Nonetheless, a one-to-one correspondence between particular territorial behaviors or markers, and stress-reducing consequences, should not be assumed. The threats or stressors to which one is responding (or anticipating) are more enduring, or prevalent, in some settings. Consequently, actions or markers may result in less stress-reduction in some settings than others. See:
Brower (1980).

[60] Appleyard, D. (1979c). Home. *Architectal Association Quarterly, 11* (no. 3), 4–20.
Appleyard (1979b).
Cooper, C. (1974). The house as symbol of self. In J. Lang (Ed.), *Designing for human behavior: Architecture and the behavioral sciences.* Stroudsbourg, PA: Dowden, Hutchinson & Ross.
Rapoport, A. (1977). *Human aspects of urban form.* New York: Pergamon.
Becker, F. D. (1977). *Housing messages.* Stroudsbourg, PA: Dowden, Hutchinson & Ross.
Tuan, Y. (1974). *Topophilia: A study of environmental perception, attitudes, and values.* Englewood Cliffs, NJ: Prentice-Hall.
Rapoport, A. (1982). *The meaning of the built environment.* Beverly Hills: Sage.

This expression is richly textured, including macro- as well as microscale features, and obvious as well as more subtle aspects of the exterior dwelling and the space around it. Personalization or individuation is facilitated by the fact that the available lexicon is virtually limitless: flowers, gardening, chairs, witch balls, figurines, metal grillwork or ornaments, and so on.

In revealing or communicating the individuality of the household two key themes can be discerned: how much the household cares for the block; and how sociable the household is, its preferred level of openness versus closedness vis-à-vis the local society. This can be indicated by the condition of the boundaries between the house site itself, and adjoining public space, like the sidewalk. When a resident puts up a fence its height is carefully noted by the neighbors, and corresponding inferences made about the resident. (The relevance of boundaries for local social dynamics is discussed at more length later in this chapter.) Boundary conditions, depending upon the surrounding context, can be reliably used as cues to the attitudes of the resident towards his or her neighbors.

Social psychological consequences

Two key social psychological consequences emerge from territorial functioning in outdoor locations near home: the group-level expression of solidarity and the reinforcement of group norms. These two effects are interrelated.

Group-level expression

In spaces outside and around the home, coresidents can express their involvement in and commitment to the immediate local society, i.e., the on-block grouping. They can express their shared goal of a well-maintained, varied, and visually rich but tasteful living environment. They can express their solidarity as a group, on block-level matters and other issues as well. On July 4th a majority of households may hang flags out. On holidays like Christmas a majority may decorate their exteriors. With such territorial behaviors and the resulting markers residents reassure one another and express their shared values and concerns. They underscore the existence of a *consonant*, rather than a *dissonant*, context.[61] They express group solidarity and cohesiveness. (See the following box and Figure 8.5.)

[61] Rosenberg, M. (1972). *Society and the adolescent self-image*. Princeton, NJ: Princeton University Press.

Territorial markers and behaviors as expressions of group solidarity: an example

Territorial behaviors and spaces in near-home public spaces can serve to express group identity and solidarity. The Afro-Am Clean Block Contest, sponsored by the *Afro-American* newspaper in Baltimore, is an excellent example of this. In the yearly contest, blocks compete for prizes and widescale publicity. To participate, a block must have an organization, with leaders. The organization goes to the offices of the paper, registers, and is given two "official" contest colors. Curbs, steps, and sometimes even windowsills will be painted with the colors. Often, planters and flowerboxes, also painted with the official colors, will be placed at regular intervals. If there are vacant lots to be cleaned and trash to be hauled away, that will be done too. The paper, during the course of the contest, features regular write-ups on the activities in various blocks. Tension mounts as the judging time draws near. Competition is keen, and the winners are announced with considerable fanfare. For a block to have been the winner of the Clean Block Contest is a label that conveys status and esteem, and greatly enhances the reputation of that block in the local community. In general terms, through the vehicle of this contest, and the accompanying beautification efforts and surrounding hoopla, each block is expressing and accentuating its own particular collective identity, just like the blocks in Columbus, Ohio, described by McKenzie in World War I, where the local flower and garden clubs held contests. Levels of pride and feelings of accomplishment and social solidarity are enhanced.

Clarification of group norms

Related to the expression of solidarity is increased salience of group norms. Territorial behaviors such as upkeep and beautification express these norms. Comments are made to neighbors when such norms are not upheld.[62] The behaviors, comments subsequent to nonadherence to the norm, and positive feedback when the norm is upheld, all direct attention to group norms, and increase compliance.

Cleaning as a group-enhancing ritual

A host of norms pertinent to cleanliness and attractive appearance probably operates on each block. These norms cover such matters as shov-

---

[62] Gans (1967) observed that the reminders are often made in a joking vein.

Figure 8.5. Signs of collective action. The "Etting Street Crew" worked hard to clean up and beautify their street, and left behind a reminder covering the doorway of a vacant house. The sign was done in red and white, which were the official block contest colors that year. Note also the flower logo on the chairs, planter, and window flowerbox at right. *Source*: Urbter Associates. Copyright 1987.

elling snow, trimming the lawn, disposing of leaves and garbage, washing the steps, and so on.

The comments here about cleanliness norms dovetail well with the anthropological analysis of "dirt" carried out by Mary Douglas.[63] Three points are pertinent.

First, Douglas suggests that every society makes distinctions between what is clean and what is unclean, what is respectable and what is abominable. Uncleanness is defined by particular cultures and subcultures. "If uncleanness is matter out of place, we must approach it through order. Uncleanness or dirt is that which must not be included if a pattern is to be maintained."[64] In other words, rituals of cleaning and beautification serve a key maintenance function for the block social group.

---

[63] Douglas, M. (1966). *Purity and danger: An analysis of concepts of pollution and taboo.* London: Routledge & Kegan Paul.

[64] Douglas (1966), p. 40.

Through these activities uncleanness and total anonymity are exorcised. These evils, however, are recurrent, and rituals must be regularly reenacted to maintain the setting. Residents cooperate to act against these pollutants.

Second, Douglas has suggested that such rituals serve as framing or focusing techniques.[65] They draw attention to the issue at hand, delineating it as a matter worthy of attention. Maintenance, upkeep, and beautification efforts focus coresidents and outsiders on the issue of cleanliness versus pollution.

And, third, Douglas suggests that there is a close linkage between pollution and morals.[66] Engagement in ritual activities to exorcise dirt and other forms of pollution is a cue to "good" persons. Everyone who is a good citizen will engage in such rituals. Widespread participation provides mutual reassurances about how much everyone cares about where they live, and what "good people" they are.

Douglas' analysis provides a wider understanding of how territorial behaviors in this zone can further buttress and enhance feelings of solidarity, or at least minimal trust, among residents on a block. Her insights convey a more universalistic perspective on the relevance of territorial activities such as beautification, upkeep, and maintenance, close to home. They suggest that these activities have ritualistic overtones, serving social functions comparable to those served by formal rituals, or customs, in other societies.

Ecological consequences

Territorial functioning in outdoor locations near home maintains the behavior setting of the streetblock. It contributes in several different ways.

Vetoing mechanisms

Territorial behaviors are used to ask people to leave particular synomorphs within the behavior setting, as when children are told to stay out of the yard. And, in the case of corner gangs, territorial behaviors may even be used to keep people off the streetblock altogether.

Deviation countering

Countless forms of territorial behaviors remind coresidents or outsiders of the setting program, and encourage adherence to it. The notification

---

[65] Ibid., p. 63.
[66] Ibid., p. 138.

may be subtle, as when a neighbor leaves out a trash can for youths who gather nightly and drink beer on a corner near his yard, and perhaps even humorous, as when neighbors make comments about "elephant grass." Or they may be harsher, and perhaps more direct, as when a resident threatens to call the police unless a neighbor moves her disassembled car from the street in front *immediately*. But, regardless of the form or content, the impact is to "remind" people about the setting program, to make salient the behaviors that are appropriate there.

Markers as social learning–based cues

Territorial markers act as physical reminders of the appropriate behavior in the setting.[67] Through past learning experience we have learned to associate physical elements with residents who care and are vigilant. Some individuals have "learned" these associations "better" than others, and the actual cues used vary depending upon subcultural context and class level. So, on blocks where the grass is trimmed and edged, and the sidewalk well swept, we may be less likely to throw litter. Physical elements in the setting, such as territorial markers, suggest to us which behaviors are appropriate for the setting.

Support for the setting program

To state the preceding points more generally: Territorial behaviors and markers serve to maintain the standing pattern of behavior, or setting program, in streetblock behavior settings. By directive and nondirective channels individuals receive information about what behaviors are appropriate in what locations.

Summary

Spaces outside and adjacent to the residence are finely differentiated. The "neighborhood" is not psychologically uniform. Neither is the streetblock itself. Territorial functioning in outdoor spaces near the home reflects this differentiation. Territorial behaviors, markers, and cognitions are highly location specific.

Territorial functioning itself is a complex product of physical, social, cultural, and class-related conditions in the residential context. All of these factors have clear influences on the spatial extensiveness of ter-

---

[67] Wicker (1979), *An introduction to ecological psychology*. Monterey, CA: Brooks/Cole, Chapter 4.

ritorial functioning, or the gradient of resident influence as one moves away from the dwelling unit.

Territorial functioning links the household members to the immediate local society and, at the same time, reduces the likelihood of exterior stressors negatively influencing interior household functioning.

Small groupings of residents on streetblocks, or at the subblock level, generate social forces that result in the establishment of norms. Adherence to or deviation from these norms, as evident in territorial behavior and marking, allows group members to gauge one another's commitment to locale and potential helpfulness in time of need. They also express group solidarity. Thus, in exterior residential settings, as in interior residential locations, territorial functioning emerges from and shapes social dynamics.

From an ecological psychological perspective, these norms are part and parcel of the standing pattern of behavior or setting program and, in addition, provide physical and behavioral cues to outsiders about how to behave appropriately there.

9
REGULAR USE SETTINGS

We used to go to a bar off Grant Street. Gays used to hang out there.
Over several months my wife started getting more approaches, and I
fewer, when we visited there. It changed over to a lesbian bar.
– former San Franciscan

When your desk, shelves, and wall space are covered with mementoes,
photographs, trophies, humorous mottoes, and other decorative effects,
you are probably not beautifying the office; rather, you may be giving it
a jumbled, untidy look.... The proper atmosphere for a business office
is one of neatness and efficiency, not hominess.
– Business Etiquette Handbook[1]

Proceeding down the centrality continuum brings us to regular use settings. These are places frequented on a more or less regular basis by an individual or group, where the individual or group plays some role in maintaining the setting, and/or encounters known others. Territorial functioning in those settings is the focus of this chapter. The settings included in this portion of the centrality continuum are diverse, and more geographically dispersed than the interior residential settings and outdoor spaces near home examined in the previous two chapters. Nonetheless, commonalities across these locations in terms of territorial functioning are evident. It is the relative position of these settings on the centrality continuum that helps explain similarities in territorial functioning in the settings.

The nature of regular use settings is examined and the characteristics of territorial functioning in those locations are outlined. Following the same practice used in the preceding two chapters, evidence of personal, social, physical, and "cultural" predictors of territorial functioning in these settings is presented. The types of places covered include work settings of different types. Arenas in which athletic contests are held are, however, also included. Then, psychological, social psychological, and ecological consequences are noted. Attention is given to the role

---

[1] *Business Etiquette Handbook* (1965). West Nyack, NY: Parker. Quoted in Sundstrom, E. (1986). *Work places: The psychology of the physical environment in offices and factories.* Cambridge: Cambridge University Press, p. 221.

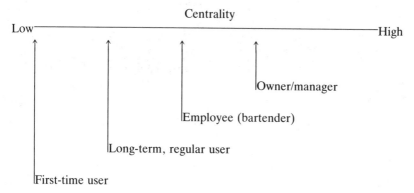

Figure 9.1. Centrality of a regularly used place as a function of setting role: the neighborhood bar.

of territorial functioning in organizational life. In the concluding section, similarities with territorial functioning in interior residential settings are noted.

Centrality and regular use settings

Centrality is higher for locations whose loss is more stressful or more disruptive to the individual or group. The loss of such locations is more keenly felt. Centrality, albeit intimately linked with setting characteristics, is not a characteristic of settings per se. It is a characteristic of the *transactions between the individual or group and the setting*. It is a *person–place* or *group–place* characteristic.

Consequently, the same location may have a very different centrality value for the different persons or groups who use it. Let's take a neighborhood bar and consider four different types of persons we might find in the setting; the owner/manager, a bartender, a regular customer, and a first-time customer (see Figure 9.1). The centrality will vary for the different individuals. They have different degrees of association with the site. In the total lifespace or psychogeography of each, that setting is differentially salient. The variation in centrality for the various users is greater in the case of regular use settings than it is in the cases of interior and exterior residential settings.

Consequently, some of the settings discussed here will also be discussed in Chapter 10, under the heading of temporary territories. Thus, territorial functioning of a first-time or infrequent user in a neighborhood bar will be discussed in Chapter 10, while territorial functioning of regular users, and those playing maintenance roles in a neighborhood bar, will be discussed in this chapter.

In the regular use setting there is an ongoing, face-to-face group structure and a familiarity based largely upon the *particular* location and, to a lesser extent, on extrapolations from other comparable behavior settings.[2]

Elements of territorial functioning in regular use settings

The elements of territorial functioning in regular use locations are similar in many respects to the elements discussed in interior residential settings, and adjoining outdoor locations. *Relevant cognitions* include concerns of privacy, controllability and security, social legibility, responsibility, and that the location does or does not adequately express the position and individuality of the occupant. *Relevant behaviors* include those geared towards allowing entry versus excluding others, manipulating the environment or one's position so as to increase or decrease visual or auditory access to others, cuing others about appropriate behavior in the setting, and embellishing or enhancing the setting. These latter behaviors result in *markers* that signal relative status or power, or individuate the person or subgroup in the setting.

Maintenance and upkeep behaviors are not included as territorial behaviors in regular use settings because they are often allocated to specific others, such as janitors or maintenance personnel.

Predictors of territorial functioning

Again, we will use the now-familiar tactic of examining each of our four clusters in turn and will identify specific determinants of territorial functioning.

Personality factors

People arrange, configure, and mark their regular use territories differently. These differences are expressive but also have functional consequences, such as increased congruence between the setting and the behaviors performed by the individual, which are pertinent to his or her role there.

---

[2] One also brings to a particular setting a host of expectations based upon the type of behavior setting (Wicker [1979], *An introduction to ecological psychology*. Monterey, CA: Brooks/Cole, p. 4). But, it is not that knowledge we are addressing here.

Faculty offices

A small number of studies of faculty offices suggest that arrangements in these regular use territories express the individual personality of the occupant, have functional benefits, and also shape the social perceptions of the occupant. The focus of these studies has been on who has "open" versus "closed" office arrangements. *Open* arrangements are those where the desk is pushed against the wall, and visitors can sit in a chair at the side of the desk. Work on seating arrangements has suggested that such "kitty-corner" seating arrangements are perceived as the warmest, friendliest, and potentially most intimate.[3] *Closed* arrangements are those where the officeholder sits behind the desk, with the visitor seated opposite; the visitor is confronted or blocked by the desk.

Faculty who have open interior office arrangements are

Of lower status, as indicated by being younger and of junior rank, and are more highly rated by students;[4]
Perceived as friendlier and more extroverted by visitors;[5]
Likely to be higher on the personality variables of internal control and extroversion;[6] and
more likely to have a less traditional orientation to education.[7]

In short, results indicate that faculty favoring an open arrangement appear more self-confident, sociable, and operate more effectively in, or are more committed to, their organizational milieu.

These findings can be recast into a more explicitly territorial framework. Some individuals are less concerned than others about controlling access once visitors are actually inside their territory.[8] This more relaxed disposition is indicated by the open arrangement of the office interior. Access here means visual and nonverbal access, once the two persons, officeholder and visitor, are together. These less concerned individuals,

[3] Sundstrom, E. (1986), pp. 274–280.

[4] Zweigenhaft, R. (1976). Personal space in the faculty office: Desk placement and student-faculty interaction. *Journal of Applied Psychology, 61*, 529–532.

[5] Morrow, P. C., & McElroy, J. C. (1981). Interior office design and visitor response: A constructive replication. *Journal of Applied Psychology, 66*, 646–650.

[6] McElroy, J. C., Morrow, P. C., & Ackerman, R. J. (1983). Personality and interior office design: Exploring the accuracy of visitor attributions. *Journal of Applied Psychology, 68*, 541–544.

[7] Hensley, W. E. (1982). Professor proxemics: Personality and job demands as factors of faculty office arrangements. *Environment and Behavior, 14*, 581–591.

[8] An interesting question is how does interior access control relate to access control at the boundary of the territory. Do those faculty with more open interior arrangements also leave their doors open more frequently?

with more open offices, are more comfortable with others and more effective working with others in the roles prescribed by the organization. Consequently, they feel less threatened and adopt the open interior arrangement.

But there may be limitations to linkages between office arrangements, interpersonal effectiveness, and personality. These limits are twofold. First, the relative salience of the open–closed dialectic, as reflected in desk and chair positioning, can be "swamped" or overwhelmed by expressions of individuality. When offices are highly personalized (macramé hangings, fish tanks, and posters), whether the desk–chair arrangement is open or closed appears to have little impact on visitors.[9] Highly individualized offices make visitors feel more welcome, comfortable, and positive towards the occupant than do open desk–chair arrangements. Second, job requirements may mediate between the personality and attitudes of the officeholder, and the office desk–chair arrangement.[10] A faculty member with traditional attitudes towards education, who would favor a closed interior arrangement, is more likely actually to display an open office arrangement as the number of his or her advisees increases. Since the mechanics of advising – looking at transcripts, signing forms, and so on – are more convenient from a conversational or "kitty-corner" arrangement, faculty confronted with such job demands appear to modify desk–chair placement accordingly, even if it goes against their grain.

In sum, faculty adopt interior office arrangements that maximize person–environment congruence, and/or express the personality of the officeholder. Both the degree of personalization, as well as the open versus closed nature of the arrangement, influence the social perception of the officeholder, although the former appears more influential.

Business settings and personalization

Personalization of office work spaces – modifications, embellishments, decorations – is extensive. Evidence to date suggests that about three-quarters of employees personalize their office space to some extent.[11]

Nonetheless, in business settings there are often explicit limits on the degree of personalization by employees.[12] The assumption, unsupported so far, is that the less personalized setting will be more businesslike and

---

[9] Campbell, D. E. (1979). Interior office design and visitor response. *Journal of Applied Psychology*, *64*, 648–653.

[10] Hensley (1982).

[11] Sundstrom (1986), p. 220.

[12] Ibid.

efficient.[13] In fact, limits on personalization of office space may be associated with lower levels of job satisfaction, and less commitment to the organization.[14]

In sum, different people configure work spaces differently. Although the degree of openness and personalization is undoubtedly linked to individual differences, it is also a reflection of rules governing the setting, and links between the individual and the setting.

Social determinants

Relative position and status in work spaces

Undoubtedly the most important determinant of territorial functioning in work settings is the relative status, power, and prestige of the individual or group within the organization. In many organizations, the amount of physical supports one may have for effective territorial functioning – number of walls, presence of a door, size of office, degree of personalization permitted – is explicitly tied to rank within the organization.[15] (See the following box.)

The linkage between status and supports for effective territorial functioning

Eric Sundstrom, in *Work places*, provides several examples of how organizations rigidly link physical features of the workplace with relative status within the organization.

"One of the most widely recognized (and emotionally loaded) perquisites of rank is the private office, which apparently symbolizes inaccessibility. Physical enclosure seems to correspond closely with rank, even in open-plan offices. At Provincial Property & Casualty Company, for instance, an employee with the job of manager is enclosed on two sides by 72 inch panels. An associate director has three panels; a director has four. Only the vice presidents have walled offices with doors."[16]

"At the offices of CBS in New York City, [i]f the individual's rank is high enough, he or she may have a wood-veneered desk top instead of formica, and perhaps a potted plant."[17]

---

[13] Ibid., p. 221.
[14] Ibid., pp. 222–223.
[15] Ibid., pp. 240–248.
[16] Ibid., pp. 241–242.
[17] Ibid., pp. 234–235.

"In the Canadian Ministry, the deputy minister receives a minimum of seven windows, assistant deputy ministers get six, directors have four, and the luckier of the less senior officers make do with a three window bay."[18]

Empirical investigations support the connections suggested by these examples. An investigation of offices of high-status (supervisory) and low-status (nonsupervisory) personnel in a range of organizations found that personnel status correlated quite well with office features. High-status personnel had:

Better access control, as reflected in a more secure boundary (i.e., door instead of opening), lower levels of visual exposure, and a better ability to screen visitors;
More space;
More furnishings; and
More room where personal decorations or items could be displayed.[19]

What these examples and the preceding study demonstrate is an allocation of physical characteristics that make boundary regulation and personalization more or less difficult, and functioning in the space more or less comfortable, based on relative social position. Or, to put the point graphically:

Relative social position (power)	→	Physical amenities: location inaccessibility personalization	→	"Strength" of territorial functioning

Physical parameters tied to relative position are subjectively important for those holding them because they *support their perceived status within the organization*. They function as *status supports*. The more of these physical amenities available to a person, the more he or she feels that the physical surrounds of the workplace are an accurate reflection of his or her status within the organization.[20]

In addition to influencing the physical characteristics of the office space itself, relative status also influences the positioning of adjoining spaces,

[18] Ibid., p. 235.
[19] Konar, E., Sundstrom, E., Brady, C., Mandel, D., & Rice, R. W. (1982). Status demarcation in the office. *Environment and Behavior, 14*, 561–580.
[20] Ibid.

which may further insulate the occupant. Once a person reaches a certain level within an organization, he or she is usually allocated a personal secretary or administrative assistant. The office of this person is, for maximum effectiveness, interposed between the person in question and the rest of the organization. Thus there is a *chambering effect* such that those wishing to gain access must traverse progressively more private spaces in order to reach the officeholder in question. Such arrangements further buffer the officeholder, reducing outside noise and unwanted intrusions.

An important question, of course, is whether the differential distribution of physical parameters makes territorial functioning more effective. We will turn to this issue shortly.

Relative status or power within the organization also influences the distribution of human resources pertinent to territorial functioning, such as secretaries or administrative assistants. And, when the officeholder desires privacy, these personnel can be used to maintain territorial boundaries – to screen or hold incoming calls and/or visitors, allowing the officeholder to seclude him- or herself, or to hold confidential conversations with others.[21]

In sum, relative status or power results in the differential distribution of physical and nonphysical attributes allowing more effective territorial functioning. The physical parameters linked to status, and most pertinent to territorial functioning are location, inaccessibility, and scope of personalization permitted.[22]

Audience effects

In a very different type of regular use setting – the sports arena – dynamics between the home audience and the home team can be helpful or harmful. They can result in either a *home court advantage* or a *home court disadvantage*. The advantage turns to a disadvantage if expectations about the home team's performance are high. Then, the home court advantage can "backfire."

An analysis of athletic contests by Schwartz and Barsky supports the concept of a home court advantage.[23] They made an extensive analysis of wins and losses and found that teams were more likely to win at home than on the road (see Table 9.1). But the magnitude of the home ad-

---

[21] Justa, C. F., & Golan, M. B. (1977). Office design: Is privacy still a problem? *Journal of Architectural Research, 6*, 5–12.

[22] Sundstrom (1986), p. 241.

[23] Schwartz, B., & Barsky, S. F. (1977). The home advantage. *Social Forces, 53*, 641–661.

Table 9.1. *Home advantage by sport*

Sport	Home wins (%)
Professional baseball (AL, NL)	53
Professional football (NFL)	55
College football	59
Hockey (NHL)	64
"Big five" basketball	82

Note: Data are for the year 1971. Ties are excluded. The "Big five" basketball teams are LaSalle, University of Pennsylvania, St. Joseph's, Temple, and Villanova.
Source: Barry Schwartz and Stephen Barsky, "The home advantage." *Social Forces, 55* (March 1977). Copyright © 1977 the University of North Carolina Press. Adapted with the permission of the University of North Carolina Press and Barry Schwartz.

vantage appeared to vary as a function of type of sport, being greater for basketball and hockey than for other sports. And the advantage seemed to be stronger the greater the discrepancy in skill level; the more the quality of the home team exceeded that of the visiting team, the greater the home advantage. The authors concluded that the home advantage could contribute more to performance than team quality itself.

It is one thing to establish that a home advantage exists, and quite another to explain it. The authors consider several explanations, such as fatigue of visiting team and better knowledge of playing area by home team, and reject them after considering relevant data. *They conclude that it is basically an audience-related effect.* Audience support results in the home team players being more physiologically aroused, leading to better performance. And, the more supportive audience cues the home team players that potential reward or reinforcement will be forthcoming should they perform well, and so they do. The authors further suggest that audience support and team performance are both expressions of "the integrity, vitality, and self-consciousness of the home community."[24]

The home advantage, however, may turn to a disadvantage when the stakes are *very high*. Baumeister and Steinhilber have suggested that if one individual or group is before a supportive audience, and self-presentational concerns are salient – if the person or group performs well

[24] Ibid., p. 658.

it counts as a major accomplishment, and a significant enhancement of image – then, in such a situation, self-attention may take attention away from environmental cues, and/or interfere with well-learned skills.[25] Testing their hypothesis by examining the outcome of fifty years of World Series data, they found that more home teams won the first games, and lost the last games, than vice versa. The home advantage in early games became a home *disadvantage* in later games. A consideration of fielding errors suggested that the home team, when on the verge of winning, would "choke." Although visiting teams made more errors in the first games, home teams made more errors in the last game.

So, there is evidence of a home advantage in athletic contests, and it seems bound up with audience–team dynamics. But when the stakes are high, and a win by the home team portends a major change in their status, the advantage can turn against them. When it comes down to the big game, the team may be better off without its fans.

Physical factors

Extent of work space enclosure

Perhaps the most important physical support for effective territorial functioning is the degree to which an individual or subgroup is physically bounded and insulated. As degree of enclosure increases, probabilities of intrusions from outside decrease, and the occupant is allowed more behavioral freedom. One's behavior is less scrutinized. The impact of physical enclosure on territorial functioning in office spaces is well documented. Eric Sundstrom and his colleagues observed a monotonic relationship between the number of partitions or walls surrounding a work space, and the rated privacy of the work space.[26] Such feelings of increased privacy are functionally important, being associated with greater satisfaction with the work space.[27] The more enclosed an office worker is, apparently, the happier he or she is with the work space.

[25] Baumeister, R. F., & Steinhilber, A. (1984). Paradoxical effects of supportive audiences on performance under pressure: The home field disadvantage in sports championships. *Journal of Personality and Social Psychology, 47*, 85–93.

[26] Sundstrom, E., Town, J., Brown, D., Forman, A., & McGee, C. (1982). Physical enclosure, type of job, and privacy in the office. *Environment and Behavior, 14*, 543–559.

Sundstrom, E., Burt, R. E., & Kamp, D. (1980). Privacy at work: Architectural correlates of job satisfaction and job performance. *Academy of Management Journal, 23*, 101–117.

[27] Ferguson, G. (1983). Employee satisfaction with the office environment: Evaluation of

The dynamics underlying the enclosure/privacy satisfaction link, I would suggest, center on territorial behaviors and territorial marking. The more enclosed the space, the easier it is to regulate who enters. One's territory itself is more clearly defined. And, more walls provide more surfaces to be personalized with markers. As a result, satisfaction, a psychological outcome, is enhanced.

Open offices

Given the enhancement of territorial functioning offered by physical enclosure in an office setting, it is no surprise that those working in open offices – where different work locations are *not* separated by walls and doors – find the experience less satisfying than working in a "closed" office setting. Over the last 30 years or so, there has been a considerable movement towards doing away with the walls and doors of the conventional office and instituting a more "open" office plan.[28] Originally, it was hoped that an open office plan would result in "warmer" social relations in the office, and a "cozier" or more familylike atmosphere.[29]

From a territorial perspective one might expect that an open office arrangement would be disadvantageous. Recall from Chapter 7 that people defined territories at the level of a room, or of a specific piece of furniture, and the conclusion that a territory, to be perceived and to function effectively as a territory, had to be physically bounded. The same holds true in an office.[30] There, to go from a closed to an open arrangement is to take away the physical props that are necessary for a person to be able to define, and others to perceive, a territory. As the door and the walls disappear, so too does the possibility for easy control of access. One no longer has an office of one's own; one is left with only a clear claim to a desk and chair.

Consequently, it is no surprise that workers moving from a closed to an open office plan report less psychological privacy, and less satisfaction with the work site. One study by Eric Sundstrom and his colleagues

a causal model. In D. Amedeo, J. Griffin, & J. Potter (Eds.), *EDRA 1983: Proceedings of the Fourteenth International Conference of the Environmental Design Research Association*. Washington, DC: Environmental Design Research Association, pp. 120–128.

[28] Sundstrom (1986), Chapters 13 & 14.

See also Wineman, J. D. (1982). The office environment as a source of stress. In G. W. Evans (Ed.), *Environmental stress*. Cambridge: Cambridge University Press, pp. 256–285.

[29] Oldham, G. R., & Brass, D. J. (1979). Employee reactions to an open office plan: A naturally occurring quasi-experiment. *Administrative Science Quarterly, 24*, 267–284.

[30] Goodrich, R. (1982). Seven office evaluations. *Environment and Behavior, 14*, 353–378; see p. 365.

compared "before" questionnaire responses, when the workers were in a closed office arrangement, with "after" responses, gathered after the workers had been in the new open arrangement a few weeks.[31] Results revealed decrements in acoustical privacy, satisfaction with privacy, and ability to hold confidential conversations.[32] People were more visually exposed, and a loss of access control was accompanied by increased "leakage" of visual and auditory information.

The open office plan was more bothersome for some than others. Higher-level employees showed the largest decrease in satisfaction with privacy.[33] The decrease in satisfaction on their part could have been because the feature that they "lost" in the open office – the ability to hold confidential talks – was more central to their job role. Or, alternatively, they may have changed the most because the shift they experienced in going from a closed to a open arrangement was more dramatic than that experienced by lower-level workers. Secretaries, for example, were already for the most part working in an "open" work site before the move. Higher-status employees then, relative to employees of lesser station, may have had their cognitive expectations about what they "deserved" in terms of an office space more radically disconfirmed.[34] For them, the physical change resulted in the more substantial loss of *status support*. In short, the impact of the *physical* characteristics of the work space on territorial functioning is conditioned by the *social role* of the individual in the setting.[35]

---

[31] Sundstrom, E., Herbert, R. K., & Brown, D. W. (1982). Privacy and communication in an open-plan office: A case study. *Environment and Behavior, 14*, 379–392.

[32] Acoustical privacy was measured using on-site test equipment. As acoustical privacy decreased, conversations were more likely to be heard in adjoining workspaces.

[33] Sundstrom, Herbert, & Brown (1982).

[34] Thibaut, J., & Kelley, H. H. (1959). *The social psychology of groups*. New York: Wiley. The higher status personnel had a higher comparison level (CL) against which they compared the new office arrangement.

[35] One might argue, however, that the open office plan could still be justified because it can result in better communication among co-workers. Unfortunately, even this benefit has not materialized. The open office plan may result in *decreased* interpersonal satisfaction (Oldham & Brass [1979]). Persons in more accessible, open office arrangements do not report greater levels of contact with co-workers, although they do report greater levels of contact with supervisors (Sundstrom et al. [1980]). Apparently, then, the more open, more accessible office arrangements, resulting in higher visual exposure of workers, allows supervisors to keep better tabs on them. Because of this, or perhaps as a simple strategy for coping with possible information overload, workers do not interact more with co-workers, even though they are more accessible. The open office has by no means resulted in an arrangement that allows for cozy chatting, like a family gathered around a hearth.

"Open" classrooms

Curiously, there has been a move towards *"open space" classrooms* as well as "open" offices in the last two decades. Classrooms have more of an open space design when desks are not arranged in traditional rows, and boundaries between different activity areas are absent. The results of the research on open space classrooms, focusing mostly on consequences for achievement, are mixed and beset with a variety of conceptual and methodological limitations.[36] There have been no studies directly examining territorial functioning in these open space classrooms.

Nonetheless, indirect evidence suggests that territorial functioning of students may be less efficient in open classrooms. Interruptions of classroom activities appear more frequent the more open the design, suggesting that the closed design provides physical cues to pupils and others delineating in- and out-of-class spaces. These physical referents may help remind them what behaviors are appropriate where.[37] Lacking boundaries, it is more difficult to "create" territories, and exclude others, at the classroom level, and at the level of the individual pupil.

In the same way that closed classroom designs create boundaries and facilitate access control, boundaries at the level of the individual student may likewise enhance territorial functioning and permit more on-task behavior in the classroom. Being able to create a demarcated territory is rewarding at least, and can be used as a reinforcer of appropriate behavior. In one behavior modification study pupils were allowed to decorate their desks, put up signs, and mark off the area around their desk with tape. The privilege was earned by staying in one's seat more often and was effective in reducing out-of-seat behavior.[38]

"Cultural" and "subcultural" factors

Work settings

Different organizations have different operational styles, and are perceived differently by workers. Some organizations are seen as having

[36] Ahrentzen, S., Jue, G. M., Skorpanich, M. A., & Evans, G. W. (1982). School environments and stress. In G. W. Evans (Ed.), *Environmental stress*. Cambridge: Cambridge University Press, pp. 224–255.

Weinstein, C. (1979). The physical environment of the school: A review of the research. *Review of Educational Research, 72*, 577–610.

[37] Evans, G. W., & Lovell, B. (1979). Design modification in an open-plan school. *Journal of Educational Psychology, 71*, 41–49.

[38] Nay, W. R., Schulman, J. A., Bailey, K. G., & Huntsing, G. M. (1976). Territory and classroom management: Exploratory case study. *Behavior Therapy, 7*, 240–246.

more "open" management styles, whereas others are perceived as stratified and autocratic, for example. One might expect that the different styles or "cultures" in different organizational contexts would be reflected in differences in territorial functioning. Unfortunately, there is no research on such a connection.[39]

Nonetheless, what connections *might* exist between territorial functioning and organizational climate? Some possibilities are as follows.

1. Perceived "openness" of the organizational climate is linked with territorial functioning. For a particular person, the extent to which he or she is buffered from co-workers behaviorally, physically, or locationally will be reflected in his or her perceptions of a "closed" organizational climate. That is, as co-workers have more inaccessible (i.e., enclosed) work locations, use screening devices (secretaries, answering machines) more extensively, or are inconveniently located (i.e., distant) vis-à-vis one another, the worker in question will experience the setting as more cold, distant, and isolating.

2. In more rigidly stratified organizations territorial functioning is more multilayered or redundant in character. Control over access by others is likely to involve several mechanisms simultaneously (chambering, physical barriers, screening secretaries, etc.) rather than just one or two.

Special "subcultural" groups "taking over" settings

Moving away from work settings, we can consider a variety of public settings that particular user groups convert into regular use settings. In such instances the subgroup taking over makes distinctions between themselves and outsiders, and may communicate their claim to the setting through a variety of mechanisms.

An example of such dynamics is found in Cavan's analysis of how a bar in San Francisco became a predominantly gay bar.[40] For example, newcomers were sized up quickly as either fellow homosexuals, non-homosexuals who might be interested in homosexuals, or "straights." Those in the latter group, by the demeanor of the waiters, and loud comments about them or those accompanying them, were made to feel uncomfortable. Such instances of a supposedly public place being "taken over" or dominated by one user group are not uncommon. The public arena is converted, sometimes with and sometimes without the consent

---

[39] Sundstrom (1976), pp. 354–355.

[40] Cavan, S. (1963). Interaction in home territories. *Berkeley Journal of Sociology, 8,* 17–32.

of the management, into a semiprivate space where only certain types of individuals, or members of certain groups, are made to feel at ease.[41]

Parallel dynamics probably come into play when, for example, bikers take over a beach and exclude surfers, or corner groups take over particular corners, and so on. There is a homogenization of the predominant user group, and it is maintained by their interpersonal ties. Via such ties and the attendant solidarity they can discomfit or exclude dissimilar others. Although public by definition, the setting is "taken over" by a particular subcultural group.

Consequences of territorial functioning

In keeping with our framework, the psychological, social psychological, and ecological consequences of territorial functioning in regular use settings are described. Inasmuch as the bulk of evidence concerning regular use settings comes from office settings, the consequences discussed here are best thought of as applying most clearly to such settings. Following this examination, similarities between territorial functioning in regular use settings and interior residential settings are noted. We consider whether these similarities are points of homology or analogy.

Psychological consequences

Task relevance

The portion of territorial functioning concerned with *access control* is enhanced by physical parameters increasing enclosure and inaccessibility. Consequently, task completion is facilitated. In the terminology of Stokols' contextual-stress model, thwarting is decreased, and actual facilitation of motivationally significant needs in the setting is increased. One can get more done with fewer interruptions.

The types of tasks protected by enclosure vary as a function of the job responsibilities in question.[42] Individuals in "higher" status job categories require privacy for more reasons (see Figure 9.2).[43] Basic work-

---

[41] For a general discussion of the dynamics involved in such transformations, see Lofland, L. (1973). *A world of strangers*. New York: Basic Books. For other commentary on this process see Lyman, S. M., & Scott, M. B. (1967), Territoriality: A neglected sociological dimension. *Social Problems, 15*, 236–249.

[42] Sundstrom, E., Town, J., Rice, R., Konar, E., Mandel, D., & Brill, M. (1982). Privacy in the office, satisfactions, and performance. Paper presented at the annual meeting of the American Psychological Association, 1982, Washington, DC.

[43] Sundstrom (1986), pp. 309–310.

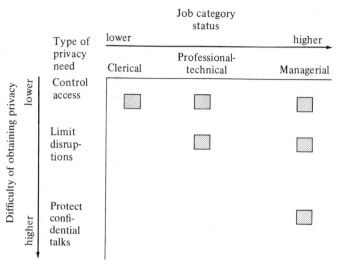

Figure 9.2. Reasons for varying levels of privacy. In an office setting, needs for privacy vary as a function of job category and associated job requirements. *Source*: E. Sundstrom (1986), *Work places*. Cambridge: Cambridge University Press. Copyright 1987 by Cambridge University Press. Adapted with permission of the author and Cambridge University Press.

ers need to be free enough from interruptions to do simple tasks such as typing, filing, and answering phones. Physical distance from others provides this. Technical or clerical workers need to be free from distractions in order to complete more complex tasks, which may be more involved, or may suffer more from interruption. Some degree of physical enclosure, and/or a private office, are required to complete these tasks. Finally, managerial workers need privacy where they can hold confidential discussions without fear of interruptions. Private offices and/or additional screening mechanisms such as secretaries are required in order to carry out these tasks comfortably. In other words, as the status of the job category increases, tasks requiring more secure access control mechanisms are required. Effective access control, buttressed by physical and human components, facilitates the completion of different types of tasks for different job categories.[44]

[44] Persons will not always exercise effective boundary control, even if they have the means to do so. One study found that middle managers, even when they were pressed and had tasks to complete, would leave their doors open. They did this in deference to

Table 9.2. *Markers and related features linked to perceived status support*

Status marker	Correlation with perceived status support
Private office	.41
Door	.44
Capacity for personalization	.51
Desk size	.58
Storage capacity	.43
Quality	.26

Note: Data come from a survey of 100 supervisors. Figures shown are zero-order correlations. The multiple correlation of status markers with perceived status support, which included some other markers not shown in this table, was .72.

Source: E. Konar et al., "Status demarcation in the office." *Environment and Behavior 14* (1977), 561–580. Copyright © 1977 Sage Publications, Inc. Reprinted by permission of Sage Publications, Inc.

Satisfaction

The *marker* component of territorial functioning is associated with higher levels of satisfaction with the work space, which in turn is associated with overall job satisfaction. The role of markers is to individuate the officeholder in the setting. More specifically, markers function as *status supports*. That is, they underscore the relative status of the person in the organization. They provide an external, symbolic referent indicative of the relative prestige of the officeholder within the organization. Physical parameters increasing inaccessibility, and enclosure, in addition to facilitating access control, also function as status supports, as do the availability of space for personalization, desk size, quality of furnishings, and so on (see Table 9.2). Lacking such congruent supports, an officeholder may feel stress or discontent.[45]

Territorial markers may also increase satisfaction for an additional reason. Modifying, beautifying, and decorating the work space, apart from their effects on perceived status support, may decrease the alien-

norms operating in the setting, which dictated that managers "be available." The managers often compensated by staying late to finish reports.

Justa & Golan (1977).

[45] Sundstrom (1976), p. 240.

ation of the worker from the work setting. The standard Marxist critique of modern work settings highlights the alienation of the worker from the work process. The segmentation of work, such that an individual rarely nurtures a product from start to finish, makes the work experience less satisfying. This dissatisfaction with the workplace, posited as a given for most jobs by Marxists, may be decreased in settings where higher levels of personalization and individuation are permitted. Such personalizing may help bridge the gap between work and home, by allowing, at least on a visible level, a greater interpenetration of the two spheres. (Unfortunately, I know of no evidence bearing on this point.)

Social psychological consequences

Displaying of relative status

Several of the agreed accoutrements of status are pertinent to territorial functioning: degree of inaccessibility and enclosure, availability of screening mechanisms such as personal secretaries, space for personalization and degree of personalization permitted, and so on. In white-collar offices people agree on what types of items are linked to status. In particular organizations, the link between work space features and relative status is even more highly codified. "In organizations like CBS and the Civil Service, workspaces can be read as literally as military insignia."[46] This facilitates interpersonal functioning by making explicit the relative position of the person with whom one is interacting.[47] A visitor waiting in an office to see someone can gather a lot of information about the officeholder, and his or her position, from the work space itself.[48] A visitor taking in these cues forms status-relevant person perceptions, which help him or her get primed, or preset, for the interaction. The cues and the attendant perceptions help set the "tone" of the interaction, and shape expectations about its outcome.

Individuation

But there are other facets to a person besides his or her relative status within an organization. The person's identity itself is also important.

---

[46] Sundstrom (1986), p. 237.

[47] Lacking these cues, one can make embarrassing gaffes. A former colleague was visiting a city planning department one day. While waiting for the elevator to come up, he began chatting casually with another person. In an offhand way the visitor asked the other person what he did "around here." The latter replied, somewhat less casually, that he was the director of the department.

[48] Rapoport (1982).

And, territorial markers that personalize the space and "express" the personality of the occupant individuate him or her from the others in the setting. These items – a six-foot pop-art poster of Flash Gordon; a suspended, inflated banana; an eight-foot rubber plant; a floor-to-ceiling mural of the seashore; pictures of family members; or a stuffed and mounted swordfish – provide useful conversational gambits and further sharpen visitors' perceptions of the occupant. The information can be used to "gauge" characteristics of the occupant, and can provide some initial focus or structure for the interaction.

Ecological consequences

The ecological consequences of territorial functioning in regular use settings such as work spaces are the *organizational* consequences stemming from these processes. It is the organization that functions as the larger context or setting. The differential efficacy of territorial functioning, in particular, boundary regulation and personalization, resulting in part from the differential distribution of physical and nonphysical supports for territorial functioning, serves organizations well. It clarifies and supports the "vertical" or stratification-relevant dimension of the organization. It makes clear who has power over whom. Such clarity is important for an organization.

The importance of a clear power structure in an organization was discussed by Max Weber, one of the "founding fathers" of organizational sociology. He gave considerable attention to the issue of power in formal organizations.[49] Weber suggested that one important characteristic of a *bureaucracy*, which he thought of as an "ideal type" of formal organization, was a system of *hierarchical statuses*. Given the division of labor in many organizations – different people and different offices do different things – a system is needed to link the various functions. With a status hierarchy, each office (or rank) takes orders from, and is controlled and supervised by, the office (or rank) that is "higher," and controls and supervises the office (or rank) that is just "below" it. In this way there is an orderly flow of communication. Further, Weber suggested that as a consequence of such a structure there is less interpersonal friction and work proceeds more smoothly. The taking of orders is legitimated and sanctioned by this arrangement.

[49] Weber, M. (1947). *The theory of social and economic organization*. New York: Free Press.
    See also:
    Gerth, H. H., & Mills, C. W. (Eds.) (1946). *Max Weber: Essays in sociology*. Oxford: Oxford University Press.

Consequently, from an organizational perspective, physical and non-physical office characteristics relevant to territorial functioning externalize, underscore, and further legitimate the existing status hierarchy, which is necessary, according to Weber, if the organization is to function effectively. Territorial functioning in regular use settings such as work spaces in effect "drives home" the presence of the operating status hierarchy.

Would the functional efficacy of an operating status hierarchy be diminished if territorial functioning did not exist? Business magazines occasionally run stories about a company president who eschews an office and personal secretary, placing his desk in the middle of the main floor and sharing the work space of his managers and employees. Are lines of information and decision making more muddled, or less clearly perceived in these situations? I know of no "hard" data bearing on this point. My suspicion is that such "nonterritorial" arrangements would not impair organizational efficiency in small businesses, with small numbers of employees. In these cases it does not take long for all employees to learn the position and relative status of co-workers. In larger organizations, however, such "nonterritorial" arrangements *may* be harmful. It would be more difficult for employees to easily determine the relative position and functional responsibilities of various co-workers. This may result in more conflict and less organizational efficiency.

Similarities and dissimilarities with territorial functioning at other points on the centrality continuum

Territorial functioning in regular use settings such as workplaces can be compared and contrasted with territorial functioning in interior and outdoor residential settings. The parallels highlight the underlying structural similarity of the processes operating at different points along the centrality continuum. The differences underscore the impact of context on territorial functioning.

Similarities

1. As in interior residential settings, in regular use settings such as workplaces, there is a mapping of the social structure onto the spatial ecology. More specifically:

a. The spaces one can claim depend on one's relative position in the social group.

Higher-status workers can claim corner offices on higher floors, with more space, and so on. In interior residential settings, more dominant persons in a group had more frequent access to valued locations. The priority access hypothesis is supported in both the high and medium ranges of the centrality continuum.

b. Related to the preceding: Since access to valued locations is a function of relative status, there is a differential distribution of stressors stemming from a lack of privacy. The efficacy of territorial functioning varies across members of the group in the setting, so some experience more powerlessness than others. Parallel to mothers' lower levels of satisfaction with the residential environment because they are more accessible to others, are the lower privacy and satisfaction levels of clerical workers and secretaries, who have more public work spaces.

2. In outdoor residential settings, and in workplaces, there is widespread agreement on the interpretation of territorial markers. The "meaning" of various markers is not idiosyncratic, but rather is shared, allowing different individuals to similarly interpret physical and nonphysical elements of territorial functioning. People "know" what to think about a person who has a well-trimmed lawn and eye-catching flower garden, and what to think about an executive who has a top-floor, corner office with two secretaries outside. Absent these shared cognitions, territorial markers would be useless, and territorial functioning would be highly inefficient.

3. In interior and outdoor residential settings, territorial functioning serves to maintain the setting. Inside homes, it allows daily routines to be carried out with minimal fuss. Outside the home, it helps maintain the setting program. In regular use settings such as offices it serves to accentuate the existing structural hierarchy, a key element of effective operations in many organizations.

Differences

1. Territorial functioning in regular use settings such as workplaces is much more highly regulated than in interior and outdoor residential settings.

In work settings "leaders" in the setting can lay down guidelines concerning different aspects of territorial functioning. They can "outlaw" personalization, or marking, of the work space for certain classes of employees. They can enforce strict rules concerning physical dimensions of territories. In interior residential settings, parents may decide which child gets the larger bedroom, but these allocation rules are much less formalized than those of the workplace.

2. Territorial functioning in regular use settings such as work places serves to differentiate occupants along a vertical, status-related dimension, whereas territorial functioning in outdoor residential locations serves to differentiate persons mainly on a horizontal, in-group versus

out-group dimension. This is because there is no "threat" posed by outsiders in workplaces. Mail carriers, couriers, and visitors do not jeopardize the setting itself. By contrast, in outdoor residential sites occupants are continually striving to determine who "belongs" and who does not. In this respect, territorial processes in public regular use settings, such as the gay bar described by Cavan, are closer to those operating in outdoor residential sites than those functioning in workplaces.

Remaining questions

Territorial functioning in regular use settings has been less researched than territorial functioning in indoor or outdoor residential settings. Outside of workplaces, and in particular, offices, little evidence is available. Studies such as Cavan's are highly illuminating. But, lacking other available studies it is difficult to know how generalizable her results are across settings.[50]

And, even within work settings, there is room for considerable empirical development. For example, on an organizational or setting level, territorial functioning could be profiled and its association with measures of efficiency examined. The effects of personalization on the occupant's link with the workplace remain unexamined. Processes similar to those discussed by Vinsel and her colleagues, who found that college students with displays indicating stronger commitment to the college locale were less likely to drop out, may also be operating in the workplace. Or, somewhat less specific, it may be that freedom to personalize a space, and the extent of personalization, net all else, are linked with decreased alienation from the work site. The hypothesized link between an impersonal environment and organizational efficiency has not been proved. If personalization results in less alienation from the work site, a change from "businesslike" to "homey," decorated work settings may result in more satisfied employees.

Finally, in work settings and elsewhere, links between territorial functioning and other setting conditions remain unexplored. For example, how is territorial functioning linked to the staffing level, i.e., the ratio of available people to requisite roles?[51] Over the last five years ecological psychology has become better integrated with industrial/organizational psychology and, it seems, could profitably be integrated with research on territorial functioning. For example, the research on over- and un-

---

[50] It may well be that, outside of work settings, the only viable method for collecting information is field research of a participant nature. Given the difficulties of field research, the lack of available evidence is not surprising.

[51] Wicker (1987).

derstaffing suggests that in overstaffed settings criteria for entry into the setting are more stringent. This heightened stringency might be manifested *within* the setting itself, with participants in particular synomorphs seeking to exercise greater excludability of others, and tighter boundary control.

Summary

In regular use settings occupants appear periodically, and are surrounded by many known others. They may have functional roles involving them in maintaining the setting. The bulk of empirical evidence relevant to regular use settings comes from white-collar workplaces, i.e., offices. Territorial behaviors and markers in these settings serve a variety of functions, including isolating the individual or group to facilitate task completion, organizing space so as to make roles and tasks congruent with the environment, reflecting the overarching hierarchy of the organization and its subunits, and individuating the occupant from his or her surroundings, and/or other actors in the setting. Key shapers of territorial functioning in these settings are physical boundaries, relative social position in the setting, the personality of the person in the setting, and the "culture" of the larger organization. Psychological consequences of territorial functioning include enhancement of privacy for task completion and confidential communication, leading to enhanced actual facilitation of needs significant to the setting. Major social psychological consequences include supporting social perceptions of particular individuals that are congruent with their relative position and/or goals in the setting. Major ecological consequences include clarification and support of the organizational hierarchy.

Several parallels between territorial functioning in regular use settings and in interior residential settings are apparent. Most notably, in both locations, social position is "mapped onto" physical space. Higher-status persons are more likely to have access to the more valued spaces (the priority access thesis). And, territorial functioning of higher-status persons is likely to be more effective at excluding others. In both types of settings, these similar aspects of territorial functioning are undergirded by a known group structure; that is, they rely upon mutual recognition of the relative social position of others in the setting. They also further support that structure.

10
MINIMAL TERRITORIAL FUNCTIONING

Territorial functioning in settings where the person–place transactions are of low centrality is the focus of this chapter: how people create and maintain minimal territories in settings that are by definition public. In the round of our daily lives, we are constantly "laying claim" to spaces for short periods of time. (For some examples, see the first box in this chapter.)

Organization of the chapter

The nature of the low centrality person–place bond is reviewed. The components of territorial functioning in locations where centrality is low are examined. Although territorial functioning may in some instances shade into other person–place processes such as jurisdiction, group space, and personal space, it is nonetheless clear that territorial functioning operates in these public settings. Following our model, evidence of the physical, social, cultural, and personal determinants of territorial functioning, and the consequences of such functioning for individuals, groups, and settings, are considered.

Settings where person–place bonds are of low centrality

We spend considerable amounts of time in public places and spaces; these locations are open to all or almost all of the citizenry. The sheer number and variety of these places is staggering: buses, trains, planes,

221

bus and train stations, airports, stores, restaurants, classrooms, banks, post offices, libraries, resorts, stadiums, theaters, bars, playgrounds, and beaches, just to name a few. Since these are "public" spaces, our "claim" to a particular "spot" in a location is not backed by any law or legal statute. We have no defined legal "right" to any particular site within these settings. And yet we, and many others, "claim" positions within these settings. We use such spaces, for the most part, with few "hassles" or confrontations. How is this possible? The current chapter addresses this question.

Minimal territorial functioning in these locations plays key roles in facilitating usage and minimizing conflict. *Minimal territorial functioning involves asserting some form of temporary and spatially very limited "claim," while using a space or resource in a public setting, such that others are discouraged from sitting or standing close to us while we are there, or from using that spot should we vacate it for a brief time.*[1] It is the laying of such claims, and the respect of others for those claims, that allows each of us to use public settings, patronized or occupied by many other people, with minimal conflict or annoyance.

In these settings where minimal territorial functioning is evident, the person–place or group–place bonds are of low centrality. Were an individual or group to lose access to such a location, the negative impact would not be substantial. Such sites are often replaceable (e.g., there are other seats available in the bar) or serve a low-level need or are needed for only a brief time.

Sites where the person–place transactions are of low centrality are distinguished by:

1. Short durations of usage, a few hours at one time at the most;
2. The space in question being, by common agreement, and with few limitations, open to a substantial number of users (e.g., a library at a college is open to students of that university), and perhaps even the general public (e.g., a state beach); and
3. A nonexistent or low level of acquaintanceship between the individual occupant or small user group, and other occupants in the setting.

---

[1] Goffman has suggested that in such locations we establish *public territories*. Altman has described them as *temporary territories*. Goffman's term focuses on the nature of the setting where the territorial functioning operates; Altman's term focuses on the temporal dimension. I prefer the term *minimal* territorial functioning because it is more holistic and places the territorial functioning relative to functioning in instances where the person–place bonds are more central.

Goffman, E. (1963). *Behavior in public places*. New York: Harper.

Altman, I. (1975). *The environment and social behavior*. Monterey, CA: Brooks/Cole.

These sites differ from regular use settings in two ways. First, usage need not be regular, although it may be, as in the case of the business colleagues who lunch at the same restaurant, at the same time and at the same table, once a week. Should regular usage persist, the person–place bond may shift from minimal to medium centrality (Chapter 9), thus altering the territorial functioning. Second, given the public nature of the setting itself, and its irregular use by the individual or group in question, as well as others, one is surrounded almost totally by strangers when in such locations. An individual, or a small group, knows few specifics about the surrounding others.

A day of life in public

The variety of locations where you might claim minimal territories is illustrated in the following outline of the activities of a college student.

Darlene is an undergraduate at a large California state university. She lives on campus. During her first and second morning classes, both in large lecture halls, she occupies a seat towards the front of the room where she can see better. After these two lectures she goes with a couple of friends to the cafeteria where they sit at a table and talk about upcoming midterms. In the afternoon she studies for two hours in a carrel in a remote corner of the library. That evening she goes with her roommate and another mutual friend to the student union on campus where they play some video games (she thinks "Donkey Kong" is much harder than "Starfighter"), and later they head to a bar just off-campus. Despite the crowd, after a wait they manage to get a table near the door where they are later joined by her roommate's boyfriend and one of his "brothers" from his fraternity. They make arrangements to go to the beach the next day. The next morning at ten Darlene and her two friends meet the men they were with the night before and the five of them drive to Huntington Beach. Upon arriving they spread out blankets, radios, Frisbees, and a cooler. The day passes with some swimming, chatting, Frisbee throwing, and napping.

Darlene was probably engaged in minimal territorial functioning:
In the classroom;
At a table in the cafeteria;
At a carrel in the library;
At the video machines;
At the table in the bar; and
At the beach.

Minimal territorial functioning

Some clarifications regarding minimal territorial functioning are in order before describing its elements.

Must a site be "assigned" for territorial functioning to operate?

Some researchers have objected to the concept of territorial functioning in public settings.[2] They feel that the space in question must be assigned before it can legitimately be labelled a territory, or before one can conclude that territorial functioning is operating.

But such a criterion is too restrictive. It means that territorial functioning can occur only in locations where spatial prerogatives are explicitly recognized. Territorial processes, however, are not dependent solely upon such acknowledgments. How people interact in a location, and appropriate or do not appropriate space there, may be influenced by the explicit rules of the setting, as well as by the informal norms operating in the setting and the needs of the individuals who are there. In fact, informal arrangements, and individual and group needs, can sometimes overcome the explicit rules applied to the setting. It is not at all unusual to see groups of men hanging around on a corner near a bar or liquor store where a "No Loitering within 50 Feet of This Building" sign is conspicuously displayed. Many inner-city playgrounds, with a "Playground Closed from Dusk to Dawn" sign near the entrance, are used regularly after dark by preteens or teens for socializing or drinking.[3] How people move through, utilize, and appropriate space is a subtle, shifting process, and does not tidily unfold in accordance with official acts of legitimization or assignment.

How temporary is temporary?

Some researchers have suggested that temporary occupancy of a spot in a public space is too short lived to qualify the place as a territory.[4] This objection seems arbitrary. Time is a continuum. It is capricious to

---

[2] Shaffer, D. R., & Sadowski, S. (1975). This table is mine: Respect for marked barroom tables as a function of gender of spatial marker and desirability of locale. *Sociometry*, *38*, 408–419.

[3] Lofland (1973) provides a delightful collection of incidents where transients set up house in train stations and bus stations. She discusses one situation where a person discovered that if he was continuously reading a newspaper in Grand Central Station he could stay there throughout the night.

[4] Shaffer & Sadowski have made this suggestion.

cut it at one point and say that processes during occupancies of shorter duration do *not* qualify as territorial functioning. There is no sound basis on which to make such a distinction.

Overlap with other sociospatial processes

In some instances minimal territorial functioning "shades into" related sociospatial processes at work in public settings. Related processes include personal space, group personal space, and jurisdiction. The determinants and consequences of group personal space, in particular, seem similar to minimal territorial functioning. (See the next box for a summary of pertinent findings.) Nonetheless, minimal territorial functioning is distinguishable from these related processes.

Minimal territorial functioning reflects the subjective value of the space for the occupant or group in question. In other words, minimal territorial functioning is highly dependent upon the nature of the extant person–place or group–place transaction. Stated differently, minimal territorial functioning is more likely to be evident the greater the subjective utility of the location in question. The related sociospatial processes of personal space and group personal space, albeit somewhat tailored to the surrounding context, are not as dependent upon the subjective utility of the location in question.

In addition, personal space and group personal space cannot be left behind; a temporary or public territory can be.

Group personal space

Minimal territorial functioning, when exercised by a small group, such as Darlene and her friends at the beach (preceding box), seems in several respects quite similar to the establishment of *group personal space*. The latter refers to the creation by small face-to-face groups of a zone around themselves that nongroup members would rather not invade. The existence of such a group personal space can be inferred based on the fact that others avoid walking through it.

If two people are standing fairly close together and chatting, passersby are more likely to go around rather than between them.[5] As the individuals stand farther apart, passersby become more likely to walk between them. It's as if the two talking at the distance appropriate for a personal con-

---

[5] Efran, M. G., & Cheyne, J. A. (1973). Shared space: The cooperative control of spatial areas by two interacting individuals. *Canadian Journal of Behavioral Science, 5*, 201–210.

versation are perceived as one "cell" by outsiders; as they stand farther apart the "cell" fissions, and instead of perceiving one group space, outsiders perceive two personal spaces. Should the two individuals not be conversing, passersby are less likely to perceive a group space, and more likely to walk between them.[6]

Passing through a group personal space is aversive.[7] Invaders use agonistic nonverbal expressions, such as grimacing, while walking through a group's personal space, and are in a worse mood afterward than noninvaders.[8]

Group personal space becomes more solid, or less permeable, as the size of the group increases.[9]

Also dependent upon group size is the spatial extent of the group's personal space. When the group is composed of strangers, the size of the space increases as group size increases.[10] This expansion does not occur if the group is composed of friends.[11]

In addition to group size, other social characteristics of the group, most

[6] Cheyne, J. A., & Efran, M. G. (1972). The effects of spatial and interpersonal variables on the invasion of group controlled territories. *Sociometry, 35,* 477–489.

[7] Efran, M. G., & Cheyne, J. A. (1974). Affective concomitants of the invasion of shared space: Behavioral, physiological, and verbal indicators. *Journal of Personality and Social Psychology, 29,* 219–226.

[8] Why does passing through a group space cause discomfort? Are passersby worried that people will think them rude? Are they worried that the conversants might physically threaten them? The pattern of findings for sex effects suggests that neither of these explanations is totally satisfactory. Mixed-sex dyads are least likely to be invaded, female–female dyads being the most likely. If male passersby are worried about being thought rude, this concern would lead them to intrude least upon female–female dyads. With regard to physical threat, if this concern were uppermost, male–male dyads, where the invader would be the most vulnerable, should be the least invaded; they are not. A third possible explanation has to do with simple interpersonal distance. But if this were the correct explanation, going behind two people who were talking, in separate groups, should be just as bothersome as walking in between two conversing people. But it isn't; the latter appears to be experienced as more disagreeable. Thus, the theoretical rationale for the spatial deterrence power of group space is not yet clear.

[9] Knowles, E. S. (1973). Boundaries around group interaction: The effects of group size and member status on boundary permeability. *Journal of Personality and Social Psychology, 26,* 327–331.

[10] Knowles, E. S., Kreuser, B., Haas, S., Hyde, M., & Schuchart, G. E. (1976). Group size and the extension of social space boundaries. *Journal of Personality and Social Psychology, 33,* 647–654.

[11] Edney, J. J., & Grundmann, M. J. (1979). Friendship, group size, and boundary size: Small group spaces. *Small Group Behavior, 10,* 124–135.

notably its sex composition, influence the "invadability" of its personal space.[12] Space around a mixed-sex couple is less likely to be invaded than the space around a same-sex couple.

These findings confirm the existence of group personal space and high-light the factors influencing its extent and permeability.

What it involves

Minimal territorial functioning involves an individual or group "laying claim" to a site located within a public or open, accessible setting. Such a claim, albeit legitimate, is also bounded or conditional in several respects.

The major limitations placed on the claim stem from the nature of the behavior setting in which the claim is made, and the roles others play in the setting.

1. The setting must be open for the claim to be operative. And, when the setting closes, the claim is terminated. A student preparing for a midterm must leave the library study hall when it closes at midnight.

2. The setting shapes the spatial extent of the claim. No one expects to be able to occupy two seats on a crowded commuter train.

3. The claim is contingent upon the occupant's behavior being in accordance with the setting program. A person wishing to sleep on a long library study table has a less legitimate claim to the site than another student who wants to spread out books there for studying.

4. In addition, one's claim can be voided or suspended temporarily by a person who plays a more central role in the behavior setting. A student sitting at a CRT in a computer activity room can be "bumped" by an assistant working there who needs to access the system to check its status. A claim can also be contested by others in the setting – those in a rush, who were there earlier, or who have a special need. In light of a legitimate counterclaim, most would "give up" their claim.

Behaviors

1. Minimal territorial functioning involves, at the least, the *use or oc-cupancy* of a site in a public or accessible location, for some period of time. The use may or may not accord with the behavior setting program. In the latter case, the use may subvert or be counter to the goals of the setting, as in the case of homeless people sleeping in a train station.

---

[12] Cheyne & Efran (1972).

Important parameters of the usage include its spatial extent – how much of a space is claimed – as well as the duration and frequency of usage.

2. When the occupant's or group's site is threatened or usurped by another user who does not have a superior, prior, or more legitimate claim, the occupant or group will *actively defend* the site *if the site is valuable*. The person or group will not allow themselves to be pushed out unless it is for a good reason. Examples of "good reasons" are people who were there prior, or who have an emergency, or who run the setting.

3. The occupying individual or group may *mark* the space (see below).

4. The occupying individual or group, prior to departure may, if they expect to return, *enlist coprotectors*. They may ask neighboring occupants or persons "in charge" to watch their place, keep their place in line, or tell intruders they expect to return.

Cognitions

Individuals or groups feel that they have some *conditional or bounded, but nonetheless legitimate, claim to a particular site*. As mentioned earlier, such claims are bounded in several respects.

The constraints on what a person or group can "claim" as "theirs" in a public setting are reflected in territorial cognitions, and can be gauged by responses to questions about the possibilities of being interrupted or invaded, or about how long one expects to remain at the particular site.

Markers

In public or open-access settings *territorial markers* are items at the site that clearly belong to someone, or clearly indicate to others, if no one is present, that the place is occupied. Markers include books, coats, handbags, briefcases, packs, and other items. In a bar, a pack of cigarettes or an unfinished drink may serve as a marker. Items that are *personal* markers and more clearly belong to an individual, such as a coat, hat, scarf, calculator, or bookbag, are thought to be more effective at communicating occupancy than markers that could be part of the setting, such as books in a library. Markers may reduce or eliminate space conflict, except where users grossly outnumber available seats, by signalling occupancy and thus acting as a "warning device" to others.[13]

[13] Becker, F. (1973). Study of spatial markers. *Journal of Personality and Social Psychology, 26*, 439–445.

Potential invaders are warned off and will delay occupying marked sites.[14] People prefer to sit at unmarked tables, as has been observed in libraries and in other settings.[15] For example, at the opera in Vienna, where standing room tickets are very cheap, students will line up outside the opera house. The doors open two to three hours before curtain time. Students will go in and wrap a scarf or two on the railing to indicate that they have claimed a spot, and then go and have dinner. Only rarely will they return to find that another has ignored their markers and is standing in their marked spot.

Markers, like actual people, have a protective effect. Marking a seat at a table will not only protect that seat from intruders, but may also, except under conditions of high user density, ward potential intruders off from the *adjoining* area. Markers in libraries have "protected" entire tables.[16]

Of course, markers are just proxies for people; they leave a trace saying, "Someone was here, and that person will be back." An even stronger "marker" is the actual occupant. Actual occupancy communicates an even stronger territorial claim: "I have been here, and I'm here now." It is not surprising then that others avoid infringing upon the occupied temporary territory of others.[17]

Markers are quite crucial in settings where minimal territorial functioning occurs because the occupying individual or group has few others to rely on. They are surrounded largely by unknown persons, who, unless "enlisted" to watch or protect the claim, provide no support. When individuals lack the support provided by known others in the setting, markers must play a greater role in "protecting" the claim.

Predictors of territorial functioning

In this section, we use our fourfold clustering of variables and consider the physical, social, cultural, and personality predictors of minimal territorial functioning.

Physical predictors

In public or open-access settings, various physical characteristics can make a particular location more or less desirable, and thus more or less

[14] Sommer, R., & Becker, F. (1969). Territorial defense and the good neighbor. *Journal of Personality and Social Psychology, 11*, 83–92.

[15] Sommer, R. (1969). *Personal space.* Englewood Cliffs, NJ: Prentice-Hall.

[16] Sommer & Becker (1969); Becker (1973).

[17] Becker (1973).

worthy of occupying and "defending." Since different activities are pursued in different behavior settings, and the nature of the behavior setting program varies, what makes a site desirable and worth "defending" in one setting may not make it so elsewhere. The setting-dependent nature of the link between physical characteristics and desirability of location is highlighted by contrasting territorial functioning in libraries and bars.

Enclosed and private study settings more defended in library

Many go to libraries to read and study. Study behaviors are facilitated by a setting that is better isolated from nearby traffic, discourages social contact, and affords privacy. A study carrel, where one is enclosed on two or more sides from others nearby, provides a more private setting for studying than does sitting at a table with three to ten others.[18] Consequently, given the relatively higher value or desirability of a carrel as opposed to a table in a college library, one would expect the former to be more vigorously defended than the latter.

And, indeed, this turns out to be the case. In a field study carried out by Debbie Brooks and myself, a confederate (Brooks) invaded seats temporarily vacated in a library.[19] We had earlier confirmed that students at the university valued carrels more highly for serious studying. In accord with their cognitions, students were more likely to "defend" a carrel by asking for it back, as compared to a table. All of those returning to a carrel asked for their seat back, whereas only half of those returning to a table "defended" it by asking for it back.[20]

In sum, in a library, increased physical enclosure and separation from high-volume areas makes a site better for studying, and thus more desirable. Consequently, occupants are more likely to "defend" such a location by asking intruders to leave.

Barrooms: more demand for more central, sociable sites

By contrast, people go to bars or pubs to socialize with one another. Thus, one might expect that more desirable sites within a bar would be those where one has more of a chance of meeting others.

[18] Sommer, R. (1968). Reading areas in college libraries. *Library Quarterly, 38*, 249–260.
[19] Taylor, R. B., & Brooks, D. B. (1980). Temporary territories? Responses to intrusions in a public setting. *Population and Environment, 3*, 135–145.
[20] These behavioral results accorded well with differences observed in the earlier questionnaire study. Of the participants in the questionnaire study, 68% indicated that if they left their carrel for a few minutes, came back, and found someone there, they would ask that person to move; at a table only 29% thought they would defend by asking the person to move.

Table 10.1. *Delaying invasion in barroom: marker efficacy and sociability of site*

	Potential for socializing at site	
	High	Low
Marked	8.4	10.3
Unmarked	1.5	2.1

Note: Figures indicate the delay, in minutes, between the time the confederates left the barroom table, and the time it was occupied by another person or group. Tables high in interaction potential were those located "along the aisles near the center of the room." Tables low in interaction potential were located "in the rear of the room on the main aisle but along the wall" (p. 411).
Source: D. R. Shaffer and S. Sadowski, "This table is mine." *Sociometry, 38* (1975), 408–419. Adapted with the permission of the American Sociological Association and David Shaffer.

A field study at a "college" bar confirms the higher desirability of more social regions within the setting.[21] The value of sites for socializing was directly determined by asking patrons where they would sit if they wanted to socialize and meet others, and if they wanted to be left alone. The authors hypothesized that since the more sociable spots were more desirable, territorial markers left behind by occupants would be less effective at delaying occupancy by others. The stronger "demand" for the social tables would render markers left behind less effective at preserving a claim. And, the results supported this expectation (see Table 10.1). Markers did delay occupancy by others, as shown by the contrast with invasions of unmarked tables. But if the site was more desirable, affording better chances of meeting and greeting others, markers were less effective at "preserving" the claims of those who had left.

By implication, if the authors had conducted an experiment where experimental confederates invaded marked but unoccupied tables, returning customers would have been more likely to "defend" and ask for their table back, if the table was in a more social position.

In a barroom, a more central location is more valued because it provides for potential opportunities for interaction. More central lo-

[21] Shaffer, D. R., & Sadowski, S. (1975). This table is mine: Respect for marked barroom tables as a function of gender of spatial marker and desirability of locale. *Sociometry, 38*, 408–419.

cations appear more desirable in classrooms as well, although for different reasons.

Classrooms: more central sites more defended

Those seated in more centrally located seats in a classroom obtain higher grades. This was the conclusion reached over 60 years ago by Griffith,[22] after examining data consisting of 20,000 grades. (And this was *before* the age of computers!) Those seated in the very front, back, and on the sides did not do as well. Griffith speculated that those in more central locations were more involved in and more attentive to the material being discussed, while those on the periphery were more distracted, and not as integrated into the social group attending closely to the professor. Subsequent studies have replicated this finding, and it appears to hold both under conditions of self-selection, when students choose their own seats, and under conditions of alphabetical or random assignment.[23]

Given the functional value of more central seats in a classroom, it is not surprising that intruders of more central seats are rebuffed more frequently.[24] A study in which confederates invaded temporarily vacated seats found that if invadees had been sitting in a central seat in the classroom, 55 percent defended their seat by asking for it back. Only 19 percent of the invadees in peripheral seats defended. Defenders tended to stop and stare at the intruder first, and then to verbalize ownership.

Conceptualizing the link between physical characteristics and territorial functioning in open-access settings

The preceding studies, carried out in different contexts, illustrate a conditional linkage between physical characteristics of a site within a setting, and territorial functioning. The nature of this conditional linkage is depicted in Figure 10.1.

Figure 10.1 makes the following linkages. (Numbering in the following discussion corresponds to numbered arrows in the figure.)

1. The behavior setting itself, its program or standing pattern of be-

---

[22] Griffith, C. R. (1921). A comment upon the psychology of the audience. *Psychological Monographs, 30*, 36–47.

[23] See Knowles, E. S. (1982). A comment on the study of classroom ecology: A lament for the good old days. *Personality and Social Psychology Bulletin, 8*, 357–361. He reviews relevant studies and also comments on their theoretical barrenness.

[24] Haber, G. M. (1980). Territorial invasion in the classroom: Invadee response. *Environment and Behavior, 12*, 17–31.

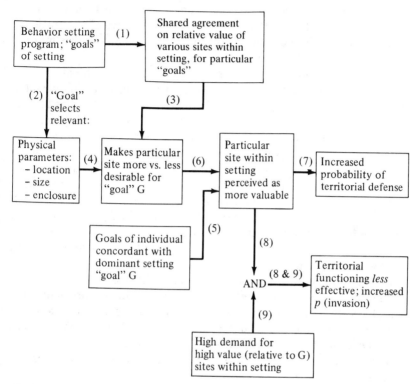

Figure 10.1. Linking physical features and territorial functioning in "public" settings.

havior, and/or the "goals" of the setting suggest to users in the setting what portions of the setting, or what sites nested within the setting, will be more valuable than others. A large proportion of users within a setting will agree with one another on the relative "value" or desirability of a site for a particular goal. Users of a bar will agree on the best spots for seeing and greeting others, library users will agree on the best spots for serious studying, and so on.

2. The particular "goal" that may be satisfied in the behavior setting is pertinent to particular physical characteristics. Given a particular goal in a setting, some physical characteristics are more pertinent than others. For the "goal" of solo studying in a library, whether the table where one is seated accommodates four or twelve is irrelevant. But, if one wants to study with a group, this feature is relevant. Seats at the back of a barroom are best for being left alone, seats nearer the bar itself are better for chatting with others.

3. The shared agreement on better versus worse sites within a setting, combined with (4) the actual configuration or features of the particular site or locus within the behavior setting, makes it perceived as more or less desirable.

5. At this juncture, the "goals" of a particular individual or small group within the behavior setting become pertinent. If the individual or group enters the setting with goal G in mind, and (6) the site has the physical characteristics that make it valuable for goal G, then that site will be perceived as desirable by the individual or group.

7. Consequently, they will be more likely to "defend" their site should it be unjustifiably "invaded" by another.

8, 9. At the same time, the heightened desirability of the particular site for goal G, if many others came for the same purpose, will result in decreased efficiency of territorial functioning in that spot. While at the table in a bar, for example, one may be asked to share the table. Or, if one leaves the site, even if it is marked, it is likely to be invaded sooner by other parties.

In sum, territorial functioning at a particular locus within a public setting like a library, bar, restaurant, or classroom is contingent upon the physical characteristics of the site. The nature of the contingent linkage turns upon the particular behavior setting goal, how that meshes with the goal of the individual or group in question, and the overall demand, stemming from that goal, for desirable sites within the behavior setting.

Social predictors

In an open-access setting, participants in the setting can be broken down into two groups: the individual or small group whose territorial functioning is of interest, and others in the setting. Since social ties between the individual or group of interest, and others, are usually minimal or nonexistent, most of the research on social factors has focused on characteristics of the target individual or group.

Gender

Women's markers less respected. The group personal space research has suggested that female groups are more vulnerable to invasion than are all-male groups. Women's relative vulnerability to invasion is also apparent here. The barroom study found that tables where women's markers were left behind were invaded about five minutes sooner than tables where men's markers were left behind.[25]

Women's territories more vulnerable? Some findings from two field studies carried out on beaches (see the following box) suggest groups including a woman, as compared to all-male groups, display more restricted minimal territories.[26] (1) Lone women "claimed" smaller areas than lone men. (2) Groups including a woman – all-woman groups and mixed groups – "claimed" smaller areas than all-male groups. (But, when considering space per person, mixed groups claimed less than same-sex groups.) And, (3) one researcher, investigating beaches in different countries, had difficulty finding "lone and paired females to sample. This in itself attests to the territorial vulnerability of females, as does the over-representation of females in triads in all three samples."[27]

Sex differences in behavioral research are often difficult to interpret. The more evident constriction of minimal territorial functioning in groups including women may reflect their relative vulnerability. But, alternatively, it could be an indication, in the case of mixed groups and all-female groups, of a stronger bond between the members of the group. And, the relative paucity of lone women and pairs of women may have more to do with implicit norms pertinent to the setting: Men interpret lone women or pairs of women on the beach as interested in being "picked up." To avoid such "hassles," women may go to the beach in groups of at least three.

A beach study: the "ultimate" summer research project

Are you looking for the "ultimate" summer research project and interested in territorial functioning? Two field studies of territorial functioning on beaches attest to the fun (and tanning opportunities) researchers can have if they put their minds to it.

The first "beach" study was carried out in the early 1970s by Julian Edney and Nancy Jordan-Edney at Hammonassett State Park (Connecticut), a large public beach. Working as a pair, the research team approached groups on the beach. While one researcher interviewed the

---

[25] Shaffer & Sadowski (1975).

[26] Edney, J. J., & Jordan-Edney, N. L. (1974). Territorial spacing on a beach. *Sociometry, 37,* 92–104.

[27] Smith, H. W. (1981). Territorial spacing on a beach revisited. *Social Psychology Quarterly, 44,* 132–137; see esp. p. 134.

group, the other researcher recorded group size, sex composition, markers, and distance to nearest neighbor. The procedure used to estimate size of the group's claimed space was novel.

"The experimenter mentioned to the respondents that when people settle on the beach, they often consider an area surrounding them to be their own. To get an idea of this space, in their case, the experimenter said that he would start to walk slowly backward from the group, and that the group should indicate the point at which he appeared to step out of their space, thus enabling the experimenter to get an idea of where the perimeter lay. The experimenter then proceeded with this method, first walking backward from the group in the direction its members were facing, then repeating this at right angles from the first direction."[28]

To examine cross-cultural differences, H. W. Smith took this methodology to a beach in Germany (Westerland Beach on the island of Sylt) and one in France (Pampelonne, near St. Tropez).

Group size

Studies done with naturally occurring groups, as well as with experimentally created groups, indicate that characteristics of minimal territorial functioning are linked to group size.

Sense of ownership and mood. One experimental study allowed individuals or groups of four to "create" territories.[29] Participants were shown to a room and provided with materials to decorate. Experimental instructions created the impression that participants would return to the room at a later time. Individual participants felt a stronger sense of ownership of the created territory than people who had participated in a group; those in the individual condition felt the room was more "theirs." Single subjects also showed more elevated moods – happier, more aroused, rating the room as more pleasant – than group subjects.

Space and markers. Links between group size, space, and markers were investigated in the two "beach" field studies discussed in the preceding box. In the American study, larger groups of people put out a larger (total) number of markers. But the number of markers per person *de-*

[28] Edney & Jordan-Edney (1974), pp. 94–95.
[29] Edney, J. J., & Uhlig, S. R. (1977). Individual and small group territories. *Small Group Behavior, 8,* 457–468.

creased as group size *in*creased. Further, larger groups felt a larger area was "theirs" on the beach, but per capita space was less with larger groups.[30] Smith's study of beachgoers at German and French beaches found, as in the American case, that as group size increased, the per capita space claimed decreased, and the per capita number of markers decreased. Overall, total territory size increased as group size increased in the French groups, but not in the German groups.[31]

The decreasing number of markers per person, and space per person as group size increases, may come about because markers and space per person are less necessary to highlight the group's spatial claim as group size increases. Increasing group size by itself may make the group's claim salient enough.

Taking over. Public or open-access settings can be diverted from their intended functions by subgroups of users. Beaches can be turned into football fields, or motorcyclist hangouts; parking lots can be turned into dragstrips, and so on (as discussed in the following box). Subgroups of users can turn open-access settings into regular use territories for themselves, making special claims on the setting. There are many ways this can be achieved.[32] One mechanism involves traveling in *packs*.[33] Sheer numbers can enable individuals in a group to occupy and to some extent "take over" a setting.

Packs and the use of open-access settings for alternate purposes

One means for groups to establish a territory in a public setting is to travel in packs. The image of a squadron of rowdy and slightly drunk conventioneers invading a quiet restaurant is a familiar one. Teenagers taking over a shopping mall parking lot on Friday and Saturday nights are another. In one rural Maryland location, "hundreds of teenagers in hot rods, jacked up trucks and family station wagons . . . form two bumper-to-bumper rings that slowly circle in opposite directions. Traffic can get so heavy that it takes an hour to travel the 1/3 mile circuit. . . . Neighbors have reported seeing teenagers drinking beer in their cars, urinating in the parking lot, and parked in dark corners."[34]

---

[30] Edney & Jordan-Edney (1974).

[31] Smith (1981).

[32] Lofland (1973) discusses the different ways this can be accomplished. See also Scott & Lyman (1967).

[33] Lofland (1973), pp. 138–139.

[34] Robinson, R. (March 19, 1984). Parties in parking lot anger residents. *Baltimore Sun*, pp. C1, C3.

> The youth in this location report that they can be sure to be seen, and see others if they "make the scene" on a Friday or Saturday night. Although the neighbors admit that most of the teens are probably not "bad," on some nights the noise is so loud they can't hear their TVs. The teens contend that if the police chase them out of the center they'll just go somewhere else. Their sheer numbers, and limited police resources (the area is under the jurisdiction of the spread-out state police), allow the teens to define the setting for whatever purposes they wish.

Enlisting others: good neighbors

Others who are close by can be enlisted as allies to help maintain a claim to a space in an open-access setting, but they are neither long-term nor willing allies.[35] Studies carried out in college libraries suggest that "neighbors" on the whole prefer to remain uninvolved. But, if a potential invader, approaching a marked but unoccupied seat, directly queries the person sitting next to the marked location, the "neighbor" will indicate that it is taken, although he or she is less likely to render this judgment the longer the original occupant has been away. Thus the "neighbor" can assist in the "defense" of minimal territories.

The reluctance of "neighbors" to assist in the defense of the minimal territory unless directly queried suggests that such spatial claims are supported only by informal norms of the immediate social system. This is in contrast to "permanent" territories such as residential dwellings, which are supported by legal statute. Most of the time this informal system is latent or not called into play, and thus immediate neighbors of marked-but-unoccupied territories prefer to remain uninvolved. It can be "activated" or articulated, however, by direct inquiry of the neighbors, who will then respond in accordance with the system.[36] The social, norm-based underpinnings of claims in public settings are not only highly context dependent but also informal and thus fragile.

In sum, increasing group size makes a claim to a site more salient. This heightened salience perhaps explains the decrease in space and markers per capita for larger groups. Very large groups, through sheer numbers, can "take over" a public setting. Sex composition influences perceived extent of a claim, but the underlying rationale is not evident. Nearby others can be enlisted to help "defend" a claim while an occupant is away, but are reluctant to become involved.

[35] Sommer & Becker (1969).
[36] Ibid., p. 92.

Cultural variation

Cross-cultural variation in minimal territorial functioning exists, and is well demonstrated in studies of territorial claims on American, French, and German beaches, as discussed in an earlier box.[37] The variation was evident in two ways.

First, the size of the site claimed differed markedly in the three cultures. In fact, differences in mean claim size and variation in claim size *across* cultures were far larger than differences *within* cultures.[38]

In addition, the applicability of territorial notions to a public setting were also highly variable across cultures as demonstrated by differences in how people marked and bounded their territories. A full 99 percent of the German sample built sand walls around the space they claimed as "theirs"; none of the French sample were observed to do this. Further, 20 percent of the Germans put up "reserved" signs, indicating that they would be there on such and such a date, such and such a time, and left these behind. None of the French were observed to do this. The French were also more likely to ignore signs about which groups (nudists, people with dogs, etc.) could use which portions of the beach.

The same culturally dependent application of territorial concepts was reflected in people's attitudes as well as their behaviors. German participants seemed readily to understand the concept of territory when interviewed, saying "A man's home is his castle." (It appeared to the investigator that in some cases this was the only English they knew.) While saying this they would gesticulate towards their sand walls. The French, on the other hand, seemed totally confused when asked about this idea. They emphasized that the beach was public, and open to all.

Thus, although there are similarities across cultures in terms of how territorial claims are linked to group compositional variables, there are also cross-cultural differences in types of display and ease of understanding the applicability of the idea of minimal territorial functioning.

Personality

I have not found any empirical investigations linking personality variables with minimal territorial functioning in public or open-access settings. I would, however, expect such differences to exist. Some people may be pushier than others, for example, claiming larger areas, even in a crowded setting.

---

[37] Edney & Jordan-Edney (1974); Smith (1981).
[38] Smith (1981), p. 136.

Time

An additional parameter pertinent to minimal territorial functioning is time. It is relevant in several ways.

1. As time passes for an occupant he or she becomes more strongly linked to the site in question. In a classroom invasion study, only 12 percent of invasions occurring before class actually got under way were countered by the returning occupant, whereas 60 percent were countered if the invasion occurred later, during a mid-class break.[39]

2. The longer an occupant is away from a site, the weaker his or her claim is seen to be.[40] When neighbors are asked about a vacant site by a potential invader, the longer the original occupant is away, the less likely the neighbor is to "defend" the site in question.

3. The longer the occupant *expects* to be in the site, the more vigorous will be his or her territorial functioning. In a laboratory experiment, if subjects were in a room to which the experimenter had given them the key, and to which they anticipated returning in the next few weeks to "help out" the experimenter, they responded more aggressively to the intrusion of a (bogus) telephone repairman.[41]

This link between heightened defensiveness and future time commitment obtained in a lab setting parallels the field findings by Edney: Those who anticipated living longer at a residence had more territorial displays, and responded more quickly to an intruder.[42] The extent of future time commitment to a locale then, no matter what the setting, appears linked with vigorousness of territorial functioning.

Consequences of territorial functioning

Psychological outcomes

Use setting more effectively

Minimal territorial functioning allows individuals, or small groups, to retain valuable sites within a setting for their own use, and thus to *use the setting more effectively*. Behaviors such as marking, and discouraging intruders, help preserve functional benefits for the occupant(s) in the

---

[39] Haber (1980).
[40] Sommer & Becker (1969).
[41] Edney, J. J. (1972). Place and space: The effects of experience with a physical locale. *Journal of Experimental Social Psychology, 8*, 124–135.
[42] Edney, J. J. (1972). Property, possession, and permanence: A field study of human territoriality. *Journal of Applied Social Psychology, 2*, 275–282.

setting. Students in classrooms can focus better on teaching, library users can study more effectively, and bar patrons can have a better chance of meeting others.

The enhanced use of setting resources provided by territorial functioning is demonstrated in a study carried out in a video arcade. Even though, given the layout of the setting, displaying markers is not possible, machine users use nonverbal channels to maintain their "claim."[43] Using both naturalistic observation and actual experimental interventions Carol Werner and her colleagues observed that:

Many players, about 40 percent, spontaneously touched the machines before actual play began;
When threatened with an invasion while not playing, individuals were more likely to touch their current machine; and
If a confederate, even though not playing, was standing close to a machine, and touching it, others were less likely to "invade" and ask to use the machine.

So, in settings where markers cannot be spread out to delineate a territory, due to the nature of or arrangements in the setting, nonverbal channels can be used to preserve access to resources in the setting.

Preserving access to a valuable site within the setting increases the actual need facilitation a person or group is able to achieve in the setting. And, markers reduce potential thwarting when the occupant leaves the site temporarily.

Distancing

Minimal territorial functioning results in a distancing between different occupant groups within the setting. Thus, different individuals or groups are less likely to interfere with one another's usage of the setting. This distancing reduces the chances of one's activities being thwarted by another user, thus increasing environmental controllability.

Ecological outcomes

The preceding two psychological consequences can also be viewed from an ecological perspective that takes into account their impacts on the setting.

---

[43] Werner, C. M., Brown, B. B., & Damron, G. (1981). Territorial marking in a game arcade. *Journal of Personality and Social Psychology, 41*, 1096–1104.

Preserving setting from overuse

By distancing user groups from one another, overuse of the setting is avoided. Since spacing is preserved, the total number of users or user groups in the setting is controlled. Under special conditions these spacing mechanisms can be overridden. But in most instances they help keep down the total "load" on the setting, or on particular sites within the setting.

This load-control function may keep setting usage at *less than* optimal levels in some instances. Would-be users of a setting, whom the setting has room to accommodate, may be deterred. For example, a person thinking about studying in a library where there are eight- and ten-person tables may be discouraged from studying there if he or she sees only two or three persons per table. The person opts not to use sites within the setting because persons there are claiming more space than perhaps they need.

Differentiation within the setting

From the perspective of the setting, territorial functioning, and in particular markers, clearly differentiates the setting into used and unused portions. Thus, entrants to the setting can easily discern which sites are currently in use, and which are not. Stated differently, the overall legibility of the setting is enhanced, and the entry of newcomers into the setting is channelled effectively towards the unused portions.

Social psychological outcomes

The foregoing psychological and ecological consequences, by implication, will reduce interpersonal and intergroup conflicts over spatial matters. If people or user groups are better distanced from one another, and if it is made clear which sections within a setting are currently in use, users within the setting are less likely to come into conflict about which space is whose. Up to a certain point, there is mutual recognition of and respect for the claims made in the setting.

And, when encroachments are necessary, informal protocols structure the transactions between the occupant and others. Norms about giving up a seat if a person claims he was there first, asking a neighbor if someone is using an empty seat before occupying it, and other rituals geared towards occupying, reclaiming, and ceding sites also reduce potential disagreements.

Minimal territorial functioning: similarities to and differences from functioning on other points of the centrality continuum

Differences

In public or open-access settings, territorial functioning is much more constricted than in interior or exterior residential settings. These limitations stem from the fact that the setting is usually, by definition, open to all. And, the time of occupancy is minimal. Thus, territorial functioning in locations where the person–place bond is of low centrality is different from instances where centrality is higher.

1. Marking is less extensive and elaborate. The range of elements that can be used as markers is limited to what the users can easily bring into the setting. And since markers are portable, they can always be taken by others. So, very valuable or personal items are not likely to be used as markers.

2. Thus, markers in an open-access setting provide less information about the occupant than do markers in other settings. Little about the occupant is revealed – perhaps sex, age, and something about taste – but not much more.

3. Related to the "bare-bones" markers and the public nature of the setting in question, there is little correspondence between territorial functioning and extant social structure. The spatial ecology, apart from indicating which places are used and by whom, does not mirror the local social structure. The close social–spatial correspondence evident in interior and outdoor settings, and in regular use locations, is not evident when person–place bonds are of low centrality.

4. The minimal social structure of open-access locations results in fewer social supports for territorial claims. Since usage is irregular, and there is turnover in the other persons present, one's claim does not automatically receive support from adjoining others, although their support can be enlisted through direct query. Before leaving, one can ask one's neighbor to "watch" a spot, or a potential invader can ask a neighbor if an empty seat is "taken."

5. The spatial extent of the claim is quite restricted, and limited usually to how much space one "needs" in the setting.

6. The temporal extent of the claim is limited by the setting program. In addition to the setting program, informal norms operating in the setting may further limit how long one can claim a site within the setting. In a video arcade, for example, it may be considered very selfish to stay at a popular game for more than, say, five games in a row, when others are waiting to use the machine.

There are instances in which claims are legitimately projected forward some time in the future. The German beach people "reserving" a spot for a future date is a case in point. Another example is spot reserving at the Vienna opera. But, when such claims are projected forward for a considerable amount of time, more than just a few minutes, there is either cooperation on the part of those who manage the setting, and/or strong informal supporting norms in operation.

Similarities

There are numerous similarities between territorial functioning when centrality is low and territorial functioning at other points on the centrality continuum. These similarities highlight the conceptual linkages between minimal territorial functioning and territorial functioning at higher points on the centrality continuum.

1. Markers play a key role in highlighting and reserving claims to a site.
2. There is widespread agreement on how to "read" or "decode" markers.
3. Territorial functioning is highly context specific. It is tailored to the behavior setting, and to the values of the specific site within the setting.
4. Territorial behaviors match territorial cognitions. The latter are reflected in the perceived desirability of a locale.
5. At a general level – stress reduction, reduction of interpersonal conflict, and enhancement of setting legibility and functioning – the consequences of territorial behaviors are similar.

Summary

Minimal territorial functioning occurs in public or open-access locations where individuals or small groups "lay claim" to a space and/or a resource in the setting, and the person–place transactions are of low centrality. The claims made are limited spatially, temporally, and behaviorally. The limitations on territorial functioning stem largely from the open nature of the surrounding behavior setting, the operating setting program, and the person or group's use of the setting for functional purposes only. Minimal territorial functioning serves no expressive function. In addition, in these settings a person or group is most usually surrounded by strangers, and thus has minimal social support for defending a claim.

The nature of the setting program, and the goals of the individual or group in question, determine what physical (including locational) factors make a particular site within the setting more or less desirable. More desirable sites are more stoutly defended by returning occupants.

Social factors of sex composition and group size are linked to how a claim is manifested. The proper interpretation of sex differences is not yet clear. In the case of increasing group size, the presence of the larger group highlights the claim. Thus, it is less necessary to advertise the claim by increasing space or markers per person.

Broad-ranging cross-cultural differences in *relevance* of territorial functioning to public settings, and in *extent* of claims, have been observed.

Past time and anticipated future time at a site are both linked with behavioral vigor of claims to the site.

PART IV
APPLICATIONS TO SOCIAL
PROBLEMS

In the preceding four chapters we have considered territorial functioning in a variety of settings, ranging from sites where the person–place transactions are of highest centrality to places where they are weakest. This examination has explored how territorial functioning is shaped by context and in turn influences intrapersonal, interpersonal, and ecological outcomes.

This section considers two current social problems to determine if territorial functioning:

Helps us better *analyze* or *dissect* social problems; and
Suggests *new solutions* to these problems.

Exploring the potential applicability of territorial functioning to "real-world" issues is important on two grounds. First, it may yield new insight into the causes and solutions of a particular problem. It may allow policymakers to view a concern in a new light, increasing their leverage by suggesting new points of intervention.

Second, application to extant social problems is one of the most powerful means for improving a theory. Examining a theory in a practical context suggests new conceptual refinements that would not have been evident otherwise. In other words, application is a powerful engine for theory development.

Two social problems are addressed in this section. Chapter 11 examines three aspects of disorder: crime (including both "street crimes" such as muggings and assaults, and property crimes such as burglary),

247

fear of crime, and vandalism. The relevance of territorial functioning to these outcomes is reviewed, and processes underlying this influence are outlined. This chapter builds on and extends the material discussed in Chapter 8 on the outdoor residential environment.

Chapter 12 addresses territorial functioning and issues of resource conservation. Particular attention is devoted to an allocation strategy – a *territorializing strategy* – based on territorial functioning. The strategy permits segmentation of space and resources. Experimental studies have demonstrated the beneficial impacts of such a strategy. These findings, and their potential applicability to energy dynamics in everyday settings, are scrutinized.

Stepping back from the particular issues addressed, this section underscores the continuing viability and expanding applicability of territorial concepts. They can capably address everyday problems and contain a richness conducive to theoretical articulation that meshes well with practical concerns. (The reader, after digesting the next two chapters, may wish to return to this statement, and consider to what extent he or she agrees with it.)

11
DISORDER

The first criminal is the landlord.
– Lena Boone, long-time president of the Upton Improvement Association (Baltimore)

This chapter considers disorder, in particular, the issues of crime, fear of crime, and vandalism. It addresses the question: How is territorial functioning relevant to these outcomes? Where territorial functioning is "stronger," are crime, fear of crime, and vandalism less evident? If so, why?

Organization of the chapter

The chapter opens with an outline of the three related social problems to be addressed. Following this introduction a general model linking territorial functioning to these outcomes is presented. The model constitutes an application and extension of the general model we have been relying on throughout the volume. Next, the theoretical processes linking territorial functioning to crime, fear of crime, and vandalism are outlined. This preliminary orientation completed, we examine the empirical work on each of the "predictors" of disorder used in our model: physical and social factors, context, territorial functioning, and offender perceptions. The final sections of the chapter consider the practical implications of research to date, future research needs, and conclusions.

The nature of the problems

Crime

Crime has insinuated itself into the lives of millions of Americans. The Bureau of Justice Statistics estimates that about one quarter of all households in America are "touched" by crime in a year.[1] Luckily, the number of households experiencing serious or violent crime is much smaller.

Nonetheless, it is clear that in the last 25 years this country has witnessed a sizable increase in crime rates (Figure 11.1). The rates for most major crimes rose sharply from the late 1960's through the mid-1970's, leveling off somewhat in the latter 1970's, and climbing again in the early 1980's.

Although the recent increases in crime rates and levels of fear of crime are indisputable, there is less agreement on the reasons for these changes.

There are many theories about what has "caused" this increase in crime. Some suggest that it is largely a function of better and more uniform crime-reporting practices. Others suggest that it is due to baby boomers entering the crime-prone ages of the late teens and early twenties.[2] Still others suggest that changes in routine activity patterns, such as more households with two adults working, and technological changes, such as more portable electronic equipment, have been responsible.[3] But, regardless of the cause, there can be no doubt that the impacts of these changes on American society have been wide reaching and complex.

Behind these numbers, such as those presented in Figure 11.1, are people whose lives have been changed. With society's penchant for numbers and statistics, it is easy to forget the human impact of this social change. As a result of being victimized, people's activity patterns, attitudes towards neighbors, and mental health can be altered, often irrevocably.[4] Even a burglary, considered by police to be less serious than person-to-person crimes such as shootings, stabbings, or armed robbery, can be extremely traumatizing for the victim. It is not uncommon for a burglary victim, even months after the incident, to be afraid to come home alone at night, or to have trouble sleeping.[5]

In addition, there are societal costs to consider. Some have sug-

[1] Rand, M. R. (1986). *Households touched by crime, 1985*. NCJ–101685. Washington, DC: Department of Justice, Bureau of Justice Statistics.

[2] Blumstein, A. (1984). Sentencing reform: Impacts and implications. *Judicature, 68,* 129–139, esp. p. 137 and fn. 20.

[3] Cohen, L. E., & Felson, M. (1979). Social change and crime rate trends. *American Sociological Review, 44,* 588–608.

[4] Karmen, A. (1984). *Crime victims: An introduction to victimology.* Monterey, CA: Brooks/Cole.

[5] Waller, I., & Okihiro, N. (1978). *Burglary: The victim and the public.* Toronto: University of Toronto Press.

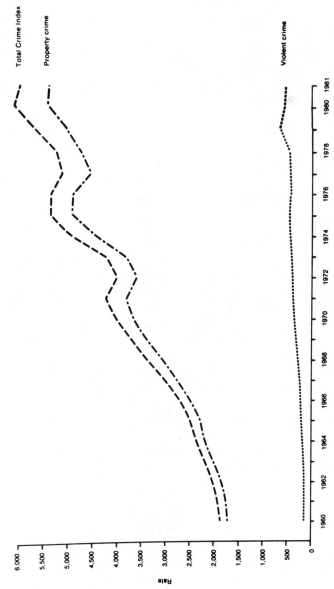

Figure 11.1. Crime in the United States in recent years. Rates shown are per 100,000 inhabitants, based on crimes reported to the police. *Source:* E. J. Brown, T. J. Flanagan, and M. McLeod (Eds.), *Sourcebook of criminal justice statistics: 1983.* Washington, DC: U.S. Government Printing Office.

gested that crime "atomizes" a community, heightening levels of mutual suspicion and distrust, and making it more difficult for people to work together to solve local problems.[6] Other, more indirect costs may accrue as well. Public funds spent on law enforcement and corrections are funds taken away from improving educational or vocational opportunities. Crime may contribute to the deterioration of urban neighborhoods, and reduce residents' willingness to invest in their property,[7] resulting in lower property taxes and therefore fewer resources to combat other urban ills.[8] In a variety of ways then, both direct and indirect, crime hurts: It hurts individuals, cities, and society. But the reader is surely not surprised by this bad news; the pervasive and increasingly violent nature of crime in our society is widely acknowledged.

Fear of crime

As crime has risen over the last 20 years, so too has *fear of crime* (Figure 11.2). Fear of crime refers to a portion of people's responses to crime; it is an emotional or affective concern for one's safety. It is more than an awareness of or concern about crime. Most typically, fear of crime is gauged by responses to a question such as: "If you were out, alone, at night, in your neighborhood, how safe would you feel? Would you feel very unsafe, unsafe, safe, or very safe?"

As with crime itself, there are numerous "explanations" for the origins of fear of crime, and its recent increases (see the following box). Although none of these explanations is completely satisfactory, it is nonetheless evident that fear of crime is not simply a straightforward reflection of crime. Although victims of crime are more fearful than nonvictims, at an areal level, such as neighborhoods or streetblocks, the linkage is much weaker than people have expected.[9]

---

[6] Conklin, J. E. (1975). *The impact of crime.* New York: Macmillan.

[7] Taub, R., Taylor, D. G., & Dunham, J. (1984). *Paths of neighborhood change: Race and crime in urban America.* Chicago: University of Chicago Press.

[8] Some have suggested that crime may cause people to "flee" the city. Research to date, however, indicates that this is not necessarily the case. See, for example, Guterbock, T. M. (1976), The push hypothesis: Minority presence, crime, and urban deconcentration. In B. Schwartz (Ed.), *The changing face of the suburbs.* Chicago: University of Chicago Press.

[9] For example, at the streetblock level, the correlation between the rate of crimes of violence on the street, and block fear levels, was around .2.

Taylor, R. B., Gottfredson, S. D., & Brower, S. (1984). Understanding block crime and fear. *Journal of Research in Crime and Delinquency, 21*, 303–331.

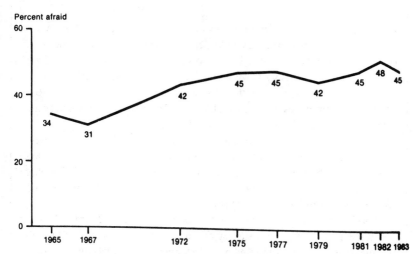

Figure 11.2. Fear of crime in the United States in recent years. Line graphed indicates percent of those questioned who responded positively when asked: "Is there any area right around here – that is, within a mile – where you would be afraid to walk alone at night?" *Source*: George H. Gallup, *The Gallup report*, Report No. 210 (Princeton, NJ: The Gallup Poll, March 1983), p. 6. Figure appears in E. J. Brown, T. J. Flanagan, and M. McLeod (Eds.), *Sourcebook of criminal justice statistics: 1983*. Washington, DC: U.S. Government Printing Office. Figure constructed by *Sourcebook* staff. Reprinted by permission of George H. Gallup, Inc.

Fear of crime:
different views on the causes[10]

When fear of crime, as an issue separate from crime itself, first emerged in the early 1970's, it was thought that fear was largely a "reaction" to crime, that is,

Crime → Perception of crime → Fear of crime

But, this early model foundered on two repeatedly observed findings.

---

[10] For more detail on this material, see Taylor, R. B., & Hale, M. M. (1986). Testing alternative models of fear of crime. *Journal of Criminal Law and Criminology, 77*, 151–189.

For more information on other responses to crime see:

Du Bow, F., McCabe, F., & Kaplan, G. (1979). Reactions to crime: A critical review of the literature. Washington, DC: U.S. Government Printing Office.

First, fear of crime was more widespread than crime itself. Many more people were afraid of crime than had actually been victimized. In addition, fear of crime and crime rates did not correlate very well at the areal level, even if the units of analysis were quite small, such as streetblocks.

Subsequently, several models were developed suggesting potential "multiplier" variables, that is, variables causally interposed between crime and fear that explained the higher fear levels.

Wes Skogan and his colleagues proposed an *indirect victimization* model.[11] The essential idea is that crime victims tell neighbors and acquaintances about what has happened to them. The latter then become more fearful. Thus, local communication about crime and crime-related issues boosts residents' fear levels.

Another perspective has concentrated on *perceptions of disorder*. Developed independently, and in slightly different forms by Hunter and his colleagues,[12] and by Wilson and Kelling,[13] the kernel of the model is that if people see more physical and social signs of decay around where they live, they will feel more vulnerable and fearful. Physical signs of decay include abandoned houses and cars, graffiti, vacant lots littered with trash, and so on.

A somewhat more complex variant of the disorder model, discussed by Conklin[14] and by Lewis and Salem,[15] has been proposed that draws on the concept of *community concern*. The notion is that if people see lots of signs of disorder around where they live, and if these "cues" make them more concerned about the viability of the local community, then those people will be more fearful.

All three of these models contain a "kernel of truth." An analysis of the causes of individuals' fear levels, carried out by Margaret Hale and myself, found that the key variables in each model were indeed predictive of fear levels. The "strength" of the models, however, was not overwhelming. Although some models were better at predicting fear levels than others, in general the models explained only about 10 percent of the variation in fear levels. In short, much remains to be learned about the causes of fear of crime.

[11] Skogan, W., & Maxfield, M. (1981). *Coping with crime*. Beverly Hills: Sage.

[12] Hunter, A. (1978). Symbols of incivility. Paper presented at the annual meeting of the American Society of Criminology, Dallas, November.

[13] Wilson, J. Q., & Kelling, G. (March 1982). Broken windows: The police and public safety. *Atlantic*, 29–38.

[14] Conklin (1975).

[15] Lewis, D., & Salem, G. (1980). Crime and urban community. Unpublished final report. Evanston, IL: Center for Urban Affairs, Northwestern University.

Fear, like crime, has numerous costs for individuals and society. People may buy unnecessary security hardware or private protection services. Second, individuals or households may, as a result of fear of crime, restrict their activities. They may be less willing to go out at night, or willing to go only to certain locations, avoiding others. This means lost social opportunities for the individuals affected. And, third, from the community perspective, fear may contribute to higher levels of suspicion, or distrust, thereby weakening the neighborhood "fabric." Fear of crime has its own identifiable individual and societal costs.

Vandalism

Vandalism is "the willful or malicious destruction, injury, disfigurement, or defacement of any public or private property."[16] Vandalism, like divorce or herpes, is a social problem that does not respect class boundaries. All neighborhoods are vulnerable. (The following box discusses an example in a suburban, upper-class community.)

Vandalism and graffiti are not just inner-city problems

In 1981, in a very respectable neighborhood in affluent, quiet Severna Park, Maryland, youths went on a vandalism spree after a local person was convicted in a highly publicized burglary/arson/theft trial. The front of the local Episcopal church was spray painted. Perhaps the "high" point of the rampage was when "vandals stole a 1979 Cadillac Eldorado, spray-painted 'Free Dave' on the sides, top and rear, and drove it through a chain link fence and into a partly drained Chartridge community swimming pool."[17]

No neighborhood is immune. And neither are college campuses. In the last ten years campus vandalism has emerged as a major problem in college residential life. Some universities have commissioned special task forces to investigate the problem.[18] In Boston, the president of a major university refused to repaint the student dormitories or replace destroyed fixtures because he was convinced that the surfaces and items would be immediately revandalized.

[16] *Uniform Crime Reporting Handbook* (1978). Washington, DC: FBI.

[17] Ettlin, M. D. (October 22, 1981). Severna Park vandalism spree mounts. *Baltimore Sun*, pp. C1, C10.

[18] See, for example, *Task Force on Vandalism: Summary report* (May 1980). Storrs, CT: University of Connecticut.

In cities, vandalism has recently been recognized as a major problem and has gained the attention of several top officials. When Philadelphia Mayor Wilson Goode assumed office, he worked with citizens to scrape and wash graffiti off public buildings. In Baltimore, William Donald Schaefer "declared war" on vandalism. He noted: "The problem of vandalism is of great concern to me. It negatively affects the attitudes of our communities and businessmen, and is a source of costly unattractiveness in our city. The eradication of vandalism and its causes would result in a healthier and more attractive Baltimore, and that is my top priority."[19] He mounted a widely publicized campaign that allied businesspersons, communities, and schools.

Despite the widespread attention given to the problem by the public and private sectors, proposed solutions have not always been well thought out. For example, in the South Bronx, thousands of dollars were spent for life-size decals to put on vacant, boarded-up housing. Blank facades with red wood over the doors and windows suddenly sprouted flowerboxes and curtains.[20] The idea was to make the vacant houses look occupied. It is doubtful that neighbors were convinced. What are needed are solutions solidly based on empirically supported, generalizable theories.

Several theories of vandalism have been formulated. Two that are particularly pertinent to environment–behavior linkages are briefly described.

Allen and Greenberger have developed an *aesthetic theory of vandalism* that is basically concerned with vandals' choice of objects to be broken.[21] They hypothesized that, all else equal, vandals will choose to break those objects that look more interesting as they are being destroyed. More complex patterns of destruction are assumed to be more enjoyable. In an experiment where participants saw different types of glass breaking, they indicated they would be most interested in actually breaking the type whose disintegration was judged by others to be more complex.

This theory, although not empirically supported in field settings, has already been put to use. In some locales, school supervisors have tried turning outside lights *off* so that vandals cannot see what they were breaking. Vandalism rates have not declined, and residents living near the darkened schools often feel less safe.

---

[19] Personal communication, January 13, 1981.

[20] Hess, J. L. (November 17, 1983). False images. *Baltimore Sun*, p. A17.

[21] Allen, V. L., & Greenberger, D. B. (1978). An aesthetic theory of vandalism. *Crime and Delinquency, 24*, 309–321.

Greenberger, D. B., & Allen, V. L. (1980). Destruction and complexity: An application of aesthetic theory. *Personality and Social Psychology Bulletin, 6*, 479–483.

A second relevant psychological theory is Fisher and Baron's *equity theory of vandalism*.[22] The basic assumption of this model is that vandalism is not, as some have suggested, a "senseless" crime; rather, the authors suggest, it has clear motivations. In particular, the authors propose that those who experience inequity – getting less than their fair share – will be motivated to seek redress. If, in addition, those individuals experience moderate-to-low levels of perceived control, they will seek compensation through vandalism. Those who are very low on perceived control will revert to a state of learned helplessness. Those who are very high on internal control will seek retribution through socially accepted means. That is, whether or not vandalism is chosen as a "channel" for redress of perceived inequity depends upon the individual's level of perceived control. Architectural and group factors come into play in determining the type of vandalism committed (malicious vs. tactical/ideological) and actual site choice.

Simply put, if an individual perceives that he has been treated unfairly or unjustly by an institution, and if he also feels only a moderate amount of control over his own life, he may "pay back" the institution by vandalizing institutional property.

A third perspective on one aspect of vandalism – graffiti – has been offered by two social geographers, Ley and Cybriwsky.[23] Very simply, the authors have suggested that gang graffiti serves as group territorial markers. They have observed that graffiti is more intense nearer the core of a corner gang's domain; in disputed zones one group's graffiti is amended, often obscenely, by another group; graffiti expresses and is spatially coincident with a group's boundaries; and graffiti is an indicator not only of underlying sentiments but also possible harassments that will be perpetrated on intruding individuals, or groups, in the case of racial succession in a neighborhood (Figure 11.3).

Linking territorial functioning and disorder

Extending the general model

The organizing scheme we have adopted throughout can be applied to problems of disorder. The main elaboration of the model required is the inclusion of offender- or delinquent-based processes.

The modified model is presented in Figure 11.4. It predicts, in keeping

[22] Fisher, J. D., & Baron, R. M. (1982). An equity-based model of vandalism. *Population & Environment*, 5, 182–200.

[23] Ley, D., & Cybriwsky, R. (1974). Urban graffiti as territorial markers. *Annals of the Association of American Geographers*, 64, 491–505.

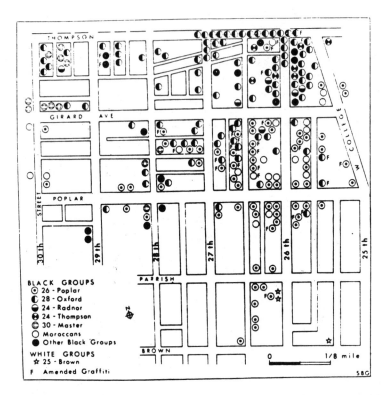

Figure 11.3. Gang graffiti in northwest Fairmount, Philadelphia, in the early 1970's. Note that the distribution of each gang's graffiti is uneven, becoming more concentrated near the center of activity. Note also overlap in several places between the graffiti of different groups, indicating contested areas. *Source*: D. Ley and R. Cybriwsky (1974), Urban graffiti as territorial markers. *Annals of the Association of American Geographers, 64,* 491–505. Reprinted with permission of the Association of American Geographers and Roman Cybriwsky.

with the earlier evidence reviewed, that social, physical, and contextual factors influence territorial functioning, and that these same factors influence offender- or delinquent-based perceptions. Territorial functioning, and these other parameters, have impacts on disorder *in part* because of their influences on offender- or delinquent-based processes. In other words, territorial functioning, and the other social, physical, and contextual predictors, have an influence on the outcomes; some of the influence is direct, and some is mediated by offender- or delinquent-based processes.

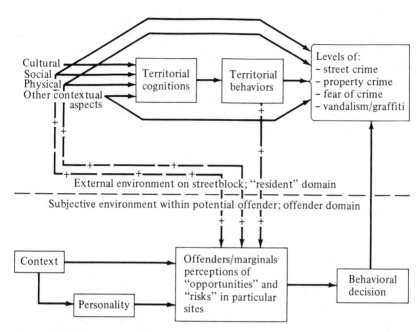

Figure 11.4. Extension of the general conceptual model: understanding crime and related outcomes. *Dashed lines* (—+—+—+—) indicate conceptual links as yet unverified.

Conceptualizing the links between territorial functioning and disorder

The model in Figure 11.4 suggests that territorial functioning is linked to disorderly outcomes through its impact on offender perceptions and behaviors. This relationship is multistranded. Territorial functioning can be connected to disorder in many different ways. This section outlines the various causal pathways involved in these linkages. In some instances, there is little evidence for the proposed influence; in other cases, there are some supporting data.

Crime

Eyes on the street. How people use the outdoor space adjoining their residence is part and parcel of territorial functioning. Those who are outside more often find the setting more socially "legible." They have a better sense of who's who. It appears that offenders against persons, as well as property offenders, view the mere presence of people outdoors as a risk factor. In the case of street offenders like muggers, the evidence is indirect. Since muggings occur in more deserted areas, with fewer natural guardians, it can be inferred that offenders were choosing sites that lacked "eyes."[24] Interviews with suburban burglars have provided direct confirmation of offenders' desire to avoid well-peopled blocks.[25] Offenders' avoidance of places where there are lots of "eyes on the street" vindicates Jane Jacobs' suggestion, made over 25 years ago, about the safety-enhancing benefits of "eyes on the street."[26]

Vigilance and surveillance. Although offenders unfamiliar with a particular locale may avoid committing offenses on blocks where many people are present, as they learn about a site they may gain insight into people's willingness or unwillingness to keep an eye on street events, and/or to intervene in incidents. The mere presence of people, albeit a deterrent in and of itself to crime or related incidents, does not mean that residents or bystanders will intervene in an incident, either directly or indirectly.[27] And it appears that offenders familiar with a locale avoid committing offenses where residents or users *would* intervene. Supporting evidence comes from Sally Merry's ethnographic study of a multiracial housing project outside Boston.[28] Clearly evident in her interviews with local offenders was their awareness of where residents lived who would intervene or call the police, and their avoidance of such locations within the project. (No direct evidence on the sensitivity of burglars to surveillance per se is available.) Some folks are more vigilant and responsive than others, and street offenders are aware of these differences. This constitutes a second channel by which territorial functioning is linked to disorderly outcomes.

Empirical links between territorial functioning and crime have been observed from the residents' perspective as well. A Baltimore study

[24] Rhodes, W. M., & Conly, C. (1981). Crime and mobility: An empirical study. In P. J. Brantingham & P. L. Brantingham (Eds.), *Environmental criminology*. Beverly Hills: Sage.

See also:

Shotland, R. L., & Goodstein, L. I. (1984). The role of bystanders in crime control. *Journal of Social Issues, 40*, 9–26.

[25] Rengert, G., & Wasilchick, P. (1986). *Suburban burglary*. Springfield, IL: Thomas.

[26] Jacobs, J. (1961). *The death and life of great American cities*. New York: Vintage.

[27] Shotland & Goodstein (1984).

[28] Merry, S. E. (1981a). *Urban danger: Life in a neighborhood of strangers*. Philadelphia: Temple University Press.

Merry, S. E. (1981b). Defensible space undefended. *Urban Affairs Quarterly, 16*, 397–422.

found that crimes of violence to persons were lower on streetblocks where residents felt a stronger sense of responsibility for events occurring in near-home, public spaces like the sidewalk in front of the house and the alley behind.[29]

Markers suggest caring, vigilance, or willingness to intervene. Potential offenders, just like residents, can probably "read" the territorial markers in a location such as signs of beautification or upkeep, and make inferences about how likely residents are to "look out" for things, and/or how willing they might be to do something should an incident arise. Lacking direct behavioral evidence of residents' or shopkeepers' willingness to intervene, potential offenders can use the much more broadly available presence or absence of territorial markers as a "proxy" measure of how residents will act. Absent these signs of upkeep, etc., a potential offender will more quickly assume that residents are vulnerable, or relatively helpless. The quotation from the community organization president at the beginning of this chapter reflects this line of reasoning: Uncaring landlords who let properties deteriorate are encouraging offenders to view the site as more vulnerable.

Indirect evidence in support of this connection comes from Barbara Brown's analysis of burglarized and nonburglarized households in a suburban neighborhood.[30] The attitudes of nonburglarized residents – they reported feeling more pride, compared to burglarized residents, in the appearance of their homes – suggested they kept up the outside better. In addition, nonburglarized sites had more extensive real and symbolic barriers, and thus were more clearly "set off" from the adjoining public arena of the street. So, although offender perceptions have not yet been directly examined, the available evidence suggests that potential offenders are sensitive to territorial markers such as barriers and upkeep.

In short, the mere presence of people, the presence of people who are known to keep an eye on things or to intervene in one way or another, and the presence of territorial markers represent three different ways that territorial functioning can impinge upon potential street or property offenders. The strength of the evidence in support of these three channels varies, being stronger for the first two than the last.

---

[29] Taylor et al. (1984).

[30] Brown, B. B., & Altman, I. (1983). Territoriality, defensible space, and residential burglary: An environment analysis. *Journal of Environmental Psychology, 3,* 203–220.

Brown, B. B. (1982). House and block as territory. Paper presented at the annual meeting of the American Psychological Association, Washington, DC, August.

Fear of crime

Residents are reassured by the behaviors and markers of coresidents.
Residents have continuous access to information about how much coresidents keep an eye on street happenings, intervene or get help when
it is needed, and keep their place up. That is, the three aspects of
territorial behavior available to potential offenders are also apparent to
coresidents. The latter – territorial markers – are a form of continuously
available "evidence." We discussed in Chapter 8 how residents make
inferences about their neighbors based on such evidence. One such
inference is how likely coresidents would be to help out.[31] They can
estimate how likely it is, were they themselves not home, that their
neighbor would chase a suspicious-looking stranger out of their backyard. Or, they can gauge how likely their neighbor would be to rout
some bottle-tossing teens out of the alley. Evidence from surrounding
coresidents of "vigorous" territorial functioning is reassuring and thus
reduces the fear of crime experienced by a particular resident. The
resident does not have a sense of being completely surrounded by an
unlimited, overwhelming threat. Thus, at least in the area close to home,
on the block, or perhaps in the neighborhood, he or she will feel safer.

The lack of territorial signs may be fear inducing for two reasons.
Not only will the resident be more likely to conclude that coresidents
would not help were there a need. He or she may also come to feel
more threatened by the coresidents themselves. One's greatest potential
enemy is one's neighbor. Neighbors see when you leave, when you come
home, what kind of new purchases you make. A close neighbor has all
the information needed to carry out a successful burglary. Perhaps territorial markers serve to reassure residents about one another; they are
symbols of commitment to the locale, and indicate adherence to public
norms of right conduct.

Empirical links between fear of crime and territorial functioning have
been observed at the individual and areal level, and in the commercial
as well as residential environment. In the residential context, fear of
crime is lower on blocks where residents feel more responsible for what
happens in near-home public spaces.[32] At the individual level, *controlling for differences between blocks*, individuals who could better recognize insiders and outsiders in the private spaces – front yards and

---

[31] They can make inferences about what Mann calls the *latent neighborliness* of their
coresidents.

Mann, P. H. (1954). The concept of neighborliness. *American Journal of Sociology,*
60, 163–168.

[32] Taylor et al. (1984).

backyards – immediately adjoining their homes, and who felt more responsible for what happened there, had lower fear levels.

Moving from the residential to the commercial environment, a Minneapolis-St. Paul study of small commercial centers examined links between fear and "weak" territorial functioning.[33] In commercial centers where residents living nearby felt less responsibility for what happened on the sidewalks in the center, and less recognition of and control over intruders, those residents also expressed greater fear of crime. And, *controlling for differences between commercial areas*, individuals whose territorial cognitions concerning public space in the commercial center were "weaker" – lower sense of responsibility, less control over intruders – were more fearful of crime. Links between fear and territorial functioning were observed for commercial proprietors as well. Controlling for other factors, those who felt less responsible for what happened on the sidewalk in front of their store were also more fearful of crime. Thus, for nearby residents as well as businesspersons in small commercial centers, the extent of perceived effective territorial functioning was inversely linked with fear of crime.

Vandalism

The spatial distribution of territorial functioning creates "weak points." The spatial distribution of territorial functioning is stronger in some places than in others. The places where it is weak provide areas of opportunity for delinquents and potential vandals; places where, due to low levels of surveillance, natural guardianship, vigilance, or the infrequent presence of others, they have a better chance of committing vandalism without being detected.

In other words, from a spatial point of view, areas of low control by residents or occupants, and/or which they view as potentially dangerous, are areas of potential opportunity for vandals. (Note that the areas vandalized in the Severna Park sprees [described earlier in this chapter] *lacked* natural guardians at the times of the incident.)

Empirical links. An analysis of the spatial ecology of stripped cars provides support for the suggested link between "holes" in the territorial fabric and vandalism.[34] Although car theft is a crime, separate from the

---

[33] McPherson, M., Silloway, G., & Frey, D. L. (1983). Crime, fear, and control in neighborhood commercial centers. Draft final report. Grant no. 80-IJ-CX-0073. Washington, DC: National Institute of Justice.

[34] Ley, D., & Cybriwsky, R. (1974). The spatial ecology of stripped cars. *Environment and Behavior, 6*, 53–68.

Table 11.1. *Land use and stripped cars*

Rank/type of land use	% stripped cars ($N = 138$)
1. Institutional	22.5
2. Vacant house or store	21.0
3. Doorless flank (side of building)	20.3
4. Vacant/parking lot	13.0
5. Occupied apartment or store	12.3
6. Occupied house	10.9

Source: David Ley and Roman Cybriwsky, "The spatial ecology of stripped cars." *Environment and Behavior, 6* (1974), 53–68. Copyright © 1974 by Sage Publications, Inc. Reprinted by permission of Sage Publications, Inc., and Roman Cybriwsky.

theft process is the process of abandonment and subsequent vandalization of autos. A survey of one part of Philadelphia revealed that stripped cars were most likely to be found where there was minimal territorial control (see Table 11.1).

If car-stripping is one manifestation of delinquent or criminal activity, we conclude that this form of behavior does indeed make its own distinctive bid for space, and that this bid is located in zones and at points where space is otherwise weakly claimed and poorly surveilled – at the interstices between local control systems.[35]

Graffiti and vandalism can serve as markers. Groups of delinquents or those viewed as "marginal" by most occupants are engaged in their *own* territorial functioning, "sending messages" to one another (see Figure 11.3).

Determinants of territorial functioning: their links to territorial functioning and disorder

In this section, factors hypothesized to bolster territorial functioning and decrease disorder, either directly or through territorial functioning, are considered.

---

[35] Ibid., p. 65

Physical determinants

Physical supports for territorial functioning have received considerable attention. *Defensible space theory* is concerned with events on a small scale: the site, or the streetblock. The theoretical nucleus of defensible space theory was first proposed by Jane Jacobs. Based on one case study – her observations in Greenwich Village in the late 1950s – she concluded that certain design guidelines could be effective in reducing crime in urban residential areas.[36]

The specific "principles" articulated appear in the accompanying boxes. Although this perspective did embody some fundamental misunderstandings of human territoriality, it is important because it suggested how territoriality might be relevant to the crime problem.[37] And, more important, it forced people to examine the contribution of features of the physical environment to crime.

Origins of defensible space

Jane Jacobs has suggested the following design and siting principles for "safe" residential environments:

1. If buildings were oriented towards the street this would encourage surveillance by residents indoors; there would be more "eyes on the street." Knowing this, people would be less hesitant to use the street, and there would be more surveillance by outdoor users as well as indoor residents.

2. Public and private domains should be clearly separated. It will then be clear to transients and others which spaces are owned, cared for, and watched over. The clarity of these delineations would deter casual offenders.

3. Outdoor spaces for use by the public should be placed in proximity to intensively used areas. Parks, playgrounds, and rest areas that are "cut

---

[36] Jacobs (1961).

[37] For a detailed discussion of the theoretical shortcomings of defensible space theory see Merry (1981b) or Taylor, R. B., Gottfredson, S. D., & Brower, S. (1980). The defensibility of defensible space. In T. Hirschi & M. Gottfredson (Eds.)., *Understanding crime*. Beverly Hills: Sage. Or see:

Mayhew, P. (1979). Defensible space: The current status of a crime prevention theory. *Howard Journal of Penology and Crime Prevention, 18*, 150–159; or

Mawby, R. I. (1977). Defensible space: A theoretical and empirical appraisal. *Urban Studies, 14*, 169–179.

off" – by distance, buildings, or foliage – from more active locations will not "feel" safe. If people feel vulnerable due to a lack of nearby (potential) assistance, they will not use those locations.

Evidence supporting the relevance of defensible space features was gathered in the 1970s by Newman and colleagues. Limited largely to the public housing context, the results from these studies were mixed.[38] At about this time there were several other studies seeking to link defensible space attributes to crime outcomes. Many of these found consistent but modest links between design features and crime rates, explaining anywhere from 1 to 10 percent of the variation in crime. For example, a British study comparing burglarized households and a general (nonburglarized) household sample found that burglarized houses were characterized by significantly poorer surveillance opportunities, and significantly easier access from nonresidential land uses.[39]

Thus, by the end of the 1970's it was clear that particular design features were linked with lower crime rates. It was not yet clear, however, whether this linkage depended on the physical features "activating" or facilitating residents' territorial functioning.

Defensible space

Jacobs' ideas were later elaborated and labelled "defensible space" by Oscar Newman,[40] who provided additional suggestions why the physical environment should be manipulated: Such manipulations would have a major impact on the residents themselves. Newman proposed that physical design changes could "release latent attitudes in tenants which allow them

[38] For details on this research see Taylor et al. (1980).

[39] Winchester, S., & Jackson, H. (1982). *Residential burglary: The limits of prevention.* Home Office Research and Planning Unit Report: Home Office Research Study no. 74. London: Her Majesty's Stationery Office. See esp. Table 4.2.

[40] Newman, O. (1973a). *Defensible space: Crime prevention through urban design.* New York: Macmillan.

Newman, O. (1973b). *Architectural design for crime prevention.* Washington, DC: Government Printing Office.

Newman, O. (1975). *Design guidelines for creating defensible space.* Washington, DC: Government Printing Office.

to assume behavior necessary to the protection of their rights and property."[41]

The design ingredients in defensible space are fourfold:[42]

1. *Real and symbolic barriers* were to be used to separate the residential environment into smaller, more manageable sectors or segments. This would "encourage tenants to assume territorial attitudes and prerogatives." Residents would be more willing to look out for, and keep control of, the space in question if it was more manageable, and more clearly demarcated from surrounding spaces. "Real" barriers include physical features that would impede access, such as fences, high walls, locked gates, and so on. "Symbolic" barriers did not actually impede or prevent entry, but rather symbolized where the public domain ended and the private domain began. Such barriers might be obvious, such as a low hedge or railing, or more subtle, such as a change in materials from cement to brick, or a modest change in elevation. In short, residents will act territorial if they can see the boundaries of a territory and it is of manageable size.

2. Opportunities for *residential surveillance* must be provided. This applies both to interior spaces, such as hallways, lobbies, and stairways, and exterior spaces. Consequently, spaces adjoining buildings must be situated so that residents can easily overlook them. Lighting must be adequate. (But see Figure 11.5.)

3. The exterior *design of sites must not stigmatize* the residents. In other words, public or low-income housing projects should be built in such a way that nonresidents do not readily perceive the site as such. Stigmatization can be avoided through use of materials, changing the height and size of the buildings, or through other means.

4. Residential structures should be placed in *proximity to safe or non-threatening areas*, and away from unsafe areas. Examples of threatening areas would be industrial sites that are vacant at night, parks that are not well lit or well used, and commercial areas that draw unsavory patrons. Proximity to threatening areas will, it is assumed, increase residents' sense of vulnerability, and therefore make them less likely to watch out over adjacent outdoor spaces.

Subsequent research reported in the early 1980's addressed this gap. Newman himself modified the theory somewhat and included additional design and social "principles." For example, he proposed that the num-

---

[41] Newman (1973b), p. xiii.
[42] Newman (1973a), 9; [1973b], xv.

Figure 11.5. Defensible space features, such as improved street lighting, may serve a variety of purposes. *Source*: *Quincy*. Copyright 1985 by King Features Syndicate, and reprinted by permission.

ber of people who shared a claim to a particular space be reduced.[43] This could be achieved, for example, by reducing the number of apartments that shared a single outside doorway. Such a change would, it was hoped, make residents more willing to act territorial.

Research carried out by Newman and Franck has confirmed the essential "logic" of defensible space.[44] Examining 63 federally assisted or public housing projects in three cities, they focused on physical features such as building size and accessibility.[45] Lower building size, and less accessibility, were expected to be associated with a safer residential context. They observed that the features were linked with resident interaction in and perceptions of control over outside space. (The building site was the unit of analysis.) These attitudes and behaviors were linked to outcomes such as personal crime rates. Thus, the physical features were associated with more "vigorous" territorial functioning, which, in turn, was associated with lower crime rates and fear.

In a residential nonsubsidized housing context, a study of 63 Baltimore streetblocks found that defensible space features were linked to indices of attachment to the neighborhood, and that these in turn were linked to crime and fear.[46]

Thus, in a variety of residential contexts, it does appear that defensible space features are linked to territorial functioning or related processes, such as attachment to place, and via this channel of influence are associated with lower levels of disorder.

[43] Newman (1975), p. 55.
[44] Newman, O., & Franck, K. A. The effects of building size on personal crime and fear of crime. *Population and Environment, 5*, 203–220.
[45] The accessibility measure included many different measures such as real and symbolic barriers, and number of apartments sharing an outside entrance.
[46] Taylor, Gottfredson, & Brower (1984).

Social determinants

We discussed in Chapter 8 how social factors may enhance territorial functioning. The relevant parameters of local social ties include not only network characteristics (extent of network, network density, etc.) but social climate factors as well: perceived homogeneity versus heterogeneity, perceived levels of caring for locale, and so on. Residents, each from their own perspective, may consider the streetblock to be a *consonant or a dissonant social context*.[47] A consonant social context is one in which the individual perceives that others are like him or her on certain critical dimensions (race, class, values, etc.) and in a dissonant social context one perceives that others are dissimilar on key dimensions.

Social factors may directly reduce street crime. If the block is more cohesive, strangers or suspicious persons may be more readily spotted, decreasing their ability to surprise potential victims. Offenders themselves may be aware of relative levels of social cohesion on various blocks, and avoid locations where residents are "tight" with one another. Hypothetically, through territorial functioning social factors may have indirect as well as direct impacts on street crimes.

Perhaps the clearest empirical support for the proposed linkage comes from the Baltimore study of 63 streetblocks.[48] More extensive local social ties were associated with stronger territorial functioning, as measured by stronger feelings of responsibility for near-home spaces such as alley and sidewalk, with a lower rate of crimes of violence to persons (muggings, yokings, purse snatchings, etc.), and with lower levels of fear.

Thus, more extensive local social ties are directly associated with lower levels of disorder; at the same time, they are indirectly linked because they strengthen norms of responsibility for adjoining public spaces.

Intrapersonal factors

Little work linking intrapersonal variables, territorial functioning, and disorder has been carried out, although there are some tantalizing exceptions.

Elderly and fear

The linkage between "stronger" territorial functioning and *lower* fear levels applies to the elderly. Elderly persons who exhibit more territorial

---

[47] Rosenberg, M. (1972). *Society and the adolescent self-image*. Princeton, NJ: Princeton University Press.

[48] Taylor, Gottfredson, & Brower (1984).

markers,[49] or who feel more territorial control,[50] have lower fear levels. The dynamics linking territorial functioning with fear of crime appear to persist, then, even for older persons who generally experience lower levels of environmental mastery.

Perceptions of equity and vandalism

Those who have a low sense of control, and experience inequity, are more likely to report engaging in vandalism.[51] This is in accord with Fisher and Baron's theory about who engages in vandalism.[52]

Context

Territorial functioning viewed as having less deterrent impact in a high-threat setting

Brower suggested that in a residential context where disorder and threat were higher, more redundancy would be required for territorial functioning to maintain its effectiveness.[53] And, this turns out to be the case empirically.[54] Supporting this idea are results from a study by Sidney Brower, Kathleen Dockett, and myself. When asked what would happen in various scenarios depicted with line drawings, those living in a high-threat context felt that multiple territorial cues – fencing *and* plantings – would be necessary to keep intruders out. In other words, the context influenced the perceived adequacy of particular territorial elements.

Stability of context

As stability of context increases, local social ties are strengthened, and territorial functioning becomes more vigorous. For example, on street-

[49] Patterson, A. H. (1978). Territorial behavior and fear of crime in the elderly. *Environmental Psychology and Nonverbal Behavior, 2*, 131–144.

[50] Normoyle, J., Lavrakas, P. J. (1984). Fear of crime in elderly women: Perceptions of control, predictability, and territoriality. *Personality and Social Psychology Bulletin 10*, 191–202.

[51] Warzecha, S., Fisher, J. D., & Baron, R. M. (1984). The equity-control model as predictor of vandalism among college students. Paper presented at the annual meeting of the Eastern Psychological Association, Baltimore, April.

[52] Fisher & Baron (1982).

[53] Brower, S. (1980). Territory in urban settings. In I. Altman, A. Rapoport, & J. Wohlwill (Eds.), *Environment and culture*. New York: Plenum.

[54] Brower, S., Dockett, K., & Taylor, R. B. (1983). Residents' perceptions of site-level features. *Environment and Behavior, 15*, 419–437.

blocks where there were higher proportions of homeowners, we found that residents were more likely to belong to local groups that their neighbors belonged to and that they felt more responsible for what happened in near-home spaces.[55] Stability of context, by increasing social legibility and strengthening norms about involvement in immediate public spaces, contributes to lower levels of disorder.

Subcultural factors

Sometimes territorial functioning can be impeded by subcultural factors, leading to subsequent high fear levels. This is exemplified in the work of Sally Merry.[56] In the multiracial housing project she studied, the different cultural groups in the project were afraid of each other. More specifically, the fear between various pairs of groups was roughly proportional to the cultural distance between them. Thus, the Chinese were most fearful of the blacks, whose customs and language seemed the strangest.

Due in part to this fear and strangeness, the Chinese, who were the most numerous cultural group and thus potentially the strongest group in the community, misperceived the situation. They felt that the blacks were the most dangerous group, and that black youth controlled most of the exterior spaces. Consequently, when the offenses committed by members of one cultural group (blacks) were witnessed by members of another cultural group (Chinese), many instances went unreported because of fear of retaliation. Subcultural differences, and perceived "strangeness" of other groups, inhibited the exercise of territorial control and increased fear of crime.

Thus, to date, a variety of contextual factors have been linked with territorial functioning, and outcomes related to disorder. An important direction for future theory is to develop a comprehensive theory linking areal dynamics – at the neighborhood, streetblock, and subcultural group level – to territorial functioning and disorder.

Practical implications

Indices of territorial functioning have been linked to crime and fear of crime in subsidized housing environments, in more "standard" residential environments, and in small commercial centers. These connections have been observed at both the areal and the individual level. Consequently, it would seem appropriate to move forward with action research

---

[55] Taylor et al. (1984).
[56] Merry (1981a, 1981b).

to see if *changes* in territorial functioning can result in lower levels of crime, fear, or vandalism. The essential thrust of such action research would be to encourage "stronger" territorial functioning, either on the part of individuals, or local organizations.

Two demonstration projects have already been carried out, with mixed results. A longitudinal study designed to implement some defensible space concepts in a public housing setting was carried out in the early 1970's.[57] Two public housing projects with a rowhouse layout were modified in accord with defensible space guidelines (better lighting, fences around housing, individual colors on houses, etc.). (Unfortunately, residents were not involved in the modifications, and one morning awoke to find bulldozers digging away at their doorsteps.) Behavioral and crime changes in the modified locations were noted, and compared to events in physically similar but unmodified sites. The results were complex and equivocal. The modifications did not have a clear-cut enhancing effect on territorial behaviors such as planting and gardening.[58] Impacts on crime were ambiguous. It appeared, then, that the modifications did not disinhibit territorial behavior of residents as planned, and that overall there was no demonstrable deterrent effect.

A second study carried out in an inner-city neighborhood in Hartford, Connecticut, implemented physical changes to make the neighborhood more defensible, reduce through traffic, and "turn the streets back to the people.[59] Again, the results were mixed.

Working from the perspective of this volume, these two demonstration efforts to enhance residents' territorial functioning can be faulted on two grounds. First, and perhaps most importantly, the researchers failed to grasp that territorial functioning is a small group dynamic and that it does not make sense to encourage it at the neighborhood level. Effective boundary regulation depends upon face-to-face ties, such as exist at the streetblock level. Second, the studies relied too heavily on physical

---

[57] Kohn, I. R., Franck, K. A., & Fox, A. S. (1975). *Defensible space modifications in row house communities*. Unpublished final report. New York: Institute for Community Design Analysis.

[58] There were some effects of design on behavior, but these were unanticipated and not mentioned in grant reports. For example, along the backs of row houses large fences were put up to keep out intruders. But this meant that residents had to walk all the way around the group of homes to put their garbage out in the alley. Many residents cut a hole in the fence to get through more easily.

[59] Fowler, F. J., & Mangione, T. W. (1981). *An Experimental effort to reduce crime and fear of crime in an urban residential neighborhood: Re-evaluation of the Hartford neighborhood Crime Prevention Program*. Draft Executive summary. Boston: Center for Survey Research.

changes alone, seeing the physical environment change→territorial functioning change link as stronger and less contingent than it actually is.

Having a much better chance of "success" is an action research project carried out in Brooklyn in the mid–1980's.[60] The researchers there sought to identify ways that could "boost" local block clubs that were involved in anticrime efforts, as well as other activities. Such clubs boost territorial functioning with their emphasis on upkeep, beautification, and watching out for what happens on the street. And, these groups appear to have an impact on outcomes such as fear of crime.

In sum, although there have been some early missteps, action research linking *changes* in territorial functioning with changes in disorder is under way and appears promising. Thus, it may be possible to develop guidelines to help streetblocks "strengthen" territorial functioning and use the territorial functioning–disorder linkage for practical ends. There will be, undoubtedly, many complexities in developing such guidelines, but at least the direction is theoretically sound, and appears worthy of further investigation and application.

Research needs

What is most needed now is research linking offender perceptions and actions with resident territorial dynamics. We need to know, for the purposes of estimating deterrence value, how offenders perceive and evaluate various cues to territorial functioning – markers, surveillance, and so on; and how their valuation of these parameters varies as a function of their own motivations, their background, and other contextual factors. The initial theoretical groundwork in this area has been delineated,[61] and there have been some promising empirical gains.[62]

---

[60] Rich, R. C., Chavis, D., Florin, P., Perkins, D., & Wandersman, A. (1986). Do community organizations reduce crime and fear through crime prevention efforts and informal social control? Paper presented at the annual meeting of the American Society for Criminology, Atlanta, October.

[61] Brown, B. B., & Altman, I. (1981). Territoriality and residential crime: A conceptual framework. In P. J. Brantingham & P. L. Brantingham (Eds.), *Environmental criminology*. Beverly Hills: Sage.

Taylor, R. B., & Gottfredson, S. D. (1986). Physical environment, offenders, and communities. In A. Reiss & M. Tonry (Eds.), *Crime and justice: An annual review of research*, vol. 7. Chicago: University of Chicago Press.

Taylor, R. B. (1987). Toward an environmental psychology of disorder. In D. Stokols & I. Altman (Eds.), *Handbook of environmental psychology*. New York: Wiley.

[62] See, for example, Bennett, T. W., & Wright, R. (1984). *Burglers on burglary: Prevention and the offender*. Farnborough: Gower. See also: *(cont. on p. 274)*

Understanding the resident-environment-offender connections is crucial for a complete grasp of the links between territorial functioning and disorder.

Summary

Territorial functioning is linked to crime, fear of crime, and vandalism. Research and theory suggest that potential offenders are sensitive to the presence of witnesses, territorial behaviors such as surveillance, and territorial markers, and may use the latter as a proxy for residents' willingness to intervene. Both street criminals and property offenders may "take in" or be sensitive to resident territorial functioning.

Territorial functioning probably influences *fear* of crime more directly, based on how residents decode the territorial behaviors and markers of coresidents. Research strongly suggests that vandals use sites where territorial control is weak or nonexistent – areas lacking natural guardians – as opportunity areas for their actions.

In keeping with the evolutionary perspective on the origins of territorial functioning, links at the small group level between territorial indices and disorder have been observed. At this level, territorial functioning can be supported or "strengthened" by local social ties, and particular physical features and site arrangements, although the physical features–territorial functioning link is not as strong as some have proposed. Contextual factors, such as level of perceived threat, overall stability, and subcultural composition, also influence territorial functioning and its link with disorder.

Early efforts to enhance territorial functioning and thereby decrease disorder were aimed at a theoretically inappropriate level – the neighborhood. But current efforts under way focusing on assisting block groups suggest that it may be possible to bolster extant levels of territorial functioning and thereby reduce indices of disorder.

(cont. from p. 273)

Weaver, R., & Carroll, J. (1985). Crime perceptions in a natural setting by expert and novice shoplifters. *Social Psychology Quarterly, 48*, 349–359.

12
RESOURCE CONSERVATION

For that which is common to the greatest number has the least care bestowed upon it.
– Aristotle[1]

Territorial functioning, at the most basic level, involves a segmentation of space; locations are differentiated into those "belonging to" or used by one person or group, or another. As part of this allocation process boundaries are created or maintained. They are selectively permeable: Certain people at certain times, or for certain purposes, are allowed to enter one spatial segment from another, or to cross the boundary. The boundary may be clear-cut or fuzzy, agreed upon or disputed, acknowledged by others or ignored, and consistent or variable. Nonetheless, this process of spatial differentiation is fundamental to territorial functioning.

Focus of the chapter

This chapter considers issues of resource conservation from a territorial perspective.

How is resource conservation related to territorial functioning? Many natural resources are distributed spatially; that is, they are more plentiful in some places than in others. Oysters, growing on oyster beds, are an excellent case in point. Lobsters and crabs, although they migrate, are more plentiful in some locations than others. Wood is a resource clearly fixed in place. Energy resources such as oil and coal, although their refinement and distribution are often centralized, are more plentiful in some parts of a country than others. So, since territorial functioning

[1] Jowett, B., trans. (1885). *The Politics of Aristotle*, vol. 1. London: Clarendon, p. 30.

275

involves the segmentation of space, and many resources are distributed unevenly in space, at certain levels differentiation into territories has implications for resource allocation, and, more importantly, resource conservation. As we will see in this chapter, if a resource is "divided" or segmented into allocations, using a scheme that resembles territorial functioning, such division has implications for how well that resource is managed.

Organization of the chapter

The chapter opens with a couple of "real-world" examples of the impacts of resource segmentation strategies. These examples strongly suggest that the allocation of some resources into "territories" results in better resource management, and fewer chances of resource overuse.

We then consider results from lab experiments that corroborate the patterns observed in these examples. They provide strong evidence of the advantages of a *territorializing strategy*. Such a strategy and its consequences, ecological and psychological, represent an *analog* of territorial functioning observed in settings of varying centrality. The effectiveness of territorializing strategies is illuminated by considering some concepts from microeconomics.

Further, other experimental findings from research on social traps, commons dilemmas, and social dilemmas suggest ways that territorializing strategies could be effectively implemented with small groups, as well as individuals. These findings have implications for applying territorializing strategies more broadly.

The chapter then turns back to the "real world." First, we address the question that many may have been asking: Do we need to worry about resource conservation anyway? Is not this a nonproblem? This is an issue on which sharply differing views are held. We also address policy questions.

Finally, future research needs, both in the laboratory and in the field, are noted. Possibilities of linking territorializing strategies with other approaches to resource conservation, such as an applied behavioral analysis viewpoint, are discussed.

Resources in the real world

Oysters in the Chesapeake: a change from segmented to open waters

In the 1960's the Chesapeake Bay was not a pacific body of water. Watermen,[2] who collected oysters in sail-powered skipjacks, were re-

---

[2] The term "watermen" refers to both men and women who harvest and sell oysters for a living.

stricted to oystering within the region of the bay claimed by their particular county. Thus, the productive oyster bars in the Choptank River, for example, could be dredged only by watermen in the counties bordering the river. Oyster bars are beds of crushed oyster shells; oysters grow productively only on such beds. Occasionally there would be altercations and, literally, running gun battles between different boats. Life was exciting on the bay.

A 1968 court decision, however, struck down the traditional county-line laws. The Maryland waters of the bay were opened to all Maryland watermen. As a result, almost two decades later many sections of the bay have been "fished out."

"There were bars full of big, beautiful oysters in the West River and Herring Bay [on the Western Shore], and the Eastern Shoremen couldn't stand not to get at 'em," said Mr. Harrison, in recalling the events leading to the 1968 decision. "Now," he added, "those bars are long gone, wiped out, and the tables are turned on the Eastern Shore."[3]

Oyster harvests have declined significantly in the succeeding years. In 1983 the catch was 868,000 bushels, "the lowest, by a substantial margin, since oystering began in earnest after the Civil War."[4]

Of course, other factors besides the court decision, such as increasing pollutants and runoffs, may be involved. Nonetheless, many feel that the legal change is a crucial element leading to the current situation. And the legal decision has led to occurrences such as were observed in December 1984 in the little Tred Avon River, near Oxford, Maryland. The modest estuary was clogged with an estimated 400 workboats in the first few weeks of the oyster season.[5]

Even as watermen express concern that the shellfish stocks . . . cannot stand such pressure, they acknowledge there is little they can do except continue to "get yours, or somebody else will."[6]

In short, the 1968 legal ruling "desegmented" the Chesapeake Bay for the watermen, allowing them to catch oysters wherever they wished, instead of limiting them to the waters between their county lines. This has led to increased pressure on the oyster stock and "overfishing," resulting in a subsequent reduction in oyster catches.

It seems plausible to causally link the desegmentation of the bay's wa-

[3] Horton, T. (December 9, 1984a). Baywide scarcity of oysters forces some crewmen to seek jobs ashore. *Baltimore Sun*, pp. 1D, 4D.

[4] Horton, T. (December 9, 1984b). The hunt for oysters brings the "tragedy of the commons" close to home. *Baltimore Sun*, p. 3N.

[5] Horton (1984a).

[6] Ibid., p. ID.

ters with overfishing and reduced catches. But establishing such a connection is complicated by many factors. A simple pre-desegmentation versus post-desegmentation comparison of oyster harvests, though tantalizing, is inconclusive[7] because many *other factors* besides the ruling may also have affected the size of oyster harvests: changes in levels of pollutants, natural cycles, and so on. In short, the impact of the ruling cannot be separated from other *historical influences* that may have been operating.

Fortunately, there is an excellent study available, providing more conclusive evidence of the relative advantages of a highly segmented approach to resource management. The resource in question is lobsters, and the location is Maine.

Lobstering in Maine: island groups versus harbor gangs

James Acheson, an anthropologist, has carried out a number of studies of the Maine lobstering industry. In one study along a stretch of the coast from Boothbay Harbor on up to Seal Harbor, Acheson investigated the consequences of two different types of lobster fiefs.[8] He observed that groups of lobstermen banded into two types and that each type of group fished a particular type of region.

Two types of groups, two lobstering arrangements

Along the coast lobstermen from each harbor or from nearby harbors were likely to form "harbor gangs." These were groups with fluid boundaries. To gain entrance one simply had to live in the area, hang around long enough, and have the proper equipment. The groups could be large, including up to 90 boats or more. The men in these groups had little in common, save for their shared occupation in the same locale. They lobstered in *nucleated territories*. That is, they had a core area that all in the gang agreed was exclusively theirs, whereas towards the edges of the lobstering area there was likely to be overlap with other harbor gangs. (Since the buoys marking lobster pots must have registered designs, it is easy to tell whose traps are whose.) The sharing of the areas along the perimeters is not a great source of concern; rather, it appears to be accepted. The costs of totally excluding outsiders from an area – rigid

[7] Cook, T. D., & Campbell, D. T. (1979). *Quasi-experimentation*. Chicago: Rand McNally.

[8] Acheson, J. M. (1975). The lobster fiefs: Economic and ecological effects of territoriality in the Maine lobster industry. *Human Ecology, 3,* 183–207.

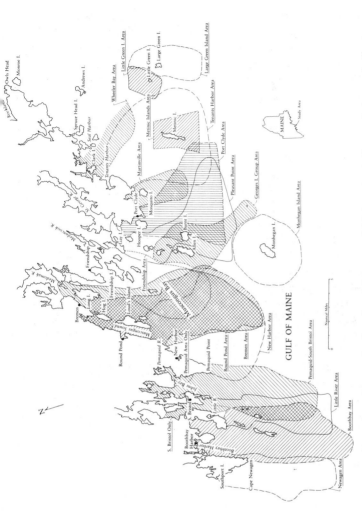

Figure 12.1. Lobstering territories along the central Maine coast. James Acheson indicates that the territories, over a period of more than a decade, have remained for the most part locationally stable. *Source:* James Acheson (in press), *The lobstermen of central Maine.* Hanover: New England Universities Press. Reprinted by permission of the publisher and the author.

boundary maintenance – could be high; one could risk retaliation and the loss of one's traps, which are an expensive investment. Intruders attempting to lobster in the core of another gang's territory are repulsed, but along the boundaries, where the sense of ownership is weaker, invaders are tolerated. Some harbor gangs maintain more clear-cut boundaries than others, but the point is that in all these cases there is a territorial gradient, stronger near the harbor where the boats are anchored, and becoming progressively weaker towards the perimeter. There is *not* a rigid, impermeable segmentation of the lobstering areas.

On the offshore islands, however, the territorial structure, socially and spatially, is quite different. The islands are owned and controlled by a small number of families, many of whom have resided there for several generations. On an island it is not at all unusual for different households to share bonds of kinship. The resident groups are thus smaller, "tighter," or more cohesive, and with less permeable group boundaries than is the case landside. All of these factors facilitate coordinated defense of an area.

And defend they do. For the island group, the entire lobstering territory is equally valuable. Waters along the perimeter are defended as vigorously against interlopers as are waters close to the island. If men from a harbor gang put pots in an island *perimeter defended territory*, members of the island group can quickly communicate with each other about the threat, since they live close together and are a small group. They take concerted action, which might be very costly to the intruder. Their lobstering areas are *completely* segmented. So, along the coast of Maine, as in inner-city neighborhoods in Baltimore, stronger ties with local others facilitate territorial control. The social factors facilitating territorial control are similar in the two cases. In both, the presence of cohesive groups allows the emergence of a group-based or superordinate goal, which takes precedence over individual goals.

Economic consequences

Microeconomics as well as social psychology is relevant to this arrangement and cannot be dismissed as a partial cause for the vigorous protection of perimeter-defended territories (some microeconomic concepts are defined in the following box).

Microeconomic concepts, part I

Microeconomists are concerned with patterns of resource use and conservation as an example of how people use or conserve a "good." They invoke various concepts to explain the patterns of behavior they observe. In the case of the lobster fiefs, and in other resource situations, these concepts are useful for describing the economic impacts of various behavior patterns. Some of those concepts are introduced here; additional ones are explained in the next box (p. 286).

Externalities. In economic terms an externality is present in situations where my behavior has an impact on you, even though you have not allowed this or agreed that it could happen. Externalities can be positive or negative. *Negative externalities* abound in the real world. Residents of Love Canal who lived downwind from the Hooker chemical dumpsite and saw the new paint blister off their homes suffered a negative externality. You suffer a negative externality when your neighbor is grilling on his back patio, suffocating you as you sit chatting on your back porch.

Examples of positive externalities also exist in the real world but are somewhat rarer than negative externalities. In the real world, the renovator who fixes up an unsightly building is creating a positive externality for neighbors whose property values subsequently increase (unless neighbors cannot afford the higher taxes). Externalities affect others.

Utilities. Externalities must be distinguished from utilities. The *utility* of my behavior or my group's behavior is the sum of all the positive and negative things that happen to me as a result of what I do, or my group does.

Think about a herdsman grazing his cow on the common. Assume that there are already N herdsmen, each grazing one cow on the common. If the herdsman adds one more cow to the common, the resulting positive utility is $+1$. The herdsman will realize one more unit of profit when he sells his cows. But there is also a negative result: The added cow means there may be some overgrazing; his cow cannot get as much grass as it needs. Therefore, as a result of overgrazing, his cow will not be as fat as it should be, slightly reducing his profit.

But, since this negative result is spread out over all the herders, the negative utility to the particular herdsman is $-1/N$; the negative externality to all the others is $-([N-1]/N)$. So, if the individual herdsman adds together the partial utilities, the profit from adding a cow is $(1 - 1/N)$. The negative utility is much smaller than the negative externality, and much smaller than the positive utility.

Exactly the same calculations apply to a waterman deciding whether to add another boat to an oyster bed that is already being heavily dredged. Thus, since a herdsman or waterman experiences only his positive and negative utilities, and is not influenced (directly) by the negative externalities experienced by others, it is profitable to send another boat to the oyster bed in danger of being dredged out.

> Ironically, in the long run the herdsman or waterman *is* negatively influenced by the externalities because the resource dries up or can no longer replenish itself. But, in the short run, it is only the immediate utilities that matter to the herdsman or waterman.

On the islands, alternative, lucrative occupations are not as available as they are ashore. The islanders are thus more likely to be full-time lobstermen and to depend more heavily on the lobster income to support themselves. Ashore, more of the lobstermen are parttimers who can hold down other jobs in the off season. Stated differently, the marginal utility of the revenue from lobstering is much more significant for islanders than for those in harbor gangs. Likewise, if lobsters were overharvested, the negative utility for those on the islands would be higher than it would be for those ashore. Also, since the island groups are smaller, negative externalities from one individual's overharvesting, influencing another member of the group, are likely to be greater than they would be for shorebased groups.

It is not surprising, therefore, that some of the island groups have worked out cooperative strategies that limit harvesting. One island group agreed that each member would only set out a certain number of traps. Another island group agreed only to put their pots in the water during the first lobstering season (April to June), when prices were highest and their catch would bring the greatest return, and to haul their pots during the second season (August to November).

These different social arrangements indicate a different relationship between the lobsterers and their resource pool (the lobsters). Most significantly, Acheson found that the density of pots per unit of bottom area was less in perimeter than in nucleated territories. This is a function, in the former case, of smaller group sizes, less overlap between groups, and self-imposed limits on harvesting machinery (pots). The last difference also means less cost per boat, and potentially more profit.

Consequently, lobstermen from perimeter-defended territories do better because they

catch more lobsters per trap;
catch larger lobsters, which are more profitable; and thus make more money.

Preliminary estimates made by Acheson suggested that the gross per capita income differential, between those lobstering in nucleated and in perimeter-defended areas, in 1972 dollars, was over $6,000. The net difference may have been even greater given the lower overhead of those in island groups.

Summing-up on lobstering

To recast the findings of this study in a more explicitly territorial terminology: The island-based groups agreed upon clear segmentation of the common resource (lobstering grounds) and effectively prevented "poaching" by others. They maintained exclusive control over a segment of the overall resource. The boundaries of the resource pool were clearly coextensive with the group boundaries. Further, they developed cooperative strategies to limit withdrawals from the resource pool, resulting in a more productive pool (a higher replenishment rate), higher levels of harvesting, and, probably in the long run, a healthier, more viable pool. These strategies were grounded in tradition, kinship, and tightly knit social arrangements. All of these factors facilitated the development of ecologically sound practices.[9]

Implications

As with all case studies, the preceding results are limited. They are nonetheless encouraging and significant. The import of the case study is twofold. First, it indicates that a clear-cut territorializing strategy can have beneficial impacts on the resource pool in question. The pool can be better managed, and with more positive results. Second, the factors conducive to cooperation, and a group-based management of a resource segment, appear to be exactly the same factors relevant to territorial functioning in other situations, with person–place bonds of varying centrality.

Acheson's study is extremely suggestive. He contrasted two different resource arrangements, one based on complete spatial segmentation, the other based on partial spatial segmentation, operating in the same time frame. The former, from resource conservation and economic standpoints, appeared superior.

Can we garner even *more* support for territorializing strategies? To explore this possibility, we turn to results from lab experiments and simulations.

[9] For an example of equally sound ecological practices, also grounded in tradition, from the other side of the world, see Thompson, L. (1949), The relations of men, animals, and plants in an island community (Fiji). *American Anthropologist, 51,* 253–267.

From the real world to the lab

The psychological nature of the problems investigated: social traps, the commons dilemma, and social dilemmas

People–resource links when there is competition for resources have been viewed as a specific type of social dilemma and have been investigated in laboratory studies and simulations. Much of this research has focused on how quickly resources are harvested and on the influences of various social psychological parameters. Before going on to examine research on territorializing strategies, some background conceptual perspective is needed.

Social dilemmas

The most general possible social psychological perspective on problems related to resource conservation is to treat these issues as social dilemmas.[10] Social dilemmas have two key characteristics. First, if one individual in the group does not do what is best for the group, that is, if he or she acts selfishly and "defects," then he or she receives a higher "payoff" or reward than if he or she "cooperates," that is, does what is most advantageous for the group. This outcome is independent of what the others in the group do. Second, if all the individuals cooperate, each individual's payoff is higher than it would have been had all the individuals defected. The dilemma is at the individual level, or within the individual.[11]

Stated more generally, social dilemmas focus on situations in which there is a conflict between individual rationality and collective rationality.[12] Social dilemmas apply to situations where two or more people are involved, and are thus more general than the well-researched, two-person prisoners' dilemmas used in social psychology.

The social dilemma approach is limited, however, in some important respects. Most notably, the concept is *static* rather than *dynamic*.[13] It fails to consider how the conflict between individual and collective rationality might be modified over time. Nor does it consider how, with

[10] Dawes, R. M (1980). Social dilemmas. *Annual Review of Psychology, 31*, 169–173, pp. 169–170.

[11] Ibid., p. 170.

[12] Stern, P. C. (1976). Effect of incentives and education on resource conservation decisions in a simulated commons dilemma. *Journal of Personality and Social Psychology, 34*, 1285–1292.

[13] Ibid.

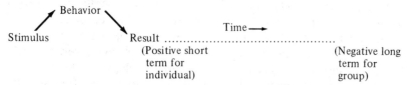

Figure 12.2. The nature of a social trap. *Source*: J. J. Edney (1980), The commons problem: Alternative perspectives. *American Psychologist, 35,* 131–150. Copyright 1980 by the American Psychological Association. Reprinted with the permission of the author.

the passage of time, what was once viewed as rational becomes increasingly irrational, as increasing numbers of others act in their own individual interest.

The social trap perspective

In contrast with the social dilemma perspective, the *social trap* perspective takes into account temporal factors, and thus is inherently dynamic.[14]

A social trap exists in a situation where certain behaviors result in immediate positive consequences for an individual, but in the long run, the consequences are negative for that individual's group (see Figure 12.2). Over time, because so many individuals are seeking short-term reinforcement, a negative consequence for the group builds up. A classic example of this is commuting by car and air pollution. All individuals seek the comfort and convenience of taking their own transportation to work. But, given the right environmental conditions, a negative consequence for the entire group ensues: air pollution and smog. "Individual goods lead to collective bads."[15]

Social trap theory has been explicitly couched by some (e.g., Platt) in a Skinnerian reinforcement framework. But it is not necessary to apply notions of reinforcement to a social trap analysis.[16] The focus is on the conflict between short-term and long-term rationality, and between individual and collective rationality, with an emphasis on the former. Thus, the social trap perspective has a dynamism that is missing from the atemporal social dilemma focus.

[14] Platt, J. (1973). Social traps. *American Psychologist, 28,* 641–651.

Cross, J. G., & Guyer, M. J. (1980). *Social traps*. Ann Arbor: University of Michigan Press.

[15] Platt (1973), p. 645.

[16] Stern, P. Personal communication. September 27, 1985.

Nonetheless, despite the fairly high level of generality and broad applicability of the social trap perspective, it is limited in a couple of important respects. When utilized within a Skinnerian orientation, it places reward over reason.[17] It assumes that people are governed solely by reinforcement contingencies and cannot develop expectation states about what will happen if they go on doing something (but see the following box). This seems to be an unduly depraved view.

Microeconomic concepts, part II: the issue of time

The social trap perspective explicitly considers how the consequences of behaviors change over time; what is good for an individual in the short run is bad for a larger group in the long run. In its most explicitly Skinnerian formulation, it assumes that people fail to develop expectations about the future and are governed merely by reinforcement contingencies. Julian Edney criticizes the formulation on these grounds.

People *do* develop expectations about the future. For example, the president of a large steel manufacturing plant considers: "If I keep polluting the air the way I have been, and fail to install scrubbers on my stacks, the air around here will soon be really polluted, which is bad." But will the president act on the expectation and take steps to avoid a future that is "bad" for the group?

Often people do not. Microeconomists have a concept that makes this seemingly irrational behavior appear "rational." It is the concept of *time discounting*. This refers to

the phenomenon of . . . the inverted telescope through which humanity looks to the future, estimating the present worth of objects to be enjoyed in the future far below their worth if they could be instantly transferred to the present. This consequent devaluation of the future is considered to be an entirely rational response to the uncertainties of life.[18]

In psychological terms, the reinforcement of delayed gratification is less salient than the reinforcement of immediate gratification. In economic terms, the estimated positive utility of a good decreases the further in time that good is placed from the present.

The time discounting also applies to disamenities – things that happen to us that we do not like. The further off in time certain bad consequences

---

[17] Edney, J. J. (1980). The commons problem: Alternative perspectives. *American Psychologist, 35,* 131–150.

[18] Heilbroner, R. L. (1980). *An inquiry into the human prospect.* New York: Norton, p. 134.

are the more we devalue that negative impact, the more trivial it seems to us. The uncertainty we might have about whether such a future bad consequence would in fact ensue, and the lesser psychological salience of a future as compared to immediate punishment, help to drive the time-discounting process.

Time discounting is a postulated psychological process to explain various economic behaviors. It need not, however, be accepted as a universal psychological fact. There may be instances where people do not discount future positive or negative consequences.

Given that individuals usually engage in time discounting, it seems plausible to assume that the same process also goes on at the collective level – with small groups, companies, neighborhoods, communities, cities, and nations.

Boniecki has suggested that one reason people are doing so little about environmental and resource issues is because they do not care about the future.[19] The economist would reply that people care about the future but that they just do not care as much, in dollar terms, as they do about the present. Thus, the future is "mortgaged."[20]

More importantly, from a societal perspective, the social trap perspective does not address the distribution of environmental rewards and costs. Those who benefit from patterns of environmental utilization and consumption of resources are from a different class than those who must pay the costs.[21] For example, toxic chemicals are used in the degreasing of microchips found in personal or microcomputers. The people who

[19] Boniecki, G. J. (1977). Is man interested in his future? The psychological question of our times. *International Journal of Psychology, 12*, 59–64.

[20] There are, of course, other factors at work here besides economic ones. Natural hazard research suggests that people cannot imagine anything happening to them worse than what they have already experienced. There is a failure of imagination. "Thus the worsening environmental situation offers paradoxical hope: the leading edge of disaster may prod people to action." Stern, P. C. (1978). When do people act to maintain common resources? A reformulated psychological question for our times. *International Journal of Psychology, 13*, 149–158, p. 152.

And, of course, given a large volume of social psychological research on slippage between attitudes and behavior, people may care about the future but not do anything. Diffusion of responsibility may also be operating.

[21] For a discussion of this see:

Schnaiberg, A. (1980). *The environment: From surplus to scarcity.* New York: Oxford University Press.

Humphrey, C. R., & Buttel, F. R. (1982). *Environment, energy, and society.* Belmont, CA: Wadsworth.

buy and enjoy these appurtenances will be from a very different class of society than those who live near the toxic waste landfill where those chemicals are stored after use in the factory.

Nonetheless, despite these shortcomings, the social trap perspective highlights a very important point: In pursuing their own goals people may create long-term negative consequences for themselves and others. But since the reward for the behavior in question is immediate, and the punishment does not come until later, people are not aware of the latter. (The microeconomist would say they devalue the latter.)

The commons dilemma

A focus on the commons dilemma goes beyond the dynamism of a social trap framework to take into account resource-relevant parameters. More specifically, in addition to the conflicts between short-term and long-term rationality, and individual and group interests, the commons dilemma considers *resource renewability and exhaustibility*.

"A commons problem arises when a number of individuals, relying on a common pool of resources, arrive at a point at which their collective demand exceeds the supply and their rate of consumption is sufficient to threaten the future functioning of the pool itself."[22] Probably the most popular example concerns New England townsfolk of days gone by grazing their cattle on the grassy area, or common, open to all, at the center of town. As more farmers added their cattle, resources (grass) were consumed faster, and a commons problem developed when consumption rates, or the number of consumers, exceeded the carrying capacity. Ultimately the commons was destroyed.

The problem becomes tragic when individuals cannot stop consuming.[23] Like the watermen in the Chesapeake, everyone wants to get theirs before it's all gone. To hold oneself back while others harvest seems useless. The balance between demand and supply is upset as a result of the condition of joint use. It is only when the resource is exhausted, completely barren, that users come to a halt. And by then it is too late, if the resource cannot renew itself through natural means.[24]

---

[22] Edney, J. J. (1980), pp. 131–132. As the quote at the beginning of the chapter shows, Aristotle was aware of the nature of commons problems. In the last century Lloyd gave attention to the problem. Lloyd, W. F. (1833). *Two lectures on the checks to population.* Oxford: Oxford University Press.

[23] Hardin, G. J. (1968). The tragedy of the commons. *Science, 162,* 1243–1248.

[24] There has been considerable dissent regarding Hardin's "tragedy of the commons" arguments. These arguments suggest that a "tragic" outcome is not inevitable whenever people have access to a common resource. More specifically: (1) the logical and historical

Summary

To summarize these three different perspectives: The social dilemma framework pits individual rationality against collective rationality, but is static and ignores the dynamism of user–resource relationships. The social trap perspective considers the conflict between short- and long-term consequences, as well as the individual–group conflict, and tends to focus on the former. A commons dilemma perspective incorporates these two conflicts, and also considers what happens to the resources themselves. The exhaustibility of resources is highlighted in particular. Inasmuch as the commons dilemma captures most fully the important parameters of user–resource relationships, we are particularly interested in how it has been investigated in the lab.

The commons dilemma in the lab

A simple approach to capturing the commons: the nuts game

Julian Edney has created a very precise *analog* to the commons dilemma for use in experimental or classroom situations.[25] As described in the following box, the nuts game is highly involving and captures the social, psychological, and resource dynamics of real-world resource-depletion situations.

The nuts game

The nuts game, in a scaled-down form, has all the essentials of the commons dilemma. A number of individuals, say four, gather around a large bowl. In the bowl are many large metal nuts (as in nuts and bolts). (Real nuts, poker chips, plastic packing squiggles, or any other suitable material could also be used.) These nuts represent the *resource pool*. The experimenter explains the rules as follows. The goal of the game is for each individual to gather as many nuts as possible within a specified time period, or trial. The number of nuts gathered by each individual represents his or her *harvest*. The experimenter replenishes the remaining supply of

---

assumptions of Hardin's analysis have been questioned; and (2) certain cultural values and arrangements are necessary to produce scarcity in the first place. See Fox, D. R. (1985). Psychology, ideology, utopia, and the commons. *American Psychologist, 40,* 48–58, esp. pp. 51–52.

[25] Edney, J. J. (1979). The nuts game: A concise commons dilemma analogue. *Environmental Psychology and Nonverbal Behavior, 3,* 252–254.

nuts in the bowl by adding a certain amount of nuts to the remaining pool every so often. For example, he or she may double the number of nuts in the pool every ten seconds, providing that the total number of nuts in the bowl does not exceed some specified limit. The addition of new nuts represents *resource replenishment or renewal cycles*, and the maximum possible number of nuts in the bowl reflects the environmental *carrying capacity*. At the end of the experiment the harvested nuts may be turned in for something valuable such as money or course credit.

The game, however, has a "catch." Should the resource pool be "wiped out," the game is up. If the experimenter goes to add more nuts to the pool remaining in the bowl, and the bowl is empty, no resources are added and the trial is ended. This is analogous to the situation in which a species of mammal or bird or fish has become extinct, or a regenerating resource in a niche has completely run out. Such total depletion is tragic in the real world. In the nuts game the consequences are negative but less dire; participants in the trial can earn no more points. The total number of points they can earn in a whole session has been drastically diminished.

What is intriguing about the nuts game is that, first time around, people tend not to be very good at it. Edney reported that in his pilot trials, about 65 percent of the groups never got to the first replenishment stage. Everyone grabbed as many nuts as they could in the first few seconds of the game and emptied the bowl. (I have had similar experiences with students at an eastern university where the undergraduates were touted as quite "bright.")

A potential solution: a territorializing strategy

One approach to avoiding the tragedy of the commons is to dismantle it. One can directly divide the space in the commons, thereby, indirectly but nonetheless effectively dividing the resources. Portions of the pool are assigned to particular individuals or groups; each is responsible for a portion of the resources. And *poaching* – consuming resources that belong to another – is forbidden. Thus, each individual or subgroup has control over a portion of the space and the resources therein. This is the essence of a *territorializing strategy*.

How might a territorializing strategy come into play in a nuts game? Imagine that the bowl was divided into quarters using a cardboard divider, and that there were four nuts in each quarter at the beginning of each trial. Each member of the group "owns" one-quarter of the bowl, and the resources, or nuts, therein. Each may harvest only his or her own nuts and may not "poach" other resources. It does not take too much reflection for each individual to conclude that the harvesting strategy resulting in maximum gain is to withdraw or harvest two nuts each replenishment period, and wait for the remaining nuts to be replenished to the allowable maximum of four.

Most obviously, such a strategy, as mentioned, segments or apportions the resource pool to particular individuals. But there are other, less apparent consequences of this strategy that might also emerge. A psychological linkage is created between each individual, his or her space, and the resource portion. This connection is analogous to the relationship between an individual and a space he or she considers to be his or hers. The space, and consequently the resource within the space, is apportioned to or appropriated by the individual (or group). Given this linkage, people may take better care of the resource in question.

Second, one might expect enhanced feelings of control and responsibility as a result of the segmentation. One may feel more responsible for the resources that are in one's own space than for the resources in common.

In short, a territorializing strategy dismantles the commons and the resources therein. Consequently, the user–resource linkage may be strengthened, resource usage moderated, and psychological feelings of enhanced control and responsibility may ensue.

Rigorous tests of the territorializing strategy

The first rigorous test of territorializing strategies in a commons dilemma was carried out by Robert Cass and Julian Edney in a computer simulation.[26] Subjects were seated at terminal screens that displayed twelve independent resource cells; subjects could "harvest" points from the resource cells.[27] The cells were periodically replenished. If a cell was completely wiped out (points remaining equal to zero), it then remained empty for the rest of the game. The experimenter clearly indicated to participants that the optimal strategy was to maintain two points per cell throughout the game, and that if everyone followed the optimal strategy, all participants would earn full credit for the session.

The territorializing strategy was accomplished by assigning each participant three adjoining cells in the display, and limiting harvesting to those three cells. In the "no territories" condition each participant could

---

[26] Cass, R. C., & Edney, J. J. (1978). The commons dilemma: A simulation testing the effects of resource visibility and territorial division. *Human Ecology, 6*, 371–386.

[27] Harvested points could later be converted to extra credits in a psychology course, and thus were assumed to be valuable.

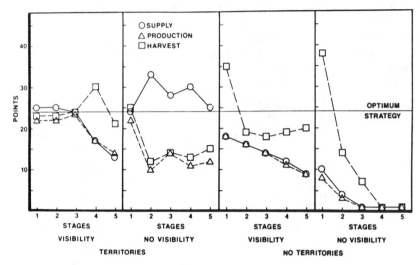

Figure 12.3. Results of territorializing strategies. The means for supply, production, and harvest by condition (territories/no territories; visibility/no visibility), across stages, from the Cass and Edney experiment. *Source*: R. C. Cass and J. J. Edney (1978), A commons dilemma: A simulation testing of the effects of resource visibility and territorial division. *Human Ecology, 6,* 371–386. Reprinted with permission of Plenum Publishing Corporation and Julian Edney.

withdraw or harvest points from any of the twelve cells. A second experimental manipulation was resources visible versus not visible. In the "visible" condition, when a participant desired, he or she could get information about how many points remained in the various resource cells. Outcomes of interest, for each group, were total points harvested, total number of points left in the pool or supply at the end of each trial, and the number of points replenished, or the productivity of the pool.

The results are presented in Figure 12.3. A significant main effect for the "territories" condition indicated that points harvested, replenished, and left at the end were all higher when resources were segmented rather than unsegmented.

Not only did territorializing result in a better outcome, but significant interactions between territorializing and visibility indicated that participants followed the optimum production (replenishment) strategy most closely when resources were territorialized and visible (far left panel of Figure 12.3), and an overcautious harvesting strategy, resulting in maximum supply (points left), when resources were segmented but not visible (second panel from left). The resource pool fared worst under conditions of no segmentation and no visibility. In this condition (far right), most supply cells were zeroed out by the third replenishment round. By the time the game was half over, there were no more points left to be harvested.

Participants also reacted to the experiment in a postexperimental questionnaire. Visibility and segmentation both contributed to perceiving the game as fairer, and more controllable, and heightened perceptions of success in resource management. Segmentation also resulted in individual participants feeling more responsible for what happened. Participants perceived the game as fairest, most controllable, most successful, easiest, and themselves as most responsible when resources were segmented (territorialized) and visible.

These results are important on several counts. First, territorializing resulted in the kind of changes in cognitions one would expect if dealing with spatial territories rather than resource "territories"; the territorializing strategy resulted in enhanced feelings of control and higher levels of personal responsibility. This finding underscores how the psychological dynamics involved in spatial territories, and in the segmentation of resources, may be similar. Second, the expected beneficial impacts on the resource pool were evident. Territorializing resulted in behavior changes that lengthened the life of the resource pool. And, third, the manipulation of visibility, which made the resource in question more concrete, resulted in participants matching their behavior more closely to the optimal strategy. The authors suggested that the positive effect of visibility was due simply to the fact that it provided respondents feedback on the consequences of their action.

In another lab experiment by Julian Edney and Paul Bell, mechanical strategies such as territorializing and equal outcomes were weighed against situations where moral rules were emphasized.[28] Participants, in groups of three, each took turns withdrawing resources (actually points) from a slowly regenerating resource pool. In addition to being able to withdraw points, a subject could also act "altruistically," signalling his or her intention to forgo two consecutive turns to withdraw.

There were five conditions in the experiment: *territorialized* (the resource was segmented into three individual pools, one for each participant, and no "poaching" was allowed); *equal outcomes* (participants

---

[28] Edney, J. J., & Bell, P. A. (1983). The commons dilemma: Comparing altruism, the golden rule, perfect equality of outcomes, and territoriality. *Social Science Journal, 20*, 23–33.

For related studies, see Edney, J. J., & Bell, P. A. (1984). Sharing scarce resources. *Small Group Behavior, 15*, 87–108. Edney, J. J., and Bell, P. A. (1987). Freedom and equality in a simulated commons. *Political Psychology, 8*, 229–243.

were told that the best way to make a lot of points was for everyone to request the same number); *Golden Rule* (participants were told that the best strategy was to choose the number of points they would want others to withdraw); *altruism* (they were told that the best way to accumulate points was to make choices that helped people who were doing less well than themselves); and a *control* condition (no particular instructions were given on the best strategy).

In the segmented resource (territorialized) and equal outcome conditions, groups did the best, earning the most points and keeping the resource pool viable the longest. The conditions emphasizing moral suasion were less successful, but they were more successful than the control condition. In the segmented condition *no* resource pools were destroyed (i.e., zeroed out before the end of the game), whereas sixteen resource pools were destroyed before the end of the game in the control condition. Postexperimental questionnaires indicated that the condition where resources were segmented or territorialized was perceived as the fairest and most controllable.

The Edney and Bell study replicates, using a different experimental setup, the results of the earlier Cass and Edney study. Consequently, it underscores the viability of a territorializing strategy for conserving resource pools, in an experimental commons situation.

The questionnaire data gathered in the sessions also suggest that the equal outcome and segmentation approaches, although roughly equal in terms of efficiency at preserving the resource pool, were experienced quite differently. The equal outcomes condition was rated as the most cooperative but also least fair. Territorializing was rated as the fairest but also most competitive. This suggests that despite the behavioral equivalence of the two strategies, the psychological experiences in the two conditions were divergent.

These two studies indicate that, in a lab setting, territorializing strategies have psychological consequences that fit with the view of territorial functioning developed in this volume. It results in "stronger" territorial cognitions. Participants feel more responsible for what happens, and greater control over the outcomes. Stated differently, the territorializing strategy *does* result in a fundamental shift in the nature of the person–resource bonds. The strengthening of these bonds results in a different utilization pattern, with resources being consumed more slowly. The slowdown in consumption is probably a result, in part, of two interrelated factors. Participants feel a greater sense of ownership and stewardship over the resource, and thus have more of a vested interest in making the resources last longer. Second, participants need not worry about what others are doing. Their response patterns are uncoupled from the action patterns of others. They need not concern themselves about keeping up with others, or about others consuming their resources while they are not looking.

There are numerous ways a small group can be linked to a commons or a portion thereof, and in their more recent studies Edney and Bell have explored these influences. Forced equity of outcomes, free versus linked consumption choices, and the possibilities of stealing from others within the group instead of harvesting one's own, all have influences on either harvest quantity or resource longevity. Thus, these studies indicate that a territorializing strategy, where a small group has a portion of a commons, could be structured in several different ways, and these structural differences will have impacts on consumer–resource transactions.

Understanding why a territorializing strategy works from a microeconomic perspective

Why does a territorializing strategy result in more successful resource conservation? The evidence points to some psychological dynamics that are helpful in shedding light on the issue. But a very different "explanation" can also be offered, from a microeconomic perspective.

The consequences of applying territorializing strategies to resource pools can also be analyzed in microeconomic terms, using the concepts discussed earlier in the chapter. Perhaps the most salient consequence of territorializing is a *reduction in total negative externalities*. An individual can wipe out his or her resource cell but cannot wipe out the whole resource pool, which is protected from the consumption habits of one individual or one subgroup. To return to the example of oysters in the Chesapeake Bay, before the county lines were struck down greedy watermen in one county were only able to "fish out" one part of the bay; they were not able to deplete the oyster beds in the rest of the bay. By contrast, after the laws were struck down the amount of damage they could do was much higher.

At the same time, positive externalities are also reduced. If your crop is doing well, that has no positive impact on how much your neighbor can harvest. What is happening, in effect, is that a territorializing strategy *internalizes externalities,* negative and positive, so that only the particular user or group is affected by their behavior.[29]

Second, when resources are territorialized and segmented, each individual or subgroup is likely to realize a *higher positive utility*. Since the resource is more controllable, and lasts longer, each individual or subgroup can harvest more "points" (or oysters or lobsters). This point

[29] I am indebted to Paul Stern for suggesting this terminology.

was amply demonstrated in Acheson's study of the offshore lobstermen who maintained perimeter defended lobstering areas.

Third, there is an *increase in the negative utility* of overconsuming for each individual or subgroup, under the territorialized arrangement as compared to a pure commons situation. To the extent the individual's or subgroup's consumption rate results in replenishment rates below the maximum possible, the individual or group suffers more than would be the case in a pure commons situation.

In sum, a territorializing strategy, by dismantling the commons, changes the economic structure of the resource situation in several respects. These changes are likely to result in lower probabilities of overconsumption and resource exhaustion, and higher productivity both within resource segments and across all resource segments.

From individuals to small groups: factors that might make territorialization a more effective conservation strategy

In both of the preceding experiments portions of the resource pool were allocated to individuals. In the real world, to which we shall turn shortly, it is unlikely that a spatial resource allocation will fall to an individual; it is much more likely to fall to a group. There is no a priori reason why a resource segment cannot be allocated to a small, face-to-face group.

Assume for the moment that we are preparing to carry out studies in which a territorializing strategy is used, and the commons is dismantled and allocated to small groups of users, rather than single individuals. We might wonder, given social psychological research, whether there are any parameters that might be manipulated to make the group function *more effectively as resource conservers*. Fortunately, the experimental work on social and commons dilemmas provides several leads.

Information about potential consequences. Informing participants about the consequences of behavior does result in reduced patterns of consumption. For example, in an experiment where the task for participants was to decide whether to carpool, Stern found that giving subjects full information about the structure of the game, and thus long-term consequences, resulted in higher levels of conserving (carpooling).[30] The

---

[30] Stern, P. C. (1976). Effect of incentives and education on resource conservation decisions in a simulated commons dilemma. *Journal of Personality and Social Psychology*, *34*, 1285–1292.

It has been suggested that information will be influential only if it is "backed up" by a fine, but this has been observed only in one study.

Powers, R. B., & Boyle, W. (1983). Generalization from a commons-dilemma game:

availability of information increases the salience of less obvious, longer-term dynamics that are at work, and of which people are often unaware.[31]

Communication. Allowing members of a consuming group to communicate results in more conservation behavior.[32] If communication is permitted, only one group member needs to be aware of the relationship between players' behaviors and the state of the resource pool; he or she can pass that information along. But if no communication is allowed, all group members must be aware of what is happening to avoid eliminating the resource pool.[33]

Communication may be more effective than simply providing information about the resource dynamics. Apparently, communication, as compared to providing information, results in more active information processing on the part of the subjects.[34]

Salience and direction of group norms. If participants lack actual information about the state of the resource pool, they will use the actions of others, such as number of points harvested per turn, as a rough guide for their own behavior.[35] Lacking a clear, objectively based strategy, social comparison processes, resulting in conformity to a group norm,

---

The effects of a fine option, information, and communication on cooperation and defection. *Simulation & Games, 14,* 253–274.

[31] Such an interpretation is in keeping with a large volume of cognitive social psychology, which has demonstrated that people tend to ignore relevant information when trying to predict events, or to attribute causes for observed behaviors. See, for example, the following:

Kahneman, D., & Tversky, A. (1973). On the psychology of prediction. *Psychological Review, 80,* 237–251.

Nisbett, R. E., & Borgida, E. (1975). Attribution and the psychology of prediction. *Journal of Personality and Social Psychology, 32,* 932–943.

Weary, G. (1981). The role of cognitive, affective, and social factors in attributional biases. In J. H. Harvey (Ed.), *Cognition, social behavior and the environment.* Hillsdale, NJ: Erlbaum, pp. 213–226.

[32] Brechner, K. C. (1977). An experimental analysis of social traps. *Journal of Experimental Social Psychology, 13,* 552–564.

[33] Edney and Harper have reported a similar finding: Edney, J. J., & Harper, C. S. (1978a). Heroism in a resource crisis: A simulation study. *Environmental Management, 2,* 523–527.

[34] Edney, J. J., & Harper, C. S. (1978b). The effects of information in a resource management problem: A social trap analog. *Human Ecology, 6,* 387–395.

[35] Schroeder, D. A., Jensen, T. D., Reed, A. J., Sullivan, D. K., & Schwab, M. (1983). The actions of others as determinants of behavior in social trap situations. *Journal of Experimental Social Psychology, 19,* 522–539.

determine consumption levels. Although most of the research so far has focused on how the emergence of group norms results in *lower* consumption levels,[36] norms could also facilitate *higher* consumption levels, if the norm that emerged was biased in that direction.

Trust. The relevance of group factors to cooperation and conservation in commons dilemma simulations may rest in their linkage to the more general construct of interpersonal trust.[37] People may be more likely to forgo immediate gain and to conserve if they have a reasonable assurance that others in their group (however that may be defined) will do likewise. Stated differently, everyone may have a deep-seated fear of being made a chump, of (voluntarily) riding mopeds while others cruise in Cadillacs. The best way to avoid this fate is to exploit all one can. It is only when groups form, and minimal levels of interpersonal trust are established, that this fear is sufficiently allayed to permit conserving, and less harvesting, rather than exploitation.

Other factors. In addition to work done explicitly on commons dilemmas, there is a host of additional social psychological research that has implications for the question of which types of groups will be more likely to conserve than others. *Smaller groups*, for example, will probably be more effective because individual contributions to conservation are more noticed,[38] and because there is less diffusion of responsibility.

Group processes, superordinate goals, and conservation

We have observed, in its evolutionary origins, and in a variety of settings, that territorial functioning rests on small group processes. For example, on urban streetblocks where coresidents know one another better, they feel more responsible for nearby public spaces like the sidewalk in front of the house. The group formation process "drives" the development of a superordinate goal to which all members contribute, even though at some cost to themselves. The result is a better environment for the group.

It appears, from the commons dilemma research, that superordinate *conservation* goals can also emerge, under certain conditions – communication, information, clear-cut, proconservation norms, and so on.

---

[36] Samuelson, C. D., Messick, D. M., Rutte, C. G., & Wilke, H. (1984). Individual and structural solutions to resource dilemmas in two cultures. *Journal of Personality and Social Psychology, 47,* 94–104.

[37] Dawes (1980), p. 191.

[38] Sweeney, J. W., Jr. (1973). An experimental investigation of the free-rider problem. *Social Science Research, 2,* 277–292.

If we merge these patterns of results with what we know about the efficacy of territorializing strategies in promoting conservation of resources, it suggests that resource pools can be segmented and allocated to subgroups of users, and that those users, particularly when certain conditions are present, will conserve resources.

In other words, the experimental evidence suggests that resource pool segmentation into territories allocated to small, face-to-face groups, coupled with conditions that inform the group about the conditions of the resource and that foster group cohesion, would be an extremely effective intervention strategy for encouraging resource conservation.

From the lab back to the real world

We have now considered evidence suggesting that territorializing strategies, in which the commons is "dismantled" and resources allocated to particular individuals or subgroups, result in higher levels of resource conservation and can be effective in avoiding the "tragedy of the commons." Further, the psychological impacts of territorializing strategies appear remarkably similar to those that accompany territorial functioning in various settings. And we have made the case that territorializing strategies could effectively be used where small, face-to-face groups have access control over resource portions.

Now, however, comes a most difficult task. We must move from the lab back to the real world, and think about how territorializing strategies can be used to conserve various kinds of resources, and what the consequences might be.

Do we need to worry?

But first, we need to confront a question that has probably lingered in the mind of the reader. Do we need to worry about conserving resources? Don't we have plenty of oil and coal and wood to last us for some time?

There IS a problem

This question is as difficult to answer as it is easy to ask. There are many opinions. On the "Yes, there is a problem" side we have, for example, the authors of the *Global 2000 Report to the President,* who suggest:

In many LDCs [less developed countries], water supplies will become increasingly erratic by 2000 as a result of extensive deforestation.... The world's forests are now disappearing at the rate of 18–20 million hectares a year (an area half the size of California), with most of the loss occurring in the humid tropical forests of Africa, Asia, and South America. The projections indicate that by 2000 some 40% of the remaining forest cover in LDCs will be gone. . . . Serious deterioration of agricultural soils will occur worldwide. . . . Already, an area of cropland and grassland approximately the size of Maine is becoming barren wasteland each year, and the spread of desert-like conditions is likely to accelerate.[39]

NO problem!

Many, however, reject such a scenario. They may believe, as the late Herman Kahn did, and as Julian Simon has argued, that people are the ultimate resource, and therefore we will somehow avoid dire disaster.[40]

Or, in the specific case of energy supplies, they may feel that the disappearance of the gas lines of the 1970's, and the stability of gasoline prices coupled with adequate supplies through much of the 1980's, "prove" that there is no energy crisis, and that what Americans experienced in the 1970's was a shortage manufactured by suppliers. Given all of these factors they may feel, therefore, that there is nothing to worry about.

No problem?

This counterargument – "People are the ultimate resource and technology and innovation can get us out of any problem" – is flawed, however, in several respects.

1. Simon's critics have pointed out that he assumes resources, in essence, to be infinite.[41] This misses the distinction between resource existence and practical availability. Although an extractable resource may exist, as it becomes relatively less abundant it is more difficult to extract, requiring more energy and technology, and creating more pollution and heat. In short, it is a situation of diminishing returns.[42]

2. As Riley Dunlap has pointed out, persons such as Julian Simon and the late Herman Kahn approach the question of resources, environment, and population from a basic set of assumptions that are

[39] Barney, G. O. (1982). *The Global 2000 report to the President: Entering the twenty-first century, vol. 1.* New York: Penguin, pp. 2–3.

[40] Simon, J. L. (1980). Resources, population, environment: An oversupply of false bad news. *Science, 208,* 1431–1437.

[41] Bad news: Is it true? (1980). *Science, 210,* 1296–1308.

[42] Schnaiberg, A. (1980).

not testable and cannot be shaken.[43] Simply put, they think the human species is not governed by ecological limits, as other species are.

3. With regard to the question of energy, and specifically oil supplies, the current "glut" is an understandable consequence of market forces, was predicted at the outset of the decade, and will, most expect, last through the 1980's. But this simply spells a hiatus rather than an end to the energy crisis that, many experts expect, will descend upon us with renewed fury in the 1990's.[44]

In summary, those who argue that resource conservation will *not* be a problem in the future are basing their arguments on an untestable set of assumptions and are ignoring the costs of extracting "available" resources. Consequently, we would probably do well to take seriously the problem of how to conserve resources.

[43] Dunlap, R. E. (1983a). Ecological "news" and competing paradigms. *Technological Forecasting and Social Change, 23*, 203–206.

See also:

Dunlap, R. E. (1983b). Ecologist versus exemptionalist: The Ehrlich-Simon debate. *Social Science Quarterly, 64*, 200–203.

The paradigm used by Simon, and the societal worldview of those who agree with him, assumes that "the 'exceptional' characteristics of Homo sapiens, particularly our knowledge and technology, largely exempt us from the ecological limits that constrain other species and insure our successful adaptation to ecological change" (Dunlap [1983a], p. 204).

By contrast, those who do not share Simon and Kahn's views are working from a competing set of assumptions – a different paradigm "that does not view the unique characteristics of humans, important though they are, as exempting us from ecological constraints or insuring our continued survival as a species. This paradigm leads one to see ecological limits as real and, for example, efforts to extend such limits via technology as temporary solutions that in the long run are likely to create more problems than they solve" (ibid).

For a fuller description of these competing paradigms see:

Dunlap, R. E. (1980). Paradigmatic change in social science: From human exemptionalism to an ecological paradigm. *American Behavioral Scientist, 24*, 5–14.

Catton, W. R., Jr., & Dunlap, R. E. (1980). A new ecological paradigm for post-exuberant sociology. *American Behavorial Scientist, 24*, 5–14.

Catton, W. R., Jr., & Dunlap, R. E. (1978). Paradigms, theories, and the primacy of the HEP–NEP distinction. *American Sociologist, 13*, 256–259.

[44] Kissinger, H. A. (February 3, 1985). OPEC's problems should not cause the West to relax; difficulties remain. *Baltimore Sun*, p. 4E.

The problems in moving from the lab to the field

The generalizability of results of lab studies on resource conservation to real-world situations is not yet established. There are always questions about the generalizability of social psychology experiments. But, in addition to these vagaries there are some particular features of resource conservation experiments that make these questions even more poignant.[45] But, of more central interest, given our focus on territorial functioning, is the feasibility of territorializing strategies in the "real world."

Would territorialization strategies work?

In the "real world," would territorializing strategies, where a resource is segmented and allocated to smaller subgroups, actually promote resource conservation?

There are reasons to think that it would, particularly if (1) the subgroup in question were small, and (2) the relationship between the subgroup and the resource in question were expected to remain in place over a long period of time.

The smaller the group charged with husbanding a segment of the resource, the more quickly that group can develop moderate levels of trust. Thus, the group members would be less suspicious of other members getting more than their share.

The long-term subgroup–resource relationship would probably result in the subgroup members being more concerned about careful resource management. Knowing that, with a territorialized arrangement their "externalities" will be "internalized," they can be assured, for some time to come, that they will only hurt themselves if they overexploit the resource. In addition a long-term relationship allows a *stronger* bond between the subgroup and the resource to develop, suggesting that, all else equal, they would be more concerned about what might happen to the resource.

A lot more research is needed, including considerable field experimentation, before we can be confident about the applicability of territorializing strategies to existing resource issues. Nonetheless, at the current time, there are grounds for pursuing this line of reasoning.

What kinds of resources?

In lab studies on territorializing strategies, resources have been directly segmented. In the real world, however, territorializing strategies directly

---

[45] See Stern (1976) for a discussion of these issues. See also Dawes (1980), p. 189.

segment *space*, and it is as a *consequence* of this allocation that resources are segmented. The division of the Chesapeake Bay into county-level oystering jurisdictions, such as existed pre–1968, is a case in point.

Thus, the resources to which territorializing strategies would most effectively apply would be those that are distributed and harvested in a decentralized spatial arrangement – that are fixed rather than fluid. Lobstering areas, oystering areas, woodlands, farmland, and ground-water are cases in point. Less applicable would be resources such as air quality, which is heavily influenced by activity elsewhere (cf. Canada's finding that much of its pollution problems "come from" the United States), or resources that rely upon centralized processing and distribution facilities, such as oil.

Issues of policy

Although much more research clearly needs to be done on the feasibility of territorializing strategies in the real world, for various kinds of resources such strategies may be able to provide viable, real-world policy alternatives in situations where overuse or depletion of resources is threatened. Of course, it is much too soon to have a more concrete idea of what such policies might be, or whether they would be worthwhile.[46] Nonetheless, important questions about such potential policies can be formulated.

1. *Would the policies allow for protection of territorialized arrangements that had "naturally" emerged, or would they actually seek to territorialize resources?* In the first case, the policies would simply support extant arrangements, such as those of the Maine lobstermen or the pre–1968 division of the Chesapeake Bay oyster beds, on the grounds that these arrangements result in better use of resources. In the second case, the policies would actually seek to segment and allocate space and resources. In this scenario, a host of problems emerges: deciding on equitable allocation schemes and built-in mechanisms to punish poaching, to name just two.

2. *If a policy actively to territorialize resources were adopted, for the purposes of increasing resource conservation or environmental quality, the costs and benefits of those strategies would need to be compared to the costs and benefits of other policies, based on other mechanisms.* There

---

[46] Shippee has criticized Edney's (1980) policy suggestions on the grounds that they are basically unworkable. See Shippee, G. (1981). Energy policymaking and Edney's dilemma. *American Psychologist, 36*, 216–217.

   Edney has replied that it is too early to tell: Edney, J. J. (1981). Reply to Shippee. *American Psychologist, 36*, 217.

are already a variety of policies in place that seek to reduce environmental pollution, or to promote resource conservation: clean air standards, bubble plans for air quality (a certain region must have acceptable air quality), effluent charges (for every X many particles per million of chemical Z dumped into a stream, a company must pay Y dollars), and so on. The costs and benefits of policies based on a territorializing approach must be compared with these other approaches.

This comparison becomes particularly difficult because *some of the benefits of a territorializing strategy cannot be stated in monetary terms.* It is very difficult for a policymaker to attach a monetary value to the benefit of increased feelings of responsibility and control that accompany a territorializing strategy.

3. *Widespread, active territorializing of resources implies social reorganization on some scale.* Here we get into issues of political philosophy. Some suggest that as resources become scarcer, stronger and more centralized authorities will be necessary to control the distribution and consumption of these resources.[47] Others suggest a radically different alternative, with social reorganization into smaller, autonomous, villagelike communities.[48] It is too early to tell whether a territorializing strategy necessitates, and under what conditions, one or the other of these arrangements. The point can nonetheless be made that widespread implementation of territorializing strategies has implications for the basic fabric of our society.

Territorializing arrangements in the past have worked quite well, as indicated by recent analyses of the forest-management practices of the New England Indian tribes in the sixteenth and seventeenth centuries.[49]

4. *Territorializing is not privatizing.* Considerable attention has been given lately to the concept of "privatizing" various public resources. The proposals to sell off wilderness areas and to turn parks over to private companies are cases in point. These proposals have nothing to do with the territorializing of resources. In the latter instance, the welfare of the managing group is tied inextricably to how well it manages and conserves the resource with which it is entrusted. When a resource is privatized, this condition does not obtain; the managing entity may

---

[47] Heilbroner, Hardin, and Edney all fall into this camp. See: Heilbroner, R. W. (1980). *An inquiry into the human prospect*, 2nd ed. New York: Norton.

Edney, J. J. (1981). Paradoxes on the commons: Scarcity and the problem of equality. *Journal of Community Psychology, 9*, 3–34.

[48] For a discussion of some of these views, see Fox, D. R. (1985). Psychology, ideology, utopia, and the commons. *American Psychologist, 40*, 48–58.

[49] Cronon, W. (1983). *Changes in the land: Indians, colonists, and the ecology of New England.* New York: Hill & Wang.

be better off exploiting rather than managing and husbanding the resource in question.

Research needs

In the lab

Work on territorializing strategies is in an early stage. The results appear promising, but much more work is needed. In particular, the following issues could be cleanly investigated in a lab setting:

Can small groups (two, three, four, or five persons) manage their portion of a territorialized resource as well as an individual?

What kinds of small groups are more effective resource managers? More homogeneous groups? More cohesive groups? Groups with a history of successfully working together? Groups with designated leaders?

What conditions allow the group members to operate more effectively? What levels of communication are needed? What levels of public commitment to conservation?

What is the importance of the temporal duration of the group–resource link? Do groups who have husbanded a resource longer become more committed to its continuing viability? Do groups who know that resource mismanagement will have negative consequences for them in the future act more conscientiously?

In the field

Field research on the territorializing strategy has not even begun and is sorely needed. Two types of evidence are needed.

1. *Information on costs and benefits*. Although research so far has demonstrated "savings" in resources that can be gained from territorializing strategies, it has not weighed these against the cost of setting up such a segmentation in the first place. This kind of information is crucial for a policymaker. He or she needs to know, in rough terms, what the savings will be, measured in resources conserved, if a territorializing strategy is implemented, and how these compare to the costs of the implementation and management itself, and to the costs of alternative strategies.

The findings, to be relevant, must be sensitive to local social, cultural, and physical factors. That is, experimenters must be sensitive to contextual factors. One of the major themes of this volume has been that territorial functioning is context dependent. Consequently, future territorializing policies should have the same orientation. There will be no one policy that is likely to work everywhere.

2. *Information on complementing territorializing strategies with other techniques.* Field researchers should pursue the possibilities of melding territorializing strategies with other techniques to enhance effectiveness. To take just one example out of many: An immense number of studies, carried out within an applied behavioral analysis framework, has examined the impacts of feedback on conservation behavior.[50] It would seem worthwhile for researchers to consider how territorializing strategies might make feedback strategies more effective, and vice versa. There is nothing theoretically incompatible between the two perspectives that prevents such an alliance. (See Chapter 14.)

Summary

Commons dilemmas are resource situations where there are conflicts between individual and collective rationality, and between short-term and long-term gains. One way to avoid the tragic outcome of a commons dilemma, where the resources are exploited and completely depleted, is to dismantle the commons and allocate particular portions of the resources therein to particular subgroups or individuals. Such a process of spatial and (consequently) resource segmentation is referred to as a territorializing strategy. The case study of offshore Maine lobstermen suggests that such a strategy is undergirded by cohesive, small group functioning, and results in more effective resource management. Lab studies of the strategy suggest that it results in higher levels of resource conservation behavior, as well as greater feelings of responsibility and control. Although much more experimental and field research remains to be done on territorializing strategies, they may provide a basis, for particular resources, in particular settings, for resource conservation policies that are more cost effective than those currently in effect.

Territorializing strategies in lab situations – where resources are al-

---

[50] For a review of this work see Geller, E. S., Winett, R. A., & Everett, P. B. (1982). *Preserving the environment: New strategies for behavior change.* New York: Pergamon.

Some of this work has been criticized from a policy perspective. It has been argued that the behaviors assessed represent only a modest fraction of the behaviors and decisions that determine national levels of energy consumption. See:

Stern, P. C., & Gardner, G. T. (1981). Psychological research and energy policy. *American Psychologist, 36,* 329–342.

This point may be correct, but it does not obscure the fact that if people are motivated to save or conserve (i.e., if consumption is costly enough to them), then feedback will result in increased levels of conservation.

located but space is not – represent an analog of territorial functioning in settings. The points of similarity are enhanced feelings of control and responsibility, and more care exercised in the allocation. Territorializing strategies in real-world situations – where space and consequently the resources therein are segmented – are bona fide instances of territorial functioning, when based on small group arrangements. They suggest a heretofore unsuspected benefit of territorial functioning: resource conservation.

PART V
REVIEW AND PROSPECTS

This section is both retrospective and prospective. It reflects on the contents of the volume so far, and the general conclusions about territorial functioning that can be drawn from the evidence. At the same time, it looks forward to consider unresolved theoretical issues, and potential areas of application.

Chapter 13 summarizes the general line of argument advanced in the volume. The clarification of the origins of territorial functioning revealed by an evolutionary perspective, and the limiting parameters on territorial functioning, as a result of that heritage, are discussed. An evolutionary framework highlights the small group–based, context-sensitive, and flexible aspects of territorial functioning. It also brings to the fore the functional benefits of laying claim to territories.

Chapter 14 considers research and application futures. First, I attend to a theoretical "loose end" – the influence of time on territorial functioning. This is an important conceptual concern meriting attention. And, to date, it has been relatively neglected. I then sketch out three practical areas of application, social problems where a reliance on territorial functioning, coupled with other conceptual "tools," might lead to more effective solutions. Those areas are stress or friction within households, disorder reduction by privatizing streets, and energy conservation. The first and third case each require careful construction of multidisciplinary models to accurately capture the dynamics surrounding the issue. The reader, as an exercise, may wish to delineate a particular social problem, other than the three pursued here, and develop an intervention strategy based on a merger of territorial concepts and other theoretical models.

13
SUMMARY OF THE GENERAL LINE OF ARGUMENT AND ITS IMPLICATIONS

Organization of the chapter

This chapter outlines the general perspective on human territorial functioning developed in the volume. The first portion examines how territorial functioning "fits" into an evolutionary framework, and the implications of that framework. Then, examining certain implications in more depth, the associations between physical environment and territorial functioning, and between social environment and territorial functioning, are reviewed. In both cases these connections, albeit amply evident across the full range of the centrality continuum, are variable or *contingent*. Finally, the outcomes associated with territorial functioning are reconsidered.

What does it mean to work within an evolutionary framework?

From the outset, I have argued for the importance of viewing territorial functioning through the lens of evolutionary theories. Such a footing is important for two reasons. First, by considering *human* territorial functioning in the context of other species, important "baseline" information is provided. Similarities can be pinpointed. If such parallels turn out to be based on homology they focus us on generally adaptive behavior patterns. Second, a wider stance for grappling with territorial functioning is particularly important for this area of work because *strong miscon-*

311

ceptions and misleading analogies have abounded. An evolutionary vantage point provides a broad enough footing to set the record straight.

What does it mean to work within an evolutionary framework? Given the scope of this volume, there are three elements. First, it means considering human behavior in the context of the behavior of other species and, as a corollary, using explanatory mechanisms that are similar for the different species. We should try to explain human behaviors with the same tools used to explain other species' behaviors. Second, it means considering in what ways the behaviors in question were adaptive in our environment of evolutionary adaptedness: What advantages did they provide to protohominids and early hominids in the ecological niches they occupied? What advantages over the species with which they competed for resources, and which sought them as prey were provided by territorial functioning? And, third, working with such an outlook mandates explaining, prior to the development of a capacity for culture, *and* after, how the behavior patterns of interest spread throughout the species.

Major points emerging from evolutionary analysis

1. In looking at territorial functioning in various species – ranging from ants to birds to primates – it is apparent that *territorial functioning is not universal*. Some species exhibit it (e.g., howler monkeys), others do not (e.g., mountain gorillas). In addition, even among those species that do exhibit territorial functioning, it may not be continuously manifest. Whether it is operative depends upon extant resource and competition levels. In other words, territorial functioning is an adaptive constellation of behavior patterns; its presence or absence, and its particular manifestation, are adaptive responses to the surrounding context.

2. Some of the species that are phylogenetically closest to humans, mountain gorillas, for example, do not exhibit territorial functioning. Our *closest* relatives, chimpanzees, were thought not to be territorial, until Jane Goodall's recent analyses questioned this generalization. Nonetheless, the less than universal pattern of territorial functioning, across primate species, suggests that the common ancestors of hominids and pongids were *not* territorial. Thus, as protohominids and, subsequently, early hominids emerged, it seems likely that they developed the rudiments of a small-group-based territorial system. If they did, what advantages did this confer on the species; in what ways did it make the hominids "better adapted" to the environmental pressures they faced, allowing them to compete successfully with the pongids and avoid predation?

3. Merging Lovejoy's analysis of human origins with King's analysis

of social carnivores, a picture of territorial functioning among early hominids can be developed. The model suggested involves a sociospatial system with the following attributes.

a. The behavior pattern is home centered rather than nomadic. Sequestration allows more intensive parenting and reduces caloric demands on adult females, allowing them more calories for breast feeding of infants. Hazards of travelling are avoided, thus decreasing infant mortality. Increased familiarity with the environment allows better avoidance of hazards and more efficient utilization of the setting.

b. Women and children can forage close to the home base, while males forage farther afield.

c. The absence of males from the home base would be acceptable only under conditions of assured paternity. Strong monogamous pair bonds and an equal sex ratio would provide such assurances. Paternity can also be highlighted by the male parent spending time with his infants while at the home base. The emergence of a rudimentary toolmaking capacity and of bipedality allows males to carry provisions from far afield, to the home base.

d. The diets of social carnivores, such as lions and hyenas, include a substantial proportion of meat. In diet, early hominids evolved towards a more efficient diet, with more meat. Thus, in this respect they were more like social carnivores than they were like primates.

e. Social carnivores support their dietary habits with a socioterritorial arrangement. The arrangement involves the defense, by a moderate-sized group, of a delimited prey area.

f. For early hominids then, socioterritorial arrangements allowed them to catch large and quickly moving prey, *and* to defend an area that contained feeding resources.

g. Hunting in groups was facilitated by several mother-father-infant clusters sharing a home base, with the males cooperatively working a particular feeding area.

h. Such an agglomeration into small, face-to-face groups not only facilitated cooperative hunting and the defense of a sizable hunting area against "poachers"; it also provided for better defense of the home base and protection against predators.

In summary, then, territorial functioning centered on a home base and a defended feeding area. It was based on small-group functioning and gave early hominids an advantage over other species by increasing their inclusive fitness.

4. Territorial functioning was elaborated subsequent to the emergence of a capacity for culture. Being transmitted culturally, it could adapt more quickly and successfully to local conditions, although the particular variants of territorial functioning transmitted through culture need not

always be adaptive. Probably one of the major "advances" in territorial functioning permitted by cultural emergence, putting aside of course the advantages that would accrue from language, was the use of *markers*. With them people could signify ownership, intention to return, symbolize danger to potential intruders, and so on. By serving as proxies for actual occupancy they allowed territorial functioning to progress to a higher level of efficiency.

Implications of evolutionary analysis

The foregoing remarks suggest several general points about human territorial functioning. Some of these points are directly counter to "popular" views on human territorial functioning.

1. Territorial functioning is not inherently individuocentric; it is an environment–behavior system grounded in small group structure and function. In its earliest form it emerged as a result of *cooperation* not competition, and facilitated group functioning.

2. In its present forms, it is still a *group-based process*, and still serves to reduce intergroup and within-group conflict. One way it does this is by "mapping" the group's social structure onto the physical environment, determining who can go where and when. Even territorial markers, such as inner-city gang graffiti, serve to keep disagreeing groups apart, warning them of potential consequences.

3. Related to the preceding point is that the social and spatial scale on which territorial concepts can be comfortably applied is *restricted*. Since territorial functioning originated within, and is "driven" by, small group structures and processes, to apply it to larger social entities, or more extensive, spatial domains is to take the concept beyond its focus of convenience.[1] In addition, application of territorial functioning to matters beyond its range of convenience is not warranted by any empirical evidence. For example, neighborhood dynamics, even those centering on mobilization, are much more effectively explained by political science processes than territorial processes.[2]

4. For millions of years, human and protohuman territorial functioning has centered on *spatial issues*. This concentration is highlighted in the definition of territorial functioning offered. Consequently, given this vantage point, it would be incorrect to *de*spatialize the concept. When

---

[1] Kelly, G. (1955). *A theory of personality*. New York: Norton.

[2] Henig, J. (1982). *Neighborhood mobilization*. New Brunswick, NJ: Rutgers University Press.

  Crenson, M. (1983). *Neighborhood politics*. Cambridge, MA: Harvard University Press.

we talk about people being "territorial" about ideas or projects, we are speaking metaphorically.

5. Territorial functioning is a highly place specific, flexible set of processes. This adaptability is shown, for example, in the sensitivity of territorial cognitions and behaviors to physical environment parameters. Territorial cognitions "match" the locale, and territorial behaviors emerge where and when "needed." Stated differently, it is highly context specific in its manifestations.

This does *not* mean, however, that different territorial processes are invoked in different locations. Rather, and as argued in Chapters 7 through 10, *the same underlying processes are at work in various settings,* where the person–place transactions are of varying centrality.

6. Given that territorial functioning is part of our evolutionary heritage, although it is *not* wired into our biogrammar, it can often operate "out of awareness" in the same way that other environment–behavior processes, such as personal spacing, also do.[3] So, the nature and impacts of various territorial behaviors are often unintended.

A comment on restriction of range

Throughout, I have emphasized the limited application of territorial concepts, to a range of issues more restricted than proposed by others. (See point 4 in the preceding section.) The spatial range of territorial functioning is a legacy of its long evolutionary heritage. And further, to go beyond this range is to exceed the available empirical evidence. Concepts other than territorial functioning work admirably well for spatial domains of larger scope. In the case of neighborhood, for instance, concepts of *attachment to place* fit nicely. But this does not deny that territorial concepts overlap with these related concepts, such as attachment to place, and that there may be instances where they both work well.

This overlap exists at both ends of the spatial continuum. Although territorial functioning is appropriate to a particular range of environment–behavior, sociospatial processes, there are points of overlap with *related* processes. This shared coverage is indicated in Figure 13.1

By implication then, there may be matters where *either* territorial concepts *or* related concepts may be applied. For example, people can be attached to their streetblock and still exhibit territorial functioning there. One's perspective depends on one's purposes. If concerned about the negative mental health effects of leaving a valued streetblock setting,

---

[3] Processes operating "out of awareness" should not be confused with unconscious processes.

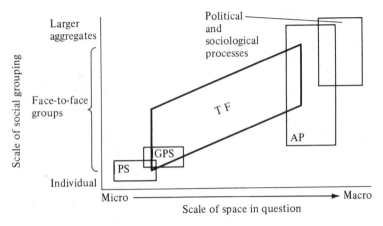

Figure 13.1. Scale and person–place processes. *PS*, personal space; *GPS*, group personal space; *TF*, territorial functioning; *AP*, attachment to place.

attachment concepts work well. But if, instead, one is interested in how residents on the streetblock manage a littering problem, a territorial perspective is more suitable. Likewise, at the more micro end of the spatial scale, one can choose between territorial concepts, personal space, or group personal space. Nonetheless, these points of overlap do not overshadow the range of behaviors, cognitions, and sentiments that are solely or most adequately analyzed using concepts of territorial functioning.

Expansion on some specific points within the argument

In this section three key points in the general argument developed in the volume are discussed in more detail.

Territorial functioning–physical environment links are contingent upon setting conditions

Territorial functioning – in inside and outdoor residential settings, regular use settings, and "public" settings – is shaped by specific physical parameters of the site in question. *But this connection is highly contingent upon other setting conditions.*

To provide just one example from the material covered: Oscar Newman postulated that real and symbolic barriers and surveillance opportunities would facilitate more effective territorial functioning on the part of residents. But as Sally Merry observed in the multiethnic housing project she studied, many sites with excellent defensible space features went undefended, due in large part to cultural factors. Other examples, from other points along the centrality continuum, could also be supplied.

Several aspects of setting conditions play a role in shaping the physical environment–territorial functioning linkage. The goals held by the person in the setting are pertinent. For example, the barroom study in Chapter 10 found more demand for tables located in places where there were more chances to socialize, and markers there were less effective, keeping vacated tables free for a shorter time interval. But this dynamic probably did not apply to those in the setting who were not there to socialize.

Views of others in the setting are probably crucial as well. The study using abstract pictures of backyards, for example, found that perceptions of the efficacy of physical markers and barriers depended upon perceived threat. Those who saw themselves surrounded by troublesome others expected these physical elements such as fences to be less effective at deterring intruders.

Given the role of these and other setting conditions, the physical environment–territorial functioning association is by no means invariant or deterministic; rather it is probabilistic. And we can identify several of the other elements that influence the connection.

Social structure–territorial functioning links depend upon setting conditions

In numerous settings the linkage between relative position in the social structure and territorial functioning is extremely clear-cut. The highly codified allocation of physical and nonphysical status supports in large corporate offices provides an excellent case in point. And, in many other settings, territorial functioning allows a mapping of the social structure onto the physical environment.

But whether or not this mapping occurs, and the degree to which it occurs and articulates social position in a particular situation, *depends on other setting conditions*. The following are just a couple of examples. The home court advantage provided by the hometown audience becomes a *dis*advantage when the stakes are high. Instead of a resident advantage a *hospitality effect* emerges when the task structure is cooperative rather than competitive. And, although Sundstrom and Altman found support for the priority access hypothesis in their field study, the dispersion hypothesis was supported only under conditions of stable overarching group structure. As in the links with physical environment, so too with social structure: In many instances, it depends. But at least research has begun to pinpoint the specific factors influencing the strength of the linkage.

Territorial functioning has multilevel outcomes

Three classes of consequences have been discussed throughout: psychological, social psychological, and ecological. These consequences occur at different levels of analysis: within the person, between individuals or groups, and at the level of the setting itself.

Intraindividual outcomes

The psychological consequences that flow from territorial functioning accrue because the processes help to buffer individuals from adjoining individuals, groups, and activities. In other words, the internal consequences ensue, not because the territorial processes change the individual, but because they change his or her "position" relative to surrounding others; in this case it is the person-in-group that is the focus of territorial functioning, not the person per se. A person in isolation has no need for territorial functioning.

And yet, these person-in-group shifts have internalized consequences for individuals. The person can better do what he or she wants to do in the setting; actual facilitation is increased. The probabilities of being interrupted, feeling crowded, or of having to compete for a spot are reduced. In Stokols' terminology, there is reduced thwarting. Consequently, the environment is more controllable, and the person is less stressed in the setting.

Social psychological outcomes: between individuals or groups

By indicating to whom various spaces belong, or by communicating the characteristics of the various individuals who occupy or have claim over various sites, potential conflicts are reduced and group structure is clarified. Expectations about the extent or type of influence can be manifested so that others may respond appropriately.

At the simplest level, for example, territorial markers in public settings indicate that the space is occupied and that the occupant will return and reclaim the location. Even while a site is occupied, the spread of markers can be used by others as a rough index of how extensive an area the person feels he or she needs for setting-specific purposes. And when intrusions do occur, rules about reclaiming or ceding sites help make such transfers orderly and less conducive to disagreements.

Somewhat more complex are the dynamics in the outdoor residential environment, where markers and behaviors, or the lack thereof, indicate which spatial segments are private, cared for, and watched over, and which are public. The signalled relationship between occupants and various portions of the setting constitutes, in effect, a cue about the range of expected behaviors in the setting. If followed, the cues result in fewer conflicts between various user groups, or between various individuals, in the setting.

Ecological consequences

Several social psychological consequences have implications for the *ongoing viability of the behavior settings within which they occur.* If we adopt a setting-level focus, we can reinterpret these social psychological outcomes as playing key roles in setting maintenance. The example developed in Chapter 7 focused on streetblocks. Attitudes such as feeling more responsible for what happens in adjoining public spaces like alleys and sidewalks, behaviors that redirect the behaviors of others or seek to eject others from the setting, are crucial elements supporting the behavior setting program. Even behaviors such as making joking comments to a neighbor about his "elephant grass" can be relevant to setting maintenance.

Further, elements of territorial functioning, in particular markers, also help maintain streetblock behavior settings by indicating the *bounds* of the setting. This is important because in the interstices of behavior settings, particularly in urban areas, there is a competing order of settings. The locations in between the settings maintained by "regulars" are themselves areas of opportunity for those viewed as "marginal." This point is well demonstrated in Ley and Cybriwsky's analysis of stripped cars. As they suggested, there is a micropolitical, ongoing conflict between these two dissimilar orders. Each order, by clearly marking the central zones within its area of influence, is communicating its respective claim. Graffiti, broken glass, and damaged playground equipment, and well-trimmed lawns and cared-for flower beds result, for the opposing group, in patterns of behavioral avoidance.

This point is illustrated graphically in Figure 13.2, which presents the spatial contour of territorial control resulting, in part, from this conflict. The psychogeography of a long-term household, which backs onto the playground, is depicted. Like their neighbors, residents of the striped house feel that they have more or less control over their front yard, the sidewalk in front and across the street, and their backyard, but their control wanes rapidly as they cross the alley and consider the playground, where the local teens gather nightly and many people from adjoining blocks, strangers to the residents, come to play during the

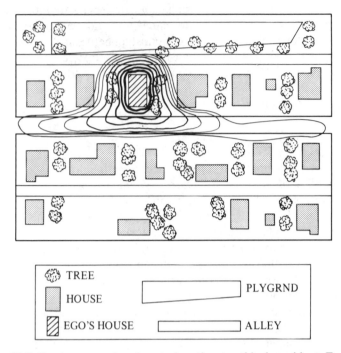

Figure 13.2. Psychogeography of control on the streetblock: resident. From the perspective of *ego*, who lives in the *striped house*, territorial control is higher closer to the home, and declines farther from the home. The higher degree of territorial control is indicated by *darker lines*; less control by *lighter lines*. The "slope" of the decline in control is a complex function of physical and social environment.

day. By contrast the psychogeography of the local teens is almost the reverse (Figure 13.3). They feel they can do pretty much as they wish on the playground at night, since the playground is obscured by trees. They know, however, that were they to carry on out on the street itself, they would probably be chased off. Thus, the two competing orders, each aided by its lexicon of markers, are distanced from one another. This segregation helps maintain the integrity of the streetblock behavior setting.

Summary

In this chapter I have recapped some of the main elements in the line of argument developed in the volume. The evolutionary origins, group-

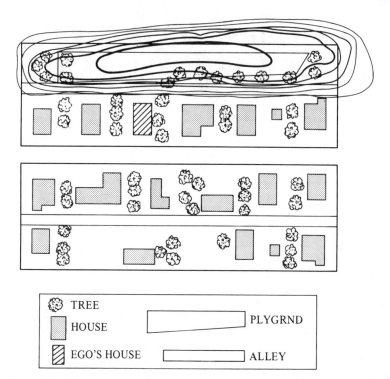

Figure 13.3. Psychogeography of control, from the perspective of teens who gather nightly on the playground. The higher degree of territorial control is indicated by *darker lines*; less control by *lighter lines*.

based processes, contextual sensitivity of territorial functioning, and its multilevel adaptive or advantageous outcomes were highlighted. Reasons for limiting territorial functioning to spatial issues of a delimited nature were summarized.

In the final chapter I outline some issues to be addressed in future research and application efforts.

14
FUTURE DIRECTIONS FOR RESEARCH AND APPLICATION

This chapter addresses two matters: future conceptual issues deserving attention, and areas of potential application. One area of investigation is singled out with regard to the former: *time*. A detailed look at one area may be more fruitful than providing a laundry list of areas deserving investigation. Moving over to practical concerns, three potential areas of research application are highlighted. First, the role of explicit territorial arrangements in interior residential settings as a way of reducing or managing household stress is explored. To develop such an intervention fully, territorial concepts would need to be merged with concepts from family therapy. Second, the possibility of disorder reduction through a privatizing of streetblocks is considered. There have already been some efforts in this direction in St. Louis, but a more complete implementation and evaluation of such an arrangement is needed. And third, a resource conservation program involving feedback, reward, and a territorializing strategy is developed, using a particular hypothetical context. Complete delineation of such a program necessitates merging a territorializing strategy with an applied behavior analysis approach.

Time: a theoretical loose end

Although some theoretical attention has been given to the connection between time and territorial functioning,[1] and it has appeared in the empir-

[1] For example, Werner, C. M., Altman, I., & Oxley, D. (1985). Temporal aspects of

ical literature in different places, it is by and large a neglected topic. In what ways might it tie in to territorial attitudes and behaviors? The conceptual framework we have used throughout (as introduced in Chapter 5) can be expanded to incorporate temporal issues.

Short-term association

Social changes

The organizing framework used throughout includes as one of its components the following linkage:

$$\text{Social factors} \xrightarrow{\ \pm\ \pm\ \pm\ } \text{Territorial behaviors}$$

where "$\pm \pm \pm$" summarizes the various intermediate steps. Social factors, particularly within-group parameters, *change*, sometimes in relatively short time frames. Incompatible roommates can grow to hate each other within a matter of days. Siblings (or parents for that matter) can fight bitterly, and then "make up" soon after.

An interesting question is whether, and if so, to what extent and how soon, these changes in within-group ties are reflected in territorial functioning. In other words, is it the case that

$$\text{Change in social factors} \xrightarrow{\ \pm\ \pm\ \pm\ } \text{Change in territorial behaviors?}$$

Figure 14.1 suggests a scene in which the two changes *are* coupled. I would expect, particularly in cases where group structure is informal, that changes in the strength and valence of ties would be reflected in variations in territorial behavior, *provided* the environment in which they are operating is capable of expressing those changes. If there are four people on a life raft, and three of them hate the fourth, there is not much they can do about it. If, in fact, it *is* the case that shifts in ties are reflected in changes in territorial functioning, isn't that too obvious to be of even rudimentary interest?

I think not, the reason being that changes in territorial functioning may be linked with *subsequent* changes in social climate. Or, to use the example in Figure 14.1, Brother and Sister Bear agreeing to "undivide" their tree house *itself* contributed to the process of patching things up, playing a role in a speedier improvement in relations. This kind of linkage, depicted in Figure 14.2, becomes considerably more interesting.

homes. In I. Altman & C. Werner (Eds.), *Home environments*. New York: Plenum, pp. 1–32.

Figure 14.1. Are changes in how well two people get along reflected in shifts in territorial functioning? When Brother and Sister have a fight, and make up later, it sure looks like it. *Source*: Stan & Jan Berenstain (1982), *The Berenstain Bears get into a fight*. New York: Random House. Copyright © 1982 by Berenstains, Inc., and Random House, Inc. Reprinted by permission of Random House, Inc.

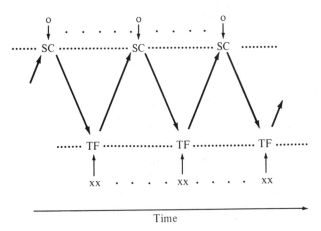

Figure 14.2. Territorial functioning and social climate over time: *o* and *xx*, other, exogenous factors; *SC*, social climate; *TF*, territorial functioning.

Such connections would also have important practical implications, some of which will be noted later in this chapter.

How could such an issue be investigated in "everyday" settings? In the case of interior residential settings, people sharing a living space could be asked to keep daily logs recording behaviors and spatial processes within the setting, for particular time intervals. These patterns could be coupled with periodically completed Mood Adjective Checklists, and other measures tapping social climate. On-site observations of how the room or apartment is "partitioned" could also be useful. Then, variations in how roommates feel about one another could be linked with patterns of spatial behavior, or changes in arrangements in the setting.

Physical changes

The organizing framework used in the volume also postulates linkages between physical environment and territorial functioning:

$$\text{Physical factors} \xrightarrow{\pm \ \pm \ \pm} \text{Territorial behaviors}$$

Again, we can expand this and include a time dimension by asking if:

$$\text{Change in physical factors} \xrightarrow{\pm \ \pm \ \pm} \text{Change in territorial behaviors}$$

The physical environment is constantly being altered. People add on extra rooms to their houses, a roommate drops out of school and his former apartment mates now each have a separate bedroom. People build and take down fences, replace garages with patios, or rehab a house while they are living in it. Such alterations in the physical environment are ever present.

The effects of these changes on territorial attitudes and behaviors are largely unknown, however. If a family of four adds on a new room, or decides to convert a garage into an extra room, how are the allocation and use of the new space decided? What aspects of territorial behavior patterns will be influenced? For example, a dormer is put on the third floor of a family house. The mother, who spends much of her time writing, decides to use the expanded space as a writing room. How did this decision come about? And, since she is farther away from the rest of the household, will she need as many "markers" to keep away the other family members since they are less likely to interrupt her?

One area where we have some initial insight into these longitudinal dynamics is in the movement from closed to open plan offices, based on studies carried out by Eric Sundstrom and his colleagues. And, although some of their results were as one might expect from cross-sectional studies, there were some important wrinkles. Satisfaction and privacy levels dropped, as one might expect. But, less predictably, the impacts of the change were contingent upon position within the organization. The lesson here, a familiar but important one, is that the patterns observed in longitudinal studies cannot always be easily extrapolated from cross-sectional investigations.

Impacts of time itself

Time *itself* may be an important predictor of interest. I have argued throughout that territorial functioning has adaptive aspects. If this is so, modifications of territorial functioning in a short time frame should be evident as people adapt to a new setting. Agreements worked out by roommates sharing a dorm room or an apartment for the first time, and their actual behavior patterns, may shift considerably in a short time frame. We have, of course, the experiments by Altman and his colleagues using Navy personnel in isolation, in which it was found that groups that started out acting "territorial" later eased off, and were less likely to ask to leave the experiment. Such results make one wonder: What happens when real groups, in everyday settings, start off in a shared living space? Undoubtedly, the connection between time and territorial functioning is highly context specific, but if, for a variety of settings, "healthy" patterns of adaptation over time or adaptive territorial behavior profiles could be noted, they could be used to identify individuals who were *failing* to adapt. This could be a particularly useful diagnostic tool in institutional settings.

Long-term association

Long-term past and expected temporal association with a site emerged as a predictor of territorial functioning in Edney's field study, with residents who expected a longer tenure at a site responding more quickly to an intruder. Apart from this finding, effects of long-term association with a site remain largely uninvestigated.

By contrast, in the research on attachment to place, length of residence has emerged repeatedly as a key variable. To provide just one example: Kasarda and Janowitz in their analysis of a British survey found length of residence to be the strongest predictor of sentiments of attachment.[2]

But how does length of residence fit into territorial functioning? An initial framework is developed in the next section. This model will be articulated specifically with regard to the outdoor residential context, but could also be adapted to work with other settings with which an individual or group is associated over a long period of time.

A model of time passage and territorial functioning

In very general, global terms, there are two types of contexts in which people can live. They can live in a congruent or *consonant* context, or

---

[2] Kasarda, J. P., & Janowitz, M. (1974). Community attachment in mass society. *American Sociological Review, 39*, 329–339.

in a *dissonant* context where there is a lack of congruence. In a consonant or congruent context the individual or household perceives that they "fit in" to the setting. *Physically*, it provides the right amenities: enough yard space, nearby playgrounds, convenient location, and so on in the case of a household with young children. *Socially*, people also feel they fit in. On important parameters, they feel that they and their neighbors share the same background, values, and similar conceptions of what it means to be a good neighbor. And sociologically, or in terms of *class or status*, they feel matched. They feel that their house, property, block, neighbors, and neighborhood adequately reflect their own relative status in society. They perceive that the setting functions as an adequate *status support*. People may also live in a setting that is consonant socially and dissonant physically, or vice versa, but such "in between" situations are not of interest here. Here, for clarification, we are focusing on extremes.

If a condition of congruence obtains, as time passes the individual or household will develop stronger local social ties and feelings of attachment. These respective external and internal changes will effect how the context itself is viewed. The setting itself becomes seen as more valued, more "appropriated" (again, in the sense of the Latin word *appropriare*). And as the place becomes more valued, territorial cognitions and behaviors should also become "stronger." Graphically:

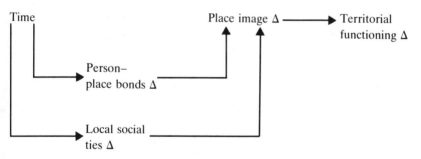

(*Note*: Δ stands for "Delta" or change.)

In what ways will territorial functioning shift over time? Cognitions will reflect increasing responsibility, and greater social legibility of the sites adjoining the house proper. Behavioral changes could include increased willingness to intervene and counter behavior that is viewed as inappropriate in the setting. As the resident or household becomes more familiar with other neighbors, and more sure of the latter's willingness to back up any corrective action taken, the likelihood of intervening increases. In short, over time the person becomes better integrated into the immediate local society, and more involved in implementing norms specific to the setting.

The passage of time, in a congruent context, results in social integration in the local face-to-face grouping, as well as deepening attachment; these shifts in turn alter territorial functioning. Some base level of territorial functioning will occur without attachment, of course. The suggestion here is that for *elevated* levels of territorial functioning to be manifest, increases in attachment are needed. Moreover, if the longitudinal model is correct, it contains a hidden irony. Although the passage of time is "driving" the territorial processes, time's impact can remain "hidden." Unless the appropriate analysis is carried out (some variant of a two-stage model), it will look as if alterations in attachment and local ties, not time itself, are causing changes.

For individuals or households in an *incongruent* context, the passage of time will have effects, but of a different sort. The individual or household will, of course, become more familiar with the site because of repeated exposure. But this will *not* lead to increased liking for the locale or neighbors *if* the individual or household in question perceives the surround as dissonant. Thus, there will not be an integration into the adjoining local face-to-face group. This persistent distance will further retard the development of any feelings of attachment to the setting as a whole. But, partly as a result of this alienation from the immediate setting, the home/beyond distinction will become more important. In other words, with the passage of time territorial functioning will "adapt" to the setting, but in a dissonant as compared to a consonant context the extent of that functioning is more constricted, centering on the home/nonhome dichotomy, rather than the on-block/off-block dichotomy. In a dissonant context, house and property take on more aspects of a "haven."

So, in both the consonant and dissonant context adaptation of territorial functioning is ongoing after the individual or household enters the setting, but the results of the adaptation are different. Graphically, what may happen in the dissonant context is:

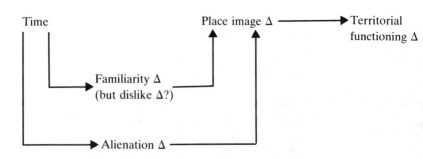

(*Note*: Δ stands for "Delta" or change.)

Over time the household becomes more familiar with the local context, but, given the perceived dissonance, feelings of alienation from the local others increase. Distaste for the setting may even develop.

Spatially what is happening over time is very different in the consonant versus dissonant context. These differences are shown in Figure 14.3.

The two scenarios depicted represent the ends of a continuum: people in a situation where perceived consonance is high, and where perceived dissonance is high. Undoubtedly, many less extreme situations exist, more towards the middle of the continuum. In those cases we would expect the territorial functioning manifested as a result of adaptation to fall between the extremes depicted here.

Summary

Time has been a relatively neglected topic in territorial research. Nonetheless, both past and expected future association with a site have surfaced as influences on territorial functioning in several investigations. By expanding the conceptual organizing scheme used throughout, time can be systematically incorporated as an exogenous variable. In the short term, several features of the linkage with time are of interest: Which aspects of territorial functioning are influenced, and how soon; how do these changes then influence the context itself over time? When thinking about the longer-term passage of time, it is appropriate to consider the interplay between territorial functioning and attachment to place. Developing a model and applying it to the outdoor residential context suggests that if the household in question perceives the block and neighborhood as a *consonant* context, the results of territorial functioning adapting to the setting would be markedly different from the results of adaptation to a *dissonant* context.

Three specific areas of research application

Three areas of potential application are outlined in this section. Each of the models and scenarios presented represents a case where *policy-relevant field research* could be carried out. Each represents a specific possible research future.

Although it is not possible to discuss each research application in complete detail, enough particulars have been provided to allow the reader to get a "flavor" of each instance. Each application is accompanied by a very "loose" conceptual model linking pivotal concepts. These models are surely incomplete. (As an exercise, the reader may find it useful to elaborate each model, pinpointing key additional variables and deciding how to integrate them into the model.) But at least

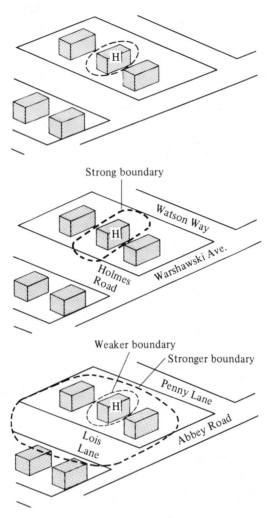

Figure 14.3. Passage of time and territorial functioning of a household (*H*) on a streetblock. *Upper panel* reveals moderate-strength household/beyond psychological boundary when household first moves onto street. *Middle panel* indicates later spatial structure of psychological boundaries in a dissonant context. A stronger household/other psychological boundary has developed over time. *Bottom panel* indicates later psychological boundaries in a consonant context. A weak household/beyond boundary, complemented by a stronger block/beyond boundary, has emerged over time.

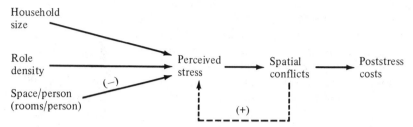

Figure 14.4. A model of household spatial stress.

they begin to join together some of the central constructs relevant to each problem area.

Reducing spatial conflicts and within-household stress

The problem

This first area of application is concerned with within-household stress management of spatial conflicts. Disagreements about who can use which spaces when for what purposes are inherently frustrating, and thus worthy of attention. Such frustrations, if chronic, can lead to stress-related consequences.[3] In addition, they can have detrimental impacts on the social relationships of those involved.[4] On these grounds it seems worthwhile to explore what can be done.

A rough modeling

A rough modeling of the problem appears in Figure 14.4.

In very stripped down form the model combines key variables from density and stress research. The three exogenous variables come from density research. *Role density* refers to the number of different functional roles within a household. Two households could each have six members. But one household may include two parents and four children, whereas the second could comprise one parent, two children, a grandmother, an aunt, and a boarder. In the latter

---

[3] Gove, W. R., Hughes, M., & Galle, O. R. (1979). Overcrowding in the home: An empirical investigation of its possible pathological consequences. *American Sociological Review, 44*, 59–80.

[4] Schiavo, R. S. (1977). Family use of the environment, related psychological experiences, and evaluation of environmental features. Paper presented at the annual meeting of the American Psychological Association, San Francisco, August.

household the role density is much higher.[5] Role density has been associated with household dysfunctioning.[6] In addition, household size and decreasing space per person (or more specifically, a decreasing ratio of rooms per person) are both associated with increased spatial conflicts within a household.[7]

From a stress perspective we employ two constructs. First, these stressors, moderated of course by a host of other factors, engender a perception of the stressful situation within the individual. (For the sake of economy two different elements of the psychological response to stress – perception of the stressor and subsequent appraisal after determining how much of a threat it is – are being collapsed here.) In addition, from the stress perspective we also include the concept of poststress effects, of a cognitive, behavioral, physiological, or affective nature.

The model assumes that perceptions of stress and actual spatial conflicts both arise as a result of the exogenous variables. As the perception of stress increases, and the person in question feels more vulnerable or threatened, conflicts over space are more likely. And when such conflicts actually occur they exacerbate the stress perception. (This is shown in Figure 14.4 as a dotted line, the "+" indicating a positive feedback loop within the system.) And, later, poststress deficits occur.

Intervention

Households where there is a high frequency of spatial conflicts may need help in managing the situation. (There may be other problems besides the spatial conflicts per se, but that is not immediately relevant to the issue here.) A counselor or family therapist might develop, in collaboration with the family members, *an agreed-upon decision about how to allocate space under various conditions.* That is, they could devise an explicit *territorial arrangement.* It might be based on a time-sharing system or a consensual prioritizing of activities. The specific form of the arrangement is not important.

What is more important is that the arrangement is agreed upon and implemented consistently. That is, when situations arise where there is

---

[5] It would seem, in general, in middle-class households, with divorce and remarriage rates increasing in the last two decades, that role density overall is increasing.

[6] Loring, W. C., Jr. (1955–56). Housing characteristics and social disorganization. *Social Problems, 3,* 160–168.

[7] Verbrugge, L. M., & Taylor, R. B. (1980). Consequences of population density and size. *Urban Affairs Quarterly, 16,* 135–160.

a potential for spatial conflict, the territorial arrangement is relied upon to settle the difference, before a full-fledged dispute erupts.

What are spatial conflicts?

The term may sound rather abstract, but it refers to a variety of situations within the household where individuals compete or conflict with one another over how a space, usually a room or a portion of a room, is to be used. Do any of the following examples sound familiar?

You are in your dorm room, a one-room double, doing some last-minute studying for an upcoming test next period. Your roommate comes in; he has already finished his classes for the day and is ready to party. His buddy from across the hall comes in with the latest *Raybeats* album. His stereo is broken, so he wants to play it on your roommate's system. They put the record on and crank it up loud. Your roommate turns to you and says: "Oh hi! You don't mind if we listen to this for a bit do you?"

You are at home, reading on the living room couch. Your baby brother's playpen is in the corner. He is asleep, but after a few minutes he wakes up and starts crying.

Dad is in the kitchen having a cup of coffee with a couple of neighbors. The children are in the living room watching cartoons. Mom comes home from work with a couple of friends she invited over for a beer. She maneuvers around the men in the small kitchen and gets the beers out of the refrigerator. She and her friends stand in the entranceway for a bit, and finally go in the living room and chase the children out.

The intervention can be integrated into the rough causal model, as depicted in Figure 14.5. From a stress and coping perspective, what we are proposing is the implementation of an additional *coping mechanism* that will *buffer* the household members from the effects of the stressor, resulting in fewer spatial conflicts and fewer poststress "costs."

What kinds of arrangements could be worked out? Roughly, two types might be developed. First, allocation based on time-sharing could be used. For example, if the extra bedroom is used for baby's naps *and* the home study, husband and wife can agree that she has sole access to the room until noon for her activities, and after that time she cannot expect to work there without interruption. Or, an activity prioritization scheme could be worked out. Two siblings sharing a bedroom may agree that one can kick the other out if the first needs to do homework, and the second is there just reading or "goofing off."

Of course, there are many details to be worked out with such an example: the actual nature of the intervention, the decision rules for

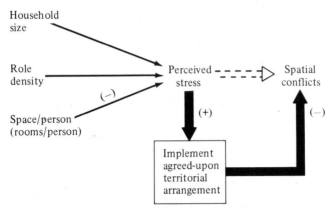

Figure 14.5. Territorial intervention to reduce within-household spatial conflicts.

implementing, ways of ensuring that household members abide by their commitment to apply the intervention systematically, and so on. Nonetheless, the general point is that an explicit territorial arrangement to sort people, places, and activities constitutes, potentially, a powerful intervention tool for reducing stress stemming from spatial conflicts within the household.

Needless to say, there are already innumerable households where such arrangements are worked out informally. But these households are not likely to be the ones in which family life is stressful and whose members go to see counselors or family therapists.

Privatizing streets and disorder reduction

The problem

Issues related to disorder were discussed in Chapter 11. In this section a specific proposal is offered that seeks to "strengthen" territorial functioning and thereby reduce crime on a streetblock, and residents' feelings of fear while they are on the block.

Modeling and intervention

The basic proposal is that residents on a streetblock can have their street "privatized." There are three components of the privatization. First, residents in toto agree that they will be responsible for various aspects of maintenance such as having the street plowed in winter, cleaning the

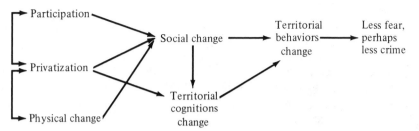

Figure 14.6. Territorial intervention to privatize streetblocks.

street periodically, and getting a contractor in to fix potholes as needed. Second, in return they receive a reduction in their property tax. This could be in the form of a rebate, or a reduction before filing. Third, and also in return, the residents, when they first "privatize" the street, can request and have granted a change in traffic patterns. For example, they may have the street closed at one end, have speed bumps put in, narrow the street and widen the sidewalk, put in symbolic gateways at the entrance to the street, and so on. These changes, of course, are implemented only after authorization by local planning officials.

An innovation similar to this was tried in St. Louis but was inadequately implemented and evaluated.[8] An effort to privatize inner-block playgrounds was recently made in an urban neighborhood in Baltimore, with mixed results.[9] But, an attempt at streetblock privatizing, in a range of neighborhoods, using techniques geared to maximizing resident participation, has not yet been carried out.

As indicated in the change model in Figure 14.6, three exogenous changes surrounding the privatization – the act of turning the street over, the accompanying participation in the process, and the physical changes made to the block – result in increased familiarity among co-residents and perceived salience of the group. These social shifts, and to some extent the privatization process itself, result in "stronger" territorial cognitions. For example, it is hoped that residents would feel more responsible for events on the street. In turn, territorial behaviors would change; for example, residents would play a greater role in keeping the street up. These altered behaviors could reduce the fear of crime. And, if potential nearby offenders are aware of these changes, crime on the streetblock could also decline.

[8] Newman, O. (1979). *Community of interest.* New York: Doubleday.
[9] Brower, S. (1986). Planners in the neighborhood: A cautionary tale. In R. B. Taylor (Ed.), *Urban neighborhoods.* New York: Praeger, pp. 181–214.

In order to provide a useful test of the application, several conditions should be met. First, the application must be implemented using an acceptable quasi-experimental design, one robust enough to allow reasonably strong causal inference. Random assignment of one block from each of, say, 30 matched pairs of blocks would be desirable. Second, since the streetblock is the unit of analysis, a large number of blocks must be included. And, the blocks should come from a range of neighborhoods, so that it can be determined if the intervention is more successful in some types of neighborhood than in others. In fact, it would probably be useful deliberately to sample different types of contexts. Third, in order to capture ongoing dynamics adequately, behaviors and attitudes should be sampled at several different points in time. And, finally, an important element of the evaluation should be a rudimentary cost–benefit analysis, attending to the full range of advantages and disadvantages. A complete analysis entails assigning a monetary value to benefits such as reduced crime and, more difficult, decreased fear. But for such an evaluation to be useful for policymakers, a detailed analysis along these lines is needed.

Such an intervention might raise concerns about possible "beggar thy neighbor" consequences. If some streets become safer, wouldn't that just mean that potential offenders are displaced onto adjoining streets? That is a possibility. But it is also possible that a "halo" effect could occur, and potential offenders would avoid not only the privatized street but also adjoining ones. And, even were displacement to occur, the question is: How much? One hundred percent displacement of offenses should not be assumed. Displacement can be factored into the cost–benefit analysis as a cost. The strategy might retain its cost effectiveness despite a low amount of displacement.

There are two reasons in particular why privatization is a potentially commendable strategy for assessment. First, the intervention itself overlaps, spatially, with the extant local groupings, capitalizing upon the existing sociospatial structure. And, second, in an era when cities are cost conscious, and undoubtedly will continue to be so, such a strategy, if viable *and* cost effective, would constitute an extremely attractive policy option.

Resource conservation and the commons:
keeping in solar hot water

The problem

The last and final area of application is *water conservation* and, by means of water conservation, *reduced electricity usage*. Water shortages are more or less of a problem depending upon where one lives. Water is much more of a concern in the Southwest than it is in Maine, for instance. Inasmuch as increased demand for water, regardless of where the demand is located, means increased outlays for public service infrastructure – dams, reservoirs, pumping stations, and so on – water usage can be viewed as a "social problem."[10]

Saving water can also mean reducing electricity consumption if the water conserved is hot water. Thus reduced consumption of hot water means a *double* savings: reduced water and electricity use.

Over the last few years *solar* units (usually placed on rooftops) for heating household water have come into use. Water is circulated in pipes through the unit, receiving heat as it passes, and is then stored in a hot water tank. If the supply of water heated by solar power is used up, electrical power starts heating water in an auxiliary unit.

Where there are multiple users, the hot water from a solar unit has some of the characteristics of a commons situation. It is a renewing resource, open to several users. And, it can be "wiped out" when all the available hot water is used up. In one way it does not capture the commons-type situation. The rate at which the resource renews itself is not dependent upon how much is left. And, second, if the resource is "zeroed out" this effect is only temporary (unless it is nighttime or very cloudy). Nonetheless, at least in some key respects a "pool" (tic) of solar-heated water represents a commons situation.

Setting

The particular setting proposed for investigation is college dormitories with solar hot water units and auxiliary electrically heated hot water backup units.

Intervention

The intervention proposed combines a *territorializing strategy* with strategies based on *applied behavioral analysis*. The particulars of the intervention are best explained by describing the proposed experimental design for the field study.

Territorialized versus not territorialized solar hot water. Two groups of equivalent college dorms are outfitted with two different types of solar

---

[10] Geller, E. S., Erickson, J. B., & Battram, B. A. (1983). Attempts to promote residential water conservation with educational, behavioral, and engineering strategies. *Population and Environment, 6*, 96–112.

water heaters. In one case, all the solar heated water for the dorm is circulated and stored in one system. That pool of hot water represents the dorm's "commons." The second set of dorms has *separate* solar water heater units on the roofs. Let's assume, for the time being, that in each dorm there are ten suites, of six rooms each, and that each suite shares one large bathroom. There is a solar water heater for each suite. In this second set of dorms the commons has been *dismantled.*

A "cue" notifying residents when the pool of solar heated water has been exhausted would be necessary. For example, a timer could be employed, so that after the pool was exhausted there was only cold water, and no hot water, for fifteen minutes. (This could result in a chilling experience for some.) After that period electrically heated water could come on line.

Other factors

The *territorialized versus not territorialized* factor can be "crossed" in the design with any number of applied behavioral parameters. A couple of possibilities are discussed here.

1. For example, some participants might be given *feedback*; a flow-meter could be hooked up outside the bathrooms indicating the amount of hot water used, or hard copy of usage on a (e.g.) daily basis could be returned to the suites participating. Or a more complex system would be to provide participating suites with readouts of the amount of solar heated water left.

2. *Extra incentives* could be offered, at the individual, small group (suite), or large group (dorm) level. For example, savings from decreased electricity use for heating water could be passed on to the user groups. Given the analysis of territorial functioning in this volume, the most appropriate unit to receive incentives would be the small group or *suite* level.

A sample experimental design is depicted in Figure 14.7. The point of the overall experimental design is (a) to test the "real-world" effectiveness of a territorializing strategy, and (b) to determine what other contingencies or conditions can increase the effectiveness of such a strategy.

Measurement. In such a field experiment it would be useful to obtain, in addition to the outcome data, details on *intervening group processes*. Through surveys one could determine how often the people in each suite talked about the issue, whether or not they discussed the feedback (if they received it), perceptions of the commitment of other suitemates, and so on. These social psychological parameters may be useful for

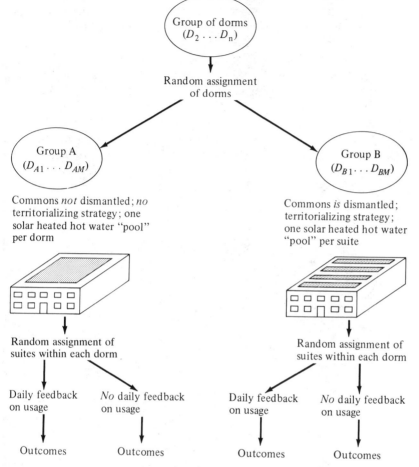

Figure 14.7. Possible experimental design for water conservation field study, using territorializing strategy: 2 × 2.

explaining, within particular conditions, the relative success (conservation) levels of the different suites.

Summary

This chapter points towards some research and application futures in the area of territorial functioning. The conceptual issue of *time* was highlighted for integration into the conceptual framework developed in the volume. Time was viewed from both a short- and a long-term perspective. The integration of the long-term passage of time into the conceptual model was illustrated using the setting of the streetblock. Impacts of time on territorial functioning were viewed as conditional on the overall level of perceived *consonance* versus *dissonance*. Turning to areas of possible application, three "social problems" were examined: within-household stress, disorder on streets, and water conservation. For each, interventions using territorial functioning were suggested. For spatial conflicts within households, explicit allocations of rooms were proposed. Privatization of streetblocks was discussed as a means of strengthening the streetblock behavior setting. And a territorializing strategy, coupled with an applied behavioral strategy, was suggested as a means for reducing water consumption. In the latter two social problems, design details for the field studies were discussed.

NAME INDEX

341

SUBJECT INDEX

access control, 130, 142, 191, 218
accessibility, 268
acorn woodpecker, 27–28
action research, xxiv, 271–272
advertisements (nonhuman), 22
aggression, *see* violence
alienation, 214–215
alleys, 189
altruism, 20, 293, 294
analogy, 48
ants, 23–25
applied behavioral analysis, 306
appropriation, 85, 180, 224, 227, 237–238
arboreal leaf eaters, 29–30
Ardrey, R., 44–47
athletic contests, 205–206
Atlanta, 175
attachment to place, 102–104, 159, 180, 315
and impacts of time, 104
audience effects, 205–207

Baltimore, 157, 189, 193, 256, 260–261, 267, 269, 335
barriers, 267
barrooms, 230–232
beaches, 235–236, 239
behavior modification, 210; *see also* applied behavioral analysis
behavior setting theory, 117, 128–129
behavior settings, 9, 127–129, 242
Berenstain Bears Get into a Fight, The, 149, 324

birds, 25–29
and territory size, 26–28
block clubs, 273
Borodino, 2
Boston, 255, 260
Brooklyn, 273
building size, 268
Bureau of Justice Statistics, 249
bureaucracy, 216
burglarized households, 261, 266; *see also* crime
burglary, 250
business offices:
and alienation, 214–215, 219
and chambering effect, 205
and ecological psychology, 208–209
and open-plan offices, 203–205
and status, 203–205, 217–218
and status markers, 214

capacity for culture, 60–61; *see also* cultural variants; culture
carrying capacity, 51
causal models, 89–91
centrality, 9, 10, 118–119, 133, 198–200, 222
centrality continuum, 10–12, 133–134
chambering effect, 205; *see also* business offices; privacy; status
Chesapeake Bay, 276–278, 303
children, 139, 142
chimpanzees, 29, 32–33
chimps of Gombe, *see* chimpanzees